THE FATHERS
OF THE CHURCH

A NEW TRANSLATION

VOLUME 115

THE FATHERS
OF THE CHURCH

A NEW TRANSLATION

EDITORIAL BOARD

Thomas P. Halton
The Catholic University of America
Editorial Director

Elizabeth Clark
Duke University

Robert D. Sider
Dickinson College

Joseph T. Lienhard, S.J.
Fordham University

Michael Slusser
Duquesne University

David G. Hunter
Iowa State University

Cynthia White
The University of Arizona

Kathleen McVey
Princeton Theological Seminary

Rebecca Lyman
Church Divinity School of the Pacific

David J. McGonagle
Director
The Catholic University of America Press

FORMER EDITORIAL DIRECTORS

Ludwig Schopp, Roy J. Deferrari, Bernard M. Peebles,
Hermigild Dressler, O.F.M.

Carole C. Burnett
Staff Editor

ST. CYRIL OF ALEXANDRIA
COMMENTARY ON THE TWELVE PROPHETS
VOLUME 1

Translated by
†ROBERT C. HILL

THE CATHOLIC UNIVERSITY OF AMERICA PRESS
Washington, D.C.

Copyright © 2007
THE CATHOLIC UNIVERSITY OF AMERICA PRESS
All rights reserved
Printed in the United States of America

The paper used in this publication meets the minimum requirements of
the American National Standards for Information Science—Permanence
of Paper for Printed Library Materials, ANSI z39.48-1984.

LIBRARY OF CONGRESS CATALOGING-IN-PUBLICATION DATA
Cyril, Saint, Patriarch of Alexandria, ca. 370–444.
Commentary on the Twelve Prophets / Cyril of Alexandria ; translated
with an introduction by Robert C. Hill.
p. cm. — (The Fathers of the church ; v. 115)
Includes bibliographical references and indexes.
ISBN 978-0-8132-0115-3 (cloth : alk. paper)
ISBN 978-0-8132-2626-2 (pbk.)
1. Bible. O.T. Prophets—Commentaries. I. Hill, Robert C. (Robert
Charles), 1931–   II. Title. III. Series.
BS1505.53.C9713 2007
224'.907—dc22

2007016972

CONTENTS

Abbreviations   vii
Select Bibliography   ix

Introduction   3
    1. The *Commentary on the Twelve Prophets* among Cyril's works 3
    2. Text of the *Commentary;* Cyril's biblical text of The Twelve 6
    3. Cyril's style of commentary 8
    4. Interpreting the Twelve Prophets 13
    5. Theological accents in the *Commentary* 17
    6. Cyril's achievement in the *Commentary on the Twelve Prophets* 20

COMMENTARY ON THE TWELVE PROPHETS

Commentary on the Prophet Hosea   25
  Preface   27
  Commentary on Hosea, Chapter One   33
  Commentary on Hosea, Chapter Two   64
  Commentary on Hosea, Chapter Three   94
  Commentary on Hosea, Chapter Four   101
  Commentary on Hosea, Chapter Five   123
  Commentary on Hosea, Chapter Six   138
  Commentary on Hosea, Chapter Seven   150
  Commentary on Hosea, Chapter Eight   164
  Commentary on Hosea, Chapter Nine   176
  Commentary on Hosea, Chapter Ten   194
  Commentary on Hosea, Chapter Eleven   210
  Commentary on Hosea, Chapter Twelve   222
  Commentary on Hosea, Chapter Thirteen   236
  Commentary on Hosea, Chapter Fourteen   249

CONTENTS

Commentary on the Prophet Joel	257
Preface	259
Commentary on Joel, Chapter One	261
Commentary on Joel, Chapter Two	280
Commentary on Joel, Chapter Three	302

INDICES

The indices to this volume are combined with the indices to volume 2, to appear in the latter.

ABBREVIATIONS

AnBib	Analecta Biblica, Pontificio Istituto Biblico, Rome.
AUG	Augustinianum.
BAC	Bible in Ancient Christianity, Leiden and Boston: Brill, 2004–.
Bib	*Biblica.*
CCG	Corpus Christianorum series Graeca, Turnhout: Brepols.
CCL	Corpus Christianorum series Latina, Turnhout: Brepols.
DBS	*Dictionnaire de la Bible. Supplément,* IV, Paris: Librairie Letouzey et Ané, 1949.
FOTC	The Fathers of the Church, Washington, DC: The Catholic University of America Press.
GO	Göttinger Orientforschungen, Wiesbaden: Otto Harrassowitz.
HeyJ	*The Heythrop Journal.*
JECS	*Journal of Early Christian Studies.*
LXX	Septuagint.
NS	New Series.
OTL	Old Testament Library.
PG	Patrologia Graeca, ed. J.-P. Migne, Paris, 1857–66.
SC	Sources Chrétiennes, Paris: Du Cerf.
StudP	*Studia Patristica.*
TRE	*Theologische Realenzyclopädie,* Berlin: Walter de Gruyter, 1976–.

SELECT BIBLIOGRAPHY

Boulnois, M.-O. "The mystery of the Trinity according to Cyril of Alexandria: The Deployment of the Triad and its Recapitulation into the Unity of Divinity." In T. G. Weinandy and D. A. Keating, eds. *The Theology of St Cyril of Alexandria. A Critical Appreciation.* London and New York: T&T Clark, 2003. Pp. 75–111.

Daley, B. E. "Apocalypticism in Early Christian Theology." In B. McGinn, ed. *The Encyclopedia of Apocalypticism* 2. New York and London: Continuum, 2002. Pp. 3–47.

Doutreleau, L., ed. *Didyme L'Aveugle. Sur Zacharie.* SC 83, 84, 85. Paris: Du Cerf, 1962.

Fernández Marcos, N. *The Septuagint in Context: Introduction to the Greek Versions of the Bible.* Translated by Wilfred G. E. Watson. Boston and Leiden: Brill, 2001.

Harvey, E. R. "Cyrillus von Alexandria." *TRE* 8:254–60.

Hill, R. C. "The Mystery of Christ: Clue to Paul's Thinking on Wisdom." *HeyJ* 25 (1984): 475–83.

———. "Psalm 45: A *locus classicus* for Patristic Thinking on Biblical Inspiration." *StudP* 25 (1993): 95–100.

———. *Theodoret of Cyrus. Commentary on the Psalms.* FOTC 101, 102. Washington, DC: The Catholic University of America Press, 2000.

———. "Jonah in Antioch." *Pacifica* 14 (2001): 245–61.

———. "Theodore of Mopsuestia, Interpreter of the Prophets." *Sacris Erudiri* 40 (2001): 107–29.

———. *Theodore of Mopsuestia. Commentary on the Twelve Prophets.* FOTC 108. Washington, DC: The Catholic University of America Press, 2004.

———. *Reading the Old Testament in Antioch.* BAC 5. Leiden and Boston: Brill, 2005.

———. *Didymus the Blind. Commentary on Zechariah.* FOTC 111. Washington, DC: The Catholic University of America Press, 2005.

———. *Theodoret of Cyrus. Commentary on the Twelve Prophets.* Commentaries on the Prophets 3. Brookline, MA: Holy Cross Orthodox Press, 2005.

———. "Zechariah in Alexandria and Antioch." *Aug* 46 (2006).

Jouassard, Georges. "L'activité littéraire de saint Cyrille d'Alexandrie jusqu'à 428: Essai de chronologie et de synthèse." In *Mélanges E. Podechard: Études de sciences religieuses offertes pour son émeritat.* Lyon: Facultés Catholiques, 1954. Pp. 159–74.

Kelly, J. N. D. *Jerome. His Life, Writings and Controversies.* London: Duckworth, 1975

SELECT BIBLIOGRAPHY

Kerrigan, A. *St. Cyril of Alexandria, Interpreter of the Old Testament.* AnBib 2. Rome: Pontificio Istituto Biblico, 1952.

Olivier, J.-M., ed. *Diodori Tarsensis commentarii in Psalmos.* I. *Commentarii in Psalmos I-L.* CCG 6. Turnhout: Brepols, 1980.

Petersen, D. L. *Zechariah 9–14 & Malachi.* OTL. London: SCM, 1995.

Pusey, P. E., ed. *Sancti patris nostri Cyrilli archiepiscopi Alexandrini in XII prophetas.* Oxford: Clarendon Press, 1868.

Redditt, P. L. *Haggai, Zechariah, Malachi.* New Century Bible Commentary. Grand Rapids: Eeerdmans, 1995.

Russell, N. *Cyril of Alexandria.* The Early Christian Fathers. London and New York: Routledge, 2000.

Schäublin, C. *Untersuchungen zu Methode und Herkunft der antiochenischen Exégèse.* Theophaneia: Beiträge zur Religions- und Kirchengeschichte des Altertums 23. Cologne and Bonn: Peter Hanstein, 1974.

Smith, R. L. *Micah–Malachi.* Word Biblical Commentary 32. Waco, TX: Word Books, 1984.

Sprenger, H. N., ed. *Theodori Mopsuesteni commentarius in XII prophetas.* GO. Biblica et Patristica 1. Wiesbaden: Otto Harrassowitz, 1977.

Wilken, R. L. "Cyril of Alexandria as Interpreter of the Old Testament." In T. G. Weinandy and D. A. Keating, eds. *The Theology of St Cyril of Alexandria. A Critical Appreciation.* London and New York: T&T Clark, 2003. Pp. 1–21.

———. "Cyril of Alexandria." In C. Kannengiesser. *Handbook of Patristic Exegesis* 2. BAC 1. Leiden and Boston: Brill, 2005. Pp. 840–69.

Zeigler, J. *Duodecim Prophetae.* Septuaginta 13. Göttingen: Vandenhoeck & Ruprecht, 1943.

INTRODUCTION

INTRODUCTION

1. The *Commentary on the Twelve Prophets* among Cyril's works

The identification of Cyril with Alexandria in Egypt arises particularly from his election to the see on the death of his uncle Theophilus in 412. At the midpoint of his episcopate in Alexandria, which lasted till his death in 444, there occurred the event that would affect the whole church of the east and embroil Cyril in theological controversy, namely, the election of Nestorius to the see of Constantinople in 428. Statements immediately emanating from Nestorius on Mary's claim to the title Theotokos prompted a response from Cyril in Alexandria that ushered in a long period of animosity between the two prelates and two major sees of eastern Christendom,[1] and that drastically altered the character of Cyril's theological writings.

Cyril's early education had been conducted under the watchful eye of his uncle Theophilus, bishop since Cyril's childhood; but, to judge from references even in the *Commentary on the Twelve Prophets*, it gave him a degree of familiarity with classical authors as well (if not sureness of touch in matters of sacred history). We find him quoting verses from the poem *Alexandra* (or *Cassandra*) of the third century B.C.E. poet Lycophron in comparing Jonah's stay in the belly of the fish to Hercules' three-day visit to the underworld; and in commentary on Zec 8.4–5 he describes the peace promised by the Lord to Jerusalem as *kourotrophon*, "nursing mother," a rare term found in Homer and later in Euripides, confirming the judgment of a well-known Cyril scholar that he "was anything but a total stranger to the humanities."[2] The rela-

---

1. It was the second ecumenical council, the Council of Constantinople in 381, that ranked Constantinople as second in Christendom after Rome, ahead of Alexandria and Antioch.
2. A. Kerrigan, *St. Cyril of Alexandria. Interpreter of the Old Testament*, AnBib 2 (Rome: Pontificio Istituto Biblico, 1952), 9.

tive peace that Cyril himself treasured in the early period of his writings after becoming bishop was rather the *pax Romana,* on which he comments favorably more than once; the promise of peace in Hos 2.18 he typically sees realized in New Testament times: "When the celebrated Roman generals were given command against all nations, they brought the whole world into subjection, with God in his plan allotting the glory to them." We find similar expressions of appreciation of this peace throughout the empire in Theodoret, who works on The Twelve with Cyril's *Commentary* before him,[3] to be broken in the next decade with incursions of Huns and Persians as he moves to comment on the Psalms.[4]

It is theological tranquillity in particular, however, which marks this *Commentary on the Twelve,* composed in the period before 428 in which it is thought Cyril wrote his biblical commentaries; we shall see him making only conventional, generic references to heretics along with Jews and pagans in applying prophetic references to enemies and conflicts, with no element of personal theological polemic ever appearing. It is thought that he began his exegetical career with two works on the Pentateuch, the *De adoratione et cultu in spiritu et veritate*[5] and the *Glaphyra* ("elegant comments");[6] in commentary on Mal 2.4 Cyril seems to refer to chapter 11 of the *De adoratione:* "Comment on the innards and the sacrifices performed according to the Law has briefly been given in our other writings." Commentaries on John and Luke also appeared in that period, as well as an extant work on Isaiah[7] (and possibly works on the Psalms and the other major prophets, no longer extant). Although Kerrigan reports that "in the course of our examination of the commentary on *Isaiah* and that on the *Minor Prophets* we have discovered no literary allusions which might enable us to decide which of these is the older,"[8] a reader

---

3. PG 81.1545–1988.
4. Theodoret mentions the invasion of Huns in 434 and Persians in 441 in commentary on Ps 18.12–14 (PG 80.977).
5. PG 68.134–1126.   6. PG 69.9–678.
7. PG 70.9–1450.
8. *St. Cyril of Alexandria,* 14. See also Georges Jouassard, "L'activité littéraire de saint Cyrille d'Alexandrie jusqu'à 428: Essai de chronologie et de synthèse," *Mélanges E. Podechard: Études de sciences religieuses offertes pour son éméritat* (Lyon:

notes that in introducing King Ahaz at the opening of this latter work, on Hos 1.1, Cyril is indebted only to 2 Kings; it does not occur to him to highlight the covenantal disloyalty of the appeal for assistance by Ahaz to the Assyrian king in the way registered by Isaiah 7, which he would surely have done if he had just come from work on that prophet. At any rate, both Isaiah and Jeremiah are cited with great frequency in this work in the period before Cyril enters the theological lists with his *Contra Nestorium* in the period following 428.[9]

Cyril is aware that he is not the first commentator on these prophets. We shall see that perhaps his most distinctive characteristic is an approach to the biblical text that, unlike those of some of his local predecessors, consistently and deliberately takes account of the factual and historical situation of the prophets and the events to which they refer, an approach we associate more with Antioch.[10] On the other hand, he reveals a familiarity with the work of his Alexandrian predecessor Didymus the Blind on Zechariah, composed for Jerome around 387,[11] as well as with Jerome's subsequent work on all twelve. And there are grounds for thinking that in taking issue with a minimalist approach to elements in the text that challenge literal acceptance, such as the marriage of Hosea, he has in mind Origen (whose twenty-five volumes on at least some of The Twelve were lost) and Eusebius—though never citing his predecessors by name.

Facultés Catholiques, 1954), 159–74; Jouassard maintains that all the OT works appeared before 423.

9. For a fuller treatment of the life and works of Cyril, see E. R. Harvey, "Cyrillus von Alexandria," *TRE* 8:254–60. Other such introductions (unlike Kerrigan's) tend to make little reference to the *Commentary on the Twelve Prophets*, a fact perhaps explained by its great bulk and (unlike the *Commentary on John*) the lack of an English translation; see R. L. Wilken, "Cyril of Alexandria," in C. Kannengiesser, *Handbook of Patristic Exegesis*, BAC 2 (Leiden and Boston: Brill, 2004), 840–69; N. Russell, *Cyril of Alexandria*, The Early Christian Fathers (London and New York: Routledge, 2000).

10. Kerrigan, *St. Cyril of Alexandria*, 110, remarks, "St. Cyril shows affinities with Theodore of Mopsuestia and Theodoretus of Cyrrhus that are really striking."

11. For details of composition of this work, see the introduction to R. C. Hill, *Didymus the Blind. Commentary on Zechariah*, Fathers of the Church 111 (Washington, DC: The Catholic University of America Press, 2006), 3–24.

2. Text of the *Commentary;*
Cyril's biblical text of The Twelve

We are indebted for our critical edition of the *Commentary on the Twelve Prophets* to the indefatigable Philip E. Pusey,[12] who performed a similar service to the readers of Cyril's work on John (but unfortunately not Isaiah). Readers (and translators) of the work on The Twelve appreciate the quality of Pusey's 1868 edition by comparison with that of Jean Aubert in the seventeenth century.[13] Differences in the two are generally not of major textual significance, and are noted in the text below.

Cyril, who appears to have had available to him not only the commentaries of Didymus (on Zechariah)[14] and Jerome,[15] but also those of the Antiochene Theodore of Mopsuestia,[16] moves through The Twelve in the order, not of the Septuagint, but of the Hebrew, which is preserved also in the Antiochene text. This decision he acknowledges when the time comes to do so, at the beginning of Joel, whom the LXX demotes in the order.[17] His Greek version (on which his lack of Hebrew makes him dependent) differs in some details from the Antiochene form of the Septuagint (if that is the correct way to speak of the Lucianic text).[18] Again the differences (also noted below) are not of great significance,[19] though the Antiochene text *suo more* removes

12. *Sancti patris nostri Cyrilli archiepiscopi Alexandrini in XII prophetas*, 2 vols. (Oxford: Clarendon Press, 1868).
13. See PG 71–72.
14. The critical edition is by L. Doutreleau, *Didyme L'Aveugle. Sur Zacharie*, SC 83, 84, and 85 (Paris: Éditions du Cerf, 1962).
15. CCL 76, 76A.
16. The critical edition is H. N. Sprenger, *Theodori Mopsuesteni commentarius in XII prophetas*, GO, Biblica et Patristica 1 (Wiesbaden: Otto Harrassowitz, 1977).
17. While the order of the last six books is the same in both Heb. and LXX, the latter seems to arrange the first six by length, not in chronological order as in the Heb.
18. Usage differs among commentators, some preferring "Antiochene" to "Lucianic," depending on the view taken as to the origins of this form of the Greek, and on Lucian's role, whether as reviser of an existing LXX or as translator responsible for an independent version. See the introduction to my *Theodore of Mopsuestia. Commentary on the Twelve Prophets*, Fathers of the Church 108 (Washington, DC: The Catholic University of America Press, 2004), 5–6.
19. Opinions differ as to whether Cyril's text represents an "Hesychian

some of the discrepancies evident, for instance, in the numbers of horses and their errands in texts and versions of Zec 6. Cyril's canon includes also the deutero-canonical books of Baruch, Sirach, and Susanna, and—in commentary on Haggai, Zechariah, and Malachi, on the return of the exiles—1 Esdras, cited substantially.

In Jerome, of course, who learned his Hebrew from a Jew while in Chalcis,[20] Cyril has the sole predecessor fully equipped to guide him through the maze both of obscure material and of the shortcomings of the LXX. Jerome systematically points out the latter, remarking of Mi 6.14, "The LXX departs considerably in this section from the *Hebraica veritas*." Cyril looks to no one else to guide him in matters of text and translation;[21] the (infrequent) citation of the alternative versions associated with the names of Aquila, Symmachus, and Theodotion is generally due to Jerome, as are Cyril's observations on the deficiencies of his own version. What is of interest is the fact that quite frequently Cyril will either ignore Jerome's reminders, apparently out of attachment to the LXX on principle, or acknowledge them while still upholding the value of his version, generally for its spiritual potential. The LXX presents its readers of the opening to Zec 5 with the unlikely vision of a flying "scythe," which Jerome and his citation of the alternative versions had informed Cyril represented rather a flying "scroll"; but Cyril insists that true scholars can gain spiritual value from his text as it stands: "There is no difficulty as far as a more obvious explanation of the revelation goes." Again, he is advised ("they say") that the LXX version of Hg 2.15 makes no sense; but he believes there is mileage in the solecism: "They say that neither the Hebrew text nor the other translators include or show knowledge of this; yet the thought

---

revision" of the LXX; see N. Fernández Marcos, *The Septuagint in Context: Introduction to the Greek Versions of the Bible*, trans. W. Watson (Leiden: Brill, 2001), 241–46.

20. Cf. J. N. D. Kelly, *Jerome. His Life, Writings and Controversies* (New York: Harper and Row, 1975), 50.

21. Russell, *Cyril of Alexandria*, 71, remarks, "Cyril does not seem to have had any knowledge of Latin, but we know that there were translators on whose services he could have called.... It therefore seems reasonable to suppose that there was a group of translators in Alexandria who made Jerome accessible to Cyril."

seems to correspond with what went before." Although he never explicitly upholds the inspiration of the Seventy, as Theodoret does,[22] nor cites the legendary *Letter of Aristeas*,[23] nevertheless a score of times he declines to accept information highlighting the shortcomings of his text, its integrity not being the prime consideration.

3. Cyril's style of commentary

For one who reveals his commitment to the pastoral care of his flock in such voluminous commentary on Scripture, the bishop rarely gives himself to direct exhortation in applying the text to their lives, as distinct from laying out its spiritual meaning, often at several levels including the moral. These prophets of the Old Testament are clearly considered to be of value to his Christian readers along with the New; in commenting on the opening verse of Zec 10, "Ask from the Lord timely rain, early and late," the two epithets are taken to refer to both testaments.

> That is to say, just as without labor there would be no grain in the fields or a fruitful vineyard producing wine, so, too, there would be no spiritual fertility in us unless God shed the revelation of his own sayings like rain on mind and heart, and, as it were, bedewed us with knowledge of the old and new Scriptures, namely, the Law and the Gospels, such being *early and late rain*. Now, the fact that knowledge and spiritual appreciation of the Law is not without benefit the Savior himself confirms.

Of course, with the commentator's often unsympathetic reference to the Jews of Jesus' time, especially scribes and Pharisees, as the realization of prophecy, there are equally instances of the presentation of the Old Testament in a negative light (as would not occur to such a degree in a *Ioudaiophron* like Theodore). When Mi 4.2 prophesies that "from Zion will issue forth a law, and a word of the Lord from Jerusalem," Cyril wants to deny any continuing validity to the Old: "Zion will be bereft even of the Law itself, and Jerusalem stripped of the divine sayings, as if somehow their Law and God's word spoken by angels had de-

---

22. In the preface to his Psalms commentary, PG 80.864.
23. As does Theodore in questioning the status of Syriac translators of Zep 1.5 by comparison with the LXX; see *Theodori Mopsuesteni commentarius*, 284.

parted. In other words, the shadow had disappeared, what was in type was at an end, the sacrifices were done away with, and what came through Moses (as far as text was concerned) was then finished."

For Cyril, despite his consistent attempt, uncharacteristic of an Alexandrian, to relate them to times and events, The Twelve are primarily not actors on a stage, but writers responsible for συγγραφή, as he remarks at the outset of his commentary. Yet for his flock experience of them comes not primarily through reading his text, but aurally, probably in the course of the liturgy; for example, they have "heard" Joel's account of the locust plague in Jl 2.9–10. As all the biblical authors and their texts are "divinely inspired," so, too, The Twelve enjoy the grace of the Spirit. Confirmation of this had, for Didymus and Theodore, been given particularly by the use of "oracle," λῆμμα, at the opening of Nahum, Habakkuk, Deutero-Zechariah, and Malachi, leading Didymus to speak of Zechariah as being θεοληπτούμενος, that is, rapt, in a state of ecstatic possession.[24] Just as Theodore quickly abandoned such an ethereal mode of biblical inspiration, which was anathema in Antioch,[25] so Cyril—alerted by Jerome to Montanist dangers in such a rarefied notion[26]—refrained from following the lead of Didymus. The closest he will come to it is, at the opening of Habakkuk, "[The prophets] are not in the habit of speaking what is from their own hearts; rather, they transmit to us words from God," a sentiment for which he has an oft-quoted precedent in Jer 23.16.

As noted above, Cyril consistently begins commentary on these prophets by situating them (as far as he is able, given his imperfect formation in this regard) in their historical situation; perhaps he has Theodore (but not Didymus) to thank partly for following this procedure. Though his editors do not recognize it as such, his opening to the work goes beyond an introduction simply to Hosea, tracing the course of events from the time of Solomon to the partition of the land into the two kingdoms in which each

---

24. *Sur Zacharie* 3, SC 84.654.
25. See R. C. Hill, "Psalm 45: A *locus classicus* for Patristic Thinking on Biblical Inspiration," *StudP* 25 (1993): 98–99.
26. CCL 76A.526.

prophet's ministry is conducted. Midway through his work he repeats the exercise in introducing Nahum and identifying his particular purpose, σκοπός:

> Each of the holy prophets was employed in some useful and demanding business at times for the purpose of ministering to the divine decrees and transmitting to people the messages from on high. Some foretold to Israel impending misfortunes so as to terrify them in their sins, and openly threatened that, unless they decided to do what was pleasing to God, they would fall foul of dire and ineluctable troubles. Others highlighted what had actually happened, and by grieving with the victims skillfully persuaded them to opt for a better life and thus appease the divine wrath from then on. Still others led Israel in its sufferings to enjoy sound hope, and brought them to the conviction that after being reduced to misery for their own sins they would in turn prosper with the return of their affairs to their original state, thanks to the mercy, grace, and power of the God who easily transforms everything to whatever he chooses. Such we shall find to be the purpose of the material provided us in this case as well.

As we observed, Cyril's admirable intention of thus contextualizing the ministry of each of The Twelve by statement of his ὑπόθεσις, narrative setting, and σκοπός falls victim to his lack of certainty in matters historical and geographical. Beyond the common interchange of the names Assyria and Babylonia that we find in ancient commentators, Cyril is inclined to use Israel and Judah interchangeably of the divided kingdoms, and is confused about the periods, events, empires, and figures involved in the fall of regimes in Mesopotamia. Nineveh, he assures his readers in introducing Jonah, "is a city of the Persians," whereas, when he comes to the next prophet, Nahum, it is "the chief city of the Assyrians, and he foretold that it would fall when the whole country was overthrown along with it, which happened under Cyrus, son of Cambyses and Mandane, who marshalled Persians, Medes, Elamites, and some other nations along with them against Nineveh. In fact, he took it by force, released Israel from captivity, and bade them return home along with the sacred vessels." Clearly, history and geography did not loom as large in Cyril's schooling as in Diodore's academy, and so his readers would have been more bewildered than would Theodore's.

Despite this handicap, or perhaps because of it, we find Cyril rarely admitting to being at a loss before details in the text; we

INTRODUCTION 11

suspect that at times he is bluffing, or being "creative," in ruling on matters better left indefinite (as we note in the text below). On the other hand, his attention to detail, even if faulty, betrays a commitment that can exceed even that of the Antiochenes; as Kerrigan remarks, "at times he seems to be more interested in these problems than they."[27] For example, in Zec 8.18–19 there is mention of a series of fasts in various months, which the Antiochenes do not trouble to identify; Cyril, by contrast, goes to great lengths to relate the occasions to critical dates in the fall of Jerusalem and subsequent events.

> I feel it is necessary for studious readers to outline once again the reasons for the fasts mentioned here, and what are the *fourth, fifth,* and those following them, *seventh and tenth;* in this way we shall then proceed to supply as well in due course and proper order the force of the directions. After the capture of the holy city, and the subsequent burning of the Temple and deportation of captive Israel along with the sacred vessels, the survivors and those left behind in Judea considered as unmentionable and oppressive the days in which their lot was to suffer such trials; assembling in groups, they kept weeping and wailing, and subjecting themselves to fasting. Now, what actually transpired on each of the days just mentioned to us, come now, let us explain from the sacred text.

If Cyril appeals as a biblical commentator for this attempt to elucidate details of the text, we warm to him no less for his readiness to admit that his personal point of view is only that; "in my view" is a phrase that occurs countless times. He will leave some decisions of interpretation to the reader, as he does in introducing Jonah: "When a text is developed at a spiritual level, and its central character is selected and adopted as a representation of Christ the Savior of us all, a person of wisdom and understanding should judge which details are irrelevant to the purpose in question, and which in turn are relevant and applicable, and likely to be of particular benefit to the listeners." What can irk a reader, on the other hand, is his wordiness and expansiveness and his readiness to quote long sections of the historical books (which often the Aubert text omits). For instance, he is alerted by Jerome[28] to the fact that in Am 3.9–11

---

27. *St. Cyril of Alexandria,* 110.
28. In explicating the background of a text Cyril can be indebted to Jerome, as he is in clarifying the Baals mentioned by Hos 2.16–17.

the LXX has wrongly seen mention of Assyria and Tyre; but, as we observed above, he feels that his version requires justifying, and so sets out on lengthy citation, even at the risk of appearing to be verbose, μακρηγορεῖν: "What is suggested recalls the facts in the second book of Kings and in the second book of Chronicles; I shall give a very brief précis to avoid the impression of being verbose." It is arguably Cyril's failure to avoid such an impression that encouraged Theodoret, who read him at least on The Twelve and Isaiah, to make and observe a commitment to conciseness, συντομία; none of this Antiochene's commentaries ever matched the length of this work.[29] He may also have been impressed by the rich intertextuality of Cyril's commentary, though again not imitating the occasional digression[30] whereby a subtext replaces the lemma to become the text, as happens in commentary on Zec 12.8—to the annoyance of the weary reader.

Slow as he is to apply the prophets' words to the lives of his readers, the bishop likewise never moralizes, even while drawing a moral interpretation from the text. He shows a readiness to unpack the imagery he finds in the text, this being another virtue that Theodoret will adopt. Where the Antiochene is inhibited in following his model is in responding to the depths of religious sentiment found in those prophets who are moved to call for social justice in particular, such as Am 8.4–6, Mi 3.1–4, and Zec 7.9–10, which has been called "one of the finest summaries of the former prophets" with its "strong emphasis on social justice,"[31] and that distillation of refined Old Testament morality in Mi 6.6–8, with its hierarchy of cultic and moral obligations, "Has it been told to you, mortal that you are, what is good, and what the Lord requires of you, other than doing justice, loving mercy, and being ready to walk behind the Lord your God?" Cyril at these places at least registers the relative richness of Old Testament teaching.

---

29. Four hundred thousand words in translation.
30. Digressions are a conspicuous feature of Didymus's commentary.
31. R. L. Smith, *Micah–Malachi,* Word Biblical Commentary 32 (Waco, TX: Word Books, 1984), 226. Admittedly, there are similar passages where Cyril fails to respond in similar fashion; see, e.g., his comments on Hos 2.14; 11.1; Am 5.

4. Interpreting the Twelve Prophets

"The prophets' discourse is generally obscure" is a conclusion reached not only by Cyril,[32] but by the Fathers generally; we recall John Chrysostom's two homilies on the subject.[33] The challenge for commentators—to find in Old Testament texts the truth, reality, ἀλήθεια—is more difficult in the case of the latter prophets. Cyril will make the overall concession that the Old Testament is but σκιά or τύπος of the reality. Yet, perhaps resisting the hermeneutic of a predecessor like Didymus, he wants to maintain that such reality can be found in factual references of prophetic texts—texts that are not to be taken simply in a spiritual sense—even in the case of the vision of the horses in Zec 1 or the inclusion of animals in the call to repentance by Jonah at Nineveh. He has hardly begun his work of commentary when he is confronted with a celebrated challenge to his herm-eneutic in the account of Hosea's marriage to Gomer. This *locus classicus* had elicited two—in his view—unacceptable interpreta-tions: that the account is not factual, and that, even if it were, it is tasteless. Cyril abjures both interpretations.

No argument would persuade us to repudiate the text, to condemn the unlikelihood of the facts, to dismiss the tastelessness of the event itself, or even to think (as some commentators do) that there was no marriage or marital intercourse with Gomer, when the sacred text says that the conception took place and the birth as well, mentions also the child's name, and cites the woman's father and in addition to that the woman's actual name. Since, however, it would be necessary to assert to those willing to concede the reality of what happened that it really happened this way, come now, by exposing the arguments of those given to mockery let us finally provide an apposite explanation of the divine plan.

At this point in the text,[34] editor Pusey cites a Florentine catena which attributes the former aberrant view to Eusebius and

---

32. The phrase "generally obscure" is applied verbatim by Cyril in comment on Hab 3 and Zec 14, as also at the opening of the *Commentary on Isaiah* (PG 70.9).
33. By προφῆται Chrysostom may be referring to all Old Testament authors. See S. Zincone, ed., *Giovanni Crisostomo. Omelie sull'oscurità delle profezie*, Verba seniorum, NS 12 (Rome: Edizioni Studium, 1998).
34. Cyril, *In XII prophetas* 1.17.

the denial of the event's factuality to Origen, while also mentioning Theodore's support for Cyril's position (with which, predictably, Theodoret concurs). Cyril also cites an acquaintance (real or imaginary) who recommends "transposing the drift of the text from factuality to spiritual import"; but he will have none of it, boldly pinning his hermeneutical colors to the mast. As he repeats when some commentators want the Jonah text watered down, "Scripture is true," even if it may at times be a spiritual meaning wherein that truth lies. He may not consistently opt for the priority of a factual/historical interpretation (as in the case of the account of the locust plague in Joel), but he has stoutly maintained that to do so is a respectable option.

What Cyril is allowing for is that a text may have layers of meaning, of which the factual is not the only one but in his view should be examined first, his invariable practice. When that layer has been examined, then one may move onwards and upwards to more "elevated" layers.[35] The advice to the shepherds in Mi 7.14 to let their flock feed in Bashan and Gilead can be taken at various levels, Cyril maintains: "Let us skillfully leap upwards from the corporeal and, as it were, materialistic level to the spiritual, and study the meaning hidden within, because the mind of the saints takes satisfaction in enjoying the meanings of the divine Scripture, and is filled, as it were, with a kind of richness, exercising abundantly, as I said, both practical and contemplative virtue, not for some brief and limited time, but, as the prophet says, *as in times everlasting,* that is, for a long and unlimited time."

In interpreting the text of The Twelve, then, Cyril's general practice is to begin with reference to the historical events (to the extent his imperfect education allows, and therefore without precision in delimiting the period and place of a prophet's ministry) before moving to other, "spiritual"[36] level or levels of meaning—christological, ecclesiological, eschatological, moral.

---

35. Cf. *Diodori Tarsensis commentarii in Psalmos. I. Commentarii in Psalmos I–L,* ed. J.-M. Olivier, CCG 6 (Turnhout: Brepols, 1980), 7: "The historical sense, in fact, is not in opposition to the more elevated sense; on the contrary, it proves to be the basis and foundation of the more elevated meanings."

36. Cyril's most frequent term is νοητός.

INTRODUCTION

In commenting on Hab 2.3 he first sees reference to Cyrus, and then takes the commentary to another level.

> As far as the historical account goes [ἱστορία], then, it was Cyrus son of Cambyses to whom reference is made in the sentence, *If he is delayed, wait for him;* it was he who took Babylon, plundering other cities along with it. But as for a mystical [μυστικός] treatment and spiritual [πνευματικός] account, I would say that the force of the expression would rightly be applied to Christ the Savior of all; he is the one "who is and who was and who is to come" [Rv 1.8], and the word of the holy prophets foretold that he is to come in due time.

The frequency of an ecclesiological interpretation among these various levels of meaning makes Ephesians a favorite reference; a reading of the *Commentary* would not confirm the view that "Cyril knew no way to speak of Christ than in the words of the Bible, and no way to interpret the words of the Bible than through Christ."[37] Admittedly, he likes to see in biblical figures a type of Christ, though admitting even of a towering figure like Moses, "Not everything in texts and types, therefore, is relevant to spiritual interpretations—only if a character is introduced who in himself prefigures Christ for us; then we properly pass over human elements and focus only on relevant details, in every case highlighting what is conducive to supporting the purpose of the text."[38]

For these reasons, then, and for this reader, Cyril's eclectic hermeneutic is more satisfying than, say, that of Theodore, whose historicism[39] precludes his acknowledging New Testament

---

37. R. L. Wilken, "Cyril of Alexandria as Interpreter of the Old Testament," in *St Cyril of Alexandria*, ed. T. G. Weinandy and D. A. Keating (London and New York: T & T Clark, 2003), 21. As suggested above, Cyril himself would probably also qualify Wilken's further remarks in this place: "Through history Christ transforms history, and after his coming a strictly historical interpretation of the Old Testament is anachronistic. For the Scriptures can no longer be interpreted as one interprets other documents from the past, setting things in historical context, deciding what came earlier and what later, relating things to what went before or followed afterward. Now interpretation must begin at the center which is also the beginning and the end, with Christ who is Alpha and the Omega. Christ imposes a new order on the Scriptures."

38. See Cyril's preface to his commentary on Jonah.

39. A result of Theodore's having been drilled in the maxim of Aristarchus, "Clarify Homer from Homer." See C. Schäublin, *Untersuchungen zu Methode und Herkunft der antiochenischen Exegese*, Theophaneia: Beiträge zur Religions- und

echoes even in *testimonia* cited by it (such as Hos 6.2; 10.8; Mi 7.6; Mal 4.2), or that of Didymus, whose arbitrary and gratuitous recourse to spiritual meanings can be seen as implying a degree of irresponsibility.[40] If Gustave Bardy awards the compliment "modéré" to Theodoret,[41] much of the credit goes to Cyril, from whom this degree of balance was learned. Predictably, there are times when Cyril is guilty of the faults of his Alexandrian predecessor, as in some arbitrary uses of allegory and in the long and irrelevant lecture he gives on spiritual blackness when meeting the puzzling inclusion of the term Ethiopians in Zep 2.12, beginning, "Since, on the other hand, the inspired Scripture is in the habit of treating of spiritual *Ethiopians*, come now, let us deal also with them, though not proceeding beyond the sense of the passage." To this Didymian arbitrariness is added the occasional recourse to his predecessor's method of interpretation-by-association, that is, arriving at a meaning of one prophetic verse by flicking through a mental concordance, as it were, as Cyril does in interpreting the sword mentioned in Mi 5.6. His invocation of number symbolism, however, is much less frequent than that of Didymus, and if, like him, he shows an interest in etymologies as a hermeneutical tool, he has Jerome to thank for being on firmer ground.

It would be surprising if the bishop did not at times see a sacramental dimension to the text. As we saw him interpreting the mention of "early and late rain" in Zec 10.1 as a reference to Old and New Testaments, so the appearance of the phrase in Jl 2.23 elicits a sacramental interpretation: "Now, it should be understood that the reality of the promise comes also in the form of sacramental fulfillment; the living water of holy baptism is given to us as rain, the bread of life as grain, and the blood as wine. Use of oil is also applied in bringing those justified in Christ through holy baptism." While we are not concerned about any lack of consistency in this, a regrettable feature of Cyril's inter-

---

Kirchengeschichte des Altertums 23 (Cologne and Bonn: Peter Hanstein, 1974), 159. Schäublin attributes to the influence of grammarians like Aristarchus the limited hermeneutical perspective of an Antiochene like Theodore.

40. See the introduction to Hill, FOTC 111, 17, 24.

41. "Interprétation chez les pères," *DBS* 4.582.

pretation of The Twelve, as also of his peers, is a failure to recognize the genre of apocalyptic—a failure that occurs frequently in these authors. Though he is in the habit of giving certain items of prophetic texts an eschatological meaning, it does not occur to him that the apocalyptic motif "Day of the Lord," which he meets frequently from Joel onwards, should be one of those; he sees such texts as having instead a proximate historical fulfillment. When he comes to one such passage in Zep 1.14–16, he finds Jerome encouraging him to see a reference not only to the Roman wars but also to the day of individual and general judgments; but he prefers to shorten his hermeneutical perspective: "Again he crushes the hope of those who in some cases are disposed to think that the prophecy will take effect only after a long delay; he presents retribution as being at the door, as it were, and the calamities of war advancing apace. He calls the time when such things will occur *day of the Lord,* referring to it as *swift* because it is coming without any delay and is due to be seen before long." While this is not the spiritualizing approach inspired by Origen, it still represents a "taming"[42] of apocalyptic and a reduction of the prophets' perspective.

5. Theological accents in the *Commentary*

As the work of one whose name is generally associated with theological controversy, not to say acrimony,[43] a feature of the *Commentary on the Twelve Prophets* that strikes the reader is the absence of polemic. Where Didymus in commenting on Zecha-

---

42. B. E. Daley speaks of "a 'taming' of apocalyptic in order to integrate it into a larger picture of a Christian world order, a 'history of salvation' culminating in the redeemed life of the disciples of the risen Christ"; see Daley, "Apocalypticism in Early Christian Theology," in B. McGinn, ed., *The Encyclopedia of Apocalypticism* 2 (New York and London: Continuum, 2002), 5. In adhering to the lifetime of the prophet in question, Cyril shows a kinship with Theodore and the Antiochenes rather than with Origen.

43. Russell, *Cyril of Alexandria,* vii, attributes contemporary perceptions of Cyril to "Gibbon's damning portrait of him in the forty-seventh chapter of *The Decline and Fall of the Roman Empire,* where he is represented as the murderer of Hypatia and the bully of the Council of Ephesus." And T. G. Weinandy and D. A. Keating believe that "for many—then and now—Cyril of Alexandria is little more than an ecclesiastical thug"; see Weinandy and Keating, eds., *The Theology of St Cyril of Alexandria,* xiii. No thug, however, wrote the *Commentary on the Twelve Prophets.*

riah can at regular intervals parade before the reader a (probably conventional) rogues' gallery of heresiarchs, Cyril, despite equal application of the prophets' discourse to the contemporary church, is satisfied with harping rather mechanically on the "errors" of Jews, pagan religions, or unspecified heretics and false teachers. This feature would, of course, support the consensus of scholars that the work belongs to the period before the outbreak of animosity between Alexandria and Antioch with the accession of Nestorius to the see of Constantinople in 428. There is, to be sure, a moral accent in the work as one of the levels of meaning Cyril allows in the prophets' message; the Old Testament people were "deceived" by false prophets and other religions, and those of the New by the devil and heretical teachers.[44] So error and deception are constant themes that occur when the commentator is dealing with his subject either ἱστορικῶς or νοητῶς; but no particular contemporary teacher or teaching is in Cyril's sights.

This absence of a polemical edge is accompanied by a positive stance on matters moral (we noted that Cyril never moralizes). The Fall has occurred, but it is the restoration, ἀνακεφαλαίωσις, that is more memorable; when the Lord in Zep 3.17 promises a restoration to Jerusalem, Cyril, who finds that term in Eph 1.10 grist to his mill more than once, bursts out with enthusiasm, "Now, 'restoring' means in a way taking up again and, as it were, reshaping to the original state. When he *renewed* us, Christ then also *brought joy* to us as though *with satisfaction as on a festival day;* how would the divinity not be likely to take satisfaction in our situation when we were rid of sin, had prevailed over death and corruption, and enjoyed a share in the Spirit and in sanctification?" Our role in this process involves faith and grace; times beyond counting, Christians are referred to as "those justified through faith," and it is only at the last gasp, in his final words on Malachi, that Cyril adds the qualification, "It is true that 'faith without works is dead' [Jas 2.20]: while faith in Christ justifies, and rids us

44. Zec 8.9 gives the commentator an invitation to inveigh against false prophets; but the most Cyril wants to say by way of application to the church of his day is this: "It also becomes us to believe the words coming from [God], and be careful to take as our guides those who would in due course be honest ministers to us of the divine oracles."

of the stain of past sins, yet if people are afterwards found to be indifferent and to have succumbed to the passions of the flesh and the world, they have put faith to death, as it were, within them, acquiring nothing deserving of commendation, but rather re-lapsing into their former depraved life."

If this commentary had been written after 428, doubtless there would have been further passages of sustained christological development than the few we find. Such passages seem to occur only when the commentator feels that readers are in danger of misunderstanding a text, such as that on the outpouring of the Spirit in Jl.2.28, where Cyril begins by asserting that the Spirit was given to Adam.

The grace given to a human being proved fruitless, however, but was renewed in Christ, the second Adam. Now, in what way was it renewed? As God, in fact, the Son is by nature also from God, truly born of the God and Father; the Spirit is proper to him, in him, and from him, according to which, of course, by "him" is understood the God and Father. In so far as he became man, on the other hand, and is like us, he is said to have the Spirit imparted to him; it came down upon him, for instance, in the form of a dove when he became like us, as I said, and in the divine plan he was baptized like one of us.

While Christ is also represented elsewhere as the second Adam, Cyril's favorite phrase here for referring to the person of Jesus is "the mystery of Christ," a term which clearly does not have the more comprehensive sense that Paul gives it.[45] We do not find, on the other hand, such accent on the humanity of Jesus as we do in the Antiochenes' commentary generally; they would, in fact, be disconcerted by one expression of it here which would strike them as docetic: namely, when Cyril is trying to elucidate the term "horns" in the LXX version of Hab 3.4 by giving it a christological bent: "The Only-begotten comes in a form like ours, then, putting up with the appearance [δόκησις] of our limitations in respect of flesh and humanity; but as God he has all the *horns in his hands,* that is, all kingdoms, in terms of all the force of the opposing activities."[46]

45. See Hill, "The Mystery of Christ: Clue to Paul's Thinking on Wisdom," *HeyJ* 25 (1984): 475–83.
46. Marie-Odile Boulnois says of Cyril, "He uses φύσις as the equivalent of οὐσία"; see her "The Mystery of the Trinity according to Cyril of Alexandria,"

As the Jewish people were on the receiving end of much of the prophets' satire and censure, so Cyril has no difficulty endorsing this stream of invective, also proceeding to apply it to the Jews of New Testament times.[47] The promise of divine wrath affecting the Old Testament people, as in Zec 13.7 LXX, is readily applied to a later generation, as of course one finds in other Fathers as well.

The fact that for the crucifiers the crime would be the source of ruin, and that those responsible for such a scheme and such exploits—namely, the leaders of the people—would be subjected to the evils arising from divine wrath, he makes clear in saying, *And I shall raise my hand against the shepherds.* It was they, remember, in the words of the prophet, who "destroyed my vineyard, turned his desirable portion into a trackless waste, it became a desolate ruin" [Jer 12.10–11]. God will *raise his hand,* as though striking with a sword and exacting vengeance for sacrilege, not only because they have vented their spleen on Christ but because in addition to this and their other crimes it was the beginning and introduction to unrestrained madness.

Such antipathy to Jews strikes one in reading the "modéré" Theodoret[48] as well, and may be a further legacy from Cyril.

6. Cyril's achievement in the *Commentary on the Twelve Prophets*

Comparisons, even if odious, are inevitable in the case of this work, which was composed in the wake of several others of differing character by eminent commentators such as Origen, Didymus, Jerome, and Theodore. Theodoret obviously found it the model to be imitated, a plausible option when one recognizes the strengths it exemplifies and the excesses it generally avoids and even decries. Not that Cyril's *Commentary on The Twelve* is a

---

in *The Theology of St Cyril of Alexandria,* ed. T. G. Weinandy and D. A. Keating, 89. Such usage occurs here in commentary on Zec 4.7: "As if someone were asking the question, '*Who are you* who promise in this way to perform great deeds without any fighting or effort?' the God and Father replies in the words, I am the *mighty mountain before Zerubbabel, to achieve,* that is, I am the φύσις surpassing everything, which to an extent proper to God surpasses everything in the glory it emits, and is destined in due course to effect the fulfillment of the promises even *before Zerubbabel.*" Boulnois, however, has not garnered universal agreement.

47. Russell, *Cyril of Alexandria,* 6–9, traces the ill feeling between Cyril and the Jews in Alexandria.

48. See n. 41, above.

INTRODUCTION 21

cut-and-paste and altogether derivative production: it adopts a consistent style of commentary and in particular an independent hermeneutic that is paralleled only in the work of his later admirer (who also chose to avoid some features, such as its prolixity). Formally it is a work of biblical commentary ("exegesis" being in this case, as in those others, a term not properly applicable);[49] Cyril is not using the Twelve Prophets as a platform for expounding theological doctrines, and the doctrinal is not one of the levels of meaning in texts that he regularly explicates, even if frequent textual mention of false prophets can elicit a conventional warning against harmful teaching.

In response to the repeated complaints that this very lengthy work has not been available in English—a lacuna this translation is meant to fill—one should not now look to it for documentation of the distinctive theological positions of the celebrated bishop of Alexandria, protagonist of polemical and conciliar wrangling of the second quarter of the fifth century. Cyril totally avoids such polemic in work on The Twelve, and in fact rarely regales the reader with sustained christological and trinitarian teaching. Instead, he constantly appears as a balanced commentator, eclectic in his attitude and his indebtedness to predecessors, and tolerant of alternative views even in his readers. If there is a fault in his style of commentary, it is the indiscipline that allows him to exceed due limits and become guilty (as he seems conscious) of being verbose, μακρηγορεῖν.

Cyril comes to these biblical authors (perhaps before work on Isaiah, his other extant commentary on the Latter Prophets) without a fully rounded formation. He had not been drilled in textual, linguistic, and even historical and literary skills to the degree required to do justice to their thinking in the original. While he has Jerome's work before him for light on the shortcomings of his esteemed LXX version—a resource he employs sparingly—he is insecure in his grasp of the factual and geographical background touched on by the authors, and, though

---

49. Cf. J. N. D. Kelly, *Golden Mouth. The Story of John Chrysostom, Ascetic, Preacher, Bishop* (Ithaca, NY: Cornell University Press, 1995), 94: "Neither John, nor any Christian teacher for centuries to come, was equipped to carry out exegesis as we have come to understand it. He could not be expected to understand the nature of Old Testament writings."

showing a refreshing interest in the history *in* the text, he predictably is unconcerned about the history *of* the text in cases where this affects meaning. It is that interest in the fortunes of the people of Israel and Judah (the distinction not always clear to him) in the centuries prior to and following the exile, and in the details of the message to them from these twelve spokesmen, that is refreshing because it distinguishes his hermeneutic from that of his Alexandrian peers in particular, who could downplay that story. Didymus showed much less interest in it before moving from the text to a range of spiritual meanings as the locus of ἀλήθεια, the reality intended by the divine and human authors. Cyril abjures an approach that dismisses the factuality of the text,[50] and consistently begins his interpretation with serious comment on it in the manner of the Antiochenes before moving to give equal attention to other levels of meaning, including the christological.

Jerome, who had requested Didymus to compose his commentary on Zechariah, but who in disappointment dismissed that work along with one on Hosea as "totally allegorical commentary, with scarcely any reference to factuality,"[51] would not have been able to find Cyril's guilty of that charge. Today's reader will need stamina to profit from it, but will judge the effort well worthwhile.

---

50. As he does in his opening defense of Hosea's marriage in comments on that prophet.

51. Jerome (not averse to allegory himself), in introducing his commentary on Zechariah, includes Origen and Hippolytus in that dismissal; see CCL 76A.748.

COMMENTARY ON THE TWELVE PROPHETS

COMMENTARY ON THE PROPHET HOSEA

PREFACE

ONE MIGHT THINK it somewhat superfluous and rash, not to say hardly vital, to endeavor to poke around, as it were, among the previous comments of many writers and make a contribution in addition to the labors of my predecessors.[1] And this despite their being quite capable of adequately clarifying the compositions of the holy prophets.[2] For my part, on the other hand, I would claim that this is not the case, and that it is very necessary; I shall recall Paul's proclaiming to those under the guidance of his sacred teaching, "To write the same things to you is not troublesome to me, and for you it is a safeguard."[3] Consider the truth of his remark: in the case where something that is required for understanding is at hand, and then lengthy commentary is given of it by many writers, there will be no harm at all in that; rather, it would be of particular benefit to the listeners. After all, if those in the business of commentary happen to make comments corresponding to one another, the comprehension by the students is surely rendered more secure. If, on the other hand, some (2)[4] new idea is pro-

---

1. Though Cyril himself refers to this preface as the beginning of his work on Hosea (see the initial sentence of the third paragraph, below), and it is thus included by Aubertus and Pusey, its function is in fact to situate all The Twelve in their respective historical settings from the division of the Solomonic kingdom to the return from exile. Cyril gives no other prophet a lengthy introduction of this kind; hence it seems best to characterize it as a general introduction, especially as Hos 1.1 attracts a further historical and hermeneutical preface.

2. Cyril is implying, as the term "Writing Prophets" used of the Latter Prophets of the Hebrew Bible also suggests, that their ministry was one of written composition *(suggraphê)* rather than of oral proclamation, which *prophêteia* might instead connote. Cyril would not have found this respectful attitude to his predecessors, which Theodoret may have learned from him, in Theodore.

3. Phil 3.1. In this disclaimer Cyril would have in mind the twenty-five books by Origen on (some of) The Twelve mentioned by Eusebius, Didymus's work on Zechariah and (part of) Hosea, and the complete coverage of The Twelve beyond Alexandria by Jerome and by Theodore in Antioch.

4. Page numbers of the Pusey edition are included in the text for ease of reference.

posed by a particular commentator that is not judged correct and acceptable by some, what harm is there if it goes into another person's mind? Rather, is it not better for there to be ample and orderly presentation of ideas?

Accordingly, even if many have written a commentary on the holy prophets before us, this is not a reason for us to keep silent; instead, we shall reject the handicap of sloth, and with the grace given us as well by the one who reveals profound and hidden things[5] we shall make this work clear to others as well, mindful of Christ's saying, "You received without payment; give without payment."[6]

In beginning our clarification of the blessed prophet Hosea,[7] then, we shall initially expose what pertains also to the compositions of the other prophets. People generally find it easy, in fact, to adapt the commentary they give to what seems the intention of the Holy Spirit, in some cases moving easily from the facts, or the visible events that happened and, as it were, fall within their vision, to interior and spiritual realities, and in other cases penetrating in quite an obscure fashion to the events at a physical level.[8] As far as possible we shall present the characters' own interventions—laments and proclamations, references to past happenings, and predictions of the future.[9] There is need, therefore, for clear discernment of each detail to the extent possible, necessarily preserving the sequence of ideas and the difference in characters, this being the way for our treatment to be completely clear, uncomplicated, and free of all difficulty.[10]

---

5. See Dn 2.22 in the version of Theodotion.

6. Mt 10.8.

7. Cyril does not advert, as does Theodoret, to the corpus of The Twelve being known as a "book" (from the time of Ben Sira), or discuss its features. (But see n. 18 on Amos 4.)

8. The introduction to Hosea thus outlines Cyril's approach to the prophets generally. He would know that in Didymus and Theodore, for example, the hermeneutical accent fell quite differently, as detailed in these two approaches. He himself is not reluctant to deal with the facts, *historia*, though usually moving to an ecclesiological and/or christological level. Kerrigan credits him with some Antiochene leanings.

9. We shall have to see if Cyril is up to this self-imposed challenge of distinguishing different genres in the material, especially apocalyptic.

10. We shall find Cyril acquitting himself well of this goal for a commentator.

I take it as necessary to give some initial explanation of what befell those of the bloodline of Israel, to prevent the readers' minds from being confused on hearing at one time of Ephraim and Israel and also Samaria, and again of Judah and Benjamin, (3) such names being frequently employed by the holy prophets.[11] Let them clearly understand all this, then, when hearing that Solomon was administering the kingdom of his father at the time in Jerusalem, and that he built in God's honor that famous and celebrated Temple. Despite being very distinguished for the splendor of his wealth and the abundance of his possessions, however, on growing old he offended God because of the scandal of his wives.

The sacred text explains to us what form of sin he was guilty of, reading this way: "The king took foreign wives in addition to the daughter of Pharaoh: Moabites, Ammonites, Syrians, Idumeans, Hittites, and Amorites. They came from the nations the Lord had forbidden to the sons of Israel: 'You shall not enter into marriage with them, nor they with you, lest they incline your hearts to follow their idols.' Solomon clung to these in love; among his wives were seven hundred princesses and three hundred concubines. In time Solomon grew old, and the foreign wives diverted his heart to follow other gods, and his heart was not true to the Lord his God, as was the heart of his father David. Solomon followed Astarte, the abomination of the Sidonians, and Baal, the idol of the sons of Ammon. Solomon did what was evil in the sight of the Lord, and did not follow the Lord as his father David had. At that time Solomon built a high place for Chemosh, the idol of Moab, for Baal, the idol of the sons of Ammon, and for Astarte, the abomination of the Sidonians. He did the same for all his foreign wives, who offered incense and sacrificed to their idols. The Lord was very angry with Solomon for turning his heart (4) from the Lord the God of Israel, who had appeared to him twice and had commanded him concerning this matter by no means to follow other gods,

---

11. Cyril is less comfortable explaining the use of "Israel" for Judah on the return from exile. Likewise, he feels free to refer to the fate of Judah as part of the message of this prophet preaching to the northern kingdom, his spiritual interpretation generally contrasting Jews as a group with Gentiles.

but to observe and do what the Lord God commanded him."[12]

Solomon's misdeeds in his old age, therefore, surpassed every form of impiety. After all, what could be more odious than such outrageous failings? How does it not beggar belief for him to deprive of honor and love the sole being who is God by nature and in truth, and accord to herds of demons the status due to him alone, and rather attach it to sticks and stones? Since he was proven to be guilty of thinking and doing what cannot be repeated, and of such disgraceful sins, the God of all then said to him, "Since this has been your mind, and you have not kept my commandments and orders that I commanded you, I shall surely tear the kingdom from your hand and give it to your servant. Yet for the sake of your father David I shall not do it in your lifetime: I shall take it from the hand of your son. But I shall not take the whole kingdom: I shall give one scepter to your son for the sake of David my servant and for the sake of Jerusalem, the city that I chose."[13] Since in fact, as I said, Solomon was in thrall to his passion for women, extremely wise though he was, and, as it were, to the full extent of his capacity he tore apart God's kingdom by attaching to idols the honor and glory due to the one God alone, consequently to be sure, and very rightly, God threatened to tear apart his kingdom, bringing him grief in equal measure, according to what is written in the prophet Ezekiel, (5) "As you have done, it shall be done to you: your recompense will return upon your head."[14]

Now, when Solomon passed away, his son was called to the throne, namely, Rehoboam. It was then, in fact, and only then, that Israel was finally divided, and the ten tribes and half of the tribe of Ephraim parted from Jerusalem. The descendants of Joseph, you see, who were sons of Ephraim and Manasseh, were reckoned as one tribe, an arrangement their forbear Jacob want-

---

12. 1 Kgs 11.1–10. Cyril is always interested in situating the prophets in their historical situation, here tracing the division of the kingdom in the tenth century before Christ.

13. 1 Kgs 11.11–13.

14. Though Cyril can be vague about scriptural references ("somewhere" being a frequent rubric), he rarely thinks in terms of the wrong author, this reference seeming to come from Ob 15 (though a similar expression occurs in Joel, Isaiah, Jeremiah, and Lamentations, but not Ezekiel).

ed to obtain; it was said to Joseph, "So now your two sons who were born to you in Egypt, before I came to you in Egypt, are mine, Ephraim and Manasseh; just as Reuben and Simeon are, they will be mine."[15] Accordingly, the ten tribes and half of one—namely, Ephraim—left for Samaria, and were outside the kingdom of Rehoboam, while those from the tribe of Judah and Benjamin stayed in Jerusalem.

Since those who remained in Samaria were without king or leader, and suspected the incursions of Rehoboam, expecting to perish along with their loved ones, they sent for Jeroboam. He was a servant of Solomon, who had fled to Egypt to King Shishak; on his arrival they immediately appointed him leader and invested the wretch with the scepter of kingship. Jeroboam was of the region and tribe of Ephraim; when he was appointed king, he then began scheming about how he could confirm his reign and achieve stability without the will of the appointers turning to some other wish or preference. Then, afraid lest Israel would be led to remember the lawful worship practices and the festivals celebrated in Jerusalem and choose to relapse into former practices and submit to the yoke of Rehoboam, (6) he made two golden heifers, forced Israel to return to worship them as in Egypt,[16] and gave orders to bow down to them and offer burnt offerings. "He erected one in Gilgal, the other in Dan."[17] These cities, which were in the region of the Samaritans, were more famous than the others.

Accordingly, the apostasy of the ten tribes and half of the tribe of Ephraim was twofold: they cut their ties not only with Jerusalem but also with the very worship of God, bowing down to golden heifers, giving sacrifices and worship to "the works of their hands," as Scripture says.[18] Those who remained in Jerusalem,

---

15. Gn 48.5.
16. There is no mention of Egypt in the PG edition.
17. 1 Kgs 12.29, though Heb. and other LXX forms read Bethel and Dan, well known as royal sanctuaries—perhaps a loose citation by Cyril (he reads Bethel below). Despite his generally confident statements about history and geography (Gilgal, for instance, is not now known), Cyril can sometimes be thought to be bluffing, even "creative." Kerrigan thinks he is indebted to Jerome for information in these areas, and a comparison of the two, cited below, supports this.
18. Jer 1.16.

on the other hand—that is, Judah and Benjamin—showed regard and attention to the oracles given through Moses, sacrificing in the Temple. They were not wholly devoted to the love of God, however, being partially given to apostasy themselves: they sacrificed to idols "on every high hill and under every leafy grove,"[19] in the prophet's phrase. So when you hear the holy prophets referring to Israel or Ephraim, you should then take it to mean those in Samaria, whereas when [they refer] to Judah or Benjamin, it is those who stayed in Jerusalem. Now, there were also prophets among them, prophesying equally among those in Samaria and those in Jerusalem; some lived in Jerusalem and some lived in the region of the Samaritans, and conveyed the words from God to the listeners.

Now, it should be understood that, after the rupture from Jerusalem of the ten tribes and half of the tribe of Ephraim, both those in Samaria and those in Jerusalem had their own kings. This obtained until the time of the final captivity, when, with Cyrus in power and permitting them to leave, they returned to Jerusalem (7) under the leadership of Zerubbabel son of Shealtiel, who was of the tribe of Judah, and with Joshua son of Jozadak as priest. It was then that they rebuilt the Temple, came under one rule, and occupied Jerusalem with the removal of all division. The following text will clearly give evidence of the number of captivities that at various times involved, on the one hand, the ten tribes and half of the tribe of Ephraim, and, on the other, those in Jerusalem, namely, Judah and Benjamin. There is need also to record the periods when each of the holy prophets spoke, for us to have a precise knowledge of the conditions when the events occurred and what the situation was when the words were delivered to them from God.[20] (8)

19. Jer 3.6.

20. It may be from Antiochene commentators that Cyril gained at least his aspiration to achieve historical "precision" in situating the prophets in their times; it would not have been from Didymus (who, Jerome tells us, wrote five books on Hosea). He seems to idealize the restored unity of all tribes; the books of Ezra and Nehemiah, however, suggest exclusivism by the south, leading to the erection of a temple on Mt. Gerizim in Samaria.

COMMENTARY ON HOSEA,
CHAPTER ONE

Word of the Lord that came to Hosea son of Beeri in the days of Uzziah, Jotham, Achaz, and Hezekiah, kings of Judah, and in the days of Jeroboam son of Joash, king of Israel (v.1).

LESSED HOSEA, then, is prophesying *in the days of Uzziah, Jotham, Achaz, and Hezekiah, kings of Judah, and in the days of Jeroboam son of Joash, king of Israel.* While the period of prophecy is understood as taking its development up to this point, my view is that a clear explanation should now be given of the events in each case, as far as we can understand it, involving, as I said before, what kind of people they proved to be, whether good and well-disposed towards God, or inclined to the opposite, and what befell each of them, both those in Samaria and those in Jerusalem. This is the way, in fact, that we shall understand in quite easy fashion what the purpose of the prophecy had in view.[1]

Although the last to be mentioned is Jeroboam son of Joash, king of Israel, he lived before Azariah, or Uzziah. It should be realized that he is different from the first king of that name, who lived in the time of the reign of Rehoboam son of Solomon, though of like mind and similar to him in impiety;[2] it is written of him these terms: "In the fifteenth year of Amaziah son of Joash, king of Judah, Jeroboam son of Joash began to reign over

---

1. Another feature of Cyril's commentary that strikes one as Antiochene is his interest, not only in the *hypothesis* or narrative setting of each prophet, but also in the *skopos* of the material. He is also very ready to expose his opinion *(oimai)* while admitting his limitations.

2. Cyril properly addresses the oddity of mention of one king of Israel, whom he rightly identifies as Jeroboam II, while four kings of Judah are cited. While he implies the respective length of reigns is the factor, his modern counterpart Dennis McCarthy believes that "the compilers of the book of Hosea significantly ignore the miserable kinglets who follow Jeroboam."

Israel in Samaria, and reigned forty-one years. He did what was evil in the sight of the Lord, not departing from all the sins of Jeroboam son of Nebat, who caused Israel to sin." Do you see how he imitated the ways of his predecessor, (9) following the same course, as it were, and, so to speak, treading in the footsteps of the other's impiety? What does the sacred text say next? "In the twenty-seventh year of King Jeroboam of Israel, Azariah son of Amaziah, king of Judah, began to reign. He was sixteen years old when he began to reign, and he reigned fifty-two years in Jerusalem. His mother's name was Jecoliah of Jerusalem. He did what was right in the Lord's eyes, just as his father Amaziah had always done. But he did not take away the high places; the people still sacrificed and made offerings on the high places. The Lord struck the king, and he was leprous to the day of his death."[3]

While Uzziah was pious and godly, he was not completely so; he did not abolish the high places, the text says; instead, those who were in error made offerings on them and offered sacrifices to the demons. Azariah, or Uzziah, was then carried away to such a degree of improper thinking as to believe that it belonged to the status of the king to perform the rites sanctioned by God and to maintain the sacred liturgy; and of course he sacrificed on his own authority in defiance of the laws of Moses. When he went up to the ritual that was in no way proper to him, however—namely, the priestly ritual—"the Lord struck him, and he was leprous to the day of his death."[4] By law the leper was unclean, and those affected by the disease were expelled from the camp; God had said to the revealer Moses, "Tell the children of Israel to banish from the camp everyone who is leprous or has a discharge, and everyone who is unclean through contact with a corpse."[5] He was punished with the disease for having presumed to do what was not proper for him, and God sentenced the king to dishonor for usurping priestly status.[6]

---

3. 2 Kgs 14.23–24; 15.1–5. The fifty-two years of Jeroboam's reign include fifteen years of regency during his father Amaziah's reign.
4. 2 Chr 26.20–21.
5. Nm 5.2. The text here reads "with a soul" *(epi psychê)*, in agreement with the LXX.
6. The account of Uzziah's temerity and punishment is given in 2 Chr 26.16–21. Cyril does not moralize on this presumptuous behavior.

COMMENTARY ON HOSEA 1

Now, since the force of the prophecy bears not only (10) on Judah—that is, those in Jerusalem—but applies also to Israel—that is, the ten tribes in Samaria[7]—come now, let us in consequence mention those who reigned over it in the time of Azariah, or Uzziah, and the awful disasters in which they were caught up for succumbing improperly to loathsome idolatry. Already in the twenty-eighth year of the reign of Uzziah, or Azariah, a different Azariah, son of Jeroboam, reigned over Israel for six months.[8] But since he, too, walked in the way of his father, and did what was evil in the eyes of the Lord, he was given over to slaughter at the hands of some of his own family, and perished.

After a lapse of time, in the thirty-eighth year of the reign of Uzziah, Shallum was anointed king over Israel and reigned one month; he was immediately done away with by Menahem son of Gadi in Tirzah.[9] The sacred text indicated that he had sons, and both were of the line of Jehu, who killed Ahab, his sons, and Jezebel; God had promised him, "Your sons of the fourth generation will sit upon your throne." Accordingly, Menahem reigned over Israel after killing Shallum; "he did what was evil in the eyes of the Lord," the text says; "he did not depart from any of the sins of Jeroboam son of Nebat, who caused Israel to sin."[10] While he was reigning—Menahem, I mean—and offending God with his extreme inclination to the false worship of idols, Pul, king of Assyria, took control of Samaria; unable to resist him by force of arms, [Menahem] persuaded him with much money to leave his country and desist from fighting.

When Menahem died, (11) however, in the fifty-second year of the reign of Uzziah, Jotham was anointed king over Judah in Jerusalem on the death of his father, of whom Scripture says, "He did what was right in the eyes of the Lord, just as his father Uzziah had always done. But he did not remove the high places,

---

7. We shall see that Cyril does not acknowledge Hosea's eighth-century ministry as directed to the northern kingdom; as a result his use of "Israel" is ambiguous, and he can see Judah's sixth-century troubles in focus as well. He is not helped in this by the double focus in v.1, and by the movement from one kingdom to the other in the text of Kings he is following closely.

8. The biblical text (2 Kgs 15.8) refers to this king as Zechariah; Cyril repeats his choice of names in introducing Micah.

9. 2 Kgs 15.8–14.   10. 2 Kgs 10.30; 15.18.

the people still sacrificing and making offerings on the high places."[11] Over Israel, on the other hand, there reigned Pekahiah son of Menahem; "he reigned two years, and did what was evil in the eyes of the Lord. Then Pekah son of Remaliah, his captain, conspired against him," the text says, "attacked him in Samaria, and reigned in his place over Israel. He did what was evil in the eyes of the Lord, and did not depart from any of the sins of Jeroboam son of Nebat, who caused Israel to sin."[12]

It was during his reign that Tiglath-pileser king of Assyria, who took control of all Samaria, deported Israel to Assyria.[13] Pekah also died when a conspiracy was made against him by Hoshea son of Elah, who came to the throne in his place in the twentieth year of Jotham son of Azariah. But, the text says, "in those days the Lord began to send against Judah Rezin king of Syria and Pekah son of Remaliah."[14] In these verses the story has gone backwards; we mentioned that Pekah had died when Hoshea son of Elah raised a conspiracy and plot against him; but the story inserts what happened in his lifetime: "In those days the Lord began to send against Judah Rezin king of Syria and Pekah son of Remaliah." Pekah son of Remaliah in fact waged war on the inhabitants of Jerusalem, though they were his neighbors; but when he saw their resistance to be fierce and unrelenting, he persuaded Rezin king (12) of the Syrians to be his ally and accomplice in mounting a joint siege against Jerusalem.

When the war broke out, then, Jotham son of Azariah died, and his son Ahaz succeeded to the kingship, a very wicked man and an idolater, so far under the influence of idolatrous errors as to make his own son pass through fire; he also acquiesced in every kind of deviant behavior and sacrificed "on the high places and under every leafy tree," as Scripture says. Taking fright,

---

11. 2 Kgs 15.34–35. 12. 2 Kgs 15.23–29.
13. 2 Kgs 15.29.
14. 2 Kgs 15.37. Cyril has been depending heavily on the annals given in 2 Kings, not thinking it could be a composite text. At this stage he notes that, after recording Pekah's death, it proceeds to speak further of his life, which an uncritical mind would find anomalous. He is also unprepared to see in the names Pul and Tiglath-pileser the same Assyrian king, Tiglath-pileser III. The Antiochenes, who for all their commitment to finding *historia* in a biblical text do not trace the succession of kings at such length or with such dependence on the text, fare no better.

therefore, Ahaz collected all the riches to be found in the house of the Lord, and sent word through messengers to Tiglath-pileser, king of the Assyrians, asking to be rescued by him. So the Assyrian took up arms against the kingdom of Rezin, captured Damascus, the capital of Syria, and did away with Rezin.[15] Ahaz then went down from Jerusalem to Damascus to see the Assyrian; noticing an altar in the shrines of the idols with novel and unusual features, he was fascinated by it, took a copy, and sent it to Uriah the priest in Jerusalem with orders to have one made like it. He brought it into the house of the Lord, showing scorn, as it were, for the one made according to God's wishes conveyed through Moses, and bade the prescribed rituals be performed on it; he also introduced other novelties in addition to this in the Temple as he chose in a manner inconsiderate and disrespectful to God.[16]

Now, in his time, when Hoshea son of Elah was still king of Israel, Shalmaneser king of the Assyrians invaded Israel, devastated Samaria, and deported Israel to the mountains and rivers of the Medes; he also killed Hoshea. What was the reason? Because, the text says, he had not sent him tribute, a sign (13) of subjection, instead summoning to his aid the ruler of Egypt.[17]

Then after this on the death of Ahaz, his son Hezekiah became king over Judah in Jerusalem; he was a pious man, so devoted to righteousness as to be without peer. "He demolished the high places, and cut down the groves," the text says, "and the Lord was with him."[18] While he was king, Sennacherib king of Assyria invaded as far as the fortified cities of Judea, besieged and took them effortlessly. At that time the Rabshakeh also made an assault on Jerusalem, opening his mouth in unbridled fashion against God and uttering those blasphemous words. At that

---

15. 2 Kgs 16.5–9. Cyril, we noted, is closely following the text of 2 Kings in developing a *hypothesis* for Hosea's ministry. It does not occur to him to highlight the covenantal disloyalty of the appeal for assistance by Ahaz to the Assyrian king in the way registered by Isaiah 7. This anomaly may suggest that Cyril's Isaiah commentary followed, not preceded, his work on The Twelve; Kerrigan (*St Cyril of Alexandria*, 14, n.3) admits, "In the course of our examination of the commentary on *Isaiah* and that on the *Minor Prophets* we have discovered no literary allusions which might enable us to decide which of these is the older."

16. 2 Kgs 16.10–16.   17. 2 Kgs 17.3–6.
18. 2 Kgs 18.4.

time also a hundred and eighty-five thousand from the Assyrian camp fell in one night, slain by the hand of an angel.[19]

So much of relevance for the time being; by anyone with skill the text of the prophecy can be fitted to each of the events, sometimes delivering a rebuke to those in Samaria, sometimes threatening those in Jerusalem with attacks. It forecasts the captivities, it foretells the fear, it promises assistance, it calls to reform; no statement or genre required for the benefit of those in error at the time is missing from the prophecy.[20]

So the text goes on, *Beginning of the word of the Lord to Hosea. The Lord said to Hosea* (v.2). God begins in fact by revealing mysteries to the prophet, as was clearly said in another prophet: "I shall stand at my watchpost, and station myself on a rock, and shall keep watch to see what the Lord God will say in me." The God of all, you see, reveals to the saints by imparting to their minds knowledge of the future; (14) blessed David, for example, says, "I shall listen to what the Lord God says in me, because he will speak peace to his people," and the blessed prophet Zechariah no less clearly comes to us in similar terms: "The angel speaking within me replied."[21] It was, in fact, the custom with the holy prophets to refer to the Word of God as an angel insofar as he announced to them and made clear the will of the God and Father. The prophet Isaiah also confirms this in saying of him, "Every garment assembled with deceit they will return with compensation, and they would prefer to be burnt alive, because a child is born to us, and he will be called angel of great coun-

---

19. 2 Kgs 19.35. Like Theodore before him, Cyril is silent on the role of Sargon II in the fall of Samaria and the deportation of the population.

20. Cyril justifiably feels that, after such a lengthy *hypothesis*, which can serve as a subtext for development of ideas in the book, he and his readers are ready to discern its movement and its various forms of expression.

21. Hab 2.1; Ps 85.8 (modern numbering); Zec 4.5 (where, in fact, Cyril does not take the angel as the Word of God, Didymus being the one to speak of it as "the angel of Great Counsel"). Having at length laid out the historical *hypothesis* of the work, Cyril—again helpfully—examines the nature of prophetic inspiration in the case of Hosea and other biblical authors. It is significant that he is not tempted to think in terms of ecstatic possession, as he will avoid it also even when the term *lêmma* occurs at the opening of Nah, Hab, Dt-Zec, and Mal, leading Didymus and even Theodore to adopt that analogue. Jerome had mentioned that it was redolent of Montanist thinking.

COMMENTARY ON HOSEA 1

sel."[22] Now, the fact that the revelation was sketchy and ambiguous in the saints, and not conveyed in language and words like ours, Paul will confirm in his letter: "Do you desire proof that Christ is speaking in me?"[23] So the coming of the word of God in Hosea would mean, in the way I understand it, nothing else than his conveying to the listeners that a revelation was given to Hosea, and knowledge of the future flashed like light, illuminating not his bodily eyes but his mind and heart.

His saying again, *The Lord said to Hosea,* leads us to the same conclusion: the instruction given did not apply generally to all the readers, nor was it proposed to those willing to carry it out at various times; it was said only and specifically to the prophet. It was, in fact, not like the command of general application and usefulness, "Thus says the Lord, Do not learn the ways of the nations, or be dismayed at the signs of heaven,"[24] by which it would be understood as right and proper to take a wife of prostitution and have children of prostitution. Instead, while the former text would usefully be applied to everyone, (15) the latter would properly be referred by God specifically to Hosea alone. The clause *The Lord said to Hosea* is in my view of such a kind as if you were to claim that it refers not simply to everyone but only to Hosea. What was said in the scheme of things to one person at a particular time, you see, should not be a pretext for many people to live a shameful and pleasure-loving life.

What, then, did God say to blessed Hosea? *Go, take for yourself a wife of prostitution and children of prostitution, because the land in its prostitution will prostitute itself by forsaking the Lord. He went and took Gomer daughter of Diblaim, and she conceived and bore him a son* (vv.2–3). No argument would persuade us to repudiate the text, to condemn the unlikelihood of the facts, to dismiss the taste-

---

22. Is 9.5–6 LXX.
23. 2 Cor 13.3. Cyril's readers might have thought it helpful for him also to say something of Hosea's background (as distinct from religious and political developments of the time), the place of his ministry, and perhaps the structure of the book. His hermeneutical approach he is almost immediately forced to expose.
24. Jer 10.2. Again Cyril shows signs of seeing the prophet putting his message in writing for his "readers." (Theodore had also spoken of Hosea "composing the book.") Jeremiah's readers were entitled to apply his verse to themselves, unlike Hosea's.

lessness of the event itself, or even to think (as some commentators do)[25] that there was no marriage or marital intercourse with Gomer, when the sacred text says that the conception took place and the birth as well, cites also the child's name, and mentions the woman's father and in addition to that the woman's actual name. Since, however, it would be necessary to assert to those willing to concede the reality of what happened that it really happened this way, come now, by exposing the customary arguments let us finally provide an apposite explanation of the divine plan.

I came across a man of some distinction, then, who wanted to clarify the question of this passage. He poured great scorn on its factuality and on those who say that things happened that way, and claimed it was clearly necessary in the case of this very chapter not to be afraid to shout aloud to the (16) lovers of continence, "The letter kills";[26] ravaging the text and, as it were, leaving it a desert, and, so to speak, falling on his face, he assembled some such texts as these. He claimed, "The divinely inspired Moses was once ordered to bring Israel, once it had been rescued from the slavery of the Egyptians, into the holy land promised of old to the fathers—I mean, the land of promise. The prophet Jeremiah also heard God saying clearly, 'Before I formed you in the womb, I knew you, and before you emerged from your mother I consecrated you, I appointed you a prophet to the nations.' How, then (he asked), are those men not commendable despite their declining such an august and fine ministry and not being averse to a delay? One said, 'O Lord, please appoint someone else fit to be sent,' while the other, citing his youth, tried to

25. Cyril is immediately forced to pin his hermeneutical colors to the mast by taking issue with the arguments of those (like Origen), on the one hand, who denied the historicity of the unusual scenario, taking it allegorically, or (like Eusebius of Caesarea), on the other, who disputed Hosea's having relations with a prostitute, real though she might be. Cyril is insistent—with predictable support from Antioch—on the factuality *(historia)* of the event *(pragma)* and its reality *(alêtheia)*, even if it may seem distasteful and therefore has its mockers. "The sacred text" vouches for it. (Cyril adopts a rather different position when it comes to interpreting the locust plague in Joel 1.)

26. 2 Cor 3.6. This text is still cited as a rubric to disallow (Cyril's and) Antioch's respect for the *alêtheia* of such biblical texts; see the article by J. J. O'Keefe, "'A Letter that Killeth': Toward a Reassessment of Antiochene Exegesis, or Diodore, Theodore, and Theodoret on the Psalms," *JECS* 8.1: 83–104.

COMMENTARY ON HOSEA 1   41

shame God. The prophet Ezekiel also (he says), when bidden to make loaves for himself on droppings of human dung, showed no little displeasure and was therefore told, 'See, I let you have cattle droppings instead of human droppings, and you can cook your loaves on them.'[27] The divinely inspired Peter, too, when the sheet was let down from heaven on which all the quadrupeds and cattle were discernible, and God was heard to say, 'Get up, Peter, sacrifice and eat,' declined in the words, 'By no means, Lord, I have never eaten anything common or unclean, nor has any profane meat gone into my mouth.'[28]

"Hosea, by contrast, on hearing that he had to have relations with a vile prostitute of execrable life, did not actually decline, did not show any reluctance, did not fall to supplication and beg an exemption. Instead, like someone quite inclined to lewd behavior, and, as it were, with no reservations, he grasped the opportunity, perhaps attracted to sexual pleasures."

Then, to reduce (17) the topic to the level of the absurd, he proceeded to add to this some unconvincing remarks, pretending to act as advocate for the prophet: "He would have shown the greatest reluctance if he thought God required physical intercourse. But since the action was a spiritual thing, he proceeds with profound godliness, as it were, and voluntarily to the execution of what was commanded. Otherwise (he claimed), the God of continence would have wanted something done of such a kind that a man like him would have been defiled by such shameful and loathsome intercourse—with a woman, I mean, who was a lewd prostitute. By transposing the drift of the text from factuality to spiritual import, however, he said Gomer was a type of those souls who opted for a shameful and ungodly life, while the prophet filled the role of the one from heaven above, that is, the Word of God the Father, who in a spiritual relationship with our souls imparts the seeds of a virtuous life."

While these were the concoctions of the person's argumentation, (18) for my part I was quite amazed—firstly, because in showing no interest in considerations of the text's reality,[29] he

27. Ex 3.10; Jer 1.5; Ex 4.13; Jer 1.6; Ezek 4.15.
28. Acts 10.13–14 plus a phrase from Ezek 4.14.
29. Cyril contests the procedure of the anonymous (and possibly typical)

presumed to claim that "the letter kills," and then further because he introduced men such as Moses, whom we just cited, as being in opposition to the revelations from on high. He was wrong, however, to keep silence about their not escaping blame in daring to challenge the divine oracles. When the revealer Moses declined, was reluctant about his mission, and cited his lack of eloquence, God charged him with weakness of faith in these words: "Who gives speech to mortals, who makes them mute or deaf, gives them sight or blindness? Is it not I, the Lord God? Go now, and I shall open your mouth." And when he was reluctant after that, and still dilatory, "the Lord was angry with Moses," and said, "What of your brother Aaron? I know that he will do the speaking for you." Again, when Jeremiah rather heedlessly said, "I am young, and do not know how to speak," God no less corrected him in the words, "Do not say, I am young, for you will go to all to whom I shall send you, and speak whatever I command you." Thus it is dangerous to say, or even merely to conceive the thought, that the divine will may be appropriately characterized as having committed an error in calling a young man to prophesy. Likewise, whereas the divinely inspired Peter, when the sheet was let down from heaven, heard, "Get up, Peter, sacrifice and eat," and in Jewish fashion called out, "By no means, Lord, because I have never eaten anything common or unclean," he was immediately corrected for daring to oppose the divine plan, and was clearly told, "What God had made clean you must not call common."[30]

After all, even if the God of all intended to chide gently, and did not immediately show considerable indignation at them for resisting, their reluctance was not without blame. (19) My view is that those under orders should without delay concede the dic-

---

commentator who in "transposing the drift of the text from factuality to spiritual import" does violence to its *alêtheia*. He will be found in the Commentary moving immediately to a spiritual dimension only when he despairs of finding a factual/historical reference, e.g., in apocalyptic material.

30. Ex 4.11–14; Jer 1.6–7; Acts 10.13–15. Cyril is directly and at (typical) length rebutting his opponent's claim that biblical characters, unlike Hosea, resisted divine commands of a factual nature, and that therefore what was required of Hosea was not factual. *Non sequitur*, replies Cyril: those other characters were chastised and had to conform.

COMMENTARY ON HOSEA 1

tates from on high to be correct and faultless, and hasten to execute the command, even if it is not altogether to their satisfaction. For example, the God of all ordered Saul to kill Agag for committing unholy crimes against the people of Israel, but he decided to treat him kindly and spared the man condemned by divine decree. He attacked the decree and thereby offended God, extremely so; he showed concern for the man condemned to death, crying aloud, as it were, and saying by his very action that God's sentence on him was not just. For this reason the blessed Samuel was very distressed and shared God's indignation, and he it was who cut down Agag, proclaiming the reason: "As your sword made women childless, so your mother will be left childless among women."[31] He predicted to Saul that he would be divested of the kingship, and pay a harsh penalty for his disobedience.

If there is need for us in addition to this to provide also another factual explanation, it is written in the first book of Kings that at one time Ben-hadad, the leader or king of the Syrians, was campaigning against the people of Israel. Ahab, who was king of Israel, was very apprehensive and afraid of the invasion, expecting to be captured before long with all his army. God promised him through a prophet to surrender the foe to him; he then captured him, and in defiance of God's will he spared him.[32] What does the sacred text say after this? "One of the sons of the prophets said to his neighbor in a word of the Lord, Strike me! But the fellow did not want to strike him. He said to him, Because you did not hearken to the word of the Lord, lo, when you leave me, a lion will strike you. He left him, a lion found him and struck him down. (20) He found another man and said, Strike me! The man struck him hard, and wounded him. The prophet went off and met the king of Israel on the way, and he had a bandage on his eyes." After an interval he spoke to Ahab on his way back, going on to say, "The Lord says this: Because you released from your custody a man set for destruction, your

---

31. 1 Sm 15.33. While we might have thought that Cyril had more than adequately dealt with the point raised by his anonymous acquaintance, he deals with another side to it.

32. 1 Kgs 20.34.

life will be exchanged for his, and your people for his people."[33]

Do you hear how the person declining to strike the prophet was done away with in pitiable fashion, falling foul of a terrifying animal? Is there no truth in claiming that the refusal to strike even a holy prophet was the fruit of piety? But it was "in a word of the Lord," and the charge of disobedience was ineluctable. Ahab was also in the wrong when he spared Ben-hadad in defiance of God's command to kill him, and he was surrendered in place of the man's life. It is therefore necessary for us to accomplish without reluctance or delay whatever is God's will. To do anything other than this and choose to follow our judgment involves a charge of arrogance; it is as though such people even opt to rebuke God for sometimes making a wrong decision. Our reply to those who claim that the factual account is not above reproach, and who ill-advisedly call it in question, is therefore, Alas for you! Does it seem to you distasteful for a prophet to live with a lewd woman? Well, then, is it not much more distasteful for some people to be slaughtered by holy prophets? How is it, then, that Samuel did away with Agag, and Elijah the prophets of Baal despite their great number? What about the prophet Isaiah, tell me, who wore sackcloth around his loins, and traversed Jerusalem naked and unshod? Surely (21) someone would have immediately charged him in such a condition with being disreputable, deranged, and out of his mind?[34] Why is there any question of everything being done with our standards of decorum, especially if it is the subject of commendation?

You will reply, however, that in those cases they performed such actions in response to divine demands. Well, tell me, what are we to think of the blessed Hosea? Surely it was not of his own choosing that he went to a prostitute and had relations with such a vile person without being bidden by God? I am none the less surprised at those who want to ridicule what is written of him, and presume to disparage the account as unseemly. In fact, by

---

33. 1 Kgs 20.35–42. The precise point of Cyril's rejoinder to his acquaintance here is that, even if God's command may seem inappropriate, it still has to be carried out.

34. 1 Kgs 18.40; Is 20.2–3, a case cited by Theodore to the same effect, and elaborated on by Theodoret with the inclusion of similar prophetic actions by Jeremiah and Ezekiel.

COMMENTARY ON HOSEA 1

rejecting the event on account of its lacking taste, and openly claiming that the prophet did not have intercourse with the prostitute, but that the Word sometimes has relations with unfaithful souls, they are probably not aware of the nonsense in which they have involved themselves. It seems that they wish the prophet to be more holy than the all-holy God. After all, would there not be the same basis for someone to claim, tell me, that the prophet had relations with a prostitute and that the Word of God chose to commune with an unclean soul? In my view there is no difference at all: either let them reject both the one and the other as inappropriate, or let human affairs proceed in obedience to the divine will.

I think there is need also to insert something from the Gospels. Our Lord Jesus Christ dined with tax collectors and sinners, but the censorious Pharisees again found fault and went to the holy disciples with the brazen statement, "Why does your teacher eat and drink with sinners?" What, then, does Christ reply to this? "It is not the healthy who need physicians but the sick."[35] While you would hardly doubt, therefore, that it is out of his immeasurable lovingkindness that God approaches those who are defiled and not yet cleansed of sin, there is particular need for us not to eliminate the distasteful character of the account given to us of the blessed Hosea, which very beautifully describes for us the divine Word's bestowing on us spiritual communion with himself while we were still loathsome and unclean.

The God of all, then, said to the blessed Hosea, *Go, take for yourself a wife of prostitution and children of prostitution.* He takes Gomer, not acting out of lustful passion, but discharging a task of obedience and service, and acting as an instrument of the type, as we shall class him by giving as far as possible a spiritual character to fleshly and earthly things. Now, no one in my view would in the future find anything shameful in the goal of the prophet; the word of the divinely inspired Scripture does not exclude marriage, sexual relations, and having children. Rather, at all points it clears them of blame and criticism; in the statement

---

35. Mt 9.11–12. Cyril's principle, of course, is of general application: the challenging elements in the Scriptures are not to be rejected but properly interpreted.

of the blessed Paul, "Let marriage be held in honor, and the marriage bed undefiled."³⁶ To those wanting to live in upright fashion and pursue a virtuous and pious life, permission is given if they also long to have children; the blessed Abraham lived this way, and his successors proved acceptable to God. So what is wrong, tell me, or how is it in any way blameworthy not to renounce marriage when God orders it described as something of vital spiritual value for the readers in bodily and material terms?

I for my part, at any rate, would have no qualms about claiming that the prophet even saved Gomer: from being a vile and promiscuous woman he raised her by means of persuasion to the level of commitment to one man; and from being a disgrace to her kind—children not being her motive for sex; instead, she sold her favors to lascivious customers, she was death's roost, (23) a door and path leading down to the very depths and ultimate darkness—he persuaded her to abstain from such despicable charms and exploits, and made her a respectable mother of children. It would seem an endeavor that befits a holy person and brings him praise not to consider himself but rather to achieve something that is of value to another and vital for their salvation. Is this, in fact, not the way we accord every commendation to the blessed prophet Isaiah for removing his tunic, undoing his sandals, paying little heed to his appearance, and walking about naked so as to present a figure of the coming captivity to the people of Israel, cause them to devote themselves to God, and persuade them in the future to embrace a cessation of sin?³⁷ Again, tell me, did not Paul in his wisdom tell us openly, "For I could wish that I myself were accursed and cut off from Christ for the sake of my brethren, my kindred according to the flesh"? Did he not say, "I have become all things to all people so that by all means I might save some, becoming as a Jew to the Jews, as one outside the Law to those outside the Law (though I am not free from God's law but am under Christ's law) so that I may save those outside the Law"? And why mention these if I omit what is

---

36. Heb 13.4. It has been a lengthy refutation of the two inadequate hermeneutical approaches that either allegorize the incident or find its factual character distasteful.

37. The final clause is missing from the PG edition.

even greater, the fact that God's only-begotten Word, to save the human race, "did not regard equality with God something to be exploited, but emptied himself, taking the form of a slave, being born in human likeness. And being found in human form, he endured the cross, disregarding the shame."[38]

There is surely nothing surprising, therefore, if by briefly departing from what is proper the prophet saved Gomer, and brought the lost woman to propriety. Now, the fact that it was a beneficial and necessary doing for God to order him to have relations with the woman he immediately confirms (24) by asserting that he commanded it for this reason: *Because the land in its prostitution will prostitute itself by forsaking the Lord.* He mentions to the prophet not a future prostitution of the land but one already committed;[39] there were the heifers at Dan and Bethel, shrines were erected to Baal, and the rites of Israel were performed throughout the whole of the country of the Samaritans. So the inspired Scripture—or as well, as is a more truthful statement, those translating it for us—is making no distinction in time. As, of course, the person of Christ himself is reported as saying in the verse from Isaiah, "I gave my back to the scourges, and my cheeks to the blows"; and the prophet himself says of him, "He was led like a sheep to the slaughter, and like a lamb that is silent before its shearer he did not open his mouth; in his lowliness his judgment was removed."[40] Do you note how the text of the prophecy introduced to us the future as already in the past? So the verse *The land in its prostitution will prostitute itself* means, The land has prostituted itself. In what way has it prostituted itself? *By forsaking the Lord,* that is, by neglecting to follow him, as one would do towards God. Scripture says, remember, "You shall walk after the Lord,"[41] that is, you shall follow him without turning from God's law from on high. So it prostituted itself *by forsaking*

---

38. Rom 9.3; 1 Cor 9.20–22; Phil 2.6–8; Heb 12.2. We shall find Cyril lending most prophetic verses a christological and/or ecclesiological interpretation. He cannot be accused of undervaluing the Incarnation.

39. Cyril is correct, despite his LXX version (which his lack of Hebrew makes him unable to critique). He will read a perfect form of the verb below.

40. Is 50.6; 53.7–8. The prophet, Cyril insists (in keeping with liturgical practice), is speaking in the person (*prosôpon*) of Christ.

41. Dt 13.4.

the Lord, being unwilling to follow; it proved rebellious and profane, and offended the Lord by devoting itself to the worship of idols. This is the reason, then, why the prophet Hosea attached himself to Gomer, *Because the land has prostituted itself by forsaking the Lord.* The action, as I said, would in fact be understood as a type of spiritual happening.

Next, Gomer gave birth. (25) *The Lord said to him, Give him the name Jezreel, because shortly I shall take vengeance for the blood of Jezreel on the house of Judah, and bring an end to kingship in the house of Israel. On that day I shall break the bow of Israel in the valley of Jezreel* (vv.4–5). In this the text delivers a twofold sense for us. Now, a different reading occurs in some manuscripts, which for the sake of precision it is necessary to mention, there being no little benefit in our referring to both readings. While the version we have, that is, of the Seventy, says, *I shall take vengeance for the blood of Jezreel on the house of Judah,* the other version says, "I shall take vengeance for the blood of Jezreel on the house of Jehu."[42] And if some commentators prefer to take it that way, there is need to give a more factual explanation. It goes this way.

Ahab became king in Israel, his wife being Jezebel. He tried to acquire the vineyard of Naboth, who opposed the request in the words, "Far be it from me to give you the vineyard of my father";[43] so he killed him, having given way to Jezebel's willfulness. After killing him, then, Ahab took over the inheritance that was Naboth's vineyard. He went on to be involved also in different ways in worship of the demons, which was wrong and raised the ire of the God of all, who then ordered Elisha the prophet to anoint Jehu king of Israel. Sending his servant, the prophet executed the divine command. On being anointed, Jehu then went to Samaria and discharged the divine wrath on those who provoked it; after killing Ahab, he threw him into the vineyard of Naboth. Then he later did away with Jezebel and the seventy sons of Ahab, who were living in different parts of Samaria. To these he added the Baal, (26) burning its pillars, demolishing the shrines, and executing the priests themselves. God found

---

42. Jerome had noted the error of the LXX in speaking of Judah rather than Jehu.

43. 1 Kgs 21.3.

COMMENTARY ON HOSEA 1   49

him acceptable in these actions, and actually made him this promise: "Your sons of the fourth generation will sit on your throne."[44] Nevertheless, though Jehu proved so acceptable, he offended God no less: he did not destroy the heifers, being involved himself in the sins of Jeroboam and following his unholy ways. Jehu's first son Jehoahaz was also an idolatrous man, who worshiped the heifers himself. In his time, however, the text says, "the Lord's wrath raged against Israel, and he gave them into the hands of Hazael king of Syria, and into the hands of Ben-hadad son of Hazael."[45] Second in line to the throne was Jehoash son of Jehoahaz, who was also an evil man. Third was Jeroboam; in his reign the prophecy of Hosea began. Fourth was Azariah son of Jeroboam, and he was an idolater; Shallum killed him.

Thus, Jehu had been anointed to avenge the blood of Naboth, who was from Jezreel, a city of Samaria, and to destroy idolatry in Israel and then persuade it to devote itself to God. But since he also had proved to be a worshiper of the heifers, and his sons were no less impious, "I shall take vengeance for the blood of Jezreel on the house of Jehu," our text says. In other words, just as he had taken vengeance on the house of Ahab through the reign of Jehu, so he would take vengeance also on the house of Jehu; in the days of his sons, Hazael king of Syria waged war, and also Ben-hadad, and they conquered Israel and laid waste to most of the cities of Samaria. Accordingly, a son is born to the prophet and is given the name Jezreel, as if God were reminding them of the sin committed against Naboth;[46] after all, how could the defender of the righteous rest when a righteous and pious man had been unjustly done away with? (27) So he promises to *break the bow of Israel in the valley of Jezreel.* The tribes of Israel were in fact defeated, as I said, by Hazael and also Ben-hadad.

While this represents an account of what happened in actual

---

44. 2 Kgs 10.30.
45. 2 Kgs 13.3. Again, as in his general introduction, Cyril is giving a précis of the text of Kings.
46. Theodoret in similar terms will make this connection. Modern commentators suggest, on the other hand, that the mention of Jezreel in the Hosea text refers to the valley that was the site of the north's loss of independence when in 733 Tiglath-pileser's armies captured the valley—a connection that Theodore had made.

fact, then, come now, let us make due comment also on the other text, raising what was said by God to a spiritual level.⁴⁷ On account of their ancestors, the assembly of the Jews was of noble birth; those of the race of the divinely inspired Abraham worshiped God living and true, were attentive to righteousness, crowned with good works of every kind, a credit to their lineage, firm in faith, and active in every form of goodness. When hunger drove them to intermingle with the Egyptians, and they had spent a long time there, they adopted from them other habits and other attitudes, and finally decided to follow the customs of the inhabitants, setting no store at all by their fathers' ways and uniquely orthodox practice of religion. They adored creation instead of the Creator, in fact, and the works of their hands, as Scripture says;⁴⁸ they took to abominations and an abominable life to such an extent as even to leave no single form of depravity untried.

To me they seem to have experienced what a woman of wisdom and noble birth would experience when, left to her own devices and, though initially given, as it were, to the pursuit of decorum, chooses rather to be seen in the appearance and trappings of a prostitute. In the way that such a woman satisfies of her own accord the appetites of everyone with no trace of disgust, so, too, the human soul neglects the pursuit of piety, despises love of God, turns to Satan, and (28) satisfies the desires of evil spirits. Thus, in a spiritual sense the assembly of the Jews played the prostitute in Egypt, giving way, as I said, to the lusts of the demons and easily involved in anything that pleased them. With them in such a desperate condition, however, God in his mercy visited them, wanting to bring them back to their senses; the most august and pure God made the loathsome creature his partner, as it were, and the mother of his children, and accorded her love on account of her firstborn, namely, Jezreel, which means "seed of God."⁴⁹

---

47. Cyril has devoted great length to justifying the Heb. text from a factual point of view, *historikôs*. He feels he can now proceed to a spiritual treatment of his own LXX text, though even this he roots in history.

48. Rom 1.25; Jer 1.16.

49. Cyril would have found recourse being made to etymologies (sometimes

COMMENTARY ON HOSEA 1   51

Observe, therefore, Hosea appointed as image and type of God's remarkably wise dispensation. A holy prophet is conjoined with Gomer, a prostitute, and she bears him Jezreel. This was the way God also through the wise Moses summoned the assembly of the Jews to a personal relationship and into spiritual communion on account of the one who would be her firstborn—namely, Christ—who is in reality "seed of God," for the Son was begotten of the Father, even though he was made flesh.[50]

Since, however, the presentation of a spiritual meaning would not prove clear and judicious in any other way than by having the facts brought to the fore, come now, I shall again rehearse them. That Jezreel was a city, therefore, the text clearly foretold to us, and by mention of the city of Jezreel it suggests Naboth; yet he also would be a type of the divine plan understood in Christ, his name meaning "coming," and by such a name the sacred text often suggests Emmanuel. It is said to the blessed prophet Habakkuk, for instance, "The one who is coming will shortly come, and will not delay"; blessed David somewhere says, "Blessed is he who comes in the name of the Lord," and even (29) the divinely inspired Baptist himself sends some of his disciples to our Lord Jesus Christ and inquires in these words: "Are you the one who comes, or are we to expect someone else?"[51] Now, that he is an image of Christ we know clearly from what is written of him; Ahab wants to acquire his vineyard and transform such a special place into a weed-infested garden. But the man was indignant at this, and clearly asserted that he would never let go of his father's vineyard: "Far be it from me to hand over to you my father's vineyard." When the ungodly and loathsome Jezebel learned this, a woman who persecuted the prophets and schemed against righteous people, she concocted devious schemes to kill the righteous man; and after arranging for his elimination she bade her partner (Ahab, I mean) take possession of it. God was rightly an-

---

popular, and often faulty, this one coming from Jerome) in a fellow Alexandrian like Didymus, but is more economical and judicious in their use as a means to spiritual development of a text.

50. In repeatedly speaking of the "assembly" of the Jews as proving unfaithful, Cyril is using the term *synagōgē*, which would be familiar to his readers in a more concrete and local sense.

51. Hab 2.3; Heb 10.37; Ps 118.26; Mt 11.3.

gered by this, and even promised to avenge the blood of Jezreel. Ahab is therefore done away with by Jehu, as I already narrated, and the most wicked Jezebel with him.

So come now, let us apply to Christ what happened of old in a type. The prophet Isaiah says, remember, "My beloved had a vineyard on a hill in a fertile place." "The vineyard was a man of Judah, newly planted, beloved."[52] But the leaders of Israel, of whom Ahab on the throne would be a type, longed to have his vineyard, not for it to be a special inheritance—namely, the vineyard—but for it to become uncultivated, that is, reduced to an incomparably worse condition, since a weed-infested garden is quite different from a vineyard. What is the worst thing about this is obvious: when subject to Christ, the Jewish populace could only (30) have been seen to resemble flourishing, productive vines, but, when living by the customs and manners of the Pharisees and drilled in human precepts, they were no different from ground-hugging weeds, which very easily fall down and die.

The leaders of the Jews, therefore, hankered after the vineyard of Christ as their own inheritance to turn it into a garden of weeds, but did not persuade him to give them the vineyard of the Father. What did the God-hating Jezebel do then—that is, the mob under the control of the leaders, or, in other words, the synagogue—in cooperation with the pains inflicted by the leaders? It treated with guile the righteous one, the holy Naboth (or "the one who is coming"), and actually had him done away with. Emmanuel was falsely accused and done away with. The fact that the deed was intolerable in God's eyes would be clear from what is said by the prophet Hosea, *Because shortly I shall take vengeance for the blood of Jezreel on the house of Judah, and bring an end to kingship in the house of Israel.*

Vengeance was taken, in fact, as I said, for the blood of Christ on the whole of Israel: since at the time when the prophecy was delivered [the two groups] were mentioned separately—the residents of Jerusalem as *Judah*, and likewise those in Samaria as *Israel*—so as to be seen to include the whole of Israel, he necessarily said he would *take vengeance for the blood of Jezreel on the house of*

---

52. Is 5.1, 7.

Judah and bring an end to the kingship in the house of Israel. The divinely inspired Jacob had also prophesied this in the words, "Government will not disappear from Judah, or leadership from his limbs, until there comes the one with whom it rests, the expectation of nations."[53] In fact, when Emmanuel shone upon us, the expectation of the nations, then and (31) only then did the kingship leave Israel; Herod, son of Antipater, of Ashkelon, was ruling the country of the Jews when Christ was born.[54] He promises to *break the* same *bow of Israel on that day,* that is, at that time; "he weakened the bow of the mighty," Scripture says, despite their believing they would get the better of Emmanuel. "The foe's swords have failed forever," and the sinews of their arms became loose,[55] for they have not conquered the unconquerable one.

Now, as though laying the foundations of the spiritual sense, he descends at once to the historical events, saying, *I shall break the bow of Israel in the valley of Jezreel;* it was there that Hazael king of Syria defeated Israel when it was coming against him.[56] Since I assume that it is proper not to switch the discourse from the vital spiritual sense, however, I say this: there is no harm done, in my view, in taking that phrase *the valley of Jezreel* ("seed of God," meaning Christ) to refer to the tomb in the garden in which the resurrection followed upon the passion and conquered every means devised arrogantly by the Jews. It was through the resurrection, you see, that their willful and bloody outrages against God were defeated; although they expected to succeed in getting rid of the Son so as to seize his vineyard as their own inheritance, after being placed in the tomb he rose to life again, rendering ineffectual the wiles of their scheme, and, as it were, *breaking their bow* because of his being unable to suffer any fur-

---

53. Gn 49.10.
54. Cyril is referring to Herod the Great, the half-Jewish son of Antipater II, who was appointed king by Rome, alive at Jesus' birth but dead in 4 B.C.E. He cites him to the same effect in comment on Zec 11.8.
55. 1 Sm 2.4; Ps 9.6; Gn 49.24.
56. See n. 46 above for the likely reference in Jezreel. Cyril's terminology of "descent" suggests that he sees layers of meaning in the text, the factual/historical being the lowest layer. The way in which he moves to other levels can be arbitrary (as in what follows immediately), if not to the extent visible in Didymus.

ther. He rejects them from the vineyard, on the one hand, as vicious haters of God and killers of the Lord, while, on the other, he gives it out to other farmers, who are good and grateful and active in good works, in keeping with the Gospel parable.[57]

She conceived again, and bore a daughter. He told him, Call her Not pitied, because I shall no longer (32) *have pity on the house of Israel, but shall be utterly opposed to them. But I shall have pity on the children of Judah, and save them by the Lord their God; I shall not save them by bow or sword or war or chariots or horses or horsemen* (v.7). After the birth of Jezreel, the prophet had a daughter by Gomer, and was instructed to give her the name *Not pitied.* He immediately supplies the reason for this, and at once clarifies the sense, saying that Israel would no longer be deemed worthy of any mercy, and that he was opposed to them, as it were, and took the role of fierce foes, and would valiantly be so hostile to their prosperity as to reduce them to utter misery and bring on them truly unbearable misfortune. With God as their adversary, you see, no benefit would come to the victims from any quarter. "If he shuts the door on someone," Scripture says, "who will open up?" And as the prophet says, "Who will deflect the hand that is raised?"[58] Or who will have mercy on the one condemned by the verdict from on high, since everything is determined by the divine decrees? Whatever the Lord chooses to accomplish, this without doubt comes to pass completely and utterly, since creation cooperates with him and follows the decisions of the one in charge of it. This is the way he punished the Egyptians: when the water was changed into blood and the soot into darkness, an unbearable hail rained down, darkness fell for nigh on three days, and all the other plagues were inflicted on them.

The girl's name, *Not pitied,* therefore, had a useful and necessary purpose; it was for them to be inquiring constantly into the reason behind it, so that when those who at that time were offending [God] by the error of polytheism learned the reason, they might be persuaded in thought and action (33) to take a turn for the better, to change in the direction of sound thinking, and by second thoughts to divert God's wrath by rendering be-

---

57. Mt 21.33–41.
58. Jb 12.14; Is 14.27.

nevolent and gentle to them the God of all, whom they had offended. Now, the prophetic passage probably suggests to us in this likewise the captivities of Israel under Tiglath-pileser and also Shalmaneser, kings of Assyria, who deported Israel from Samaria to the territories of the Persians and Medes after laying waste the cities in Samaria. They would not have encountered such dire disasters, however, if God had been willing to come to their aid, or rather if he had not been, as it were, antagonistic and ranged against them in the role of a foe, his words being, remember, *I shall be utterly opposed to them.*

On the other hand, he promises to take pity on the children of Judah and save them without recourse to the norm of war—the sense of *not by chariots or horses*. This actually came to pass when Sennacherib encircled Jerusalem, and when Rabshakeh mocked the divine glory, claiming that God was not capable of rescuing Jerusalem and those in it, and adduced as guarantee of his capturing them one and all the inability of the gods in Samaria to save their own people. Judah was saved against the odds, however—that is, the two tribes inhabiting Jerusalem; Scripture says, remember, "An angel of the Lord went out and slew one hundred and eighty-five thousand from the camp of the Assyrians on one night." Those who were saved sang a song to this effect, and narrated the course of the marvel worked in their favor in these terms: "Some take pride in chariots, some in horses, but we shall take pride in the name of the Lord our God. They collapsed and fell, but we rose and stood upright."[59] (34)

So much for the factual sense, however; let us in turn proceed to other senses, namely, to those again referring to Christ. After the birth of Jezreel—that is, "seed of God," the purpose being for you to see in this Emmanuel, whose blood he promised to avenge—there was born to Gomer, that is, to the unfaithful assembly of the Jews, a daughter, or a vast number for whom an appropriate name was *Not pitied*, for she killed Jezreel—Christ, that is. Consequently, it rightly found God hostile and very warlike; it immediately sustained insupportable calamities, was ravaged by the Roman forces, and underwent the notorious war, when wom-

---

59. 2 Kgs 19.35; Ps 20.7–8. Cyril does not tire of recounting more than once the historical background to the prophecy.

en even ate their own children and, as the prophet Jeremiah says, "The hands of compassionate women cooked their own children,"[60] hunger forcing them to set aside the law of nature and be indifferent to irresistible affection.

While all this happened to the impious ones, however, he promises to have pity on *the children of Judah*, that is, the children of the tribe of Judah born to Christ by learning and rebirth through the Spirit. After all, if through the Gospel some people are born in Christ to the holy apostles, how does it not occur rather through Christ himself? Scripture also says of them, "Lo, I and the children that God has given me."[61] They are saved, therefore, in Christ the Lord and God of all, not by wielding earthly and fleshly weapons, but through the power of the one who saves, who dislodges governments and thrones, who leads in triumph the columns of the adversaries with his own cross, overturns the evil powers, and gives to those who love him "the power to walk on snakes and scorpions and on all the might of the enemy."[62]

Now, he very appropriately likens the unbelieving and obdurate mass of the Jews who killed the Lord to a woman, namely, *Not pitied;* (35) the woman, after all, would very clearly be understood as a symbol of weakness and an unmanly and fractured way of thinking. Of this kind are all who did not accept correction through Christ, and could not bring themselves to adopt his divine and holy decrees. The prophet Hosea, for example, says, "Return, Israel, to the Lord your God, because you have been weakened by your iniquities," and again in reference to the commandments of the Savior he says, "Because the ways of the Lord are straight, and the righteous will walk in them, whereas the impious will be weakened by them." Hosea likewise says somewhere in reference to those who killed Jezreel, that is, Christ, "Israel's arrogance against him will be humbled, and Israel and Ephraim will be weakened by their iniquities."[63]

She weaned Not pitied, conceived again and bore a son. He said, Call him Not my people, because you are not my people, and I am not yours (vv.8–9). Another child close on her heels is born to Gomer

---

60. Lam 4.10.
62. Col 2.15; Lk 10.19.

61. 1 Cor 4.15; Is 8.18.
63. Hos 14.1, 9; 5.5.

within a short time, and God said it had to be called *Not my people*. Immediately a similar explanation is given for such a name: *You are not my people, and I am not yours*. It would also be clear in this case that such things were done at a factual level as a rebuke of sinners and as a sure correction of those given to contempt and drifting into error. On the other hand, they were types of what happened in due course to the people of Israel after the Incarnation of the Only-begotten and his enduring the precious cross for us. Now, if it behoves us to give a factual comment before the spiritual one,[64] we would say that when Israel was deported from Samaria to the territories of the Persians and Medes under Tiglath-pileser (36) king of the Assyrians and also Shalmaneser, those who still remained, a remnant of the endangered people, had completely lost the right to be called God's people, a result, to be sure, of their following their own inclination in forsaking God. They had, in fact, by no means relinquished their attachment to the loathsome worship of the demons.

In relation to Christ, on the other hand, you would understand the sense and the true meaning differently. After that unholy mob, who were rightly *not pitied*, because they had killed the Lord, the next generation, who were already members of the unfaithful assembly, clearly forfeited their right to be and be called God's people. The Roman war had, in fact, not wiped out all the Jewish populace, but the majority had perished in numbers beyond counting. Some of them, however, survived, and, though escaping death's net, they were scattered to the four winds, as Scripture says,[65] and were dispersed in the countries of the nations, no longer being styled God's people, as I said. Grace fell instead on those from the nations, in fact, and with them were mingled also the remnant of Israel, that is, those who were saved through faith in Christ, not a few of them becoming believers. Now, the fact that with Israel's spurning him the God of all for his part also severed his relationship with them he indicates in saying, *You are not my people*, and not only that, but necessarily

64. For Cyril it is a duty to adopt this order in interpreting the biblical text: comment first on *ta historika*, and only then on *ta pneumatika*.

65. Ezek 12.14. This is, of course, the conventional rationale for the rejection and punishment of (most of) the Jews and the acceptance of the gentiles: the execution of Jesus after earlier infidelities.

proceeding to say to them, *and I am not yours*. Instead, it is of us, namely, those who are enriched by a relationship with him, who are justified by Christ and sanctified by the Spirit, that he says in the statement of the prophet, "And I shall be God to them, and they shall be sons and daughters to me, says the Lord almighty."[66] While Christ said to Jews, at one time, (37) "Yet a little while I am with you," and at another, "Lo, your house is departing from you," it is of the nations that he said, "My sheep hear my voice, I know them, and they follow me, and to them I give eternal life."[67]

The number of the children of Israel was like the sand of the sea, which will not be measured or counted (v.10). Blessed Isaiah explains this to us in another way: "Even if the people of Israel were like the sand of the sea, the remnant will be saved, enacting the word and abbreviating it in righteousness, because God will implement an abbreviated word in the whole world."[68] But whether it is in this sense or in another that Israel is numerous beyond counting and equal to the sands of the seashore, no great account is made of them by God in their choice to act impiously, despite his granting his love and mercy in extraordinary measure to one righteous and pious person; his gaze is on one person who is humble and peaceable and who trembles at his words.[69] This was not sufficient for good and honest people, who fear and genuinely serve him; it was possible for them also to help others and sometimes rid offenders of the impending punishment. For proof of this matter you could take the words said to the Sodomites when the all-powerful God promised to release on them punishment by fire after only five righteous individuals were found in their midst. At any rate, he spared Lot together with his wife and children.[70] Why mention five righteous and good people? In threatening the inhabitants of Jerusalem with his wrath, he said, "Run about (38) the streets of Jerusalem, see and find out and search its streets in the hope of finding a man

---

66. Is Cyril citing Jer 31.1?
67. Jn 7.33; Mt 23.38; Jn 10.27–28.
68. Is 10.22–23; Rom 9.27–28. At this point Cyril does not develop the idea of the New Testament as the *verbum abbreviatum*, a familiar patristic notion.
69. Is 66.2.
70. Gn 19.

acting justly and searching for fidelity, and I shall be merciful to them, says the Lord."[71] Understand, therefore, how he prizes even a single righteous person and does not overlook anyone praying for a whole city; on the other hand, he takes no account even of a vast number beyond counting, as I said, if they are found to be profane, given to depravity, and actively involved in deception by the demons.

In the place where it was said to them, You are not my people, they will be called children of the living God (v.10). Relief was at hand from the dire wrath with its ruinous effects, and conclusion of the disasters not far off, as far as the text goes. While the fact that Israel would be rejected in due course we have clearly foretold in what has been said to you just now, he once more confirmed that it would not be completely ruined and altogether destroyed, but that there would be a time for their return to their former condition and a recovery of love for God, namely, through faith in Christ. There was need, in fact, there was need for those bent on listening to prophetic statements to have a clear understanding of the whole mystery and not be unaware of the pattern of the divine plan. The text says, then, *In the place where it was said to them, You are not my people, they will be called children of the living God.*

Of the meaning of *in the place*, come now, let us give an accurate explanation. The people of Israel, remember, were made captives for a time and deported to the land of the Assyrians, as I said. There they wept and wailed, but did nothing about the Law; blessed David made this clear to us in his words, "By the river of Babylon there we sat and wept when we remembered Zion," and went on to say, "How shall we sing the song of the Lord in a foreign land?"[72] On returning to Jerusalem, however, thanks to God's compassion, they were no worse off and were called God's people, living in prosperity, free to worship and perform the sacrifices according to the Law. It was not permissible, in fact, to discharge the requirements in any other way at all except in Jerusalem alone and in the Temple, since the

---

71. Jer 5.1.
72. Ps 137.1, 4. Again we note Cyril's habit of seeing the southern kingdom of the sixth century B.C.E. in the sights of this eighth-century prophet to the north, probably because he readily moves to the fate of all Jews in his own time indiscriminately.

Mosaic Law gave the clear instruction, "Take care that you do not offer your burnt offerings in any other place than the place that the Lord your God will choose so that his name will be invoked there. It is there that you will offer your burnt offerings."[73] So they went back at the time to Jerusalem, leaving the land of the foreigners, and duly observed the requirements of Moses, and were styled God's people.

After the crucifixion of the Savior, however, and the siege and destruction that befell them, they were dispersed with their families in the cities and countries of the nations. So how would they at that time be God's people? Surely they would not return once more to Jerusalem and assemble in the Temple, at least while living in those places to which they had been scattered in each case? What does the prophet say? *In the place where it was said to them, You are not my people, they will be called children of the living God.* They had in fact lost the status of being God's people, and were dispersed in the countries of the nations, as you could see in force even to this day. But in the endtime, "when the full number of the nations has come in,"[74] then (40) and only then the rejected Israel will be accepted as children of God, despite living in places where they are and by chance are found to be. There is, in fact, no obligation to go up to Jerusalem and still look for a temple that is made of stones, because it will not honor God with ancient customs, namely, sacrifices of oxen and slaughter of sheep. Instead, the form of worship for them will be faith in Christ, his decrees, sanctification in the Spirit, and rebirth through holy Baptism, which secures the glory of sonship for those worthy of it and called to it by the Lord.

The children of Judah and the children of Israel will be assembled together, and they will appoint for themselves a single government, and they will go up from the land, because great will be the day of Jezreel (v.11). We shall find this coming into effect both factually and spiritually: in the territory of Persians and Medes there were those made captive from Samaria, that is, Israel, and in addition to them as well those from Jerusalem, that is, Judah and Benja-

---

73. Dt 12.13–14.
74. Rom 11.25.

min. When Cyrus son of Cambyses took Babylon, however, and transferred the empire of the Persians to himself, releasing Israel and Judah from captivity and bidding them go home along with the sacred vessels, they went to Jerusalem and from then on occupied it without the division that had obtained before the captivity. Instead of having their own individual kings, they all lived in harmony in Jerusalem alone under the leadership of Zerubbabel son of Shealtiel, who was of the tribe of Judah, and, acting as priest, Joshua son of Jozadak the high priest;[75] (41) they then rebuilt the holy Temple and were occupied in domestic concerns. Accordingly, the text says, *the children of Judah and the children of Israel will be assembled together, and they will appoint for themselves a single government, and they will go up from the land*—of the foreigners, you understand, into which they had been deported when made captive.

That phrase, *because great will be the day of Jezreel,* on the other hand, does not accord with history.[76] Our view of it therefore is that when Israel will be called God's people, despite being styled *Not my people* on account of extreme impiety, as I said before, then they themselves *will be assembled* together with the children of Judah, that is, all the vast number of the Jews to be found in the endtime, and will all be under *a single government,* that is, Christ. The God of all had made some such prediction in a statement of Ezekiel in reference to Christ: "I shall set up over them one shepherd, my servant David, and he will shepherd them and be their shepherd."[77] Now, by "David" he refers to the one who is born of the line of David according to the flesh, Christ. With the mass of the nations already called, therefore, Israel will be the last to be introduced, and all will be under *a single government,* he

---

75. Cyril, who, though dependent on the historical books of the OT, can be vague where historical details are concerned, has formed this idea—against the evidence of the Chronicler—of a united people living in Jerusalem after the exile. He repeats it later.

76. The inclusion of Judah in this verse further encourages Cyril in seeing reference by this eighth-century prophet in the north to the fortunes of the south, especially as (unlike Theodoret) he does not find in Jezreel a reference to Israel's defeat by the Assyrians at Jezreel in 733, and as he is anxious in his spiritual interpretation to see Jews generally finally being admitted to Christ's governance.

77. Ezek 34.23.

says, *and they will go up from the land.* This, in my view, suggests to those interpreting it correctly either that those who accept the Savior's yoke will completely and utterly cease thinking of earthly things, and will rise above a fleshly mentality; all subject to Christ are in fact like that, as the blessed David confirms in saying, "The mighty ones of God are raised to great heights over the earth," and also Paul, "Those who belong to Christ Jesus have crucified the flesh with its passions and desires."[78] Or it means that they will also attain resurrection from the dead. (42)

Christ said somewhere, remember, "I tell you truly that everyone believing in me, even if he dies, will live."[79] Admittedly, the question must be asked, Will those not believing, tell me, stay dead and not come to life with the others? So the Savior himself revealed to us what indeed would be the abundance for those who believe when he said, "The thief comes only to steal and kill and destroy. I came that they may have life, and have it abundantly."[80] While all will rise, therefore, both bad and good, not all enjoy the bonus: those not belonging to Christ, by proving to be caught up in the crimes of unbelief, will at the endtime have a life harsher than death, paying the penalty for faults and unbelief. Those belonging to him, on the other hand, enriched with a relationship with God through the Spirit, and of good behavior, will in addition to the general resurrection and a return to life completely and utterly enjoy the consequences, namely, gifts, honors, crowns, rewards, splendor. Paul testifies to this in the words, "Lo, I tell you a mystery: we shall not all fall asleep, but we shall all be changed, in an instant, in the blinking of an eye, at the last trumpet. For the trumpet will sound, the dead will be raised imperishable, and we shall be changed."[81] Accordingly he says, *They will go up from the land,* that is, they, too, will live the life of the saints.

Because great will be the day of Jezreel, that is to say, great indeed is the day of Christ, when he will raise all the dead, coming down from heaven and sitting as Scripture says on the throne of his glory, and (43) he will render to everyone according to each

---

78. Ps 47.9; Gal 5.24.
80. Jn 10.10.
79. Jn 11.25.
81. 1 Cor 15.51–52.

one's works.⁸² If, on the other hand, you wanted to take *the day* as the time of his coming, when the forgiveness of sins is granted by Christ to Greeks, to barbarians, and to Jews who have sinned against him, you would proceed in accord with the words of truth. David also reveals the time of the coming of our Savior in saying, "This is the day the Lord has made; let us be glad and rejoice in it."⁸³

---

82. Mt 25.31; 16.27. Cyril is prepared to give to an historical event (though he is unaware of Hosea's reference to the Assyrians' victory) a spiritual meaning involving the endtime as the NT depicts it. Yet when he comes, say, in Zechariah to apocalyptic depiction of an endtime, he does not recognize it for what it is—a handicap he shares with his peers Alexandrian and Antiochene.

83. Ps 118.24.

COMMENTARY ON HOSEA, CHAPTER TWO

Say to your brother, My people, and to your sister, Pitied (v.1).

T WAS VERY necessary to add this to what had been already said: since he had said that they would all be under a single government, with no further division or separation leading to disharmony, with concord prevailing, and with faith in Christ bringing everyone together in unity of spirit, consequently the Spirit now bade those already enriched with faith and made subject to Christ to be no longer zealous in withholding peace from those who were rightly called Not my people and Not pitied. After all, once Israel was accepted, admitted to forgiveness, and made subject to Christ, what logic would there be in continuing to be separated, and not rather for those called to brotherhood in the spirit of adoption to live in harmony? O you who are enlightened by faith in Christ, he is saying, and who have attained the ornament of noble lineage, now say My people to your brother, who of old was rightly called Not my people, and say Pitied to your sister, who was Not pitied. It is, in fact, necessary (44) for the peoples subject to the Lord to be of one mind, and for those called to sonship through grace to have the same will as the Father. They should rather rejoice that the remnant of Israel is saved, as well as those formerly rejected for grave disobedience, but now made acceptable and thus sanctified in Christ. Through him and with him be glory to God the Father with the Holy Spirit, unto ages of ages. Amen.[1] (45)

Pass sentence against your mother, pass sentence, because she is not my wife and I am not her husband (v.2). After foretelling that Israel would rightly be rejected and in addition called Not my people,

---

1. Thus concludes, for reasons of length, Cyril's first volume—hence the doxology.

and in fact that the populace that killed the Lord would unquestionably be Not pitied, and rightly so, he then before long adds to this the future conversion at the endtime through faith in Christ, in saying, "The children of Judah and the children of Israel will be assembled together, and they will appoint for themselves a single government."[2] After explaining the whole divine plan from beginning to end, he then moves to revealing the charges leveled at those properly rejected, and clearly focuses on what it had been their lot to suffer. Accordingly, he says to those pitied, accepted, and made God's people despite their springing from the unfaithful synagogue, *Pass sentence against your mother, pass sentence.* In other words, he is saying, if you want to learn the reason why you were Not my people and became and were called Not pitied in the time before your conversion, you will not find me hostile to you and lacking in affection. Pass sentence instead on your own mother for not preserving (46) the sincerity of her love for me, and for denying the relationship. She definitely treated as of little account the purity of the spiritual communion with me, and was unwilling to bear the fruits of my wishes.

She is not my wife and therefore *I am not her husband.* It was not to me but to others that she bore you; I would surely have recognized you. The natural father is not slow to have pity, but he is reluctant to be kind to illegitimate offspring. While you might equally claim that this is said in the person of God, you could likewise reason, and come to a correct understanding, that when the synagogue perversely forsook God and opted instead for worship of the demons, as it were, stretching out its limbs to them like a prostitute, its members proved neither purely and constantly godly nor genuine in their behavior. Rather, they adopted the customs of their forbears, unashamedly embracing what offended God, partly by sacrificing to Baal and the golden heifers, partly by betaking themselves indiscriminately to every form of impurity. They will therefore blame their own mother, and rightly so, and not in her place the truly holy Lord, who loves virtue and who does not deign to keep a prostitute as a

---

2. Hos 1.11.

spouse. The form of prostitution, however, is altogether spiritual, even if spoken of in bodily terms.[3]

I shall remove her lewdness from my sight, and her adultery from between her breasts, so that I may strip her naked, and restore her as on the day of her birth (v.3). For those not returning to God of their own volition or unable to bring themselves to perform his will, and instead holding fast to the depravity they esteem for goodness-knows-what reason, (47) some penalty and punishment will be devised. Whereas it would have been better to adopt that approach of their own volition, the move is now made under pressure of fear. It is similar with painful and treatable wounds in the body: even if they do not show any change for the better as a result of the efficacy of medicines, they either undergo surgery by which the surgeon's skill brings them to this degree of improvement, or at least are brought around by fire. Likewise with a person's soul that has gone the way of abandoning good works: even if it does not respond to the commands of lawgivers, or choose the better path in preference to shameful behavior, it is overcome by sanctions, caught up in the snares of punishment, and undertakes conversion under pressure. This resembles what is said in the verse of Jeremiah, "By hardship and scourging Jerusalem will be corrected"; and the divinely inspired David sings a similar verse in reference to those very fond of being drawn into sin, "Keep their jaws under muzzle and rein if they do not come near you."[4] In other words, trainers are in the habit of leading about the most headstrong and untamed brute beasts on bridles to make them submit, and God treats in similar fashion those with a strong inclination to sin.

Prophets and righteous people advised the assembly[5] to abandon the worship of the idols, therefore, and to desist from the error from goodness-knows-what source it came. Not only they, however: God himself threatened to inflict on them the severest of troubles unless they decided to return to accepting and per-

---

3. Cyril has to be careful, in giving these verses an ecclesiological meaning, that he does not undermine his original thesis, namely, that for all its tastelessness Hosea's partnership with Gomer was factual.

4. Jer 6.7–8; Ps 32.9. Cyril is expansive in his treatment, making his point and documenting it not just once.

5. Cyril continues to employ the deliberately ambiguous term *synagōgē*.

forming what he willed and loved; but they were perverse, stubborn, and unbending in mind. Consequently, they were made captive by Assyrians and Medes, spending long (48) periods in that condition. When they were there, bearing the yoke of slavery, they no longer sacrificed to the heifers; how could they, after all, or with what resources, being in such ineluctable misfortune? Nor did they even invoke Baal; instead, they spent the time lamenting their own calamities. This, to be sure, is what the Lord of all meant in saying, *I shall remove her lewdness from my sight, and her adultery from between her breasts:* she will go off a captive, he says, and I shall no longer see her sacrificing to Baal or performing burnt offerings to the golden heifers, baring her breasts to her lovers, as it were, in extreme insolence. Instead, I shall take satisfaction in her grieving and suffering, experiencing intolerable calamities in a land not her own, and subject to harsh and bitter mistresses. I shall inflict these penalties, stripping her of my assistance and leaving her in such shame that she may seem to be reduced to the original condition when she was bearing the yoke of the Egyptians' oppression and lived bereft of my grace and love and of the wisdom of the Law. The assembly has suffered reversal, therefore, as though going backwards to her former situation, robbed through her stupidity of the honor and glory that had been in her midst.

The Savior himself also taught us as much in saying, "When the unclean spirit has gone out of a person, it wanders through waterless regions looking for a resting place, but it finds none. Then it says, I shall return to my house, from which I came. When it comes, it finds it empty, swept, and put in order. Then it goes and brings along seven other spirits more evil than itself, and they enter and live there; and the last state of that person is worse than the first. So will it be also with this evil generation."[6] (49) In other words, in the people of Israel living in Egypt the evil spirit dwelt as in idolaters, but was driven out from their midst, for they were called to the knowledge of God through Moses. But when they turned killers of the Lord, guilty of countless such crimes, their last state was worse than the first, with a herd of demons, not simply one, dwelling in them. Having re-

---

6. Mt 12.43–45.

jected the garment of heavenly grace, you see, the soul will be completely and utterly exposed to Satan.

I shall make her like a wilderness, turn her into a parched land, and kill her with thirst. I shall have no pity on her children, because they are children of prostitution, because their mother prostituted herself, the one who bore them disgraced herself (vv.3–5). Because of her prostitution, he says, she will be sterile, desiccated, and productive of thorns, dried up and waterless, bereft perhaps not of earthly waters but of heavenly riches from on high—that is, of the source through the Spirit, which he distributes to each wise and good soul. Blessed David somewhere sings of this to God, saying, "Human beings will hope in the shelter of your wings. They will be intoxicated with the rich fare of your house, and you will give them to drink of the torrent of your delights, for with you is a fountain of life."[7] Now, deserving of such an august and generous supply would be those who have sincerely lived an upright life and prefer nothing to love for God, whereas he says that the woman who has prostituted herself will become waterless, and will even die of thirst. This, in my view, is the sentiment of other prophets (50) about her: one said, "Lo, the days are coming, says the Lord, when I shall send a famine on the land; not a famine of bread or a thirst for water, but a famine of hearing the word of the Lord. From east to west they will wander in search of the word of the Lord, and will not find it." Jeremiah likewise says in God's person, "By hardship and scourging Jerusalem will be corrected; let my soul not turn away from you, let me not make you a trackless waste, which will not be inhabited."[8]

To each of our minds, as I said, God imparts thoughts through the Spirit, capable of nourishing us to eternal life; he also enriches us frequently through the words of the saints. He therefore said the children must perish along with the prostitute mother, with no pity shown. For what reason? Because they are the children of prostitution. We do not claim that the child is guilty of the mother's sins; we are certainly familiar with the statement of Ezekiel, "Parents will not die for children, nor children for parents; all will die for their own sins."[9] Now, it should

---

7. Ps 36.7–9. 8. Am 8.11–12; Jer 6.7–8.
9. Dt 24.16; cf. Ezek 18.20.

be realized that even if the person of the prostitute mother is understood as a type of the synagogue, no less would her offspring be likewise. In saying, *They are children of prostitution,* he clearly conveyed that they are guilty of the crimes of spiritual prostitution, impious even from their swaddling clothes, as it were, and from the womb, not ever attaining to works of piety; rather, they left virtue completely untried, and showed no respect for the way pleasing to God. The psalmist likewise says, "Sinners were estranged from the womb, they went astray from their birth, they told lies," whereas every pious person, reared on deeds of righteousness, is genuinely equipped to cry out to God, (51) "On you I was cast from birth, from my mother's womb you have been my God."[10] Just as those who live a genuinely decorous life in the light of day could rightly be considered children of light and children of day,[11] so even if some people could be referred to as *children of prostitution,* you would in turn take those whom he does not deign to pity to be living an extremely illicit life of prostitution, *because their mother prostituted herself, the one who bore them disgraced herself.* She disgraced herself, clearly, as well as the children born of her; as the righteous person enjoys the ornaments of virtue, so every impious person wears shame and disgrace.

She said, in fact, I shall go after my lovers, who give me my bread and my water, my garments and my linen, my oil and everything that belongs to me (v.5). By her *lovers* he refers to the unclean demons, using the metaphor of prostitution; following their dictates and implementing their wishes amount, in my view, to committing sins of lewdness, living in base fashion, being filled with extreme depravity, and, as it were, giving birth to every form of uncleanness. In other words, just as those who give birth to the fear of God cry aloud to God, "Because of fear of you, O Lord, we conceived, suffered birth pangs, and gave birth, we delivered a spirit of your salvation on the earth."[12] Thus, by yielding to the lusts of the demons they forthwith have their minds full of every impiety, having abandoned the divine laws and devoted themselves to utter depravity. The wicked *lovers,* therefore, who are destructive of

---

10. Pss 58.3; 22.10.
11. Cf. 1 Thes 5.5.
12. Is 26.18. Jerome and Theodore had taken the "lovers" in a similar way.

those who accede to their impiety, are the rebellious demons; if you were to choose to pay them the attention due to divine matters, you would be guilty of awful impiety, attributing to them the grace you receive, (52) often venerating them with praise, and offering thanksgiving after forsaking the only one who is God by nature, the source of life's requirements, investing us, as it were, with grace like a kind of clothing, sheltering our mind and heart with assistance from on high, enriching us, as it were, with oil, feeding us with spiritual bread in preparation for an unending life of splendor, and giving us to drink of the life-giving water that produces spiritual vigor.

Those who have opted for impiety, by contrast, like the synagogue in its prostitution, of course, cannot but follow their own lovers, he said, and offer them thanksgiving offerings, and believe that they receive from them what is needed for food and clothing. This, in my view, is the meaning of the verse, *She said, I shall go after my lovers, who give me my bread and my water, my garments and my linen, my oil and everything that belongs to me.* Wise and good people, on the other hand, God's friends and familiars, always offer to him a recompense for heavenly goods and a return for earthly ones. They will say, in fact with keen understanding, "Surely it is not possible for the idols of the nations to bring rain? If the heavens give their abundance, is it not you who does it? We shall submit to you because it is you who did all this." And they will shout aloud with the divinely inspired David, "You will visit the earth and bedew it, enriching it abundantly."[13]

For this reason, lo, I fence in her path with thorns, and shall block her tracks so that she may not even find her way. She will pursue her lovers and will not overtake them, she will seek them and not find them (vv.6-7). She plotted wicked schemes within herself, and left nothing undone of all the iniquity her nature had devised. He had said, remember, that she had no choice (53) but that of following her own lovers—that is, the unholy intentions of those deceived to direct their minds to discharging their wishes alone. So since in addition she gave thanks to the demons, who were of no benefit, for what was given to her by me, consequently I shall expose her

---

13. Jer 14.22; Ps 65.9.

planning as ineffectual and resist her forcefully; *I fence in her path with thorns* and wall up her way to prevent her from going after her lovers or finding the deceived ones useful, even if she perhaps chooses to pursue them, that is, to be zealously devoted to their honor and worship. Now, by *thorns* he refers to the harsh fate befalling Israel, by which I mean the wars, captivities, famine, dangers, life in servitude; once subject to Medes and Persians, remember, for them there was no recourse to Baal or the golden heifers. Instead, it was inevitable that, deprived as they were of the precious freedom from on high, longing for the pleasures of home, impoverished, subject to the whims of their oppressors, they would no longer be able to observe customary ways. Instead, in their grief, and carried away with their intolerable calamities, they condemned those who deceived them, since it was impossible for them to gain anything from people with vain hopes. They were no better off, in fact, either from Baal's assistance—after all, what could voiceless wood do?—or from the heifers pondering some form of aid for them, since they were made of gold, "the work of human hands," as Scripture says.[14]

Accordingly, their ways were blocked; far from smoothing the path to depravity for those addicted to sin, God to good purpose makes it rough, not allowing them to travel easily in pursuit of vain desires. The result is that their wishes are frustrated, and they take a turn for (54) the better after learning from actual experience that no sinner escapes loss.

She will say, I shall go and return to my former husband, because I was better off then than now (v.7). The text continues to adhere to the figure that is suited to its purposes, being composed from beginning to end in reference to a prostitute. Hence, he says, she will repent and say, *I shall go to my former husband, because I was better off then than now*. Observe, however, even in this the God of all correcting by his wrath, being of help in a variety of ways, pulling back the strays with the application of disasters, and causing a change for the better. In other words, he is saying, when she sees her own ways blocked by thorns, then and only then will

14. Ps 115.4.

she have a change of heart; even at a late stage and after experience she will embrace what it was better to do when the misfortunes had not befallen her. In fact, she will then love what comes from God; as though thinking wisely, she will despise sins committed in the meantime; finally she will change to choosing as she had in the beginning, and marvel at what comes from God, and, like someone recovering from intoxication, eventually discern what is incomparably different. Being corrected, therefore, is not without purpose, even if at the outset it perhaps involves distress. The prophets were aware of this in saying, "Correct us, Lord"; and the divinely inspired Paul writes, "If you endure correction, God treats us as children; after all, what child is there whom a father does not correct?" He makes clear to us the sweetness and also the usefulness coming from correction in saying, "Correction always seems painful rather than pleasant at the time, but later it yields the peaceful fruit of righteousness to those who have been trained by it."[15] (55)

She did not know that it was I who gave her the grain, the wine, and the oil, and lavished silver on her; instead, she used silver and gold for the Baal (v.8). There is no doubt, then, he is saying, that she would not choose to continue following her lovers; he will in fact achieve this without any difficulty by blocking her way, obstructing her paths and in no way assisting her progress at all. Since, however, she was inclined to prefer Baal to God, she made thanksgiving offerings to it for what had been provided to her by me, and furthermore I rightly wish her to learn who the giver was and who has power over everything. It was I who gave sustenance for her life: *grain* and *wine* and *oil* and *silver I lavished on her*. Though she should have given thanks for my generosity, she gave the credit for it to the Baal. This was surely clear proof of both extreme insensitivity and ingratitude; and her behavior was sufficient to provoke God with good reason, especially as he is the source and origin of all clemency.

It is therefore an appalling act, one that invites retribution, to seek to attribute the generous supply of graces from God to those that undermine his glory, the unclean demons, which

---

15. Jer 10.24; Heb 12.7, 11.

some people in the world also do—namely, pagans and heretics. The former devote the excesses of their fine talk to the praise of the demons, despite God's giving wisdom and speech to human beings, while the ungodly and sacrilegious bands of the heretics wreak harm on some people with the fancies of their convoluted ideas, pervert the minds of more simple people, "and with snares are bent on destroying men," as Scripture says.[16] So both groups gave honor to Baal; it was as if (56) they made a splendid offering to his glory of the things proper to God, as it were, of spiritual riches. This in my view is the clear spiritual interpretation of the verse, *It was I who gave her the grain, the wine and the oil, and lavished silver on her; instead, she used silver and gold for the Baal.* The offering should be made to God of what is his, then; it is proper to gild the giver and source of every good with all we have from him, be it brilliant discourse or a mind fit for understanding true mysteries.

Hence I shall have a change of heart and take away my grain in its time and my wine in its season, and I shall take away my garments and my linen from concealing her shame. I shall now uncover her uncleanness in the sight of her lovers, and no one will rescue her from my hand (vv.9–10). Do you see how he threatened the removal of what normally brings delight, not without benefit? In other words, he arranged to block her way with thorns to bring her to a better frame of mind, and caused her to say, as it were, even unwillingly, "I shall return to my former husband, because I was better off then than now" (v.7), knowing as she did from experience the benefit involved and where it was better to dwell. Thus, he is saying, if I take what is mine, then she will definitely search out the provider of it, and will cease feeling it necessary to offer thanks to the demons and to think that they are really gods, the result being that the people subject to them will be able to be saved. In due course I will recover *the grain and the wine and the linen,* he is saying, perhaps when the crops fail in due course and there is a delay (57) in ripening them so that it is futile expending effort in tending them.

If, on the other hand, you choose to give a spiritual meaning

---

16. Jer 5.26.

to the Jews' being deprived in due course of *grain and wine,* and stripped of spiritual blessing, your understanding would be correct.[17] By *linen* he meant defense and assistance from on high, which lends comeliness to anyone enjoying it, whereas bereft of it one is no longer attractive, but will live in the world in great ugliness and, as it were, naked. Here, therefore, you could understand the removal of the linen. This, then, is the spiritual interpretation you would give the removal of the linen so as not to cover her ugliness. He promises instead to uncover *her uncleanness,* even *in the sight of her lovers.* In what way? We just said that she would fall among thorns, that is, the misfortunes of war and the most terrifying calamities. So she would neglect even what she took to be gods, with no opportunity to offer them sacrifices or perform rituals to glorify them. Instead, mocking them as incapable of being of any benefit, and completely jeering at their weakness, she says, "I shall return to my former husband, because it was better for me then than now" (v.7). Accordingly, when I divest her of assistance from me, he says, and she encounters disasters and despises the honor and love that she had given to them, then she will be seen as ugly by them, repelling even them with her unsound and distorted thinking. Instead of being something attractive to them and lovable, she must rather be seen as wretched, and oblivious to their wishes even in extreme calamities. As far as their desires were concerned, therefore, Israel was ugly in the eyes of those she had considered gods but had ceased to love. Now, it seems to me that the blessed Elijah said something similar: "How long will you limp (58) on both legs? If the Lord is God, follow him; but if it is Baal, follow him,"[18] as he says elsewhere, "Either for Baal, Baal, or for God, God." The fact that no one would free those once subject to divine wrath, nor restore what had been rejected by God, he indicated in saying, *No one will rescue her from my hand.*

I shall cancel all her rejoicing, her festivals, her new moon observanc-

---

17. Such items in the text, for which an Alexandrian commentator would easily find a spiritual meaning, Cyril has first treated historically in reference to Israel, appreciating the imagery at the literal level. Only then does he instruct his readers to proceed to the level of the *noētos* and the *mystikos.*

18. 1 Kgs 18.21.

es, her sabbaths, and all her feasts (v.11). What basis of celebration would there be for people caught up in harsh and intolerable troubles to the extent of being under the control of savages and enslaved to the foe as captives? Or what grounds for rejoicing would they have who were burdened with such bitter cares and worn down with unbearable distress? Admittedly, how would it not be better to consider that it would instead be appropriate for those caught up in such a degree of hardship to cry aloud the beautiful sentiment sung to the psalmist's lyre, "By the river of Babylon we sat and wept when we remembered Zion." With celebration completely out of the question, they went on to say, "How are we to sing the song of the Lord in a foreign land?"[19] In my view, the Babylonians would not have permitted them to perform the worship required of them or the rites dear to them and customary at home.

Perhaps, on the other hand, you might ask, If Israel had reverted to the worship of idols, how would it not also have abandoned the festivals prescribed by the Law, Sabbaths, and new moon observances?[20] Our reply to this is that, though they had lapsed in their love for God and had bowed down to Baal and the golden heifers, they had not (59) completely rejected the requirements of Moses. Instead, they continued walking and limping in both directions, as the prophet said, thus opting not to worship Baal completely nor the God of all in unadulterated fashion. So they neglected feasts and festivals, joyful celebrations and sabbaths, allowing neither the discharge of lawful observances to God nor the performance of the customary celebrations to Baal.

Now, in another fashion as well it would very likely be true that those who abandon God and diminish their love for him necessarily feel remorse and completely lose the habit of rejoicing. "It is impossible for the impious to rejoice, says the Lord," since the worm remains with them forever. For good people with a pious and godly intention it would be quite appropriate to feel

---

19. Ps 137.1, 4. The fact that this is a lament of exiles of Judah in Babylon, not of Israel in their places of deportation, does not register with Cyril.

20. As was true also of Theodore, Cyril does not go to the trouble of explaining these festivals.

the need to rejoice in all good things; "everlasting joy will be on their heads," Scripture says; "pain, distress and groaning take their leave." The divinely inspired Paul writes to such people in these terms: "Rejoice in the Lord always, again I say Rejoice. Let your gentleness be known to everyone."[21] In other words, just as the inevitability of punishment will pursue villains, so, too, enrichment in goods from on high will attend those whose mind is bent on living a spotless life.

I shall do away with her vines and her fig trees, all the payment, she said, that my lovers gave me, and I shall turn them to witness. The wild animals of the field devour them, and the birds of heaven and the reptiles of earth (v.12). This can be put another way: "I shall take away my grain in its time, and my wine in its season" (v.9). In other words, since Israel attributed the produce of the seasons to the power and generosity of the demons (60)—a stupid thing to do—and offered thanksgiving to them instead of God, consequently he says *I shall do away with* and destroy the means by which she was so gravely deceived, claiming to have received them in payment from her lovers. The discourse is cleverly framed in terms of a lustful woman, where the reference in reality is to Israel, who believed that the abundance of the seasonal crops and the earth's enjoyment of fertility were a reward for them and a recompense for the honor and worship paid to the idols. Now, the fact that they believed that this was the sole cause of their share also in all other prosperity you would very easily understand by reading the words of Jeremiah. When Jerusalem was captured, remember, some people escaped the intensity of the fighting and went down to Egypt, the prophet accompanying them by divine command; while there he urged them to abandon the defilements of idolatry and opt to return to God. At that, a wretched and mindless crowd of women in turn opposed the advice of the prophet, and even shamelessly declared, "The word you have spoken to us in the name of the Lord we are not going to listen to, because we are bent on carrying out every word that has come from our mouths, sacrificing to the queen of heaven and offering libations to her, just as was done by us, our parents, our kings, and our rul-

---

21. Is 48.22; 66.24; 35.10; Phil 4.4–5.

ers in the cities of Judah and outside Jerusalem. We had plenty of bread and became prosperous, and experienced no misfortune. When we stopped burning incense to the queen of heaven, we were all reduced to indigence and wasted by sword and famine."[22]

Do you understand, therefore, how she says she obtained necessities, as it were, in repayment for being led astray, and prosperity in addition? Accordingly he says, *I shall do away with all the payment, she said, that my lovers gave me, and I shall turn them to* (61) *witness*—that is, what is done away with will bear witness to Israel's depravity,[23] bring notorious retribution upon them, and make manifest the divine wrath. *The wild animals of the field will consume them, and the birds of heaven and the reptiles of earth.* This should not be understood in one way; rather, there are three meanings to be taken. His meaning either is that the animals' food is in the fields, there being no one to inhabit the land on account of most people's being forced to leave homes and cities and depart unwillingly to Babylon and the Medes, and the rest wasted by war, so that the country of the Samaritans is occupied only by wild beasts and reptiles.[24] Or it means that the Babylonians like wild beasts will consume the produce of the country, while the inhabitants of the land stay within the cities' fortifications, not even daring to go out of the gates, so to speak, despite dying of hunger.

If, on the other hand, you decide to take it in a spiritual sense, you could follow a different track. That is to say, a comparison could well be made of vineyard and fig tree with the instruction given in the Law that leads to Christ; in this it acted as a tutor, according to the blessed Paul's statement.[25] A vine would be taken as a symbol of merriment, and a fig tree of sweetness; how could

22. Jer 44.16–18.
23. Despite Jerome's reminder, Cyril does not advert to the LXX's version ("witness") of a form similar to but different from our Heb. form for "forest."
24. While Cyril is to be commended for looking for several possible historical references in the text, he is indiscriminate in mention of Babylon, Medes, Samaritans (as we have noted). As usual, he then feels justified in moving to a *pneumatikos* meaning.
25. Gal 3.24. Like Theodore, Cyril is unaware of the play upon similar Heb. words for "prostitute's fee" and "fig tree."

one be in doubt that the law of God customarily brings joy and sweetness to a soul that loves God? While Israel therefore of necessity remained without participation in the spiritual goods from on high, they were, so to speak, given as food to the wild beasts and reptiles—those from the nations, I mean, who before the coming of the Savior would have been understood as little different from wild beasts and venomous reptiles on account of the depravity of their behavior. They did not persist in it, however, choosing to follow Christ, who says, "Learn of me, (62) because I am gentle and humble of heart, and you will find rest for your souls."[26] I would also add this to what has been said, that those treading the accursed path that is hateful to God of necessity forfeit every good and meet with the worst misfortunes of all.

I shall take vengeance on her for the days of the Baals when she offered sacrifice to them, put on her nose rings and her jewelry, and went after her lovers and forgot me, says the Lord (v.13). He proceeds immediately to supply the reason for such dire—or, rather, in their case most appropriate—indignation. You see, since they persisted for a long period in being deceived, he is saying, they will experience wrath for an equally extended time—the meaning, in my view, of *I shall take vengeance on her for the days of the Baals,* that is, the idols. The period of punishment and retribution, in fact, he is saying, will be exactly equivalent to the days of the deception, in which she sacrificed to Baal; she did not cease titivating herself and in many ways attracting her lovers. Now, adornment in the case of souls opting for idolatry means performing what pleases the unclean demons; just as we say that a person's soul is appealing when it is seen to be conspicuous for virtues, so, too, it must be presumed that a soul that loves sin is attractive to the herds of demons when it chooses to think and do everything that they find pleasing and lovable. Such a soul would be comparable to a woman of loose morals who is bejeweled in gold in a gaudy manner; she bewitches the heart of her lovers, as it were, with ornaments to ears and neck. Any form of uncleanness, therefore, adds luster to wicked people. Now, the fact that losing

---

26. Mt 11.29.

the very thought of God would be normal and inevitable for those who are bent on those things (63) he brought out in saying, *She forgot me, says the Lord.* After all, since she became ill in clinging to the demons, he says, or rather by completely abandoning the longing and desire for the good, she lost the very thought of God—a clear proof of her utter impiety.

For this reason, lo, I shall seduce her, and put her in the wilderness (v.14). In other words, he is saying, since she offended in many ways, I very rightly sought satisfaction for her abandonment; I took "vengeance on her for the days of the Baals" (v.13), and vented my wrath in a way commensurate with her falls. Consequently, I shall now change my attitude to one of mercy and bring her to a better frame of mind, to being capable of doing what would make her love God. What, then, he asks, will be the mode of the cure? *Lo, I shall seduce her,* not from what is required and useful for living to a life that is not of that kind, but from what is base and conducive to crime to doing what is of benefit. In other words, just as a soul is seduced from virtue to depravity, in the same way in my view by going backwards, as it were, from the practice of depravity it would seem to be seduced, as it were, bypassing its instinctive resolve and no longer following the path proposed. And just as it was of benefit for her ways to be blocked with thorns to prevent her taking her lovers, so now, too, when she is, as it were, heading down into ruin and destruction, she seems to be seduced by the mercy of God, changing to a desire for virtue, admitting into her mind and heart the light of the true knowledge of God, and, as I said, no longer following the former path.

Now, it should be realized that the phrase *I shall seduce her* is translated in different ways by different commentators, though one and the same meaning is arrived at. Some render it *Lo, I shall carry her off;* others, *I shall deceive her,* (64) which is a different version, as I said, but they mean the same thing, *seduce* being understood in a positive sense.[27] Since she is accessible and, as it were, a well-watered land for the herds of demons, he promises

---

27. The Antiochenes do not acknowledge such a range of versions, reading a text like Cyril's.

to *put her in the wilderness,* conveying to us that he will make her harsh, untrodden, and waterless for their wishes, so that they may now find no place of rest, and scorn and abandon her. Similarly, our Lord Jesus Christ also says that the unclean spirit on leaving a person wanders through waterless places, looking for rest and not finding it.[28] In other words, just as a waterless landscape is uninhabitable for human beings, so, too, the godly and holy soul would rightfully be considered bad for unclean spirits, harsh, and, as it were, inaccessible and waterless, since it is unprepared to think or do what pleases them. So the *seduction* referred to here is a form of assistance, as is placing her in wilderness country, as explained by us just now.

I shall speak to her heart, and give her from there her possessions (v.15). In this passage the text clearly promises us salvation through Christ, and mentions the time of his coming, in which we claim the prophecy will be fulfilled: "In those days and at that time I shall put my laws in their mind, and write them on their heart." This, in fact, is also the way Paul in his wisdom writes to those enriched with such a splendid grace truly worthy of acceptance, saying, "You are our letter, written on our hearts, to be known and read (65) by all people, and you show that you are the letter of Christ prepared by us, written not with ink but with the Spirit of the living God."[29] We believers, you see, are God's pupils; the divinely inspired John, for example, addresses us in these words: "You have an anointing from the Holy One, and you do not need anyone else to teach you, as his Spirit teaches you about everything." Being in receipt of the Spirit, therefore, and now having Christ himself dwelling within our heart, who introduces us to what is required, we are straightway enriched with the form of every virtue and with the generous possession of spiritual gifts not to be rejected. In addition to this Paul gives us confirmation in writing: "What eye has not seen, nor ear heard, nor has it entered into the human heart, what God has prepared for those who love him."[30]

---

28. See Mt 12.43. The Hosea text has evoked responses in Christians attracted to desert and wilderness locations in search of union with God. For all his "spiritual" interpretation, Cyril does not resonate with such aspirations.
29. Jer 31.33; 2 Cor 3.2–3.
30. 1 Jn 2.20, 27; 1 Cor 2.9; Is 64.4.

Accordingly, he promises to *speak to her heart;* the synagogue of the Jews will be called to knowledge, admitting into their mind the divine laws that have been inscribed there by the Spirit, just as is the case with the church from the nations. *Her possessions will be from there,* that is, from here, or this event—in other words, from God's speaking in us and through the Spirit making resound all that is necessary for life and the knowledge of God understood in Christ. It is through him and in him that we behold the Father and are enriched, as I said, with unfailing hope, glory, the pride of sonship, grace, and reigning with Christ himself. These are the *possessions* of the saints, this their heavenly wealth; far from bringing themselves to have any earthly thoughts, they hate the world and what is in it.

And the valley of Achor to open her understanding (v.15). The verb *give* is repeated from the passage, *I shall give her from there her possessions;* likewise, *I shall give the valley* (66) *of Achor to open her understanding.* What he means is something like this: We believers are anxious to take what happened in former times as a model for our behavior, and thus avoid offending God as productive of ruin; instead, we seek out and carefully put into action what works for his pleasure. Paul in his wisdom, remember, urges us to this in saying, "Now, these things happened to them as a type, and were recorded for our instruction, on whom the ends of the ages have come."[31] So there is a need to study what happened to the ancients as a means of guiding us to virtue.

Accordingly, the fact that those who are disobedient and rebellious, and who spurn the divine instructions, will fall foul of a dire and ineluctable accounting under Christ as Judge is very easily demonstrated at least as a type by the fate of Achan, who set at naught the divine commandment, stole some of what fell under the ban, and was punished with his whole household, Joshua son of Nun exacting the ultimate penalty of him in acting as a figure of Christ. After Moses, remember, he was in command; it was he who led the children of Israel across the Jordan, and he who distributed among them the land of promise. The

---

31. 1 Cor 10.11. In leisurely fashion Cyril is laying the groundwork for a typological interpretation of the valley of Achor and future references in The Twelve.

story of Achan goes this way: when the thief was apprehended and confessed his sin, "Joshua took Achan son of Zerah, led him out to the Valley of Achor along with his sons and his daughters, his cattle, his beasts of burden and his sheep, his tent and all his possessions, and in the company of all the people he brought them to Emekachor. Joshua said to Achan, Why did you destroy us? The Lord will utterly destroy you this day. And all Israel stoned him, and piled (67) a huge heap of stones on him."[32] Achor means distortion, then, and Emek is a prefix—hence the meaning Valley of Distortion. It was there that the children of Israel killed Achan for being hateful to God and avaricious, and along with him they placed all his possessions; Scripture says, remember, "The impious will be rooted up from the land and will perish."[33] This will also be what happens in the endtime, when from on high Christ comes from heaven, rewarding all individuals according to the deeds of each; those who have chosen to disobey the divine commandments and have instead been attached to the things of the world he will cast into Hades like a deep valley, and destroy these evil ones utterly.

Accordingly he says, *I shall give the valley of Achor* (or Emekachor) *to open her understanding;* in other words, what once happened in the Valley of Emekachor will be a great aid to her in being on the alert, as it is necessary to be, and opening the eye of the mind again after the former hardness. He called the place Distortion Valley, since it was there that not a few of the people of Israel met their end when the men of Ai pursued them and a great distortion occurred, and Joshua thought that Israel had lost God's clemency and assistance.[34] What happened in Distor-

---

32. Jos 7.24–26. Though modern commentators see in Achor in Hos 2.15 a reference to the valley mentioned also in Jos 15.7 as a gateway from the Jordan to the fertile land of central Palestine, Cyril and the Antiochenes choose not to identify its location. While Theodore just makes a lazy guess, Cyril sees a connection with the account of the disobedience of Achan at it (Achar in LXX) in Jos 7, where word play in the Heb. allows for appropriate identification of "trouble" as both a personal and a place name; Cyril gets good typological and historical value from it. Theodoret capitalizes on this, though also checking with the Syriac, but less characteristically ignoring the valley's location; he does not follow Cyril into seeing christological and eschatological dimensions of the text.

33. Prv 2.22.

34. See Jos 7.1–9.

COMMENTARY ON HOSEA 2

tion Valley, therefore, he is saying, in the case of the man who presumed to defy the divine commandment, *will open her understanding* with a view to having a clear understanding of the sort of fate that will befall those wanting to show such scorn. Now, consider how the valley of Achor was not *given to open her understanding* before he spoke to her heart; the Jewish populace would not have understood the divine commands, nor discerned the mystery of Christ in types, unless he had enriched us who already believe with a share in the Holy Spirit (68) and allowed us to participate in guidance from on high. The blessed Paul confirms us in this understanding in writing about those of the bloodline of Israel, "To this very day, when they hear the reading of the old covenant, that same veil is still there, since only in Christ is it set aside. Indeed, to this very day, whenever Moses is read, a veil lies over their hearts. But when one turns to the Lord, the veil is removed. Now, the Lord is the Spirit; and where the Spirit of the Lord is, there is freedom." Accordingly, he first promises to speak to her heart, when the Holy Spirit engraves on them the divine laws and guidance from on high; then she would in this way understand what happened in the valley of Emekachor as a type and as actual fact, which is quite capable of *opening her understanding* and ridding her of her former hardness; "a hardening has come upon part of Israel," remember, as Paul in his wisdom writes.[35]

There she will be humbled as in the days of her infancy and in the days of her ascent from Egypt (v.15). When I speak to her mind and heart, he is saying, and give her the valley of Achor to open her understanding, *there*—that is, at that time—*she will be humbled,* not subject or liable to any of the things that normally cause harm, but rather abandoning in the future any behavior that is disobedient and intractable and subject to charges of arrogance. The disobedient person, you see, is proud and, as it were, refractory and obdurate, disposed to give no account to the necessary respect for performance of the Law, (69) whereas the person who is disposed to obedience and an ardent lover of God is very humble and, as it were, compliant. He said in one of the holy

---

35. 2 Cor 3.14–17; Rom 11.25.

prophets, for example, "On whom shall I gaze if not on the one who is humble and peaceable and who trembles at my words?"[36] So when I speak to her heart, therefore, he says, then and only then will she also *be humbled* as in the beginning when, at the invitation of Moses and the command of the compassionate God to leave Egypt, she was very prompt and ready to do so, and she left the land of the oppressors. When God decreed his laws on Horeb, and they were assembled by Moses at Mount Sinai, they made a promise: "All the Lord our God told us we shall do and heed."[37] She will be humble and docile, then, as in the beginning when she took her origin through the Law for knowledge of God, and gladly accepted God's will. By *days of her infancy*, therefore, he meant rebirth through the Law to knowledge of God—hence his saying, "Israel my firstborn son."[38]

On that day, says the Lord, she will call me My husband, and will no longer call me Baal. I shall remove the names of the Baals from her mouth, and they will no longer remember their names (vv.16–17). By *day* here, then, he is referring to the time of the coming of our Savior; the moment of the Incarnation of the Only-begotten will appropriately and truly be called *day*, because that is when the mist over the world was dissipated, and the darkness removed. Bright beams, as it were, were shed on the mind of the (70) believers, and the sun of righteousness[39] shone forth, imparting the light of the true knowledge of God on those knowing how to open the eye of the mind. At that time, then, he is saying, when called to acknowledge the one who is truly God, she will abandon that hateful nonsense of former times, and will no longer be inclined to infidelity. How so? She will instead travel in an upright and sound manner and will keep her mind fixed fast on piety, the result being that not even the names of the idols will occupy the slightest of her attention. In fact, he says, *She will call me My husband, and will no longer call me Baal*, that is to say, she will cease being wanton, will desist from playing the whore any longer, will set much store on being genuine, and will confess her

---

36. Is 61.2.
37. Ex 18.8; 24.7. Is Cyril suggesting by the two names two mountains?
38. Ex 4.22.
39. Cf. Mal 4.2.

relationship—namely, the spiritual one. She will make no invocation to the Baals in the belief that things made from stone and by some people's clever skills formed in human likeness are gods. Therefore, he says, *She will call me My husband;* having come to her senses like an honest woman, she will be converted to me, will love no others in the future, and will no longer invoke the Baals.

The verse can be taken also in another way, if you prefer. *Baals,* of course, by common consent means "idols"; and it was the custom with the Hebrew women to call their own husbands by the names of the false gods, this being an extraordinary mark of respect on their part. They say that the one to begin this practice was Ninos the Babylonian, who changed the name of his father to Bel, from the idol found among them, Bel by name.[40] So he mentioned that she also gave up this vile custom when he said, *She will call me My husband,* (71) *and will no longer call me Baal;* in other words, he is saying, if she were to choose perhaps to call me "husband," she would go further to say *My husband,* no longer honoring the names of the idols. Hence he says, *I shall remove the names of the Baals from her mouth, and they will no longer remember their names.*

I shall make a covenant for them on that day with the animals of the countryside and with the birds of heaven and with the reptiles of the ground. I shall break bow, sword, and war from the land (v.18). In what was read out previously he said, "I shall do away with her vine and her fig trees, all the payment, she said, that my lovers gave me" (v.12), adding to this, "The wild animals of the field devour them, and the birds of heaven and the reptiles of earth" (v.12).[41] In commenting on the verse we said that *the wild animals, birds, and reptiles* referred indirectly to the enemy who ravaged the country of the Jews, namely, Persians, Medes, and Babylonians,[42] and the motley company of other foes, who could rightly be taken as being little different from wild animals on account of the

---

40. It is from Jerome that Cyril derives this background to his text ("they say" being his shorthand way of acknowledging such a source).
41. Hos 2.12.
42. We have noted that Cyril is imprecise in pinpointing the precise fate of the northern kingdom to which Hosea is directing his prophecy in the eighth century, and the other nations involved.

murderous character of their behavior, as birds on account of the swiftness of their flight, and as serpents for being cruel, harsh, and disposed to evil. With Israel contained within the cities of Samaria, these forces devastated everything in the fields, leaving no outrage untried. When I remove the names of their idols from the land, he says, then *I shall make a covenant* of peace for them with every cruel and savage race; the enemy attacks will lapse, (72) and they will have no further experience of war and terror. In fact, *I shall break bow and sword,* which we shall find taking effect in actual fact: when the celebrated Roman generals were given command against all nations, they brought the whole world into subjection, with God in his plan allotting the glory to them; the Persians had concern only for their own empire, while the incursions of the other barbarians against countries and cities came to an end. The blessed Isaiah makes clear reference to this event in saying, "They will beat their swords into ploughshares and their spears into pruning hooks; nation will not lift up sword against nation, neither will they learn to wage war any more."[43] In other words, after being under one yoke, they turned to productive occupation and adapted the weapons of war to use in farming. There will therefore be peace, he says, and the awful terrors of old will cease when God gives rest and gladdens those who love him with the goods that stem from peace.

Now, I think that this, too, should be added. In former times, remember, when we lived in error and were styled children of wrath,[44] the evil and hostile powers, like some evil beasts, flesh-eating birds, and fierce dragons, destroyed us. But when we came to know in Christ the one who is God by nature, and were cleansed of the crimes of the former deception through faith, then we were saved and received authority "to walk on snakes and scorpions and on all the power of the foe"; then we trod on snake and basilisk, walked on lion and dragon with Christ as protector, who (73) walls his own about with unconquerable power,

---

43. Is 2.4. Like some of his contemporaries, Cyril sees the *pax Romana* as the realization of eschatological prophecies of a golden age. The Persians remain a threat, but at this stage have not moved westward; Theodoret, also appreciative of Roman rule (at least initially), will acknowledge their invasion of 441 in his Psalms commentary.

44. Eph 2.3.

and admits peace into our mind. He says, in fact, "My peace I give you, my peace I leave with you." Paul also writes, "The peace of Christ, which surpasses all understanding, will guard your hearts and your minds."[45]

I shall make you dwell in hope, and shall betroth you to myself forever (vv.18–19). I shall not only rid you of the terrors of war, he is saying, but in addition to this I shall cause you in the future to enjoy hope in good things so as to have prosperity that is secure, permanent, and unshakable. In fact, *I shall betroth you to myself,* and this *forever.* What does this actually mean? It will be like his betrothing himself to the Israel of old, or the synagogue of the Jews, and inviting them into a relationship through the Law, which was given through the ministry of Moses and the mediation of angels.[46] The form of the betrothal was not permanent, however, nor was it for ever: far from it. In fact, the types were not intended to hold force for all time—only "until the time comes to set things right"; at "the time to set things right," that is, the time of the coming of our Savior, a different form of betrothal emerged that is permanent and irremovable, far more splendid than the former, and better than the shadow. The God of all, you see, made a gift of the removal of physical servitude like a kind of present to his bride, and in shadow and type he invited her to spiritual cleansing. But he set a time limit on the betrothal: the former one was not free of blame, according to Paul's statement,[47] nor was it proof against age and cancellation. Consequently, he looked for an occasion for a second one—that is, a new one—namely, (74) the gift and grace coming through Christ to us without time limit and without conveying a freedom that is physical; he enrolls us among the children of God, lavishes on us "the pledge of the Spirit," and prescribes abiding laws. The divine David says somewhere, for instance, "Your righteousness is an everlasting righteousness, and your word is truth,"[48] indicating clearly in my view that the contents of the Law do not abide forever, since the shadow gives way to reality, nor would

---

45. Lk 10.19; Ps 91.13; Jn 14.27; Phil 4.7. The PG text does not include the Philippians reference.
46. Gal 3.19. 47. Heb 9.10; 8.7.
48. 2 Cor 5.5; Ps 119.142.

you discern the beauty of the reality in the text of the Law, since, as I said, the Law is shadow and type. Accordingly, he betroths her to himself, annulling the initial, original marriage; the Law was not capable of cementing a perfect and pure relationship with God. We are attached to him, by contrast, through the Son and through the pronouncements he made—in the Gospels, that is—which contain also spiritual union or relationship; we are united to God in the Spirit, and enriched with a share in his divine nature.

It is reasonable, on the other hand, for us to give an elegant development of the phrase *betroth you to myself.* In this way you will understand it further, either by taking *to myself* to mean "through myself," not as in the past with the mediation of angels nor with someone acting as minister, as in the case of Moses. Scripture says, remember, "It was no messenger or angel, but the Lord himself," the Word from God the Father, who was made man like us, who presented the church to himself and "created one new humanity out of the two peoples, thus making peace and reconciling both groups in one Spirit to the Father," according to the statement of the blessed Paul.[49]

Or there is still another way to take the verse if you like. There was a betrothal, as I said, in Egypt of the (75) synagogue of the Jews, not to himself, but, as it were, to someone else—to the divinely inspired Moses, I mean—to whom he said somewhere, "Go, leave here promptly; your people whom you led out of the land of Egypt has offended."[50] Do you hear how he assigned to Moses the betrothed one, or the people, not yet according her a relationship with himself? The Law, or Moses, as I said, was not capable of making a pure and complete relationship with God; the role of the highest and truly godly achievement was kept for the mediator between God and man—namely, Christ—through whom and in whom we are united with God. He in fact "is our peace," according to the Scriptures,[51] and by removing the sin lying between us he joined us, when pure, cleansed, and sanctified

---

49. Is 63.9; cf. Eph 2.14–18.
50. Ex 32.7. Cyril politely offers yet another alternative interpretation for his readers' perusal; he could not be accused of being dogmatic.
51. 1 Tim 2.5; Eph 2.14.

COMMENTARY ON HOSEA 2   89

in the Spirit, to himself, and through himself to the God and Father.

I shall betroth you to myself in righteousness, in justice, in mercy, and in compassion. I shall betroth you to myself in faith, and you will know the Lord (v.20). He explains clearly what is the form of relationship, and in which respects the mystery of the divine plan eventuates, saying it will be *in righteousness, in justice,* and also *in mercy and in compassion.* It is probably necessary, then, to explain the meaning of righteousness, justice, and mercy. In our wretchedness we are oppressed, then, as Satan, like a wild animal of the field, seizes us, carries us off into error, and plunges us into the depths of sin of his own volition without our being able to help ourselves, since the wild beast is cruel, truly violent, and murderous. When human affairs were brought to such a state of wretchedness, however, (76) the blessed, inspired authors offered incessant prayers to the one capable of assistance, as it were, adopting for themselves the role of humanity in general, and besought the Son to come from heaven as ally and helper. The divinely inspired David, for example, said, "Rise up, O God, judge the earth," and again, "O God, by your name save me, and by your power you will judge me."[52] Accordingly, God judged in righteousness, saving the wronged and driving off murderous and destructive Satan; [God] abolished [Satan's] oppression of us and canceled the haughty and ungracious rule of the demons.

He personally made this mystery clear to us in saying, when on the point of enduring the cross for the life of everyone, "Now is the judgment of this world, now the ruler of this world will be driven out. And I, when I am lifted up from the earth, will draw everyone to myself." We do not actually claim that he said judgment of this world will be made by him at the time of his coming; as he himself said in a previous passage, "God sent the Son into the world, not to judge the world, but that the world might be saved through him."[53] Now, he speaks of judgment as correct and faultless adjudication; he ruled correctly and in a matter be-

52. Pss 82.8; 54.1. David is one of these inspired authors, *prophêtai.*
53. Jn 12.31–32; 3.17.

fitting God, as I said, in our case and his, saving us and drawing us to himself, while expelling from unjust rule against us the one who is oppressive and destructive in manifold ways.

We are therefore saved when God has mercy and compassion on us; we have been made righteous, "not because of any works of righteousness that we have done, but according to the abundance of his mercy," as Scripture says.[54] We were also summoned to the spiritual relationship through faith, and by being thus summoned (77) we came to know the one who is God by nature. Consequently, he says, *I shall betroth you to myself in faith, and you will know the Lord.* Faith made its entrance in advance, therefore, and we were enriched also in this way by knowing Christ—and this, in my view, is the meaning of what is said to some: "If you will not believe, neither will you understand." Now, the fact that the clear understanding of the mystery of Christ achieves a share in eternal life for those worthy of it the Son himself confirms in speaking to God the Father in heaven: "Now, this is eternal life, that they may know you, the one true God, and Jesus Christ, whom you have sent."[55]

On that day, says the Lord, I shall hearken to heaven, and heaven will hearken to earth; earth will hearken to the grain, the wine, and the oil, and they will hearken to Jezreel (vv.21–22). Here again by *day* he refers to the time relevant to the calling, as is customary with the inspired Scripture. So in an obscure fashion he implies that at that time Israel itself will have an abundant share in every good and the graces from God on high after being illuminated by faith in Christ. He says, in fact, that there will be an abundance of rain when he wills it—the meaning, in my view, of *I shall hearken to heaven*—and also on the earth below there will be a yield of the crops that are particularly useful and necessary for us. Without God and the will from on high, you see, heaven itself would not rain on those on earth, nor would the earth produce its characteristic crops in due season. Aware of this, (78) the prophet Jeremiah says, "Do any idols of the nations have power to send rain? And if heaven gives its abundance, is it not you, O God? We shall await you, because you have done all these things."[56] When

---

54. Ti 3.5.
55. Is 7.9 LXX; Jn 17.3.
56. Jer 14.22.

in fact the Creator agrees, as I said, and proffers his hand to those on earth, heaven will be a giver of rain, and the earth both mother and nourisher of the necessary crops. Accordingly, he says, *I shall hearken to heaven,* that is, I shall agree to send rains on those on earth; when this is done, it *will hearken to the grain, the wine, and the oil;* that is, it will yield to its inhabitants a generous crop, no one deprived of whatever is necessary and essential for life.

So much for the factual sense; from what is bodily, as though from a visible image, it is necessary to move to what is spiritual. As long, remember, as Israel was hostile, disobedient, and at odds with God, despite being the vineyard of the Lord of hosts, "the beloved plant," God instructed the clouds not to shed rain on it.[57] Now, clouds should be understood as the holy and rational powers, those from heaven on high, from whom the word of consolation would come to us—from God, that is, since spirits act in a ministerial role, according to the statement of the blessed Paul, moving hither and yon, and "sent to serve for the sake of those who are to inherit salvation."[58] When the period of punishment passed, however, the former murderer of the Lord was saved through faith and was welcomed *in righteousness, in justice, in mercy, and in compassion;* God, who lavishly distributes everything to all, sent down on him blessings from on high, instructing (79) the clouds to send down rain—that is, comfort for mind and heart.

The fact, however, that the angels by nature are not independent, and owe their riches to God, he conveyed in saying, *I shall hearken to heaven,* that is, I shall make heaven full of things from me, or the beings who live in heaven—obviously, rational and holy powers—so that they can be the ones to comfort the recipients of mercy, and then without doubt *the earth will hearken to the grain, the wine, and the oil,* in other words, those on earth will fruitfully yield hope for life, joy, and gladness. The *grain* is a type of life; *wine,* of joy; and *oil,* of happiness and good dispositions—in

---

57. Is 5.7, 6. Cyril generally follows his hermeneutical rule of thumb: first a factual *(historikôs)* interpretation, then the spiritual, the former an *eikôn* of the reality.

58. Heb 1.14.

other words, innate in believers is sound hope that is firm and unshakable. A person abandons depravity, longs for every good, submits himself to the Savior's yoke, and is nourished by a sound hope that is unwavering and completely true for future life, so as to rejoice freely in the company of the other saints and possess a joyful heart. Of the saints, remember, the prophet Isaiah said, "Everlasting joy will be on their heads; on their heads will be praise and gladness, joy will take possession of them, pain and grief and lament taking their leave."[59] It is therefore in hope of life and happiness as also of joy, consolations from on high or spiritual showers, that undoubtedly *the earth will hearken*, that is, people living on earth.

Now, the fact that the fruit of the life of the saints will also be for the glory of Christ (Scripture says, remember, "One person died for all so that those who live might no longer live for themselves but for him who died for them and was raised") he mentioned in saying, *And they will hearken to Jezreel:* to him as I said we shall bear fruit, to him we owe our life. It has been said many times that (80) *Jezreel* means "seed of God," and this is the Son insofar as he is born by nature and in unspeakable fashion of God the Father, even if the fact is described in bodily terms.[60]

I shall sow her for myself on earth, and I shall have pity on Not pitied, and shall say to Not my people, You are my people, and he will reply, You are the Lord my God (v.23). You will again understand the phrase *for myself* in two senses: I shall, as it were, make it, he says, luxuriant and fruitful—the synagogue of the Jews, that is—no longer unwillingly carrying out my laws nor insistent on being attached to the types, but opting instead as far as possible to do what is pleasing to God and in accord with his will as far as they comprehend it. Therefore, *I shall sow her for myself,* taking "my sowing" in the sense of the Gospel pronouncements and no longer the Law of Moses as in the beginning; formerly the cultivation was done in types. Or "my" could also be taken in another way:[61] I shall be

---

59. Is 35.10.
60. 2 Cor 5.5. Courtesy of Jerome, Cyril is in a position to benefit from this etymological datum to exploit the play upon the word "sow" in the Heb. in this and the next verse; but it does not register with him.
61. Again Cyril allows his readers a range of possible interpretations, mostly historical.

the farmer myself, he is saying, with responsibility for her, and, like some land that is rich and well-ploughed, *I shall sow* her by myself, not employing anyone else. The God and Father, remember, has spoken to us in the Son, though having spoken to us of old through the holy prophets "in many and various ways." The Savior himself compared the vast body of believers to the crops in the field; he said, for example, to the holy apostles, "Do you not say, Four months more, then comes the harvest? Lo, I say to you, Lift up your eyes and see how the country is already ripe (81) for harvesting. The reaper is receiving wages, and is gathering a crop for eternal life." Again elsewhere, "The harvest is plentiful, but the laborers are few; therefore ask the Lord of the harvest to send out laborers into his harvest."[62]

When Jesus Christ our Savior sent down the spiritual rain on us, therefore, we became "a land of delight," in the prophet's term; he sowed us for himself, and Israel was styled "God's field."[63] In fact, he will have pity on Not pitied, and give the name "people" to what was once Not my people; it will abandon its former deception and acknowledge the true God, *and it will say, You are my God* (v.23), despite formerly crying aloud in utter nonsense, "We know that God has spoken to Moses, but as for this man, we do not know where he has come from." Being ignorant of the Son, then, they did not even know the Father, as the Savior himself confirms in saying, "If you did not know me, you would not know the Father, either."[64] Since they have been called to knowledge, however, and have confessed the Son, through him and in him they now have a glimpse of the Father. It is true, in fact, as the wise John says, "The one who denies the Son does not have the Father, either, whereas the one who confesses the Son confesses the Father as well."[65]

62. Heb 1.1; Jn 4.35–36; Mt 9.37–38.
63. Mal 3.11; 1 Cor 3.9. 64. Jn 9.29; 8.19.
65. 1 Jn 2.23.

COMMENTARY ON HOSEA, CHAPTER THREE

The Lord said to me, Go again and love an adulterous woman in love with vice, just as God loves the children of Israel, and they in their turn look to foreign gods and take a liking to cakes with raisins (v.1).

HERE IS NEED once more to study what is meant by the incident, or the mystery; I believe there is a responsibility to get below the surface and (82) scrutinize it in detail. After the former woman, who was licentious and bold, there is presented to the prophet another woman who was involved in crimes of adultery. What was the meaning of it? The Jewish populace before the coming of our Savior proceeded incautiously and very readily into error, worshiping golden heifers, bowing down and sacrificing to the Baal, or Baal-peor.[1] So they were compared very rightly with a prostitute as though inclined to every evil and unclean spirit that wanted to indulge its own pleasures; they gave welcome to the objects of worship of the neighboring and surrounding nations as each was inclined in an unholy and uncritical fashion. They were duly punished, however, for readily entering into apostasy, being sent into slavery and trodden under foot by the enemy. God, at any rate, made clear to the prophet that at the time of the day of Jezreel, the truly great day, they would go up from the land, that is, they would proceed to the country of the foreigners. Now, once again this was to indicate obscurely that they would cease to be strangers and exiles, but rather would be captives, inhabiting a foreign clime not of their own volition; the Savior, remember, pro-

---

1. Nm 25.1–5. While insisting that he is helping the readers to get below the surface of this prophetic action, Cyril does not raise the question that occurs to his modern counterparts, that is, whether the woman concerned is the same one as before or different. He assumes the latter.

claimed "release to captives and sight to the blind,"[2] in keeping with the prophet's statement.

Now, the fact that in mercy and compassion they will also be welcomed through faith, called God's people, and indeed shown pity, he clearly stated; after the coming of the Savior, to be sure, the suffering on the cross, and the resurrection from the dead, the remnant was saved, the numbers of believers from Israel being beyond counting. (83) Yet there still remained the unbelieving multitude, which could be compared to *an adulterous woman* on account of her failure to choose the bridegroom from heaven and her scorn for the one who courted her in faith, instead surrendering her mind to the scribes and Pharisees as though to some adulterers, "teaching human precepts as doctrines."[3] So just as the prophet had had relations with the prostitute when by way of a type God tolerated the prostitution of Israel, inflicting moderate punishment with a view to conversion and bringing her back to acknowledge him, the mystery in my view is in the same way once more presented to us in elegant figurative expression.[4] While the prophet, you see, acting as a type of God, accepts the *adulterous woman in love with vice,* he cherishes her, as it were, feeding her lavishly with promises and sound hopes, and does not allow her to fall victim to desperation.

In fact, God showed the prophet that the whole mystery lies in this when he said, *Love an adulterous woman in love with vice, just as God loves the children of Israel, and they in their turn look to foreign gods and take a liking to cakes with raisins.* He says, you see, that, though they chose to be disobedient, directed their love to the false gods, and willfully satisfied their desires, in his innate kindness he loves them as the God "who wants all human beings to be saved and come to the knowledge of the truth."[5] The Word of God grants us the understanding that at the time of the Incarnation there were perhaps many among the Jews who were uncommitted, neither wholly attached to the commandments given through Moses nor totally rid of the influences of error, and in-

---

2. Lk 4.18; Is 61.1.   3. Mt 15.9; Mk 7.7; Is 29.13 LXX.
4. Once again Cyril asserts the reality of the prophetic action while acknowledging the literary expression in which it is conveyed.
5. 1 Tm 2.4.

stead fixing their eyes on foreign gods to whom they offered *cakes with raisins*, perhaps round cakes or honey cakes. They were in fact in the habit (84) of offering such cakes in sacrifice to the demons, as experience confirms.[6]

I bought her for myself for fifteen silver coins, a homer of barley, and a skin of wine. I said to her, Stay with me for many days; do not play the prostitute or go with another man, and so I will be with you (vv.2–3). The prophet therefore acquired the woman, settled her in his home, and bade her refrain from her customary lewdness and give up the defilements of adultery. He actually promises, on condition of her deciding to act continently and opting to have eyes only for him, that he in turn would be with her, that is, be united to her in marriage, Scripture saying, "The two will become one flesh."[7] What is the indirect reference? The Jewish people, unbelieving killers of the Lord, adulterous and profane after Christ's return to heaven, God required to be chaste; on condition that they no longer play the whore, that is, they no longer submit to pressure to honor false gods, he promises to join them to himself in due course—that is, when the mass of the nations has preceded them; in other words, Israel was in the rear, that is, a rearguard at the back and among the last.

Notice, on the other hand, how marital intercourse between the prophet and the sinful adulteress did not happen without conditions, and promise of its consummation after *many days* was conditional upon her not being with another man again, that is, her abstaining from the sins and defilements of spiritual prostitution; the bridegroom from heaven, as I said, in due course will accept the adulterous people as long as they have not worshiped (85) idols. After the crucifixion of the Savior, in fact, Israel has been observant of the Mosaic Law alone, though in quite a decadent and negligent way, but has not reverted to observing false worship of the demons. What was the manner of life for the adulterous woman, who was expecting a relationship with the prophet in time? What payment was made for her? *Fifteen silver coins, a homer of barley, and a skin of wine.* In other words, Israel has passed

6. The final phrase is not found in the PG edition.
7. Gn 2.14. Cyril will now move quickly to ecclesiological implications of the verses, not utilizing Jerome's explication of the Heb. measurement *homer*.

the period after its final calling, nourished on flawed instruction and paying attention to what was in effect old wives' tales from its own leaders. Her lifestyle has been that befitting cattle, her mind immersed in a drunken gloom. Now, this would definitely be a clear type, *silver* for the word of instruction in keeping with the statement of Isaiah made to them, "Your silver is flawed," and in keeping with the statement of the Savior that rightly upbraids the wicked and lazy slave, "My silver should have been deposited with the bankers."[8] So you should take the *silver* as the lessons of the teachers.

If, on the other hand, you preferred to see a reference to the Mosaic Law, you would claim that *fifteen* means that the Law is at once both perfect and imperfect: perfect if understood spiritually, speaking to us of the mystery of Christ, and in turn imperfect if the mind of those under guidance proceeds only to the letter, the concreteness of the factual meaning being, as it were, only half of knowledge. Now, the number ten is a symbol of perfection, being perfect in itself, as Scripture suggests, "Take charge of ten cities," and "To whom he gave ten talents," whereas this is not the case with the person with five, the half of ten, as I said.[9] Or you could give a different sense to (86) the statement: the number fifteen includes eight and seven, and almost always in the inspired Scripture there is a reference in seven to the whole time of the Law up to the holy prophets and to the sabbath on the seventh, and likewise in eight to the new covenant by which the resurrection of our Savior Jesus Christ happened on the eighth. This, in my view, is the indirect reference in the verse, "Divide them seven ways, or even eight,"[10] that is, let them have a place among you, the Law and the Prophets after them out of respect for the sabbath on the seventh, and let the eight have a place, that is, the apostles and evangelists after the Savior's resurrection day.

---

8. Is 1.22; Mt 25.27.

9. Lk 19.17; Mt 25.15, where the highest number of talents given is in fact five, the reading found in the PG text. Even though holding the Alexandrian view that "the concreteness (*pachos*) of the factual meaning" is only halfway to full knowledge, Cyril is not as given to exploring number symbolism as Didymus, as emerges from their respective approaches to the dates cited in Zec 1.7.

10. Eccl 9.2. Cyril is effectively saying that he prefers biblical usage to Philo's numerology when it comes to seeing significance in numbers.

Consistent with this is also the obscure sense conveyed by the prophet's statement, "Seven shepherds will be raised against him, and eight bites of human beings."[11] That is to say, when Christ our Savior shone upon us, the teaching of Law and Prophets together with the apostolic instruction rose up in some way against Satan's crippling hold on us; by these he has somehow been attacked and pillaged; and according to the Savior's statement [Satan's] property was plundered with the departure of the deceived from slavery to him,[12] and with their recognition of the one who is by nature and in truth God and Lord of all. Therefore, "seven shepherds and eight bites of human beings were raised up against him," that is, those before his coming and those after the eighth, referring by the text of the Law and the new scriptures to salvation of the deceived.

Accordingly, Israel was nourished, as I said, on the flawed statements of its own teachers, or the strict letter of the Law, despite its including also the contents of the eighth, namely, the (87) mysteries of Christ. Now, the fact that its lifestyle befitted cattle, and it inclined only to fleshly realities, is very clearly indicated by the gift of *barley* to the adulteress as food; this food befits cattle, and *wine* would be a symbol of inebriation. To them it is said, "You will keep listening without understanding, keep looking without seeing."[13] This is the experience of inebriates and the failing of drunken people, looking without being able to see and listening without being able to understand anything, their mind being thickened, as it were, and rendered hard.

Because for many days the children of Israel will remain without any king, any leader, any sacrifices, any altar, any priesthood, any signs. After this the children of Israel will be converted and seek the Lord their God and David their king, and they will be in awe of the Lord and his goodness in the final days (vv.4–5). In these verses at any rate, there is now a clear and unambiguous statement of the acceptance of

---

11. Mi 5.5 (where the LXX has confused similar forms in the Heb. to come up with "bites," *dēgmata*, for "rulers"). Theodore in comment on that verse from Micah knows of a similar interpretation of seven (possibly from Didymus's lost work on Hosea), the number of the prophets (unless he has garbled the interpretation Cyril gives it), and typically will have none of it.

12. Mt 12.29.

13. Is 6.9.

the adulteress and their living at home for many days while the prophet was with her. This, in fact, is what the text says; but the implication is of what was destined to happen in due course to the adulterous synagogue of the Jews.[14] You see, when Jesus Christ our Lord voluntarily endured the cross for the salvation of all, then it was that their country was devastated and they were scattered (88) to all quarters of the world, as it were, and even to this day they do not practice the Law, since the Temple in Jerusalem has been burnt, the *altar* overturned, *sacrifices* canceled, *priesthood* inoperative, and no *signs* to be seen. After all, since there is no high priest properly installed according to Law, how could he still see *signs*?

Now, while the studious reader perhaps knows how the *signs* are to be understood, it will not be without benefit to mention it briefly. When the God of all gave orders for the vesture of the high priest, he said at that time to the sacred Moses, "You shall make a woven product for a declaration of judgment, a span in length and a span in breadth, square in shape." Then he ordered that there be inserted with great skill into the garment stones bearing the names of the twelve tribes, and that two of them be given the names Declaration and Truth. This declaration of judgment was then suspended from the shoulder with gold chains, hanging from the chest of the high priest.[15] The Declaration and Truth were a type of Emmanuel; everything he heard from the Father he made known to us, making a Declaration of the will of the one who begot him, and making clear the way of salvation. The fact that he is also the Truth no one could doubt, since he clearly says, "I am the Truth."[16] This was the reason that it hung from the very heart of the high priest, the type, as it were, shouting and unmistakably crying aloud that in the Savior and Redeemer of everyone the sacred race will enjoy in mind and heart the Truth and the Declaration. It is therefore ab-

---

14. Cyril is still concerned that the incident be taken at face value, even if he immediately moves to another level.
15. Ex 27.15–26. Cyril is describing, in the LXX terms, the ephod with its Urim and Thummim used in divination, a subject that takes the fancy also of Theodoret in his comment on this Hosea passage and in his *Questions* on both Octateuch and Kingdoms.
16. Jn 15.15; 14.6.

solutely necessary for the ministers of Christ always to remember as well that they bear him indwelling within them through the Spirit, a pure mind (89) and a cleansed heart being his home.

Therefore, *for many days the children of Israel will remain without any king or leader,* that is, ungoverned by king or ruler; those from the tribe of Judah will not reign, nor will leaders preside appointed by Law, that is, the priests. Nor will there be, he says, *any altar, any sacrifice, any priesthood, any signs.* But although in these matters Israel will always and altogether be rejected, it will in due course be called, *be converted* through faith, and acknowledge *the God* of all, and with him *David,* that is, the one of the line of David who is Christ according to the flesh, king and Lord of all.[17] Then and only then they will be astonished at the magnitude of his generosity and the immeasurable grace of his clemency; they will have a share in the hope prepared for the saints and the vast numbers of the believers generally, and will be tended in a good pasture and a rich location.[18] For them, in fact, *the final days* will be an occasion for such splendid and praiseworthy grace in Christ, through whom and with whom be glory to the God and Father together with the Holy Spirit, unto ages of ages. Amen (90).

17. Cyril is not tempted to see any reference to Zerubbabel, a favorite nominee of Theodore's whenever there is question of Davidic succession.
18. Ezek 34.14. Cyril closes commentary on the third chapter and his second tome with a doxology.

COMMENTARY ON HOSEA,
CHAPTER FOUR

Listen to the word of the Lord, children of Israel, because the Lord has a judgment against the inhabitants of the land, that there is no truth or mercy or knowledge of God in the land. Cursing and falsehood, murder and theft and adultery are spread over the land, and blood is mingled with blood (vv.1–2).

HERE IS NEED for us in our wish to clarify the sense of the text to recapitulate, as it were, what was said initially, and summarize the whole gist of the prophecy, so to speak. As far as possible, then, this is what I have to say in summarizing: there was a "Beginning of the word of the Lord to Hosea."[1] In commenting on this we duly said that the words came to the blessed prophet Hosea from God, who was, as it were, giving him spiritual initiation and foretelling the future in types and words. Consequently, at the beginning Gomer was taken into his company, and she gave birth to Not my people and Not pitied. Then, after her a second woman, a wicked adulteress, was adopted, and the prophet was instructed in precise detail, as I said, as to the course of each relationship. As though apprised sufficiently of the force of the mystery, he then begins to predict the future for those of the bloodline of Israel, to clarify the disaster still pending for them, (91) and to explain clearly the ways in which they had offended God so that those suffering punishment would know that they were justly suffering whatever befell them. In fact, they were on the point of being captured by the enemy, and thus exposed to ridicule by people who held them in highest regard, and who thought that of all the nations Israel was the most difficult to capture.

---

1. Hos 1.2. Like Theodore at this point, Cyril feels the need to respond to the changing focus of the work, and remind the reader of the author's overall *skopos*.

Consequently, so that they should not think within themselves that the hand that assisted and saved them had lost its force, and should rather repent and choose to return to better ways in the realization that they had stupidly offended the one capable of saving them, he necessarily foretells their crimes to them as they were brought low by divine wrath even before the onset of what the future held. His words were, *Listen to the word of the Lord, children of Israel, because the Lord has a judgment against the inhabitants of the land.* Now, in judging human beings, God accuses, but does not sentence; to those guilty of impiety against him he exposes their crimes in keeping with the verse from the psalms, "I will accuse you, and lay before you" your iniquities,[2] in case they should claim that it was to no purpose that wrath was inflicted on them and was rather by way of discharging a debt, as necessarily happens to those in the habit of committing grave sins.

Now, what does he say in his *judging*, or accusing? *There is no truth or mercy or knowledge of God in the land.* He would be right to conclude, then, that there was no telling the *truth*, because at that time everybody was guilty of calumny, perjury, deceit, and dishonesty, the worst of all evils. The fact that they lacked love and compassion for one another, and were harsh, unbending, and hardhearted, would be implied (92) by there being no *mercy*. And their being in love with pleasure rather than God, and wholly devoted to the false gods, is established by his saying that there was *no knowledge of God in the land.* There would be nothing surprising in people addicted to such awful deviance giving the impression of not knowing God, especially if we say that we know him when we think rightly and follow his divine wishes. He goes beyond this in saying, *Cursing and falsehood, murder and theft and adultery are spread over the land, and blood is mingled with blood.* Do you hear how those referred to rushed headlong into every evil and surpassed the most unholy crimes, leaving none of the most outrageous untried, even what defied reason, *mingling blood with blood?* This would be a clear sign of their putting no halt to the vices, and of the guilty ones feeling no compunction for their crimes; incessantly, as it were, they piled sin on sin.

2. Ps 50.21.

So much for a rather superficial clarification. It is likely, however, that the blessed prophet goes further in offering us a more spiritual explanation,[3] blaming Israel for its frenzy against Christ and its murderous actions against him and the saints. *The Lord has a judgment against the inhabitants of the land,* note: against whom, and for what? Our Lord Jesus Christ was sent to us on mission, as he himself said, "to the lost sheep of the house of Israel,"[4] to illuminate with the torchlight of the Spirit those in darkness, to free them from the shadow of the Law, to introduce them to the forms of true worship, to justify by faith those caught up in sin, and to relate them through himself to the God and Father. To the people of Israel, however, he did not seem to have correct attitudes; the one who (93) came to them from heaven they rejected and found fault with, refusing to have among them the *truth,* the *mercy,* and the *knowledge of* the *God* and Father. Christ's being *truth and mercy,* in fact, I think does not require demonstration by means of long argumentation, since the inspired Scripture throughout its length adequately refers to Christ as our *truth and mercy.* And his being also *knowledge of God* you could learn even without effort, since he cries aloud with complete clarity and lucidity, "The one who has seen me has seen the Father."[5] So *the Lord's judgment against the inhabitants of the land* obviously refers to the land of the Jews, because among them *there is no truth, mercy, or knowledge* of the Father. While there is therefore a *judgment* against those lacking such virtues, those embracing the faith have avoided the judgment either against him or by him—something that would become clear from Christ's saying further, "Very truly, I tell you, anyone who believes in me has eternal life, and does not come under judgment."[6]

What, then, is *spread over the land? Cursing and falsehood, murder and theft and adultery, and blood is mingled with blood.* What is *cursing?* Abuse and insolence; the Hebrew mobs, remember, did not

---

3. Though it may be claimed that Cyril resembles the Antiochenes in staying with the historical dimension of the text's meaning, here he parts company with them (Theodore, at least) in moving on at even greater length to a *mystikôteros* level that is christological and ecclesiological.
4. Mt 15.24. 5. Jn 14.9.
6. Jn 5.24.

cease insulting Jesus, assailing him by word of mouth in unfettered and unbridled manner to the extent of calling him at one time a Samaritan, at another a drunkard, and offspring of prostitution,[7] being of the view that the holy virgin had committed adultery—hence the *cursing* in them. They were also guilty of *falsehood* against his reputation, claiming he had a devil, and attributing the divine signs to the powers of Beelzebul. Their having a *murderous* intent against him you could grasp from the stones frequently cast by them against Emmanuel (94) and their taking him to the very brow of the mountain with the intention of throwing him down. Nor did their crimes stop there: they held even the crime of *theft* in high regard, paying a price for him to the traitor Judas, that avaricious thief.[8] The Pharisees of the synagogue of the Jews proved to be like some destructive *adulterers*, casting away its heaven-sent Bridegroom—namely, Christ—and acting jointly in adultery by persuading them to indulge their own pleasures. *They mingled blood with blood:* how, and in what way? After killing the holy prophets, they even added to their number the very Lord of the prophets. Blessed Stephen, for instance, rightly upbraids them in the Acts of the Apostles in the words, "Which of the prophets did your ancestors not persecute? They killed those who foretold the coming of the Righteous One, and now you have become his betrayers and murderers." The Savior also said in reproach to the Pharisees and scribes, "Fill up the measure of your ancestors."[9]

As a result the land will mourn, and will be diminished along with all its inhabitants together with the wild beasts of the field, the reptiles of the earth, and the birds of heaven, and the fish of the sea will perish, so that no one will go to court and no one will be convicted (vv.3–4). Since they had led such a dreadful life that was hateful to God, impious and obdurate, he says, and had plotted and committed what was unlawful, thus provoking God, consequently and very justly they will fall into ruin. The land, as it were, *will mourn*, being devastated and changing (95) its condition and adopting an unattractive appearance, cities burnt, houses toppled, and fields laid

---

7. Jn 8.48; Mt 11.19; Jn 8.41.
8. Jn 8.48; Mt 12.24; Jn 8.59; 10.31; 11.8; Lk 4.29; Mt 26.15.
9. Acts 7.52; Mt 23.32.

bare. The inhabitants will be in sympathy with the land, lamenting and wailing; they, too, will grieve; that is, they will be bereft of all satisfaction and contentment.

Now, who are the inhabitants? *Wild beasts* and *reptiles,* and in addition to them winged creatures. We should not think, if we are to understand it correctly, that the prophetic text was crying out to us about wild beasts, reptiles, or birds; such an interpretation would be quite silly and full of misunderstanding.[10] Rather, from our ability to take a proper position, we believe it is the behavior of the Jews that is being depicted in what has just been described. By mentioning the *wild beasts* the text would be suggesting the people who are most powerful and quite capable of terrorizing others, fierce and oppressive, given to homicide and of a very cruel disposition; and by *reptiles* people who are extremely bitter in their behavior and who go to extremes of wickedness; John in his wisdom somewhere upbraids the depraved company of Pharisees and scribes when he refers to them in loud tones as "you snakes, you brood of vipers."[11] By the *birds* you would be right to understand those ready to take wing in forsaking God, or those suffering from an accursed arrogance, given to being carried away and entertaining lofty thoughts. By *fish* it probably refers to mobs and herds, those overwhelmed by life's concerns, their mind submerged, as it were, without voice or reason (fish being voiceless)—or in another interpretation those who consume weaker people, since fish are inclined to eat one another.

Accordingly, he says, *The land will mourn along with its inhabitants.* (96) What is the purpose in this? *So that no one will go to court and no one will be convicted.* In other words, since there were cursing and falsehood, theft and murder, and adultery was spread over the land, and they mingled blood with blood, consequently *it will mourn,* and there will then be an end to falsehood, deceit, and calumny. Bewailing what had happened unexpectedly, you see, and bemoaning the disaster at hand, willy-nilly they will de-

---

10. Even Theodore had accepted this view, seeing the animals referring to people (though, typically, not seeing Jews in focus). But he would not have gone as far as Cyril in his allegorical explanation of each animal.
11. Mt 3.7, the Baptist's words, or more accurately Jesus' at Mt 23.33.

sist from such sinning. *Going to court and* convicting, in fact, would, in my view, mean nothing more than accusing and condemning people, or bearing false witness. Another of the holy prophets of the bloodline of Israel, to be sure, says as much in crying aloud, "Woe is me! Piety has perished from the land, and there is no one upright among humankind. All go to court; intent on blood, they each oppress their neighbor with oppression."[12]

So much for the facts. In regard to the interior meaning, on the other hand, we give the following in determining the meaning of the prophecy.[13] In the land of the Jews, you remember, or among the Jews themselves *there is no truth or mercy or knowledge of God*, attributes we said belong to and are to be referred to Emmanuel, and instead *cursing and falsehood* are in force, *theft* is held in honor, and *they mingle blood with blood*, since they killed the prophets, as I said, and have killed Jesus himself. So now *the land will mourn* together with the inhabitants, having been burnt at the hands of the Romans. This will happen, it says, *so that no one will go to court and no one will be convicted*, an expression clearly made by one who blames the Jews for prosecuting sacrilegiously, accusing or bearing false witness against Christ: the leaders intended to prosecute and charge him, and brought him to Pilate; some came as witnesses for the prosecution, as if presuming to accuse him. Some of the cowardly slanderers claimed, (97) "He leads the people astray"; others claimed, "We heard him say that in three days he would destroy the Temple of God and raise it up again."[14] Accordingly, he is saying, court proceedings will be done away with, and accusation or slander, and false verdicts, there being no king or ruler, who normally gives judgment. Consequently, in my view, the prophetic text compares for us the people of the Jews to animals, since they have no king—namely, *wild beasts, reptiles, birds, and fish.* In similar terms the blessed prophet Habakkuk also said somewhere to the God of all, "Why do you look on the scornful? Why silent when the wicked swal-

---

12. Mi 7.1–2.
13. Cyril this time passes from the facts (*historikôs*) to an interior (*esôtatô*) meaning.
14. Lk 23.1–2; Mk 14.58.

low the righteous? You will make people like fish of the sea, and like reptiles that have no ruler."[15]

My people will be like a priest gainsaid; they will be infirm for days, and a prophet will also be infirm with you (vv.4–5). Observe, I ask you, the blessed prophet communicating in a different fashion what was said to him by God. Though he clearly heard the statement, "For many days the children of Israel will remain without any king, any leader, any sacrifices, any altar, any priesthood, any signs,"[16] for his part he downplayed, as it were, the listeners' unbridled course to wrath, reproved them with moderation, and disguised his criticism under a degree of obscurity. While in fact he subtly suggested that they would live a long time without rulers or king and remain untaught, without guidance, and he employed comparisons with those animals that had no king, he implies also that they would be excluded from sacrifices and priestly ministry, thus being in a similar situation to priests gainsaid. Who would they for their part be? Who is (98) the *priest gainsaid?* The person guilty of blame and having fleshly ailments, and consequently excluded from worship. After all, some are dismissed from the duty of serving because of impairment of legs or eyes or a crushed foot, or for another reason, even if they are members of the tribe and bloodline of Levi, this being a decision of the Law of Moses.[17]

This is the way, then, he says, they will be *my people;* despite being a priest by succession and accorded the role of sacrificing, they will be placed outside the holy tabernacle, beyond worship and priests. They will in fact perform no sacrifices, and offer no sweet-smelling fragrance to God; they bear the considerable affliction of impaired understanding and limpness of heart, and so they are justly dismissed and excluded. Now, the fact that silence of prophets also befell the people of Israel he mentioned in the words, *And a prophet will also be infirm with you,* in complete accord with the statement from God to blessed Ezekiel, "I shall bind up your tongue, you will be mute, and you will not act as

---

15. Hab 1.13–14.   16. Hos 3.4.
17. Lv 21.17–21. It may be due partly to the LXX version, and partly to the position taken by Theodore, that Cyril does not see the Jewish institutions of priesthood and cultic prophecy under criticism here.

someone to guide or reprove them, because they are a rebellious house."[18]

Now, all this will happen because of their impiety towards Christ and their crimes against the prophets. It will not be forever that Israel *will be infirm*—but only *for days*, he says; a time for salvation and conversion through faith has been kept for them.

I made your mother resemble night. My people were made like one having no knowledge. Since you rejected knowledge, I, too, shall reject you from practicing my priesthood; and since you forgot the Law of your God, I, too, shall forget your children (vv.5–6). The verse is directed against the voluble and unholy mass of the Jews, his noun *mother* being a reference to their (99) synagogue, but here he does not use it to refer to the church of those justified in Christ. Accordingly, he is right to compare the synagogue of the Jews to obscurity and gloom. Paul in his great wisdom, therefore, appropriately says of himself and of those illuminated by faith, "We are not children of the night and darkness, but of light and the day."[19] Now, he says, My people are like those who have no knowledge, despite being enriched with guidance of the Law; they have been called to knowledge of the one who is truly God, given confirmation through miracles, and nothing at all was omitted that could enlighten those in darkness, nor anything neglected that was capable of introducing commendable knowledge to willing learners. *Since you rejected knowledge,* however, he says, namely, Christ, through whom and in whom the Father is approached and known, you have now forfeited the status of being sacred, and the role of offering sacrifice, profane as you are. And since you became oblivious of the divine laws, had no spiritual understanding of Moses, nor allowed your mind to have any inkling of the teachings of Christ, I, too, shall consign your *children*, as it were, to oblivion—that is, I shall no longer remember them by according them pity and care; after all, God accords his lovingkindness to those whom he deigns to remember. To adopt a different interpretation, Israel by practicing idolatry *forgot* the divine *Law* and *rejected knowledge.*

18. Ezek 3.26.
19. 1 Thes 5.5. Cyril does not detect the confusion by the LXX of similar Heb. forms for "resemble" and "perish" in v.5.

They sinned against me in proportion to their vast number; I shall bring their glory into disrepute (v.7). The divine and ineffable nature is the source and origin of complete gentleness, and is goodness itself. He cannot bear sinners at all, however, instead inflicting due punishment on those who take that course without restraint. Hence he affirms that Israel reached such a degree of depravity (100) that its folly was no longer tolerable, its sins appearing equal in number to themselves. While they, remember, were "like the stars of heaven in multitude and like sand on the shore of the sea," as Scripture says,[20] he said that their sins were no less numerous than the multitude—the sense, in my view, of *They sinned against me in proportion to their vast number.* Since, however, they were reduced to such a degree of wretchedness and stupidity, and did not cease offending God, *I shall bring their glory into disrepute,* that is, the more they grow in self-importance, the more they will be shamed. How, and in what way? They will forfeit the credit they take in vast numbers when war consumes all their youth along with their warriors; their houses and cities will be deserted and destroyed. The prophet Jeremiah also laments this same condition of Judah: "How lonely sits the city that was full of people! She that was a princess became a vassal."[21]

By another interpretation, we lose all our good reputation by offending God and doing what is not lawful, being conceited and boasting of the very things we should be ashamed of, so that it is rightly said also of us, "Their glory is in their shame." So in this sense also you can take the clause, *I shall bring their glory into disrepute:* no one can doubt that some people surrender themselves "to a debased mind, things that should not be done," as the blessed Paul has clearly said.[22]

They will feed on the sin of my people, and in their iniquities they will take their lives. It will be thus: like people, like priest (vv.8–9). After listing the reasons for the wrath against the masses, he shifts (101) his attention to the priestly class. Now, in my view, applicable to this verse would also be what was said just now: "I shall bring

20. Gn 22.17.
21. Lam 1.1.
22. Phil 3.19; Rom 1.28. Cyril here seems content with a simple moral interpretation of the clause—a rarity.

their glory into disrepute" (v.7). The celebrated priesthood, you see, is the glory of the synagogue of the Jews, its pre-eminent and holy class—the levitical class, that is; while some members of the tribe of Judah reigned as king, human considerations counted for less and came in second place in regard to priesthood.[23] So the priestly and chosen class is the glory of the Jewish synagogue. Accordingly, he says, it will be covered in disrepute, and transformed into ugliness. For what reason? Because by neglecting what most befitted them they encouraged apostasy; they did not honor their own responsibilities,[24] they did not know the ways of priesthood, they did not take to heart the fact that *they will feed on the sin of my people, and in their iniquities they will take their lives.*

Since, however, the passage is particularly obscure, come now, let us explain as far as possible how it should be understood spiritually. From the goats, then, a he-goat was slaughtered for sin; hence the name "sin offering." But the priests of the time, in bringing the he-goat to the altar, would offer the entrails and fat but eat the rest themselves, as the divine Law provided.[25] The priest, therefore, was taken as a mediator between God and man, accepting the gifts from the people and having a share in what is sacrificed on the altar, as Scripture says;[26] he sacrificed himself, as it were, for the sins of the people, as of course our Lord Jesus Christ also did. For proof that what I say is true, I shall cite the Law dealing with the he-goat; it goes as follows: "Moses made an inquiry about the he-goat of the sin offering, and it had already been burnt. Moses was angry with Eleazar and (102) Ithamar, Aaron's remaining sons, and said, Why did you not eat the sin offering in a holy place? For it is a holy of holies, and he has given it to you to eat there for you to remove the sin of the assembly, to make atonement on their behalf before the Lord."[27] Do you see how those assisting at the holy altar and appeasing wrath for sinners with pure prayers act as mediators by eating the sin offerings, as it were, offering to God their own souls as a sweet-smelling odor for the sins of the people? As in the case of the divinely inspired Aaron, of course, when the people took ill,

---

23. All of this sentence is missing from the PG edition.
24. Jude 6.
25. Lv 4.28; 9.15; 3.3.
26. 1 Cor 9.13.
27. Lv 10.16–17.

Scripture says, he seized the censer, put on the incense, "stood between the dead and the living, and the plague was stopped." The blessed Moses likewise acted as mediator as well and placated God when the people of Israel had made a golden heifer in the wilderness; he submitted himself to justice and made an appeal, "If you will forgive their sin, forgive it; but if not, blot me also out of this book you have written."[28]

Accordingly, *they will feed on the sin of my people*—that is, the offerings made for sin—*and in their iniquities*—that is, at the time of their iniquities, namely, of the people of Israel. *They will take their* own *lives*—that is, they will offer them to God. The inspired Scripture in fact admits such a sense of the reading: what was offered to God and prepared for sacrifice was said to be *taken;* such a sense is given to the reading, as I just said, as for example in Numbers, when laws were given about the red heifer, where God said to the revealer Moses, "This is a statute of the Law that the Lord has commended, saying, Tell the children of Israel to take to you a red heifer without defect." Do you hear the word *take?* In other words, they are to bring or offer it. In reference to the leper that had to be purified, it likewise says, "The priest shall go out of the camp, and the priest shall make an examination; if the onset of leprosy is healed in the leprous person, the priest will give orders, and they will take two living clean birds for the one being cleansed."[29] So when it uses the phrase *they will take* in reference to the priests, it is duly to be understood as "they will offer." Accordingly, at the time of the *iniquities*—namely, the people's—*they will take,* that is, they will offer as a spiritual sacrifice and sweet odor to God *their lives*—properly lived, of course, and following the pattern of the Law, and as far as possible being zealous for what it behoves priests to think and do.

A priest of this character, in fact, is capable of saving the people even if they have offended God and broken the Law, whereas if they are involved in this, he is saying, they will be caught up

---

28. Nm 16.47–48; Ex 32.32.
29. Nm 19.2; Lv 14.3–4. It may have been the great length to which Cyril has gone to make this point that attracts the notice of Theodoret, though the occurrence of an extra noun ("*Peoples* will take their lives") in the Antioch text leads him to see foreign nations involved in punishment of collusion between priests and people.

with the others. Consequently, it would be just, if the priestly rites fail, for the chosen and elite people to come to an end: *It will be thus: like people, like priest,* there being nothing further to separate people from priest. This assuredly was the meaning of "I shall bring their glory into disrepute" (v.7).

I shall take vengeance on it for its ways, and repay it for its scheming (v.9).[30] By *ways* he probably means procedures, and by *scheming* likewise the faults arising from wrong ideas. Since it left the straight and narrow, therefore, he is saying, (104) embarked on a path of utter sacrilege, adopted the most shameful and absurd schemes possible, dishonored the God of all, and took to worshiping idols, *I shall take vengeance on it*—that is, I shall impose a penalty commensurate with its sins. Who could doubt that involvement in every misfortune will without any question befall those who abandon the love for God? By not having the assistance of divine wisdom and power it would neither traverse a right and blameless path nor make any wise decisions.

They will eat but not be satisfied; they prostituted themselves but will not progress (v.10). Again he has preserved the remnant for those of the bloodline of Israel; the fact that not all would perish with the priests he makes clear in saying, *They will eat but not be satisfied.* Whether in fact you take that to mean the former deportations and captivities of Israel, or the devastation of the land of Judea at the hand of the Romans in the time of Christ, you would find, preserved in those remaining, Israel itself and worship according to the Law. After the deportation at that time to the Assyrians and the Medes by Shalmaneser and Tiglath-pileser, the few stragglers from Israel kept offering to the priests what was prescribed, honoring them with what was to hand and making no exception whatsoever from what was customary. In equal fashion, when the country was devastated in the last war—in the time of Caesar Augustus, I mean—they were scattered to every quarter, in every country and city; yet they still (105) paid considerable respect to the priestly and elite class, and offered what they could. They are still involved in this, even though the ancient sacrifices have become null and void, since it is illicit for those beyond Jerusalem to offer sacrifice.

30. The PG text seems to replace this verse with the following (v.10).

Accordingly, *they will eat,* he says, *but not be satisfied;* that is, they will take hardly anything, and there will not be enough to go round. Now, this suggests the abolition of their former respect and the loss of previous prosperity. Though *they prostituted themselves,* he says, *they will not progress;* it is impossible, as I said, for those abandoning God (this in my view being the term for spiritual *prostitution* and its reality) either to have a sufficient supply of divine goods, to be able to gather nourishment from heaven above, or to *progress* in plans and actions. It is God, after all, who is the giver of every good to us, and the guide of the thoughts within us.

Because they forsook attention to the Lord, the heart of my people accepted prostitution, wine, and intoxication (vv.10–11).[31] He cites here the reasons why they were not being filled with food and why the ministers will not progress further. In other words, since even they abandoned the Lord and, despite being appointed to lead those under their control and authority, the teachers were caught up along with the taught, consequently they will duly fall under God's wrath and pay the penalty for their unremitting defection. They practiced *prostitution;* in other words, they were responsible for the continuance of the errors of those in their care, despite being obliged instead to correct and amend them. Vigilance is required of teachers, you see, in zealously removing a people's wrongdoing, and abolishing without delay what is hateful to God. (106) Now, if they cannot bring themselves to do it, if they allow the effects of error to remain and be preserved, and instead do the opposite by confirming them, the thinking of those under guidance will then give complete acceptance to *wine and intoxication,* as it were. After all, how or by what means would the disciples manage to stay vigilant and be capable of keeping the mind's eye trained on the one who is truly and by nature God if their guides and mentors in what is beneficial compounded the process of deception? This in my view is the clear statement of another prophet: "The priests did not say, Where is the Lord? Those who handle the Law did not understand me, the shepherds sinned against me, and the prophets prophesied by

---

31. The Pusey edition punctuates the verse differently from the Heb., to which the Antioch text and the PG text come closer.

Baal." And again, "My children and my sheep are no more, there is no place for my tent, no place for my curtains. Because the shepherds have lost their senses, and do not seek out the Lord. Hence the whole flock has lost understanding and is scattered."[32]

They made their requests by augury, and they reported to him through their staffs (v.12). He makes clear the way in which they left the Lord and practiced prostitution, showing the instructor to be an accomplice of those deceived. While they should have followed the divine laws—or rather were obliged to—and brought their subjects to do so, he clearly presents them, as I said, as filled with the crimes of deception. Some people, he is saying, had recourse to them in their wish to learn what would perhaps happen, that is, in their own situation, and at what time and in what events. But (107) these impious people persuaded those coming to them not to want to seek such information from God; instead, *they made their requests by augury,* that is, they sought to learn from the unclean spirits by certain signs and observations. Balaam, for example, once tried to secure a divination against the people of Israel under orders from Balak son of Zippor to do so; he said, "Make me seven altars here, and slaughter seven bulls and seven rams for me,"[33] and I shall go and take the omens. They observed smoke arising from the sacrifices, you see, how it was directed up or down, or the wretches studied palpitations of the liver, or they were occupied with flights of birds. Now, augury, divination, and suchlike things are crimes stemming from impiety, and originate in the bowels of idolatry.

And they reported to him through their staffs. To those from Israel who approached them, he is saying, anxious to find out something about their own situation, *they reported* not only *by augury* but also *through their staffs.* This was another form of deception, augury by use of a staff, an invention perhaps of Chaldean sorcery; Nebuchadnezzar in this fashion made a prophecy against Jerusalem, as the divinely inspired prophet Ezekiel says.[34] They set up two staffs, remember, then uttered some arcane incanta-

---

32. Jer 2.8; 10.20–21.
34. Ezek 21.21–22.
33. Nm 23.1.

tions at them, causing them to bend down under the influence of the demons; when they fell, they in turn watched which way they went, whether forwards or backwards, to right or to left. This was the way he now *reported* in giving the decision (108) to suppliants—the meaning of *They reported to him with staffs.* It is therefore truly dreadful that the guides of other people, who could bring them to love for God, caused them to be deceived; as the prophet says, "They established madness in the house of the Lord,"[35] by "madness" meaning false prophecy. Those in the habit of doing this, in fact, pretend not to know even where they are; some people in fact claimed they were demented and possessed, as though filled with divine inspiration, unaware that the heart is a kind of dwelling of unclean spirits, and cave for the deceived.

They were deceived by a spirit of prostitution, and prostituted themselves by leaving their God. They sacrificed on the crests of the mountains, and made offerings on the mountains under oak and poplar and shady tree, because their shade is good (v.13). The fact that such things were not done independently of the unclean and wicked spirits he clearly teaches; every form of depravity stems from them, and no vile exploit is left untried by those who opt to fulfill their wishes. Hence his saying, *They were deceived by a spirit of prostitution* and were separated from God, loving pleasure and using the practice of idolatry as an occasion of fleshly delights. They offered sacrifice, in fact, taking advantage of hills and mountains, and worshiping on the high places of the land earthly images of the demons. They next erected altars *under oak and poplar,* and offered libations to accord veneration to tree nymphs and perhaps the dryads of the Greeks' fairytales. The principal Greek poets, remember, claim to have loved the unclean spirits of plants and trees, which they called nymphs, by (109) goodness-knows-what reasoning. So they chose to frequent the shade, he says, and disport themselves under the most luxuriant trees, giving praise in the words, *because their shade is good.* Lovers of pleasure would therefore not become lovers of God; Paul confirms this of some people: "They are lovers of pleasure rather than lovers of God."

35. Hos 9.8.

So "blessed are those who mourn now," as the Savior says,[36] and who are zealous in honoring and loving as much as possible patience in bearing useful labors.

For this reason your daughters will act as prostitutes, and your brides will commit adultery. I shall not call your daughters to account for acting as prostitutes, or your spouses for committing adultery, because the men themselves also consorted with prostitutes and sacrificed with initiates (vv.13–14). Since you thought it commendable to disport yourselves in the shade of trees and to take pleasure in offending me—obviously an accursed error and uncleanness, he is saying, consequently *your daughters will act as prostitutes, and your brides* (that is, your sons' spouses) *will commit adultery*. Even if this happens, he says, I will hold my peace and *not call them to account*. Now, in this he is probably foretelling the harm that would ensue for the sinners as a result of war; once they have taken captives and won the battle, they have their way with the captives, exploiting their position without restraint, and with irresistible force doing whatever they like with them, with no respect for law and not bothering to give a thought to reason or propriety. (110) Instead, with mind hardened and set on cruelty, they accord no mercy to the abused. The fact that the children will be exposed to the foe for insult and shameful sexual abuse he clearly mentioned.

If, on the other hand, you preferred to take it another way, the God of all *will call to account* those whom he wanted to honor and love; even if he sees them adopting habits of indifference and opting to do what is unlawful, he corrects them moderately, urging them to take a turn for the better that is required for their benefit. Hence the divinely inspired Paul also says to those called to a blameless life, "If you undergo correction, God is treating you as children; for what child is there whom a parent does not correct?" The teller of proverbs in his wisdom confirms this in saying, "The one whom the Lord loves he corrects; he chastises every child he accepts."[37] To those he corrects, therefore, he also accords supervision as being wholly good and be-

---

36. 2 Tm 3.4; Mt 5.4.
37. Heb 12.7; Prv 3.12.

loved, whereas for those who gravely offend him he has no regard, saying, as it were, "I do not know you"; "the eyes of the Lord are on the righteous,"[38] Scripture says. Even if they fail, he is saying, therefore, *I shall not call them to account,* that is, I shall not care for them, I shall not turn them to me, I shall consider them of no importance. For what reason? You *yourselves,* he says, who are in the role of parents, so far abdicated respect for yourselves and your families, even if they lay claim to extreme depravity, such as to *consort with prostitutes;* in fact, they *sacrificed with initiates.*

Now, by *prostitutes* he refers specifically to the priestesses of Baal-peor,[39] Baal-peor being called Priapos; the women who honored such a vile abomination were admittedly prostitutes. By *initiates* he refers again to those initiated into the rites of Baal-peor; though males, they could not bring themselves to be what they were, instead adopting womanly attitudes, and behaving and speaking with unholy effeminacy. Some people call such men effeminate and soft; they adopt the wailing and cymbals of women, run about with torches and pretend to give esoteric guidance, acting as shameful playthings of the Baal. *They sacrificed with initiates,* then, that is, they were initiated in their mysteries, and in the company of those corrupt types they offered sacrifices to Baal-peor.

And the people of understanding were involved with a prostitute (v.14). He shifts his focus to Judah, that is, those of the tribe of Judah and Benjamin, still dwelling in Jerusalem and maintaining the divine altar, the Temple still standing. They claimed to observe the commandments of Moses and to possess understanding through the Law; but they, too, served "Astarte, abomination of the Sidonians."[40] Now, they say Astarte was somehow or other called Aphrodite by the Greeks. The statue was naked, in an obscene posture, all its members shamelessly uncovered for

---

38. Mt 25.12; Ps 34.15.

39. Hosea, as Cyril is aware, will attack at 9.10 the Israelites' association with the fertility rites practiced at Baal-peor. See also Nm 25.1–5, 16–17.

40. 2 Kgs 23.13. Cyril, who is ever concerned with the "errors" of pagan religions to which some Israelites (and Christians?) were attracted, regularly identifies the gods of Egyptians and Greeks.

the eyes of all. It was therefore not only Israel, despite its awful bout of stupidity, that *consorted with prostitutes and sacrificed with initiates;* (112) the very *people of understanding,* that is, the people that still made a claim to preserve the understanding that stems from the Law, *were involved with a prostitute.* As I said, they worshiped Astarte; Solomon in fact built a shrine to her,[41] and performed thanksgiving rites to the lewd foreign woman.

But you, Israel, do not be unaware, and Judah, do not go off to Gilgal, and do not go up to the house of iniquity, and do not swear by the living Lord (v.15). I have previously said many times that the text of the prophets refers to the ten tribes in Samaria as *Israel,* and sometimes as *Judah* and Benjamin to the two tribes in Jerusalem, namely, that of Judah and that of Benjamin. So in the present case the text refers to both, and accuses both groups of the disease; note how he upbraids Israel for being extremely unintelligent and simple-minded, and consequently rebellious as well, in that it would rightly be regarded as an example of extreme lack of intelligence to be dedicated to the worship of the idols and to abandon the love for God. The phrase *Do not be unaware* means, therefore, Do not be stupid or full of extreme unintelligence. He goes on to accuse those in Jerusalem—namely, *Judah*—of pretense and unholy insolence in going in two directions, or rather limping on both legs, as the prophet says;[42] they pretended, on the one hand, to show devotion and love for reverence to God, and performed the sacrifices prescribed by the Law, while, on the other, they did not in any way abandon their willingness even to worship the very demons, though not quite openly but secretly and furtively. The blessed (113) prophet Ezekiel was therefore bidden dig a hole in the wall; he then saw all the idols of the house of Israel depicted on the walls. What did the God of all say to him? "Do you see, son of man, what the elders of the house of Israel are doing here, each of them in their hidden chamber? Because they said, The Lord has forsaken us, the Lord does not oversee the earth." The prophet says he also observed women sitting there weeping for Tammuz, or Adonis in the Greek language.[43]

41. 1 Kgs 11.5.
42. 1 Kgs 18.21.
43. Ezek 8.14.

Consider, therefore, how, although giving attention to the divine Temple and pretending to be involved in the liturgy prescribed by the Law, they were defiled by secretly dividing their attention between exotic and demonic rites and reverence for God. Consequently he says, *you, Israel, have gone completely astray; do not be unaware,* that is, desist from your ignorance; abandon such an idle and profane attitude; accept the good sense of the Law and the Prophets, or that which comes from Christ and the Gospels. *And Judah, do not go off to Gilgal* (a city much given to worship of idols), *and do not go up to the house of iniquity, and do not swear by the living Lord.* It is, in fact, absurd on the one hand to take oaths in God's name and have *the living Lord* on one's tongue, while being devoted to idols and opting to worship lifeless heifers; Jeroboam, remember, set up one at Bethel and another at Dan.[44] Consequently, he does not allow them to pretend reverence for God by calling on the Lord while being led astray into the absurdity of false worship by going up *to Gilgal, and going up to the house of iniquity* (by *house of iniquity* referring to Bethel). For what reason? While Bethel means "house of God," (114) it proved to be a house of idols, a kind of violence being done to both fact and name, since the house of God proved to be a house of an idol, as I said. Accordingly, he said somewhere in Jeremiah about the people of Israel, "Why has my beloved committed profanity in my house?" The God of all could rightly say to those from Judah and Benjamin, "This people draws near to me; they honor me with their lips, but their heart is far from me."[45]

Because Israel was in a frenzy like a frenzied heifer; the Lord will now graze them like a lamb in a broad pasture (v.16). One of the holy ones wisely led us to the pursuit of what is beneficial by saying, "My child, do not let your heart envy sinners; instead, spend the whole day in fear of the Lord."[46] After all, how could you choose to envy those you blamed? Such is the message the God of all gives to Judah: Do not let the *frenzy* of *Israel* be an occasion of defection on your part, like abandoning the herd, as it were, in the

---

44. 1 Kgs 12.29. The LXX version encourages Cyril to see Hosea directing his words to Judah.
45. Jer 11.15; Is 29.13.
46. Prv 23.17.

manner of heifers when stung by gadfly or cattle wasp, which is a kind of bee whose bite is unbearable. [The heifer] leaves the herd, and by the rapidity of its movement it causes anyone else so inclined to move off. Will we not find Israel having this experience? It left Jerusalem, and by abandoning its herdsman—namely, God—it committed a dire and accursed defection.

Accordingly, he says, do not imitate it, O Judah: even if Israel in its *frenzy* in the manner of heifers goes off into apostasy, its exploit will not go unpunished. (115) It will in fact depart in captivity, leave its native land, and be allotted that of the Persians and Medes, no longer bold and, so to speak, hostile and rebellious (the constant manner of a *frenzied heifer*). Instead, it will become like the tamest of *lambs;* the situation of captives is lowly and fearful, with the expectation of maltreatment not remote, subject to the oppression of those in power. Now, he refers to the land of the Persians and Medes as *broad,* as if to mean something like this: it will be allotted land that is wide and spacious, and will change its location frequently, not always having the same master, but moving to the next one's land.

A person's soul could suffer the same experience after setting at naught the love for God: it will be carried in whatever direction pleases those who are beloved of demons, captive, miserable, and feeble. It will justly hear God's words, "Your apostasy will correct you, and your malice will reprove you."[47]

Ephraim is involved with idols and has set stumbling blocks for themselves, opting for the Canaanites. They added promiscuity to promiscuity, they loved dishonor in their wantonness. You are a blast of wind in her wings, and they will be ashamed of their altars (vv. 17–19). The prophet's attention is still directed at Judah,[48] which as I said pretends to observe the law and set no little store by reverence for God, though secretly inclining towards the practice of honoring the demons' images. Therefore, he is saying, *Ephraim* admittedly was *involved with idols*—Israel, that is, taking this name from the tribe in its midst that exercised control, namely, that of Jeroboam,

---

47. Jer 2.19.
48. Though in these verses the Heb. can be obscure, and the LXX no clearer, Cyril is somewhat perverse in insisting on seeing Judah in focus; this enables him to see a reference to Jews of NT times.

COMMENTARY ON HOSEA 4

who was from that district and tribe. And just as (116) by Judah he made reference to those in Jerusalem by restricting the reference to the ruling tribe, so, too, in the case of Israel when he cites Ephraim, he makes reference to the ruling tribe. He says, then, that *Ephraim is involved with idols,* adoring the Egyptians' divinity, namely, Apis, or the heifer that was their divinity. They were involved no less also in the sacrilege and unbridled insanity of the *Canaanites,* who were in the habit of giving attention and adoration to the shameful idol Baal of Peor.

In doing this, however, *Ephraim set stumbling blocks for themselves,* offending the God who assisted them and was accustomed to save them. *They opted for the Canaanites;* that is, they gave preference and priority to customs of the Canaanites, who as neighbors of the country of the Jews were impious worshipers of idols. In addition to this, the people of Israel *added promiscuity to promiscuity,* obviously by pursuing spiritual infidelity beyond the bounds of restraint and propriety and through the extent of their crimes of shameful apostasy reaching the point of depravity. They also *loved dishonor in their wantonness,* that is, with the loud boasting they uttered of God and the credit they gained from having him. Consequently, they were dishonored and abject, truly miserable and trampled underfoot, brought down by their former *wantonness;* they would no longer be called free, but rather would take the path to outrage and dishonor, and be subject to harsh masters.

Even if, however, he is saying, the uncomprehending multitude of Ephraim was subject to all this, it is you, O Judah, who, as it were, *are a blast of wind in* a bird's *wings.* Clearly, when a strong wind impels them and, so to speak, forces them, winged things definitely (117) in that case have a more rapid flight; so while Israel took a turn to apostasy and came to grief, you became to it *a blast of wind in* the *wings.*[49] How, and in what way? When she saw you, who were still under the guidance of the Law, who attended the divine Temple and performed the sacrifices according to the Law, becoming indifferent, neglectful, and guilty of like sins, it made her defection more rapid. But they will find it to be to

---

49. All the commentators have difficulty dealing with this verse.

their shame; *their altars* will be the source of disgrace and dishonor.

Whenever we who seem to stand firm, obliged as we are to live a good and irreproachable life, prove to be lazy and neglectful in doing so—or, rather, choose as much as the others to pay no heed to what is pleasing to God—far from simply wronging ourselves we bring others down as well and become liable for double punishment. To those in error or unwilling to live an upright life we ought, in fact, to have represented an image and type of virtue, but we proved an occasion of stumbling. What does Christ say, then? "Whoever puts a stumbling block before one of these little ones who believe in me, it would be better for them if a heavy millstone were fastened around their neck and they were drowned in the depths of the sea."[50]

50. Mt 18.6.

COMMENTARY ON HOSEA,
CHAPTER FIVE

Hear this, you priests, pay heed, house of Israel, give ear, house of the king, because the judgment is directed to you, since you have been a snare on the lookout, and like a net spread on Tabor. By hunting it they transfixed the prey (vv.1–2).

E HAD ACCUSED Judah of proving to be a "blast of wind" for Israel in the way just explained by us. He now directs his words of rebuke (118) to those who devised the deceit and error, and were the source of their senseless behavior. These were the falsely named *priests,* those not of the bloodline of Levi but exercising priesthood at a price, having purchased the right to act as priests to the idols. It is recorded of Jeroboam, remember, "Anyone of that mind greased his palm and was made a priest for the high places."[1] Rightly, therefore, attention moves to the ministers themselves and to the *house of the king, Israel* itself also being caught up in prosecution; some spoke and acted in favor of the continuance of idolatry, erecting altars, offering libations and sacrifices, and smoothing the path of destruction for the deceived, while the kings took the initiative in error.

Accordingly, he says to them, *You have been a snare on the lookout,* by *lookout* referring to the masses subject to the *priests* (if they really were priests) and under the supervision of the leaders.[2] They in fact were the ones to have oversight of their subjects, or were observed by those in their care: whatever those in power decided they used to mislead their subjects, since the leaders' wishes were followed by those whom they led. Therefore, he is saying, you have proved to be like *a snare* for the populace who

---

1. 1 Kgs 13.33.
2. In these verses the LXX has not picked up mention of the cult centers Mizpah and Shittim. Cyril does his best to compensate for his own linguistic inability to detect the shortcomings of his version.

were under your supervision or perhaps looking to you. You were also *like a net spread on Tabor,* a famous mountain situated in Galilee, which offered plenty of hunting of animals and birds on account of its height and the extreme density of forests and thickets.

I am your chastiser. I know Ephraim, and Israel is not beyond me (v.3). The priests, then, and also those of the royal bloodline (119) became the net and snare and hunters of the people, directing them to sacrifice to the demons, themselves giving an example, encouraging them to entertain unlawful ideas and introducing them to other forms of error in addition to these unholy novelties—namely, the high places, Baal of Peor, the abomination of the Sidonians, Baal, Chemosh.[3] But he promises that he will be their *chastiser,* and before long, inflicting on them to an unprecedented extent the evils stemming from anger and wrath. The promise proved true: some members of the royal house were involved in dire and ineluctable disasters, and others perished according to the testimony of the sacred writings, while others departed in subjugation to the oppression of the Babylonians and Medes. A miserable death—or, rather, a fitting one—befell the mercenary so-called priests, some at the hands of Jehu, others of Josiah, who was of the tribe of Judah, or David; this in fact had been prophesied by the man of God when Jeroboam was sacrificing and standing at the altar: "O altar, altar, thus says the Lord: Lo, a son is born to the house of David, Josiah by name. He will sacrifice on you the priests of the high places who offer incense on you, and human bones will be burned on you."[4]

He therefore threatened to *chastise* with anger and wrath those who proved *a snare on the lookout,* namely, priests and those of the royal bloodline, not excusing from accusation in any way the one who was deceived—Israel, that is. Consequently, he says, *I know Ephraim, and Israel is not beyond me.* Resembling that is the verse, "Who is this that conceals his intentions from me, keeping his words in his heart, and thinks he can keep me in the dark?" *I know* (120) *Ephraim,* in fact, he says, and I have not removed *Is-*

---

3. Cyril had referred to the Baal of the Ammonites, Chemosh of the Moabites, and Astarte of the Sidonians in his preface to the Commentary and elsewhere.
4. 1 Kgs 13.1–2.

rael from me; "I am a God who is near, says the Lord," remember, "not one who is far away. Can anyone hide in secret places, and I shall not see him?" And again, "Surely nothing will remain hidden from me?" For "the word of God is living and active, sharper than any two-edged sword, piercing until it divides soul from spirit, joints from marrow; it is able to judge the thoughts and intentions of the heart. And before him no creature is hidden, but all are naked and laid bare to the eyes of the one to whom we must render an account."[5]

Because now Ephraim has prostituted herself, and Israel is defiled. They did not devote their thoughts to returning to their God, because a spirit of prostitution is in them, and they did not know the Lord (v.4). Since the God of all sees into the reins and hearts, and nothing at all is out of his sight, he knew that Israel, or Ephraim, had *prostituted itself* and had reached the extremity of depravity. Yet it had not even at that stage admitted in mind and heart the need to repent because of the dominance of the *spirit* persuading it to *prostitute itself,* and its refusal to seek the true Lord. There is truth, therefore, in what the Savior says: "No one can serve two masters: either you hate one and love the other, or you are devoted to one and despise the other."[6]

Israel's insolence will be humbled before him, and Israel and Ephraim will become feeble in their iniquities, and Judah will become feeble with them (v.5). Here he calls accursed arrogance *insolence,* the proud person being a boastful one. (121) So he says that the arrogance of Israel *will be humbled* when she suffers that fate—and rightly so—which is intended to make her lowly, pitiable, abject, bereft of her boasts in God, and deprived even of the ancestral freedom from on high. Now, the reversal of its *insolence before him* should be understood as somehow resembling blows in the face as a result of every form of dishonor. He says that the people of Israel *will become feeble* together with *Judah;* the kings of Syria and of the Persians who ravaged Samaria did not allow Judah to go unaffected, including with the cities of Israel some belonging to the people of Judah and Benjamin. Now, the fact that it was

5. Jb 38.2; Jer 23.23–24; 32.27; Heb 4.12–13.
6. Mt 6.24, the PG text citing only the first clause.

undoubtedly impiety and insolence towards God that was the source of all their misfortunes he conveyed in saying that the sense of feebleness would befall them in no other way than *in their iniquities.* Reverence for God, therefore, is truly a useful and most honorable thing, because through it there would be the possibility of gaining control of nations and easily succeeding in conducting all affairs. The Savior is right to claim, "Without me you can do nothing"; and somewhere David chose to utter right sentiments: "The Lord is my strength and my celebration."[7]

With sheep and calves they will go to seek out the Lord, and will not find him, for he has turned away from them because they abandoned the Lord, because illegitimate children were born to them. Now the blight will devour them and their inheritances (vv.6–7). The facts highlight that truth that, as the divinely inspired Paul says, "It is impossible for the blood of bulls and goats to take away (122) sins,"[8] and that access to God is not granted through the Law, by "Law" referring to the ritual of bloody sacrifices prescribed by the Law. So even if the people of Israel made the prescribed offerings in supplication for forgiveness of their unholy crimes or in search of relationship with God, they would not attain it, he is saying, nor would they manage to succeed in finding God, nor would access be granted to those showing repentance in this way. He is found, you see, only through life in Christ, to which the word of faith would be taken as an introduction, and also saving baptism, which is the basis of relationship with God in the Spirit. Consequently, Israel *would not find the Lord,* at least through worship prescribed by the Law; *he had turned away from them because they had abandoned him,* departing so far as to become fathers of *illegitimate children.* Now, he calls them *illegitimate children* because they were devoted to the wishes of the idols, as it were, from the womb and their actual swaddling clothes, their parents perhaps offering them to the demons in thanksgiving and as birth offerings. Hence *illegitimate children,* not born in God, or, in another interpretation, born of foreign women; the people of Israel had promiscuous relations with the daughters of the nations, who were also idol worshipers, despite the Law's clear prohibition of marriage with foreigners:

7. Jn 15.5; Ps 118.14.
8. Heb 10.4.

"Do not give your daughter to his son, and do not take his daughter for your son, for she would take away your son from me, and he would go off and serve other gods."[9]

Since they did so, however, *the blight will devour them.* He refers obscurely once again through this to the misfortune and harm that would accrue to them from the onset of war, (123) which was quite capable of causing dreadful destruction for them and their possessions (their *inheritances*) in the manner of *blight.* The fact that war was not remote and distant but in the immediate offing he confirmed by saying, *Now the blight will devour them;* it was as if he were saying, "Experience of the disasters will follow on my words, the calamity is close and at the door." So the lot of those who offend God is an inability to *find him,* even if choosing to *seek* him, and becoming parents of *illegitimate children,* that is, not to have well-born and legitimate offspring such as would be the result of virtue and a holy life. Instead, they would perish, victims of their own vice and misery as though of a kind of *blight,* losing in addition their very *inheritances* from God, of which the divinely inspired David also sings to God the Savior of all, "In your hands are my inheritances."[10] Every *inheritance* of ours and every portion, you see, come by God's authority, and he it is who awards the crowns.

Blow a trumpet on the hills, sound it on the heights, make a proclamation in the House of Ôn. Benjamin is aghast, Ephraim has become a waste in the days of censure, among the tribes of Israel I demonstrated faithfulness (vv.8–9). It was clearly said before that in addition to the golden heifers the accursed Jeroboam also introduced the people of Israel to other forms of ruinous idolatry and error. On the mountains and hills, for example, they worshiped Chemosh and Baal of Peor "under oak and poplar and shady tree,"[11] and in Bethel and Dan there were, as I said, the golden heifers. While this was Israel's error, however, Judah, or Benjamin, was no less in error—that is, those of the tribe of Judah and Benjamin; they worshiped (124) "Astarte, the abomination of the Sidonians, and also bowed down to the sun," as will be clear to us likewise

---

9. Dt 7.3–4.
10. Ps 31.15, the reading of some forms of the LXX.
11. Hos 4.13.

from the statement of Ezekiel, who was brought to Jerusalem "in a vision of God," and then witnessed the error of the inhabitants: "I saw about twenty-five men, with their backs to the Temple of the Lord and their faces towards the east, prostrating themselves to the sun towards the east."[12] Consider, therefore, how they shared the responsibility for their ruin, offending and distressing God in many ways.

Consequently, he criticizes the delay in attacking, as it were, by those intending and eagerly looking forward to ravaging Samaria, and meaning to cause no little panic in Jerusalem—namely, Assyrians and Persians and those from Damascus (Syrians, I mean), who all attacked at various times, prompted to it by different factors at different times. He bade them begin the assault by sounding *trumpets*, and instilling the onset of terror in the souls of the deceived. When he said, "Now the blight will devour them and their inheritances" (v.7), remember, we explained that *blight* referred to the misfortunes and destruction of war. To highlight the fact that it was at the gates and would befall them before long, he was right to bid them *sound the trumpet*, as I said, and primarily in the places of the idols, either because they were due to be burnt and overturned promptly, or because they were the occasion of the war and the unbearable calamity for the deceived. So when he refers to the need to *blow a trumpet on the hills and on the heights and in the House of Ôn*, you would take it to mean the places of the idols.

Now, it should be realized (125) that the Seventy were not in accord with the other translators in regard to *the House of Ôn*, some of whom put "house of uselessness"—that is, of every idol—and others "House of Ôn." Our conclusion, therefore, is that in the present case the prophetic verse means that they should sound a trumpet not only on the hills and high places, that is, against not only the idolatry of Israel, or the ten tribes in Samaria, but also that which was current in Jerusalem among Judah and *Benjamin*. They worshiped the sun, you see, as I said (*Ôn* being the sun),[13] turning their backs on God and abandoning

---

12. Cf. 2 Kgs 23.13; Ezek 8.3, 16.
13. The Heb. term *Beth-aven* (or -*ôn*), occurring also in 4.15, was represented in Cyril's text there as "house of iniquity," but "House of Ôn" in the Antioch

what belonged to him—the sense, in my view, of having their backs to the Temple of the Lord and their faces in the opposite direction, that is, to the sun. When you hear the phrase *in the House of Ôn,* therefore, you should take it to mean the house or shrine of any false god made by human hands, or the sun. It would not be inappropriate or implausible to take a reference to the *house* of the sun as those adoring the sun, just as, of course, "house of God" would be taken as those who think and do what pleases him and who show reverence to him.

If, on the other hand, you wanted to see a reference in *Ôn* to the golden heifer, such an interpretation would also be persuasive. The ungodly Jeroboam, in fact, made the heifers in the likeness of the Egyptian deity, namely Apis; Egyptians honored Apis, claiming it was a child of the moon (and consequently it carried an image of the moon on its forehead), and believing it to be a nephew of the sun in keeping with their view that the moon was illuminated from the sun. They therefore honored Apis as child of the moon and nephew of the sun—such was the degree of error and miserable thinking to which they were reduced by the wily dragon, Satan. So he bids them (126) *blow a trumpet on the hills, on the heights,* and *in the House of Ôn,* that is, of the golden heifer. What the crimes of both were, and the basis for their being punished, he makes clear in proceeding to say immediately, *Benjamin is aghast,* that is, it has parted company with its own morals, it has slipped from a virtuous mentality, the stupor rightly being interpreted as a turn for the worse. And *Ephraim* has been left *desolate.* But it was not always so, he says: *in the days of censure* of the sins of both *I demonstrated faithfulness,* making my utterances firm and reliable; what I foretold did happen to them, and none of my statements has proved false. In other words, since they parted company with their ancient mor-

---

text. Theodoret duly noted there that it was Aquila and Theodotion who rendered it "useless house," and Symmachus "house of iniquity." Not having occasion to be more precise at that earlier occurrence (despite Jerome), here in 5.8 Cyril checks with these alternative versions (thanks to Jerome) and notes the discrepancy without being able to account for the different versions of a word that means "house of trouble," a case of what Stuart calls "a sarcastic metonymy" for Beth-El, "house of God." At a loss before the word, Cyril assumes that the sun comes into it, another version Jerome knew.

als, and lost a sound outlook, they were driven out even of their own country, and forfeited love for God and all prosperity.

The abandonment of every sound thought, and in fact every deed directed to virtue as well, will follow in a different way those who forsook God. They will proceed to become *a waste*, with God censuring and chastising them, and calling them to account for their indifference. Being with God is therefore useful and necessary for life, like that cry in the psalms, "My soul clung to you"; after all, the right hand of the one who can do all things will then protect and assist us, and no one will pluck us from it, as the Savior says.[14]

The rulers of Judah have become like those who shift boundary stones; on them I am pouring out my assault like water (v.10). In an obscure fashion this is the meaning of *Benjamin is aghast:* (127) they were like *those who shift boundary stones*, he says, and they wanted to exceed limits set in olden times. In other words, those who transfer to others what is proper to God alone and rightly devoted to him—I mean love, honor, adoration—by worshiping perhaps the sun or moon and stars are in all likelihood doing nothing other than shifting boundary stones. The fact that Judah, or Benjamin, had directed to sun, moon, and stars the glory due to God would be clearly understood from God's saying to the prophet Jeremiah, "Do you not see what they are doing in the cities of Judah and the streets of Jerusalem? Their children gather wood, their fathers kindle fire, and their wives mix flour to make cakes for the host of heaven, and they poured libations to foreign gods so as to provoke me."[15] So the leaders of the tribe of Judah *shift boundary stones,* that is, those invested with high and royal office, and the common herd probably chose to follow them in their error. But *I am pouring out my assault* on them *like* teeming *water,* he says—in other words, the effects of divine wrath will be completely unbearable, intolerable, and irresistible, just as of course the full and overflowing flood of water cannot be repelled.

Ephraim oppressed its adversary, it trampled down judgment, because it began to go after futile things. I will be like confusion to Ephraim, and

14. Ps 63.8; Jn 10.28.
15. Jer 7.17–18.

like a goad to the house of Judah (vv.11–12). While the way in which "Benjamin is aghast" (v.8) has been clearly explained (128) with his saying that "the rulers of Judah have become like those who shift boundary stones" (v.10), he comments in turn on the way in which "Ephraim has become a waste" (v.9) by proceeding to say that *Ephraim oppressed its adversary.* And attention now seems to be directed nicely to us. Accordingly, to the extent possible I shall try to unfold what charge was leveled at those of the tribe of Ephraim, or which *adversary* communicated to us in a divine oracle was the one *Ephraim oppressed.*

Some members of the tribe of Judah and Benjamin still showed some respect and attention to the laws given through Moses, and devoted themselves to righteousness. Not all defected, in fact; it would not be easy to number those who wept and lamented the defection of the deceived, and who were not a little upset, especially since some others showed no honor for the God of all and gave themselves to the forms of idolatry. As the blessed prophet Ezekiel says, for example, some people were sent against Jerusalem, axes in hand, and they heard God clearly saying that they had to follow the man clad in a frock and spare no one. In the vision, he says, "six men came through the gate facing north, each with an axe in his hand. He said to the man wearing the frock, Go through the midst of Jerusalem, and put a sign on the forehead of the men grieving and mourning all the iniquities happening in its midst. To these he said in my hearing, Go into the city behind him, cut down, and show no pity or mercy; kill old and young, women and children, to destroy them, but do not approach anyone bearing the sign."[16] Do you notice that some people were marked out as exempt from any retribution, anger, (129) or guilt, as a result of adopting correct attitudes, living a life in accord with the Law, embracing righteousness, and having an unfailing love for God? In Samaria, for instance, Israel utterly came to grief, consigning the laws of Moses to oblivion, and in a hostile manner, as it were, leading a life completely opposed to them, with the result that it considered the Law of God inimical to it, did not want even to know it, and despised the in-

---

16. Ezek 9.2–6.

structor, despite his habit of saving them and being perfectly able to bring them to a regular and untroubled life.[17]

This is the message, then, which the prophetic text is probably conveying to us, doing so nicely, as I said. The text reads, *Ephraim oppressed its adversary*, that is, Ephraim won a victory that was very wrong and productive of ruin; it *oppressed*—that is, vigorously contested—as its enemy the Law it hated. Since the expression is unclear, however, it explains it in a different way by saying, *It trampled down judgment*, that is, its attitude was definitely not one of righteousness according to the Law; *trampling down* is invariably taken to imply dishonor, and is interpreted as deserving no respect. Our Lord Jesus Christ, for example, says, "Salt is good; but if the salt loses its savor, how will it be salted? It is good for nothing any more but being thrown out and trampled under people's feet." So when you read *judgment*, take it to mean the Law. The divinely inspired David also referred to it in a similar way, crying out to God, "You have executed judgment and righteousness in Jacob," the Law being God's, even if spoken through angels.[18] What the occasion was of considering the Law inimical and *trampling down judgment* he proceeds to bring out, going on at once to say, *because it began to go after futile things*. The beginning of such an ailment, he says, was choosing to honor (130) *futile things* and follow idols; after all, it is beyond possibility to manage to follow at the same time both God and the evil and unclean spirits. Hence the divinely inspired Paul also writes, "You cannot drink the cup of the Lord and the cup of demons; you cannot partake of the table of the Lord and the table of demons,"[19] love of God being exclusive. The insecure person who is inclined to go in both directions is indecisive and unstable, ready to proceed where chance leads.

---

17. In his somewhat tentative commentary on this text, Cyril moves from southern to northern kingdoms. Modern commentators would see a reference here to the Syro-Ephraimite war (described in 2 Kgs 16.5–9 and 2 Chr 28.5–23), in which Judah invoked Assyrian aid against pressures to join a northern coalition, resulting in invasion of the north and deportation, Ephraim and Benjamin being least affected—hence the specific references in the text. Cyril adverts to it below.

18. Mk 9.50; Mt 5.13; Ps 99.4; Heb 2.2.

19. 1 Cor 10.21.

"The rulers of Judah have become like those who shift boundary stones" (v.10), he says, then, and *Ephraim oppressed its adversary, and it trampled down judgment. Now I will be like confusion to Ephraim, and like a goad to the house of Judah.* There is need to explore the meaning of this. In fact, while the other translators put "eater" for *confusion,* and "rottenness" for *goad,* the Seventy put *confusion* and *goad.* In other words, when Ephraim, or the ten tribes, were considerably alarmed by the outbreak of war against them, in one case by their neighbor (Syria, I mean) and in another by the Persians and those coming from the country of the Assyrians, Judah was in fear and trembling—or rather, under great stress, expecting to be embroiled in a similar fate in a short time, or in much worse troubles. When in fact war broke out and affected the cities in Samaria, it was absolutely inevitable that their neighbors would perish likewise, namely, Judah and Benjamin. *Confusion,* therefore, suggests the onset of war, and *goad* the pangs of distress and unease felt by them. Completely proof against it would be those wishing to have the mind of Christ, through whom and with whom be glory to the God and Father with the Holy Spirit, unto ages of ages. Amen.[20] (131)

Ephraim saw its ailment, and Judah its pangs. Ephraim went to Assyrians. It sent ambassadors to King Jarib, but he was unable to heal you, and your pain will not leave you (v.13). When God brought confusion, as it were, to Ephraim and proved to be like a goad to the house of Judah, *Ephraim saw its ailment,* or its weakness and limitations, and *Judah its pangs,* since, as I said, they raided Samaria and the territory of Benjamin. Ephraim was then exhausted by this, and, because it was unable to resist from its own resources the events befalling it, and incapable of averting the ill effects of war, it proceeded to offend the all-powerful God without understanding the benefit coming from its stripes, so to speak. When the time came for it to turn to God, however, then in particular it chose to offend him and be more determined in forsaking him. It did not acknowledge, in fact, the author and controller of its entire reputation, the generous God who was always able to overcome the adversaries; instead, it made no re-

---

20. Cyril concludes his third tome.

quest for anything, despite the exclamation of the all-wise Moses, "The Lord crushes enemies, (132) the Lord is his name," and his clear teaching that through him and in him "one will rout a thousand, and two will disperse a myriad."[21]

Then, though it should in turn have requested the customary help from him alone, and besought its Savior with prayers to assist them, it concocted drastic plans in its own head; it sent a delegation to foreigners and called on its enemies for help,[22] or by attempting to buy off the Assyrians it thought it could be rid of its pressing troubles. When Menahem was king in Samaria, therefore, King Pul of Assyria went up to Israel; then, with bribes and delegations they persuaded him to leave the country—in other words, *Ephraim went to Assyrians*. Next, Pekah son of Remaliah, king of Israel, paid Rezin king of Syria to make war on Judah and those of the tribe of Benjamin; Ahaz son of Jotham was king, and fearing an attack he persuaded Tiglath-pileser of Assyria with delegations and money to come to the aid of Jerusalem; the latter took Damascus by force, and from its midst he removed Rezin as king. But even if, as he says, *Ephraim went to Assyrians* and bought them off and by petitions secured a delay in the attack, and even if Judah *sent ambassadors to King Jarib*—that is, defender or avenger, the meaning of *Jarib*[23]—they did not overcome the divine wrath or dissuade God from requiring an account of their dire apostasy. After all, they could not (133) buy some brief respite, he is saying, nor could any other mercenary heal you; the goad of your *pains* would never cease.

It is therefore a dreadful option not rather to desire to be saved through kindness from on high, but instead to trust in help from human beings despite the Spirit's cry in the statement of the blessed David: "It is better to trust in the Lord than to trust in human beings; it is better to hope in the Lord than to

---

21. Ex 15.3; Dt 32.30.
22. At this point the PG text includes a citation of 7.11, which Theodoret seems to be aware of.
23. Cyril has gone into the details of the figures and events of international politics touched on by Hosea. Unlike the Antiochenes, he observes (with Jerome's help) that the LXX has here read an unusual Heb. form for "the great (king)" as a proper name. But like them he seems to fail to recognize in Pul a nickname for Tiglath-pileser III.

hope in rulers." Likewise in the prophet Jeremiah, "Cursed be the one who puts trust in a human being, and rests on him the flesh of his right arm, and whose heart forsakes the Lord. He will be like a shrub in the desert, or will not see when good things come. Blessed the one who trusts in the Lord, and whose hope is the Lord. He will be like a flourishing tree near water, will strike his roots in moisture, and will not fear when the heat comes; a leafy stem will grow on it, it will not fear in a year of drought, and will not cease producing fruit." It is therefore surely better to be related to God, and to utter in all sincerity that wise remark, "I am yours, save me, because I sought out your ordinances."[24]

Because I am like a panther to Ephraim, and like a lion to the house of Judah, I shall rob and make my escape; I shall take and there will be no one to rescue. I shall depart and return to my place until they are no more (vv.14–15). He makes clear the reason why those who came to the aid of Ephraim did them no good, (134) and instead their troubles did not come to an end. In fact, *I am like a panther to Ephraim*, he says, *and like a lion to the house of Judah*. So it is obvious that when God causes the downfall, there is no one who can avert it; as Scripture says, "Who will avert his uplifted hand?"[25] That it was when his clemency was utterly withheld that their fate befell them he suggests indirectly by comparing his own assault to extremely harsh and violent beasts of prey: the *panther* moves with very rapid movement against anything it wants, traveling with such rapidity as to leave no visible trace or mark on the ground, while the *lion* utters such a fearsome and depressing roar in the mountains, resembling a thunder clap and capable of alarming those who hear it. Scripture says, remember, "A lion will roar, and who will not take fright?"[26] Its leap is irresistible, and its attack quite disabling; if it catches anything, it kills it forthwith, and you would not rescue its prey. Now, the fact that the *panther* is swift in seizing its prey, almost flying, and the lion is bold, fearless, and disabling, as I said, he himself brought out by proceeding to say, *I shall rob and make my escape; I shall take and*

24. Ps 118.8–9; Jer 17.5–8; Ps 119.94.
25. Is 14.27.
26. Am 3.8.

there will be no one to rescue; the latter phrase is applicable to the lion, whereas *robbing and escaping* is something the panther would do, as I said.

And the fact that the Lord will abandon those who offend him, will, as it were, withdraw his support, and will cancel his benevolence, he mentions in the words, *I shall depart and return to my place until they are no more.* While the divinity is completely uncircumscribed by place, he is said by some authors to be present when he confers his benevolence, and likewise to be absent from sinners when he deprives them of it (135) and cancels his clemency. You see, while words are used of God in human fashion, they should be understood in a way befitting him.[27]

They will seek my face when they are distressed (v.15). Once more he conveys the fact that it is not without purpose that a terrible fate is often wrought by God on those with an unbridled inclination to depravity or in the habit of sinning unrestrainedly; rather, it is for their benefit and as a method of healing. The people in fact who despise divine clemency and do not recognize that the extent of longsuffering is a summons to repentance will not escape the effects of his wrath; rather, when shattered by the ferocity of the disaster, they will acknowledge what is for their good, and those who did not benefit from lovingkindness will be brought to a sense of the advantage by exposure to hardship. You see, just as bodily ailments that do not respond to mild remedies are often overcome by fire and knife, in the same manner and for the same reason, in my view, the passions ingrained in human souls that do not yield to positive advice and are not overcome by sensible thinking give way to hardship, scourging, and unbearable calamities. Only when subjected to distress, then, he is saying, *will they seek my face:* people without awareness have little appreciation of their prosperity when good things are within their grasp, but we come to these things with a keener desire if we have been deprived of the objects of our deepest longings, and gain a powerful and irresistible sense of loss. Accordingly, it is *when they are distressed* that *they will seek my face.*[28]

---

27. Anthropomorphic expressions in the biblical text require proper understanding, Cyril and other Fathers will insist.

28. This clause includes words in the Heb. and other forms of the LXX (in-

Now, the verse may appropriately be applied to the (136) mystery of Christ, and probably suggests very well the redemption through him and conversion to God. The *face* of God that is sought could very appropriately be understood as the Son, "who is the image, refulgence, and exact imprint of the Father's being." The Son, then, is the true face of the God and Father, especially if recognized as such; "whoever who has seen him has seen the Father."[29] The divinely inspired psalmist spoke of him in similar terms, crying out to the God of all in the words, "Shine your face on your servant"; and, in fact, speaking in the person of those who believe and are made in the likeness of the Son through the Spirit, he says, "The light of your countenance, Lord, has left its mark on us," as the prophet says, "Lord Christ, light of our countenance."[30]

---

cluding the Antiochene) that Cyril appends to the opening verse of the next chapter.

29. Heb 1.3; Jn 14.9. After considerable attention to the respective fortunes of Israel and Judah, Cyril feels justified in developing a christological dimension of the verse.

30. Pss 119.135; 4.7; Lam 4.20 LXX.

COMMENTARY ON HOSEA, CHAPTER SIX

They will arise to say to me, Come now, let us return to the Lord our God, because it is he who seized, and will heal us; it is he who will strike us and bind up our wounds, and will cure us after two days. On the third day we shall rise and live in his presence and know. We shall press on to know the Lord, for we shall find him ready as the dawn. He will come to us as early and late rain come to the earth (vv.1–3).

HE PHRASE *They will arise* here probably suggests that, as though awakening from the sleep of their dementia, and, as it were, now emerging from the darkness of night into the light of day, they will utter to one another the exhortation that it now behoves them to *return to the Lord.* This awakening is experienced by people caught up in error and involved in worship of the idols. (137) The benefit, in fact, of being awake is to seek to be rid of the mist—obviously of a demonic kind—and as though now filled with divine light to set a direct course towards knowledge of the one who is by nature and in truth God and Lord despite formerly being of the view that "there are many gods and lords" in the world, reaching such a degree of folly as "to say to a piece of wood, You are my father, and to a stone, You gave birth to me."[1]

The verse continues the figure; note how, as in the case of a lion or any other animal, they say, *It is he who seized, and will heal us.* Since he had said, remember, "I will be like a panther to Ephraim, and like a lion to the house of Judah, I shall rob and make my escape, I shall take and there will be no one to rescue,"[2] they maintained the metaphor in saying that the one *who seized* will cure; in other words, just as the wrath caused distress, he will completely gladden those who also trust in the good effects of

---

1. 1 Cor 8.5; Jer 2.27.
2. Hos 5.14.

his clemency. At the same time we shall realize that when God afflicts some, no one can do anything, whereas there would be need of him, and him alone, for restoring the fortunes of those who trust in him.

If, on the other hand, we should apply the force of the prophecy to everyone on earth, the sense we shall give it is as follows. In the beginning, remember, Adam *seized* human nature; he immediately put [the human being] under a curse, subjecting him to death and corruption. Therefore, wrath *struck* him, but grace *bound up his wounds;* he was *healed* by Christ, who called him to knowledge of the true vision of God, confirmed them in observance of the commandments through the Spirit, in turn made us devout by rendering us proof against corruption and ridding us of the ailments of the ancients, namely, sin and passions.[3] Now, this was the lot of those on earth, not (138) on the first or second occasion, but on the *third,* that is, the eventual and final one. All time, you see, is divided into three—the first, the middle, and the last, when Christ was made manifest to us. Consequently, they are saying that the time of *binding up wounds* will come to us, as it were, as a result of surgical intervention *after two days,* the prophetic verse assigning us the period of a *day.* At that time, he says, *We shall press on to know the Lord,* by *press on* meaning "hasten"; at that time, too, *we shall rise and live in his presence,* for we shall be raised with Christ. And since "one died for all,"[4] we live his life, no longer placed outside God's vision as a result of the Fall, nor cast behind him as a result of the sin; instead, we are now admitted to his sight, and have the right to speak freely to him on account of righteousness in Christ.

The fact that it is through him that we know also the Father, and that the Son has become for us the fullness of every good in us, they admit by saying, *we shall find him ready as the dawn,* that is, as a rising light, as the sun, as a sunbeam when darkness departs. He will be for us *as early and late rain:* he bedews us who have accepted the faith, and have a correct knowledge of his coming, in

---

3. As one would expect of a Greek Father, the Fall and its effects are admitted by Cyril, but the healing is presented at greater length. (The Antiochenes here do not see a reference to the Fall.)
4. Col 3.1; 2 Cor 5.14.

my view, in two senses. That is to say, he imparts in the Spirit the former teachings and laws, as well as knowledge of prophetic teachings (the meaning, in my view of *early rain*); and, as *late rain*, he gives in addition to that the understanding of the Gospel teachings and thrice-desirable grace of the apostolic preaching. We have become, as the prophet says, "a desirable land." Perhaps it was also of us that the blessed David sings, "You have visited the earth and intoxicated it; many times you enriched it." It therefore produced a hundredfold, sixtyfold, and thirtyfold yield, in the Savior's phrase.[5] (139)

What shall I do with you, Ephraim? What shall I do with you, Judah? My mercy is like a morning cloud, departing like a dew of dawn (v.4). The verse does not come from someone at a loss; God would not be ignorant of what was for the good of the deceived, nor would he have been slow to administer what was calculated to be of benefit to those ensnared in the devil's toils. Rather, he blames them for that fact that, though they lacked nothing required for their healing, they were voluntarily inclined to do with alacrity what was unlawful. It is, in fact, as if he were to say, "What manner of mercy and assistance was not devised? *What shall I do* after that? How will you fend off the disease? By what remedies will you now be healed?" Although you could have taken advantage in great abundance of my clemency and incomparable lovingkindness like an enriching *cloud* and a sprinkling early *dew*, and this without reservation, he says, you set no store by it, treating as naught such a venerable and desirable gift.

The force of the prophecy would be particularly applicable to the gift given in Christ; it is he who is the sprinkling *cloud* and the enriching *dew—early*, because after a kind of night, which is understood as diabolical gloom and darkness, he shed light from heaven, since the Word came to us from on high from the Father, and *departing*, because falling on the whole world under heaven. The saving message is, in fact, very widespread, and, as it were, travels throughout the whole world under heaven, whereas the Law was somewhat contained, embracing only the country of the Jews; "God is known in Judah,"[6] remember, according to

---

5. Mal 3.12; Ps 65.9; Mt 13.8.
6. Ps 76.1.

the psalmist's claim. (140) The whole world, on the other hand, came to know the Savior and Redeemer of all, namely, Christ.

For this reason I cut down your prophets, I killed them by a word of my mouth (v.5). The elimination of the deceivers is proof of mercy and love for them. There were false prophets at the time in Israel, remember, attending the shrines of Baal, deceiving and being deceived, as Scripture says.[7] But they were done away with in due course, something foretold by God, who delivered a holy verdict against them: some were slain by Elijah at the altar of Baal when they were babbling and crying, "Hearken to us, O Baal, hearken to us,"[8] and some were killed by Jehu, whom the blessed prophet Elisha through one of his servants anointed king over Israel at God's bidding. When he was anointed, and God was angry with the deceivers, he first disposed of Ahab, after him Jezebel, then his sons throughout Samaria. Feigning the intention to celebrate the feast of Baal, he gathered all the false prophets, and pretending to sacrifice he slaughtered them when assembled in one house; he also demolished the Baal itself, and burnt its pillars, as Scripture records.[9]

The fact that the elimination of the false prophets, therefore, was proof, as I said, of mercy and love for Israel he conveyed by saying, *For this reason I cut down your prophets.* That was well put, *cut down:* they fell in large numbers, hewn down like sheaves of corn. (141)

My judgment will go forth as a light. Because I want mercy and not sacrifice, knowledge of God rather than holocausts (vv.5–6). He outlines to us another form of mercy and love for them; if it had been observed in keeping with his will, Israel and Judah would have been completely saved. Not only, in fact, did he cut away the vast numbers of the sacrilegious false prophets by determining death as a fitting punishment for them, but the God and Father also sent in due course even his Son to indicate his good intentions to those of the bloodline of Israel before the others, and make clear his *judgment.* Accordingly, he also said in the

---

7. 2 Tim 3.13. The theme of deception is unremitting in Cyril.
8. 1 Kgs 18.40, 26.
9. 2 Kgs 9.1–2; 10.25–27. Cyril has shown imagination in dealing with the unlikely LXX version of a questionable Heb. text.

voice of David, "I have been established as king by him on Zion, his holy mountain, to announce the commands of the Lord," while he personally said on becoming like us—human, that is—"I do not speak on my own account: the Father who sent me, it is he who has given me a commandment about what to say and what to speak."[10] *My judgment will go forth as a light*, he says, therefore—that is, far from being shrouded in obscurity, my will openly and directly will be implanted in everyone's mind. Now, he makes clear that the purpose of his *judgment* is that at his coming in due course Emmanuel will not transfer to worship according to the Law those deceived, or encourage them to continue paying honor in types and shadows, but rather bring them to honesty, goodness, compassion, love for one another, and true and unambiguous knowledge of God, and he says that *I want mercy and not sacrifice, knowledge of God rather than holocausts*. What in fact did the Savior say? "So everything you want people to do to you do likewise to them"; and to show that it is love that is especially dear to God, he says, "By this all will know that you are my (142) disciples: if you have love for one another."[11]

There is no doubting the fact that he brought the mind of those approaching him to knowledge of the one who is truly God, for he had set himself for us as an image of the one who begot him, saying to his true disciple, namely, Philip, "Do you not believe that I am in the Father and the Father is in me? Whoever has seen me has seen the Father. The Father and I are one."[12] If, on the other hand, you were to say also that he means the Son is the *mercy* of the Father, better than *sacrifice* and *holocausts*, your interpretation would be correct, for thus he has been called by divinely inspired Scripture; the God and Father said of him to us, "My righteousness approaches rapidly, and my mercy has been revealed." The prophetic authors said to him, "Show us your mercy, O Lord, and grant us your salvation, O Lord";[13]

---

10. Ps 2.6–7; Jn 12.49.
11. Mt 7.12; Jn 13.35. Unlike the Antiochenes, Cyril could not be accused of failing to elaborate on what in v.6 Stuart refers to as "God's oft-quoted prioritizing of covenant requirements" and what is certainly one of the religious and moral highlights of The Twelve.
12. Jn 14.10, 9; 10.30.
13. Is 51.5; 56.1; Ps 85.7.

Christ is truly *mercy* from the Father, his purpose being to remove sins, to forgive faults, to justify by faith, to save the lost and make them proof against death. What excellent gifts, in fact, has he not given us? Therefore, *knowledge of God* is better than *sacrifices and holocausts* when achieved in Christ; it is through him and in him that we have come to know the Father, and are enriched with justification by faith.

But they are like someone breaking a covenant (v.7). We should at all points be very zealous in investigating the truth; in this case we need to say that in place of *like someone* the Hebrew text says "like Adam" *breaking a covenant,* so that we may understand that the *breaking* by the people of Israel was like that committed by Adam.[14] While it was granted to him, remember, to have a relationship with God, to live without [fear of] corruption, (143) and to be regaled with the delights of paradise, he paid no heed to the divine commandment; he then took a turn for the worse, and was unexpectedly deprived of his former condition. So, too, with *them,* that is, the people of Israel; though the God of all was benevolent and loving to them, saving and protective, and conferred his mercy on them like an *early cloud* and like *morning dew* falling, bringing forth his *judgment as a light,* and crowning them with worship according to the Law, they became indifferent about what was necessary to them and useful for their prosperity and reputation, and *they* themselves scorned the God who controls all things. This was in spite of Moses in his great wisdom saying clearly, "You shall not make for yourself an idol or likeness of anything in heaven above or on earth below or in the water under the earth," and again, "You shall have no other gods before me."[15] But since like the first man—Adam, that is—they fell headlong into apostasy, *they,* too, will be completely estranged from the one who was in the habit of making them prosper, *having broken a covenant.*

If, on the other hand, the oracle were taken in a more spiri-

---

14. The LXX has probably confused the similar Heb. terms *'adam,* "human being," and *'adama,* "soil, ground," the latter occurring here, probably as a place name such as the Adam in Transjordan. Cyril is therefore basing his "correction" on his own false reading or under the influence of Jerome.

15. Ex 20.4, 3.

tual sense in reference to Christ,[16] we would explain that sense as well in clarifying the meaning of what was said. The God and Father sent the Son from heaven to shed light on the people of Israel and make clear his judgment, his purpose being, on the one hand, to persuade them to cease their ancient sacrifices and holocausts according to the Law, and, on the other, to show mercy for them by justifying them by faith and to call them to knowledge of the one who is truly God. It is through him and in him, in fact, that we see the Father and enjoy an approach to him, as sacred Scripture says somewhere.[17] The people of Israel, however, are *like someone breaking a covenant*, the meaning of which I shall in turn explain as far as I can. The person who breaks the covenant written by another either does not have access (144) to the inheritance bequeathed by the one who wrote the will, or deprives others of the benefits described therein for them. This [crime] Jews have committed, and in the case of Christ. How, and in what way? The God and Father granted the Son leadership of the nation as an inheritance that was, as it were, wonderful and special; he cried aloud, as I said, "I have been established as king by him on Zion, his holy mount." He also gave the Son the spiritual vineyard, that is, Israel: "The vineyard of the Lord of hosts," as Scripture says, "a man of Judah, a new plant, beloved."[18] But as the blessed evangelist John says, "He came to what was his own, and his own people did not accept him," thrusting him out of the gate and giving him over to death in the words, "This is the heir; come now, let us kill him and take his inheritance."[19]

Consider, then, how they became *like someone breaking a covenant*. Did you recognize the heir? Then give him his allotted inheritance. Accordingly, they *broke* the Father's *covenant* by depriving him of his inheritance as far as lay in them. Nor did they make an approach to grace; they did not take possession of the inheritance given them by God. God said to them through the prophet, remember, "Lo, the days are coming, says the Lord, and I shall make a new covenant with the house of Israel and

---

16. Again Cyril waits until the text's historical reference has been examined before turning to its *mystikôteron* meaning.
17. Eph 2.18.   18. Ps 2.6; Is 5.7 LXX.
19. Jn 1.11; Mt 21.38.

with the house of Judah, not like the covenant I made with their ancestors on the day when I took them by the hand to lead them out of the land of Egypt."[20] Now, if the new one is compared with the former one, the difference in the promises will be conspicuous: in the one case he promised them the land of the Amorites, the Girgashites, the Hivites, and even the Jebusites,[21] whereas the new covenant (145)—that is, the promises made by Christ—summoned us through faith to God's sonship, to glory, to incorruptibility, to eternal life, to communion with God through the Spirit, to the kingdom of heaven. But they declined to have the inheritance allotted them through the Son by the God and Father. They therefore offended in *breaking the covenant* in both respects, by expelling as far as they could the heir from the inheritance given him by the Father, and forfeiting in their own case what was given them by God in Christ.

There Gilead scorned me, a city producing futile things, disturbing water, and your strength that of a man who is a pirate (vv.7–9). The text returns to outlining the crimes for which the sacrilegious band of false prophets was rightly done away with. *There*, he says—that is, at the time when Israel strayed and fell into such a condition as even to opt for worshiping demonic idols, this being a factual and not a local sense of *there*.[22] *Gilead scorned me* severely; it was one city beyond the waters of the Jordan that was allotted to the Levites according to the Law of Moses, and so it was a city of priests and Levites. Those who should have brought others from error and led them to truth and knowledge of what was to their good ("The lips of a priest," Scripture says, remember, "will preserve justice, and they will look for the Law from his mouth")[23] themselves became devotees of the idols and agents of futility, *producing futile things*—that is, the idols. They also *dis-*

---

20. Jer 31.31–32.
21. Jos 24.11.
22. Cyril's text has been divided differently from others, forcing him to call white black to justify the appearance of the adverb. He also finds Gilead in his text, as it occurs in our Heb. to the puzzlement of commentators, whereas the Antioch text has the more likely Gilgal, a nest of idol worshipers, as Theodoret remarks—but Cyril can account for his text, making a reference that is probably to Dt 4.43.
23. Mal 2.7.

turbed water, that is, (146) they became in turn an occasion of confusion to their flocks, the custom of Holy Scripture being to compare the immeasurable masses of people to water; it says, for instance, in reference to the dense population of Babylon and Nineveh, "its waters like a pool of water";[24] that is, just as a pool is full of water, so are its numbers vast.

There is also another sense in which it *disturbed water*, by proposing to its adherents a teaching that was, as it were, turbid and muddy, and by dulling the minds of the more simple; it taught them to worship idols. The God of all, for instance, once again blames them in the words of Ezekiel, proclaiming to the leaders as though to rams of the flock, "As for you sheep, the Lord says this: Lo, I shall judge between sheep and sheep, and between rams and goats. Is it not enough for you to feed on good pasture, and to tread down with your feet the rest of the pasture? To drink clear water, and with your feet foul the rest? My sheep ate what was trodden down by your feet, and drank water fouled by your feet."[25] In other words, those of the bloodline of Levi knew the Law, and by way of excellent pasture and fresh and clear water they had instruction from Moses that did not suffice for guidance to the truth, and so they trampled down their pasture, as it were. They also *disturbed the water* by proposing a teaching that was thick and slimy and full of mud to those who, though in the rank of the sheep, followed them as rams. The citizens and residents of *Gilead* are therefore accused of *disturbing water*, and charged with having *strength of a man who is a pirate*. The way in which we should understand that, I shall make clear in commenting on the following. (147)

Priests concealed the way of the Lord, they murdered Shechem because they did wrong in the house of Israel. I saw there Ephraim's horrifying prostitution; Israel was defiled, and Judah (vv.9–10). The text of the holy prophetic authors sometimes mentions some facts about which you would prefer to keep silent, and whose sense you would not be able to clarify, either. In our wish to give a clear commentary on such matters, therefore, we should overcome

---

24. Na 2.8. Ancient commentators do not trouble to distinguish Babylon from Assyria.
25. Ezek 34.17–19.

lethargy and as far as possible opt for bringing to the listeners what is of benefit.[26]

Consequently, we shall come now to some such incident. Shechem was a small town across the Jordan, then, a close neighbor of Gilead, which we mentioned before was given to those of the bloodline of Levi when Joshua son of Nun divided the land of promise. It happened, therefore, at the time of a holy feast— the feast of Tabernacles prescribed by Law, I mean—when everyone from all quarters normally went up to Jerusalem at the bidding of the Law for this celebration, that some people from Shechem, either feeling compunction and repentance for their error or called by God to observance, at that time opted to obey the divine laws and go up to Jerusalem, and intended to offer sacrifice and celebrate there the festival according to Law. This represented a beginning, as it were, of conversion and of cessation of the desire to worship the idols. In fact, to prevent some of the people of Israel—that is, the ten tribes—from going up from Samaria to Jerusalem for sacrifices and festivals in accordance with the Law and then in a short time returning to their former habits and becoming subject to the reign of Judah, Jeroboam originally came up with the idea of the heifers (148) and gave orders for the celebration of the prescribed rites with them, the wretch thus attaching to his own invention the glory due to God. In order to secure his own monarchy, God would be deprived, as it were, of his.[27]

Some of the people of Shechem, then, endeavored to go up to Jerusalem, but some people from the neighboring town of Gilead opposed their doing so, though as I said they were of the bloodline of Levi and assigned by Law to priesthood. Since they "produced futile things" (v.8), being makers of idols, and their trade would be useless if Israel now forsook the worship of idols, they were provoked to anger. As they did not dissuade them with

26. Cyril shows some delicacy in excusing himself for having to retell the events of Gn 34 alluded to here, one of the OT's more lurid incidents; the Antiochenes also see a reference to it. There is some diversity in Heb. and Antiochene and other forms of the LXX text as to division of the closing verses of this chapter and beginning of the next.

27. 1 Kgs 12. Cyril seems to be developing this account of Gilead's opposition to Shechem's reform without biblical support. *Se non è vero, ben trovato.*

words, however, they had recourse to unholy plans and actions; they made arrangements for some people to engage in acts of highway robbery and savage assaults against the Shechemites for choosing to go up to Jerusalem against their wishes. While most were killed, some survived and managed to escape their hands, but they were robbed of what they brought for sacrifice and scarcely managed to return to their own home. The Lord of all, therefore, accuses the people of Gilead, who, as Levites and priests and in their role of leaders of the others, should have made the *way* of piety clear to the deceived in obedience to the Law, but did the opposite and *concealed* it, not allowing them to have an upright attitude of their own volition or from heavenly benevolence, and in their compunction to opt now to reject the error of the demons.

Accordingly, he says, *Priests concealed the way of the Lord.* This likewise is clearly referred to in a different sense in another prophet: "The priests did not say, Where is the Lord? Those who handle my Law did not know me, and the shepherds offended against me."[28] (149) The crimes of the people of Gilead did not stop there, however: they went as far as *concealing the way of the Lord* and killing *Shechem,* doing away with them by the hands of brigands; hence his saying to Gilead, *your strength of a man who is a pirate.*

Now, observe how God reminds us of the ancient story, and mentions the former crimes of Levi. It goes like this. Dinah was the daughter of Jacob, or Israel (Jacob's name being changed to Israel). At one time she left her father's tent, wishing to see the daughters of the local people. It was in Shechem. Later, Shechem son of Hamor came upon the maiden and all of a sudden took her by force, robbing her of her virginity. The girl's brothers Levi and Simeon, therefore, were very upset at this, and hatched a plot, persuading the men of Shechem to be circumcised. When this was done, and they were still suffering and subject to pain, they killed them all, giving this reply to their father when he charged them with uncontrolled rage: "Should they treat our sister like a whore?"[29] Such is the story he now reminds us of, say-

---

28. Jer 2.8.
29. Gn 34.31.

ing with some delicacy, *They murdered Shechem because they did wrong in the house of Israel.* He says this to charge them with sinning at that time against the house of Jacob, or Israel, by robbing the girl of her virginity. Consequently, we in turn killed Shechem.

At this stage, however, they intended to return to God, he says, to love the requirements of the Law, observe feasts, and in the future abandon the defilement of idolatry. So what did the Levites do? *They concealed the way of the Lord and murdered Shechem.* Can they even now accuse them *because they did wrong* (150) *in the house of Israel?* Which young girl was now assaulted? Who was the Dinah they wronged? Which were the crimes of the Shechemites, honoring God as they were, loving a correct attitude and anxious to observe the requirements of the Law? Hence his saying, *I saw there Ephraim's horrifying prostitution;* you would rightly be astonished to see a priestly and chosen race turn away from their love for God to such extent as not only to become in their own case inventors of idols for others, but even to obstruct others from choosing to love the things of God. Accordingly he says, *Israel and Judah were defiled.* So let no one find fault with God's being angry if they suffered a predictable fate.

COMMENTARY ON HOSEA, CHAPTER SEVEN

Begin harvesting for yourself when I turn back the captivity of my people, when I heal Israel.[1]

HE VERSE addresses once again the resident of Gilead, its message being, I began as God both to *heal* and to *turn back* Israel. The Shechemites, for instance, longed to submit their neck to God in the future and to celebrate feasts, no longer those of Jeroboam but those according to the Law, and to abandon the deceit derived from goodness-knows-what source. But you, people of Gilead, so to speak, cut them back, plucked their fruit, and acquired unjust gain by brigandage. Again he proclaims with some delicacy, *Begin harvesting for yourself,* as if to say something of the kind, or rather gently insinuate instead of saying it, I shall make you the first-fruits of those punished; beginning with cutting back Israel, and harvesting those involved in such dreadful sacrilege, I shall make you the first spoils of my wrath. You need to know, in fact, that Pul king of Assyria, who was the first to come against (151) Samaria and Israel, deported the first tribes into captivity across the Jordan, and Gilead was one of those. So just as, when I *turn back* Israel and then begin to *heal,* you have *harvested for yourself,* people of Gilead, the fruits of your brigandage, so, too, I will surrender Israel to Assyria and make you the first-fruits of those sent off.

Now, the ancient crimes are of a similar kind to those of the Jews against Christ; the God and Father called the whole of Israel to opt in the future to adopt a better mentality, to cease worshiping according to the Law and choose instead the new form that is according to the Gospel. But they raised considerable op-

---

1. This sentence in Cyril's text incorporates elements of both the final verse of chapter 6 and the first verse of the next chapter.

position to those who were converted and who called them to *healing;* Scripture says, "The Jews had already agreed that anyone who confessed him to be the Messiah would be put out of the synagogue." And the leaders among them heard the words, "Woe to you, scribes and Pharisees, hypocrites, for taking away the key of knowledge; you neither go in nor allow those going in to go in."[2] So they were given over to the foe, and paid a harsh penalty for their intoxicated frenzy against Christ.

The iniquity of Ephraim will be revealed, and the wickedness of Samaria, because they were responsible for falsehood. A thief will gain entrance to him, a brigand robbing him on his way, with the result that they will be of one voice, as though singing together in their hearts (vv. 1–2). The Lord of all is surely good and longsuffering by nature, "patient and rich in mercy";[3] as long as he continues to be patient with the fallen, however, their crimes are somehow still covered over. But when he takes vengeance, calls us to account, and (152) does not persist in showing mildness, they then become obvious and seem to be laid bare, as if he likes them to be publicized and made visible to the eyes of all. This is what he is saying will happen also in the case of *Ephraim* and *Samaria.* You should take *Ephraim* here to mean the royal tribe in Samaria, from which came Jeroboam and those after him, and by *Samaria* the people in Samaria, that is, the ten tribes. He says their sins *will be revealed* for the following reasons: *because they were responsible for falsehood,* practicing a spiritless and out-of-date worship and manufacturing idols, as I said, and because *a thief* (that is, a brigand) *will gain entrance to him;* that is, a thief entered, stayed on, and caused havoc in his home, *robbing him on his way.* The purpose in this, he is saying, is that it may be clear that they are *singing together in their hearts,* meaning, *of one voice* and one mind. Some, in fact, made raids on those wanting to go up to Jerusalem; others shared their crimes with them, participating in their sacrilegious plundering.[4]

2. Jn 9.22; Lk 11.52.
3. Jl 2.13.
4. Cyril is loath to admit obscurity in the text (in both Heb. and LXX in this case), persisting in his efforts to provide some (creative) historical reference before moving to the New Testament.

The leaders of the Jews also rejoiced when those believing in Christ were under attack, and became participants in the assault and brigandage of others, taking delight in the persecution of the faithful. They welcomed Satan into their mind and *heart* as a kind of *brigand*, who robbed their mind of any pious feelings, so that they also were united in *heart* with him. In fact, just as "anyone united to the Lord becomes one in spirit with him,"[5] in the same way, in my view, anyone united to Satan will have one *heart* with him.

I remember all their vices; now their schemes have enveloped them; they have happened before my very eyes: As long as our sins are tolerable and within moderation, (153) human as we are and naturally inclined to sin,[6] God in his natural lovingkindness overlooks them; he knows, in fact, "he knows our making, he remembers that we are dust," as the psalmist says.[7] If, on the other hand, something grave, extraordinary, and truly intolerable is committed by us, which at the time even exhausts the very leniency of the Judge, and, as it were, brings him reluctantly to a state of wrath, then he comes to a recollection, so to speak, of everyone's faults. Consequently, the text says of Ephraim and Samaria, *I remember all their vices.* Now, this is probably what the prophetic oracle means to suggest to us in this verse, saying, While I lovingly passed over the slaughter by Levi of those who perished in Shechem on account of the rape of Jacob's daughter Dinah, yet since they are killing now as well, *I shall remember* also their former iniquities and call them to account as harsh and murderous for their former sins. *Their schemes have enveloped them,* in fact, as if he were to say, "They are now under siege from their own desires and unholy thoughts"; while at that time they killed the men of Shechem by guile and deceit, now it is with brigandage, even though they were turning to God. Since their sins are now beyond the bounds of reason and *have happened before my very eyes*— that is, I will not overlook such viciousness, nor put it out of my sight—I shall finally punish them.

5. 1 Cor 6.17.
6. This admission of a natural disposition to sin would not be so readily conceded by the Antiochenes, who prefer to attribute sin to free will than to human nature.
7. Ps 103.14.

COMMENTARY ON HOSEA 7   153

Their schemes have enveloped Jews, even in what was done against Christ. They killed the prophets, remember, while God was still longsuffering; but when they became murderers of the Lord, *their schemes enveloped them,* and the God of all *remembers all their vices.* (154)

By their wicked deeds they gladdened kings, and by their falsehoods rulers (v.3). Those who do good, he is saying, and opt for a lawful life should by preference win over their Redeemer and *gladden* their Savior, whose energies are directed invincibly to that end. Instead of doing this, however, they proved very indifferent about what was necessary in their own case for life and useful for prosperity, and so had no worries about offending God. Instead, they flattered their own *kings* and leaders, *gladdening* them by a concerted drive towards everything that pleased them, and bestowing on the deceivers by way of pleasure and satisfaction what was offensive to God. Once again he charges them with being in concert with Jeroboam and the rulers subject to him, and conniving at [Jeroboam's] plans for the abomination of the golden heifers and his wish to bring others sacrilegiously to a different form of worship. It was necessary, you see, it was necessary for the sincerity of love for God to offer noble resistance to their plans and very faulty schemes, and to try to obstruct their insane attempts, not to *gladden* them by readily joining them in commendation.

The sentiment is true, even if applied in turn to those who crucified Emmanuel; uttering falsehood and calumny against him, they took pains to gladden Herod, Pontius Pilate, and the heads of the synagogue. The divinely inspired Peter, remember, said somewhere to the God and Father of all, "In truth, there were gathered together in this city against your servant Jesus, whom you anointed, Herod and Pontius Pilate, together with the gentiles and the peoples of Israel."[8] (155)

They are all adulterers, like a pan heated for cooking with heat from the flame, from the kneading of the dough until it is leavened. A day of your kings (vv.4–5). In this he explains clearly to us in what way they gladdened their kings with wicked deeds and their rulers

---

8. Acts 4.27.

with falsehood. The facts correspond to this explanation; if you are familiar with them, you will have a complete grasp of the sense of the prophecy.[9] At the separation of the ten tribes, then, when the accursed Jeroboam ruled over them, he was greatly afraid that somehow by going up to Jerusalem for the festivals prescribed by the Law they would shortly transfer their allegiance back to Judah, and by recollecting their former ways they would do away with him, or eject him against his will from rule over them. For this reason the ungodly wretch took steps to consecrate the golden heifers for them, devised the forms of sacrilegious idolatry, and tried to reorganize the festivals around the heifers, according to the account given in the Hebrews' tradition. In the beginning, therefore, there was considerable fear that by advocating the original worship acceptable to the ancestors they might expel him from the throne or even do away with him, as I said, and by reversing the novelty they might choose to return to the initial situation, justifiably distressed and outraged at the offense to Moses and their trampling of the divine commandment.[10] Consequently, being an avid schemer,[11] he set a great number in Israel babbling and claiming that they had to make calves, reorganize the festivals, and petition the king for this. When he learned that the mob (156) was ready for this, and gave favor and support to those recommending it, he assembled everyone and openly proclaimed that they should adore the golden heifers, and set the day of the festival, the fifteenth day of the eighth month, as Scripture records.[12]

When Jeroboam said as much, the mob gave their commendation, and cried out, This is the king's day, and we shall support his idea; and they were bent on bringing joy to his heart by other such compliments. Those appointed as leaders were in concert

---

9. This is Cyril's simple rubric for grasping the *nous* of a text: find the *historia* behind it (even if this has to be arrived at creatively, as in the present case).

10. Theodoret may have acquired his commitment to conciseness by noting Cyril's failures in this regard.

11. The PG text refers to Jeroboam here as a fox.

12. 1 Kgs 12.32–33. In the interests of developing *historia* (he claims), Cyril proceeds to gild the lily. The story he tells he attributes to "the tradition of the Hebrews," which (in the absence of biblical corroboration) he does not document.

with the mob, lending their support and commendation. It is a reference to these the present text gives us in saying prophetically, *They are all adulterers, like a pan heated for cooking with heat from the flame.* In other words, they assented to the spiritual adultery, or apostasy from God, which is adultery. They were like *heated pans* ready for cooking anything you put in, surrounded by *flame,* which is obviously heat and, as it were, burning desire. They were also like *kneading of the dough,* which already has the leaven but is completely *leavened* on the *day of their king;* when, as I said just now, Jeroboam said boldly that they should sacrifice to the heifers and celebrate the festivals in connection with them, they shouted, "This is the *day of the king,*" as the traditional account reports, as I said.[13] Then it was that it was *leavened* completely, that is, it was completely in the grip of impiety. They were therefore *heated* in advance by their ardor in transgressing and by unrestrained desires, and *leavened* in advance in this same fashion, as it were, *on the day of the king,* and thus descended to the depths of depravity. (157)

Jews likewise committed some such offense against Christ; they misrepresented his reputation, and the scribes and the Pharisees gradually drew the mob away from love for him, thus being guilty of spiritual adultery, and turning the masses from him.[14]

Rulers began to seethe with wine, they stretched out their hands with pests, because their hearts were heated like a pan (vv.5–6). By *wine* here he probably means that from the vine of Sodom[15] that inebriates hearts, disturbs the mind, and fills it with ruinous and abominable gloom. When some people began to regret the reorganization involving the heifers and festivals, some of the rulers were moved to anger. In case the vast number of those who kept silence and who could not bring themselves to be complimentary

---

13. The plausibility of Cyril's "traditional" account is further undercut by the different division of the verses in Heb. and even LXX apart from the Antiochenes, who also (but much more vaguely) see a reference to Jeroboam.
14. Cyril has got so caught up in a "factual" reference of his own making that he has hardly a word on the spiritual interpretation. Perhaps Theodore misled him by his division of verses and mention of Jeroboam; but both Antiochenes avoided Cyril's elaboration.
15. Dt 32.32.

should seem to have better sense, *they stretched out their hands* to the mob, crying out still more loudly, "This is the day of the king," and adopted the forms of sacrilege. In their inebriation, therefore, they grew angry with unholy intoxication, and gnashed their teeth at those who did not rush to join in such vile practices, *stretching out* their *hands to pests*, meaning by *pests* the mob; they applauded them, as I said, despite being obliged to lead them to piety and open up the path that led to their benefit. Instead, their *hearts* were on fire, and they spoke, since they had welcomed into their mind the destructive flame of a desire for transgression.[16]

By toppling them all night Ephraim was overcome by sleep. Morning came, and it was enkindled like a fiery flame (v.6). I said that the ungodly Jeroboam was very fearful, (158) still entertaining only thoughts of sacrilegious exploits; he believed in fact, and with good reason, that Israel would be angered to discover something of the sort, and would not treat as a matter of no importance the violation of the ancestral customs. But when he proclaimed to the mob that they should worship the heifers, and they for their part gladly acceded to his idea and applauded it along with the rulers, choosing that way of thinking and behaving as though upright and beneficial, he abandoned his reservations and dismissed his suspicions, and from then on he was optimistic and luxuriating in his satisfaction. *By toppling them*, therefore—that is, at that time when they succumbed to ruin and destruction, aiding and abetting him, and endorsing transgression of love for God—then, he says, *Ephraim* (that is, Jeroboam, who was of the tribe of Ephraim)[17] *was overcome by sleep all night*. It was as if to say that, despite being kept awake by his reservations and suspicions to this point, he dismissed his worries, then enjoyed himself, lying on a soft bed *all night*. In the *morning*, however, he was hotter than everyone else, being *enkindled like a fiery flame*, and warmed to the task along with the mob, thinking there was no reason for

---

16. Where the Antiochene commentators are concise in their comments on these obscure verses, even in Theodoret's case declining to offer a version, Cyril seems to relish the task of developing a creative commentary.

17. The mention of Ephraim, which encourages Cyril to see Jeroboam in focus, comes from the LXX's confusing it with a similar Heb. form rendered by some modern commentators as "baker," and as "fury" by others.

delay, and instead ardently putting into effect the demonstration of his unholy exploits.

All their hearts were inflamed like a pan, and it consumed their judges. All their kings fell, there was no one of their number to invoke me (v.7). So it was true as I said: those around the accursed Jeroboam warmed to the task, and were "enkindled like a fiery flame" (v.6). So surely the extent of their impiety did not match his crimes? Quite the contrary, he says: *all were inflamed,* and (159) his successors as well, and the destructive fire of such ardor consumed all *their judges,* destroying as well all those who reigned after him. In fact, *there was no one of their number* who wished to adore me, deigned to implore the God of all, and enjoyed the privilege of true knowledge of God.

Ephraim himself was mingled with his peoples. Ephraim was a loaf unturned (v.8). He thoroughly censures those from the tribe of Ephraim invested with royal status over Israel in Samaria for adopting an attitude no better than that of the masses under their control. Instead, he says, they were in total agreement with them and easily allied with them despite their duty as leaders to guide them on the path to goodness and with more elevated aspirations to be seen to conduct them to salvation. Instead of doing so, however, they joined their ranks, all afflicted with one and the same folly, and in addition persistence in depravity and an incorrigible mindset that in no way repented of whatever they chose to do, even if it was a source of ruin and led to their destruction. So he says *Ephraim was a loaf unturned,* a metaphor from the baking of loaves on stones; if no one *turns* them, they get completely burnt, and are then found to be useless, and the foodstuff is lost to excessive heating.

Foreigners devoured his strength without his knowing. His hair turned grey without his knowing (v.9). By *foreigners* he refers to those of other tribes and races, (160) namely, Persians and the neighboring peoples, Moabites and Idumeans, and the Syrian nations, who, as it were, devoured Ephraim. Since he had said it was like a loaf, he continued the metaphor, calling its innumerable population its *strength;* the tribe of Ephraim was particularly numerous, and took great pride in this, believing it would be frightening and invincible to the Assyrian leaders and generals. When they declared war against it and came on the scene, however, it was easily consumed and taken captive. *Without his knowing,* however, he says; that is, it did not realize the cause of its misfortune, although it should have come to an appreciation of it if only from what befell it; what is not seen experience often brings to our notice. While it is better to consider what is to our advantage without waiting for experience, yet should we happen to fail in this, there remains for the sufferers the possibility of grasping what is necessary and useful from experience itself. It was therefore *without* Ephraim's *knowing,* despite *his hair turning grey,* that is, after a long life failed to give sufficient instruction and to persuade it to learn how such a fate befell it. Because it offended the one able to save it, it was caught up in dire and unexpected troubles.

Israel's insolence will be humbled in his sight. They did not turn back to the Lord their God, and did not seek him in all this (v.10). He explains clearly what he said; why Ephraim did not know, despite his "hair turning grey" (v.9), he proceeds to clarify. *Israel's insolence,* (161) he says—that is, its apostasy, with which it was afflicted through arrogance that led it to its being devoted to other gods and dishonoring the one who is God by nature and in truth—*will be reversed in his sight.* As if he were to say that it was the source of insolence and dishonor to him, which is a kind of reversal in someone's sight. Despite suffering this fate, however, it still did not acknowledge God; being hardhearted and inflexible, incurably hostile to God and obviously in a desperate condition, it gave no importance to turning to him. It was a crime of utter insensitivity, and clear proof of inveterate stupidity.

Ephraim was like a mindless dove with no heart; it called upon Egypt and went to Assyria. As they go, I shall cast my net over them, I shall bring them down like the birds of heaven, I shall correct them by the report of their tribulation (vv.11–12). It is necessary to recall once again what is written in the second book of Kings; we shall thus easily understand the sense of our text. Hoshea son of Elah became king in Samaria over Israel. Shalmaneser the Assyrian sent messengers to him, imperiously demanding the customary gifts with the intention, as it were, of imposing a tribute on Israel. Declining subjugation, however, he gave attention rather to resistance, even if he was choosing to involve Israel in war. He then sent envoys to So the ruler in Egypt to ask for his assistance, thinking that with his help he would escape the hand of the Assyrian. The latter was extremely offended by this, (162) and declared war on Israel. Hoshea then became his slave, and Israel was taken captive and deported with him from Samaria.[18] So *Ephraim was like* the most *mindless dove,* lacking true simplicity—hence Christ's saying, "Be as wise as serpents and as simple as doves."[19] In other words, simplicity of behavior and free thinking would rightly be held in high esteem, whereas when intelligence is missing, simplicity is a liability and is actually stupidity. Ephraim was *mindless,* therefore. How, and in what way? *It called upon Egypt,* but *went off in captivity to Assyria,* since So lacked the resources to help. How would it not have been better for it, then, to look for consideration, not that which is from human beings but that which is from on high and is invincible? Accordingly, the God of all said in the verse from Isaiah, "Alas for those who go down to Egypt for help, those who trust in horses and in chariots."[20] Now, the fact that it was not without God's decision that the hand of their allies proved weak he demonstrated by saying that wherever they go, he would *bring them down* like sparrows, *casting over them* a kind of *net* or snare, not allowing them to be arrogant, but bringing them down to earth from the heights, as it were, from lofty and conceited notions to a compassionate and measured mentality befitting those subject to the enemy.

He next says, *I shall correct them by the report of their tribulation,* wishing to suggest as much, in my view. In other words, rumors of what would befall them preceded the experience of it, and the report completely terrified those in Samaria. So they were *corrected* by hearing of the degree of *tribulation* that would come to them. Had they been wise, this would have been sufficient for their conversion; but being very hard of heart, (163) they were not troubled even by the actual experience, being inflexible and unbending, with their mind seriously diseased with unbelief.

Woe to them, because they have strayed from me. They are in a wretch-

---

18. 2 Kgs 17.1–6.   19. Mt 10.16.
20. Is 31.1.

ed state because of their impious behavior to me (v.13). The fact that their forsaking God was the basis of their troubles he makes clear to us in this as well. In other words, just as people with bodily illness prove responsible for it and succumb to the severity of the ailments if they do not admit physicians and the remedies that would be capable of alleviating their sufferings, so, too, we shall commit serious wrong if we remove ourselves from the love of God, since nothing saves the person who offends God. Because they forsook God, therefore, they are consequently *wretched* and *accursed*; they have been guilty of impious behavior, at least by adoring false gods and according them reverence, and so will be subject to *woes*. After all, as Scripture says, "if God shuts the door on anyone, who will open up to them?"[21]

I redeemed them, but they told lies against me. Their hearts did not cry out to me; instead, they wailed on their beds; they gashed themselves for grain and wine (vv.13–14). He once again emphasizes the fact that he inflicts punishment commensurate with each person's sins. They had slandered the God who redeemed them and led them out of the house of bondage "with a mighty hand and uplifted arm," as Scripture says,[22] and rescued them from oppression by the Egyptians. *They told lies* about his glory, according the unclean demons and the products of their own hands the praise for benefits they had received (164) by making the calves in the wilderness, as if saying dementedly by way of sacrilegious insult to the Redeemer, "These are your gods, O Israel, who led you out of the land of Egypt."[23] So it was now an insult and frenzy against God, and an open curse, to accord reverence to images and demons, offer thanksgiving to them, and direct to them the pre-eminent degree of glory. They not only slandered God, as I just said, but also denied the view that it is from him that the necessities of life come to living things in the world; *their hearts did not cry out to me*, he says—that is, they looked for nothing from me, despite feeling and believing that I am the supplier and giver of every good. Now, from this we understand that God does not require a *cry*, but rather a disposition of mind and heart.

Instead of *crying out to God*, therefore, they even turned with-

21. Jb 12.14.   22. Dt 4.34.
23. Ex 32.9.

out restraint to fleshly abuses to the extent of *wailing on their beds*. The practice is an example of vile habits, an unchecked inclination to debauchery, and a deviant bent towards pleasures. Being involved in such vile and loathsome practices would befit only people intent upon imposing on men the manners, dress, and voices of women. Such transvestites in their extreme effeminacy plumb the depths of human impurity. This, in my view,[24] is the reference in his saying *they gashed themselves for grain and wine;* by giving thanks to their idols for the produce of the fields—namely, *grain* and the fruit of the vine—they meant to celebrate the so-called rites of initiation. As though possessed and driven mad, they slashed their chest and both hands so as even to (165) offer their own blood, as it were, to the graven images and thus become guilty of extreme ungodliness. It is perhaps to such people that another prophet is referring in the ironic words, "Sacrifice human beings: there are no calves left."[25] Such practices sufficed to offend in a particular way the God of all in his great power, to whom they should instead have made thanksgiving offerings rather than ill-advisedly accord the glory due to him to sticks and stones.

They were trained by me, I strengthened their right arms, and they devised evil plans against me. They turned away to nothing, they became like an unstretched bow (vv.15–16). He attaches to them another form of their ingratitude, emphasizing their being sacrilegious and slothful. I, for my part, he is saying, despite their being formerly no better disposed than brute beasts and quite unintelligent, *trained* them with the Law and made them wise, aware of their own good and the way of righteousness, and not ignorant of the practice of complete orderliness, so that even at that stage they took pleasure in saying of themselves, "Happy are we, O Israel, for we know what is pleasing to the Lord."[26] The effects of my generosity to them did not stop there: I made them strong, quite capable of opposing any adversary wishing to make war; they conquered great and mighty nations without difficulty.

---

24. Commentators ancient and modern guess what practices are being referred to, whether those documented in 1 Kgs 18.28 and Jer 16.6 or (with Theodoret and perhaps Cyril here) pagan excesses.
25. The same prophet in fact: Hos 13.2.
26. Bar 4.4.

To me, however, the God who gave them such wonderful things, they proved *evil*, that is, scornful and disloyal; the direction of their *turning away* was *to nothing*, an image handmade from once-living wood was a *nothing*. If they had discovered something better, their offense would probably have made some sense; (166) but since such things were absolutely *nothing* compared with God, only an example of silliness and stupidity and the like, their turning away made no sense and had no plausible explanation. *They turned away to nothing*, therefore, and in addition became also *like an unstretched bow*, not reined in by repentance, not restraining the tendency that carried them to such awful shame and absurdity.

Now, it should be realized that other translators rendered it, "They became like a bow stretched backwards,"[27] the reference thus being again to Israel's committing some crime; whereas like a bow they should have been stretched against the foe, and, concentrating on discharging tautly in opposition, they failed to notice that they were severely striking themselves, as it were, with arrows from the bows. In other words, by offending God, in the aforementioned ways, what else were they involved in doing than arming their hands against themselves?

Now, the text could be taken, if you like, in another way as well: the God of all, so to speak, drew Israel as his own *bow* in battle with the devil's tyranny and in opposition to the deceit of idol worship. Israel alone of all the nations throughout the world, you see, in the Law's view, rejected worship of the idols and adhered to the one who is by nature and in truth Lord of all. But those who should have done so went instead in the opposite direction, warring against God for the sake of the glory of the idols; so "they became like a bow stretched backwards," shooting in the opposite direction.

Their rulers will fall by the sword on account of the indiscipline of their tongue. The effects of his wrath will not be directed, he is saying, only against those subject to the leaders, but will overtake—and very fiercely, too—those who normally enjoy the highest honors. *They will fall by the sword*, in fact, and the intemperance of

---

27. It is not from Jerome or Theodore that Cyril derives this rare reference to the alternative translators.

their tongue will be the occasion for their meeting that fate. It is truly a case of *indiscipline* "to say to a tree, you are my God, and to a stone, you begot me."²⁸ Now, such things could very properly be applied to Emmanuel, against whom the scribes and Pharisees directed their *undisciplined tongue*, despite his correcting and "strengthening" them (v.15)—in a spiritual fashion, that is; they took no notice, and "turned away to nothing" (v.16), preferring "human precepts as doctrines."²⁹ "They became like a bow stretched backwards,"³⁰ shooting sacrilegiously at their Lord, for whom they should have nobly fought and tried to vanquish the opposition, like the true disciples of the believers.

28. Jer 2.27.
29. Is 29.13; Mt 15.9. In a manner reminiscent of Didymus, who often passes over a text for a piece of scriptural documentation that becomes his principal text (see Hill, FOTC 111, Introduction, 11), Cyril here has developed the alternative version of the verse and found a christological dimension in it instead of in his set text.
30. Cf. v.16, above.

COMMENTARY ON HOSEA,
CHAPTER EIGHT

This is their grumbling in their bosom in the land of Egypt. Like land, like an eagle in the house of the Lord, in repayment for breaking my covenant and transgressing my Law (v.1).

HILE THIS IS expressed very unclearly in the Hebrew, in my view, causing translators much difficulty, we shall follow the order of the ideas, and state what strikes us.[1] Accordingly, *this is their grumbling in the land of Egypt;* that is, although I constantly saved and instructed them, and made them invincible to their adversaries (I empowered them, in fact), they grumbled in unholy fashion, according worship to demons and even putting their trust in the land of Egypt in the belief that it would suffice for their prosperity and assistance. Consequently, the enterprise will be thrust back *in their bosom,* (168) and they will have no good outcome to their temerity; instead, they will, as it were, get their just deserts *in their bosom.* There will come, in fact, he says, there will come the one who will ravage them, the ruler of the Assyrians, with a company of warriors beyond number; he will come to them like a whole *land* or country or fatherland, so that one might think that the entire country of the Medes and Persians was totally transported and moved to Samaria—hence *like land.*

He will also come *like an eagle in the house of the Lord,* that is, he will fly up with speed and terror even against the very Temple of God, and assault the kingdom of Judah and Jerusalem, seizing it

---

1. The Heb. is indeed "unclear," leading modern commentators to amend it (an option not open to Cyril), and the LXX offers a range of versions. The waters are further muddied by the conjunction here of the previous chapter's final clause with the opening of this one. Cyril is never one to shirk such a problem, despite being unable to resolve strictly exegetical problems of the history of the text.

without difficulty and taking it off to his own country. You see, while the country of the Samaritans was the first to be devastated, and with it Israel in particular, later as well the celebrated city was also taken, which the prophet Jeremiah lamented in the words, "How lonely sits the city that was full of people! Though a ruler among countries, she has become a tributary."[2] There is no doubt, in fact, that the Temple was burnt along with the city. He says that this will happen to them *for breaking* the divine *covenant and transgressing the Law* that was given; they set little store at all by the oracles given through Moses in his wisdom, and were zealous about living by their own desires, each of them suiting himself about worship and law.

They will cry out to me, O God, we know you. Because Israel rejected good things, they pursued the enemy (vv.2–3). They had "gashed themselves for grain and wine,"[3] performed feasts for the unclean demons, had not cried out in their hearts to God, nor acknowledged the one who was giver and controller of their complete (169) satisfaction, and instead had not even honored him with due thanksgiving, especially since they did not recognize him in the extent of their prosperity. When they experience the necessary consequences and meet the harsh and ineluctable result of their own folly, however, they will *cry out* and finally call upon me, being overwhelmed by terrible and intolerable misfortunes. Accepting the experience of their actual calamities in order to learn from it, they will then allege their own guilelessness, saying as much: *Israel rejected good things*. Though it was possible, in fact, to have these things, even in rich measure, by depending on God, they eagerly devoted themselves to following their own will, and *they pursued the enemy*, that is, as it were, willingly they went after the enemy and became subject to those who hated the God who always saved them and rendered them superior to their adversaries, thus grieving him by their infidelities. It was therefore most wise and truly beneficial not to wait for experience of the calamities, but rather to obviate its coming, and beforehand strive to consider the benefit.

They reigned as kings for themselves, and not through me; they gov-

2. Lam 1.1.
3. 7.14.

erned, and they did not make it known to me. With their silver and their gold they made idols for themselves for their own destruction (v.4). He disowns the kingship of Jeroboam and those who succeeded him in reigning over Israel in Samaria despite his having openly said, "This word came from me." This was after having threatened Solomon himself for following his preferences for foreign wives, and for sacrilegiously erecting altars in their honor, in the words, "I shall tear your kingdom and give it (170) to your servant."[4] What shall we say, then—that the God of all is a liar? Perish the thought! Rather, we shall direct ourselves to thinking correctly, taking the following viewpoint. Scripture says, remember, "Surely there will be no trouble (by 'trouble' meaning 'abuse') in the city that the Lord did not cause?"[5] In other words, while he himself of his own volition conducts his affairs, he allows some things to happen to punish some people, even if they are done in some fashion against his will. On the other hand, though he is able to hinder them, he often within the divine plan permits them to happen, being himself called the agent of them. Let us take Solomon as an example: [God] allowed him to build the Temple of stone in Jerusalem, and made him wise and incomparably conspicuous for intelligence, this being an effect of his free will. He allowed his kingdom to be torn in two, not personally conducting the affair by his own wishes, but, as it were, maintaining silence even in these ill-advised proceedings on account of his displeasure with him.

Therefore, even if Jeroboam became king like his successors, it was not with God's complete acquiescence; the effects of his wrath that befell some of them by way of retribution are susceptible of a different interpretation, and perhaps should not be understood as if they were completely in accord with his will. Accordingly, it says, *They reigned as kings for themselves, and not through me;* and although *they governed,* it was without God's knowledge, being against his will and apparently without his knowing; the

---

4. 1 Kgs 12.24; 11.11.
5. Am 3.6. This is an oft-cited text that commentators wrestle with to rationalize the paradox in its obvious sense. Chrysostom also dealt with it as bishop in Constantinople in a homily on Is 25.6–7, claiming, as Cyril does here, that "evil" in the text is not to be taken at face value; see Hill, *St John Chrysostom. Old Testament Homilies* 2 (Brookline, MA: Holy Cross Orthodox Press, 2003), 20–40.

government was weak and vulnerable, not ready to withstand rebellion, or save the subjects. "Through him kings reign, and through him rulers control the land."[6]

Now, the fact that in this they were the victims of extreme insensitivity, and through what was given by God they caused him great distress—or, rather, ruin to their own souls as well—he conveyed by saying, *With their silver and their gold they made idols for themselves for their own destruction.* You see, where they (171) could have been commended by showing compassion for their brethren, they offended God, and foolishly turned a means of salvation to inevitable destruction.

Get rid of your calf, Samaria; my anger is incensed against it: how long will they fail to be purified in Israel? A craftsman made it, and it is not God; hence your calf was a seducer, Samaria (vv.5–6). *Get rid of* is well put in the case of a stain, defilement, and extreme uncleanness, which was exactly what idol worship was, loathsome and evil-smelling, rendering a person's soul odious to God. Being compassionate and kind, therefore, he advises them to take a turn for the better, avert wrath, thus quell the cause of what would befall them, and by repentance repel calamity, if only by finally coming to their senses. *Against it,* in fact, obviously refers to his being incensed by the calf, showing that while sometimes he appears kindly and presents failings as the result of human weakness, he definitely punishes infidelity, and takes as insupportable the tendency of the insolent—namely, to adore the demons. After all, being guilty of uncleanness, how long could you remain unrepentant? What moment would be required for dismissing their folly? You believe the work of a *craftsman*'s hand to be a god, after all; and what is of no benefit—or, rather, is productive of destruction and ruin—you regard as venerable and acceptable. *The calf was a seducer,* in fact, and nothing else. (172)

They sowed seed spoiled by wind, and their overthrow will receive it; their sheaf lacks the potency to make flour, but if they do make it, foreigners will eat it (v.7). By a comparison with those laboring in vain as farmers, he suggests the fruitlessness of the false advice and the futile exertion to be found in them. Some people's working at it

---

6. Prv 8.15–16.

and sometimes showing careful devotion and honor by offerings and sacrifices would be nothing other than gathering grain *spoiled by the wind,* which is incapable of bringing the laborer any benefit at all. After all, what return is there for devotion to idol worship? Or what benefit from statues? Or how do some people find joy in what is definitely bound for overthrow? So those who are in the habit of practicing such things and devoting their attention to the honor of the idols are like people *sowing seed spoiled by wind,* and a *sheaf* of stalks containing no grain, which is not made into *flour.* If, on the other hand, anything came from them, that is, if somehow they seemed to be zealous and genuine in the practice of the error, this, too, would be done by them for *foreigners,* and would in no way bring joy to God (by *foreigners* referring to the false gods).

Our efforts among those who offend God are therefore completely without reward, and forms of clemency are completely and utterly abhorred by him because they fall short of the pursuit of good.[7] (173)

Israel is swallowed up; now in the midst of the nations it is like a useless vessel, because they went up to the Assyrians. Ephraim germinated on its own; it loved gifts. Hence they will be surrendered to the nations (vv.9–10). He says Israel has been *swallowed up,* like a pitiable shipwreck, submerged under the waves of its own sins, and smashed as though by some rock propelled by divine wrath. Or according to another interpretation, he means that it is *swallowed up* by Nebuchadnezzar as though by some terrible and implacable dragon. In fact, another of the holy prophets, speaking to us in the person of Israel, already captive and enslaved by its captors, says, "He consumed me; he tore me in pieces; a fine gloom laid hold of me. Nebuchadnezzar king of Babylon swallowed me like a dragon; he filled his belly with my delicacies."[8] In still another way it is true that the many-headed dragon gulps down in some way those who abandon love for God and makes them his

---

7. Cyril's fourth tome is concluded here. He seems to be taking a hard line on well-intentioned efforts to work with the misguided even in his readers' own community—a rigorism not typical of his approach to texts.

8. Jer 58.34. While Jeremiah has in mind Nebuchadnezzar attacking Judah, Hosea is referring to Israel falling to the Assyrians, although Cyril does not say so.

own food; the verse from the psalmist speaks of it as food given to the Ethiopian peoples: "You crushed the head of the dragon; you gave him as food for the Ethiopian peoples."⁹ Those who have in themselves a mind that is pitch-black and lacking light could (174) rightly be understood and referred to by us ourselves and by God as Ethiopians; they feed the many-headed dragon, and they in turn feed off him.

Accordingly, *Israel is swallowed up, and is in the midst of the nations like a useless vessel;* when carried off *to the Assyrians* and Medes, it was rendered completely useless, perhaps by being forced to think as the Assyrians and Medes wished. Or because it was *like a useless vessel*, it was consequently also *swallowed up;* leaving its homeland, it went off to the nations. The Lord of all says as much also in the statement of Jeremiah about one of the kings over Israel in Samaria: "Jeconiah was dishonored like a pot for which there is no use, because it was rejected and cast out into a land which it did not know. O land, land, listen to the word of the Lord, register this man as a banished person."¹⁰ So Israel was rendered *useless;* after all, what use is a soul that forsakes God, is in love with sin, and easily strays to anything wrongful at all and to what is worse than all evils, desertion of service of God? What, then, was the cause of Israel's suffering such a fate? *Because they went up to the Assyrians,* as if he were to say, they willingly betook themselves to the foe. How, and in what way? Dreading an attack by them, they did not repent and seek help from God, but instead won them over with bribes to gain a brief respite.

He then mocks such an idea as likely to be futile and useless for them, referring to the kings from the tribe of Ephraim who even sent gifts to the rulers of the Assyrians in this way: *Ephraim germinated on its own.* It is as if he were to say: The king from the tribe of Judah, like a trunk destined to be cut down and, as it were, (175) consumed by the fire of divine wrath, *germinated on its own,* that is, without me;¹¹ though having no breath of life

---

9. Cf. Ps 74.14.
10. Jer 22.28–30. Again, as the reference to Jeconiah shows (alternative name of Jehoiachin, brother of Jehoiakim, though not noted as such in Cyril's commentary), Jeremiah is referring to Judah's king in the sixth century (rather than the author's focus, Israel).
11. In explicating these verses Cyril has been at pains to unpack the author's

from me, it would live and send its root deep, and not lose its throne. It bought itself some time and slight delay in the troubles, *loving gifts*—not to receive them but to give them. What was the result of it? No good; instead, *they will be surrendered to the nations,* and would learn from the very events befalling them that one does not *germinate on* one's *own,* nor would any benefit come to those offending God from giving gifts to the foe. They will in fact pay the penalty, and before long.

Now I shall receive them, and they will shortly grow weary of anointing a king and rulers (v.10). Those from the tribe of Ephraim that reigned over them were responsible for Israel's depravity in its entirety, so to speak. The accursed Jeroboam, in fact, was the first to instigate the apostasy by setting up for them the golden heifers, and by appointing for the "high places"—that is, the groves on mountains and hills—priests not from the tribe of Levi but rather any who "tried their hand," as Scripture says. Later, when the Assyrians were expected during the reign of Menahem, they sent money to persuade them to leave the country.[12]

Consequently, the divine threat was rightfully leveled at the monarchy of the tribe of Ephraim that ruled over Israel. *Now I shall receive them,* he says, note, not as though they were keeping to the right path, or choosing to live a good life, or longing to follow the way of life according to the Law; rather, I shall act as a corrector, requiring an account and summoning them to judgment. Out of clemency I postponed the effects of divine wrath (176) in times past, but *now I shall receive them* in order that they may finally know by experience of the calamities that they are subject to the Lord and not beyond my power. The fact that the effects of his wrath would no longer be delayed he confirmed by saying *now.* So by being *received* for the purpose of correction they will then stop *anointing a king and rulers;* after all, when enslaved to Assyrians and Medes, what opportunity would they have to continue the process of apostasy, constantly bewailing and lamenting the unexpected misfortune?

---

imagery, and makes no exception of this one—unfortunately: the LXX has seen the verb "germinate" in a similar Heb. form for "wild donkey," which is intended as a pun on "Ephraim."

12. 1 Kgs 13.33; 2 Kgs 15.19.

COMMENTARY ON HOSEA 8

Now, it should be realized that after Cyrus son of Cambyses released Israel from captivity, they no longer anointed those from the tribe of Ephraim in Samaria, but were all under one yoke, namely, that of the kings of the tribe of Judah in Jerusalem; no longer divided, they all dwelt in Jerusalem. After the period of captivity Zerubbabel son of Shealtiel of the tribe of Judah was the first to exercise kingship over both, namely, Israel and Judah—in short, the twelve tribes.[13] The high priest Joshua son of Jozadak presided over the levitical ranks and administered high-priestly worship.

Because Ephraim multiplied altars sinfully, the altars were dear to him. I shall write down for him a multitude and his rituals. The altars they loved were devoted by him to foreign practices (vv.11–12). He explains the reason why those reigning had in the future to be deprived of their rule: *Ephraim* made a great number of *altars sinfully.* The verse refers firstly to Jeroboam, who became king from the tribe of Ephraim, and after him his successors, who (177) on every mountain and hill erected altars to the demons, and persuaded the people of Israel to offer sacrifice. Next, although they should have been distressed at such unlawful exploits, by which they *multiplied altars sinfully,* [the altars] even became *dear to them,* and furthermore they were *devoted by him to foreign practices*—namely, by Ephraim, to whom *the altars were dear,* meaning those positioned in the ancient tabernacle, or in Jerusalem in the divine Temple. There were two of them, one for offerings in the first tabernacle, the other of gold for incense in the second tabernacle inside.[14]

The crimes of the kings from Ephraim were therefore very numerous, firstly because they *multiplied altars sinfully,* then because [the altars] even became *dear,* things which they should have lamented and deplored as giving offense, and, still worse, as a deviation into folly, *the altars they loved* being *devoted to foreign practices* when they should have really loved and treated them as important. Now, inserted in the middle is the clause, *I shall write*

---

13. Not uncharacteristically, Cyril is somewhat astray in his historical detail: it was Judah, not Israel, that was released by Cyrus; Zerubbabel did not act as king, nor did the north join the south under his government.

14. Ex 40.26–29.

down for him a multitude and his rituals, suggesting something like this: the *multitude* of altars made sinfully and their *rituals,* namely, the sacrifices prescribed for them, or the times and forms of sacrifices on which they performed their profane rites ("they gashed themselves for grain and wine,"[15] remember, and the other things to which they gave themselves), *I shall write down* for them as crimes.

For salvation it is necessary, therefore, to cling to the divine altars and adhere to the things of God, and not to go after other things which are sinful. The latter in fact is what they do who do not live a truly Christian life,[16] lapsing, after the saving sacrament of baptism, into pagan customs and observances; (178) it behoves them to say what they find in Paul: "You cannot partake of the Lord's table and the demons' table."[17] To those who join forces with the sacrilegious heretics and partake of their altars belong *the altars that they loved and that were devoted to foreign practices;* they were *multiplied sinfully,* and they sacrifice the lamb outside the sacred and divine hall, namely, the church.

Because if they offer sacrifice and eat fat, the Lord will not accept it. He will now remember their iniquities and take vengeance on their sins (v.13). The fact that the sinful altars were made and multiplied by Ephraim he makes very clear also in this verse. He says, note, that they do not sacrifice to God; instead, offerings are made by them to the shrines of the idols; even if they celebrate with sacrifices, filled with food or drink, it has no relevance to God. In fact, they do not observe the festival, because what is done to the glory of demons the divine and untainted nature would in no way accept, but is rather provoked and insulted. It is as though God were reluctantly forced in this case to inflict the penalty of his wrath on those who provoke it, and then to recall, as it were, all the sins of the offenders. When this happens, his anger will be severe and his justice prompt, and there is no one who can escape it: "It is therefore a fearful thing to fall into the hands of the living God."[18] Rather, it behoves us, it is incomparably better

---

15. 7.14.
16. The verb used by Cyril here is *christianizô*.
17. 1 Cor 10.21. Cyril, unlike his fellow Alexandrian Didymus, does not refer frequently to Christian heretics or (as here) schismatics.
18. Heb 10.31.

and productive of complete satisfaction for us to offer to God sacrifices—clearly of the spiritual kind—and (179) celebrate festivals for him, choosing to live an upright life and zealously avoiding relapse of any kind.

They turned to Egypt, and will eat unclean food in Assyria. Once more he charges them with choosing to live a most foolish and ungodly life, and with being completely ignorant of the path leading to their benefit. For my part, he says, I threatened to subject now to my wrath those brought to such an extreme attitude, to avenge their sins and recall all their iniquities. What was expected to happen was in the initial stages, with war already terrifying Israel and, as it were, invading the country. Then, when they should have been propitiating God with prayers and repentance, been brought around to his will, and quelled his wrath with a turn for the better, something that would have been useful and capable of delivering them, *they turned to Egypt,* calling for help on "an Egyptian, a human being, not God, flesh of horses," as Scripture says. But "a king is not saved by great power, and a giant will not be saved by his vast strength. Deceptive is a horse for saving. It is better to trust in the Lord than to trust in a human being. It is better to hope in the Lord than to hope in rulers."[19] The fact that nothing of what they needed emerged from such ill-advised schemes, he says, they would learn from experience itself; deported to the Assyrians and Medes, *they would eat unclean food,* that is to say, they would pass their life rejecting any remnant of respect for the Law, and heedlessly eating what they came upon.

Perhaps, however, you will say, How would this have worried (180) the people of Israel if they had opted for idol worship? Our reply to this is that admittedly they had been deceived, but there was still some slight concern for the Law in their minds; they were not completely divorced from Jewish ways despite worshiping in the temples of the idols. Consequently, the blessed prophet Elijah also once charged them with limping on both legs, committed to following neither the Baal fully nor God completely. On becoming captive, therefore, Israel did not completely lose respect for the Law when of necessity following the ways

---

19. Is 31.3; Ps 33.16–17.

and laws of their masters. This, I think, is what Christ himself also said: "To the one who has, it will be given in abundance, but from the one who does not have, even what he seems to have will be taken from him."[20]

We must therefore not scorn the divine gifts, but rather set great store by what we have from God; the gift will be pleased to dwell in us when we show interest. If, by contrast, we prove indifferent and remiss about it, it will completely take its leave.

Israel forgot the one who made him; they built shrines, and Judah made fortified cities. I shall send fire on his cities, and it will consume their foundations (v.14). He rebukes both kingdoms, both that in Samaria and that of Judah, which is in Jerusalem; what both had done it is necessary to consider and explain. Since the outbreak of war was expected, and the terror was at the very doors, so to speak, (181) both those in Samaria and those reigning from the tribe of Judah needed to seek assistance from God the Savior; but they adopted a wrong and unhelpful attitude, and, though required to assuage him by repentance, they still further provoked the God who controls all things. Israel for its part—that is, the ten tribes and those of its members in charge—kept according greater worship to the demons as though they were offended and were capable of averting the captivity and routing the columns of the enemy. To appease them, as it were, and to make them benevolent, *they built shrines,* erected altars, and honored them with still further sacrifices. Judah, on the other hand, made their cities more fortified, trusting rather in stones, not God, despite his saying clearly about Jerusalem, "I shall be a wall of fire around it, says the Lord, and I shall be the glory in its midst."[21] While this was of no use to Israel, however, God threatened that in the future he would send *fire on the cities of Judah,* obviously when the Babylonians burned them, since they were agents of his wrath against them.

Nothing at all, therefore, will save the one who offends God. While trusting in the powers of the demons was admittedly then a waste of time and a crime of ignorance—or, rather, of extreme

---

20. 1 Kgs 18.21; Mt 25.29.
21. Zec 2.5.

impiety—no less ignorant is dabbling in appeals for earthly assistance when God is offended and alienated. There is need instead to allay his wrath with prayers and repentance; after all, he is "merciful and gracious, and relents from punishing," according to Scripture.[22] (182)

22. Jl 2.13. The final paragraph does not occur in the PG edition.

COMMENTARY ON HOSEA,
CHAPTER NINE

Do not rejoice, Israel, or be glad, as do the peoples, because you have been unfaithful to your God. You were fond of payment on every threshing floor. Threshing floor and wine vat did not know[1] them, and the wine deceived them. They did not inhabit the land of the Lord. Ephraim inhabited Egypt, and they will eat unclean food in Assyria. They did not pour libations to the Lord, and did not please him. Their sacrifices will be like their bread of mourning: all who eat it will be defiled, because their bread is for their own selves, it will not enter the house of the Lord (vv.1–4).

SINCE THE HORDES of the nations were affected by the greatest possible folly, deceived as they admittedly were, it was their custom when beginning farm work and on the point of ploughing the land to offer sacrifices to the demons and ask them for fertility for the fields. Likewise, when harvesting, as the season required, they put the grapes into the *wine vats* and poured out libations, sacrificed to the gods, and sang the vintage songs by way of thanksgiving offerings, and kept rejoicing and celebrating. God accuses the people of Israel of doing this, clearly implying they should not *rejoice* like the other nations. For what reason? While others were completely ignorant of the one who was by nature and in truth God, and were instead conceived in error, and perhaps had a plausible excuse for their malady, namely, ignorance, Israel, however, being schooled in the Law and having acknowledged the Lord of all, was guilty of infidelity and apostasy. So they could rightly be understood to be guilty of a more serious charge and to bear the inexcusable accusation of impiety. The one who knew the master's will, remember, but ignored it and did not carry it out, (183) will be severely beaten, whereas the one who did not know

---

1. Cyril is unaware that the LXX is reading "know" for a similar Heb. form "feed."

it, and therefore did not do it, will suffer a less severe beating, as the Savior says.²

Accordingly, he says, *Do not rejoice, as do the peoples:* while they have been deceived from the womb, you by contrast were schooled in the Law, and yet *you have been faithless to your God.* What was the form of its infidelity? It was *fond of payment,* not from God but rather from the heifers and Baal, despite their giving nothing to those who asked. Where did it seek *payment* from them? *On every threshing floor;* apparently it sacrilegiously and foolishly requested fertility for the fields, as I said, from the futile idols. While Israel actually asked for *payments* from the idols, then, were their requests answered? Not at all: *Threshing floor and wine vat did not know them, and the wine deceived them.* None of the more studious readers would be in any doubt that in Samaria there were lengthy periods of famine, infertility, and drought; so its hopes were disappointed, since it did not receive what it requested. Further, they left the holy land and went into *Egypt,* a land bolstering itself with still more gods; in Egypt, in fact, there were countless idols, and an extraordinary belief by their adherents in their being efficacious to the point of being easily able to do anything with their magical powers. They were therefore forbidden to *inhabit the land* chosen by God, and exchanged it for the country of idols. Even if they did so, however, they will go to *Assyria.*

They did not pour libations to the Lord: gathering the fruit of the vine in *wine vats,* they gave the initial vintage to the demons and not to God, its giver. They also offered *bread* by way of the firstfruits of the harvest; but this will be defilement and abomination, he says, and the offerings will be reckoned as *bread of mourning,* (184) that is, loathsome, profane, and odious. For what reason? The Law declared unclean a person who came close to a corpse, a closeness by way of blood relationship or even actual touching of the body.³ Family members were necessarily defiled, therefore, or friends of the deceased gathered about the corpse

---

2. Lk 12.47–48.
3. Nm 19.11; Lv 21.1–3. Theodore had failed to appreciate the reference to ritual uncleanness deriving from association with the dead as outlined in the Law.

in grief, who wanted to do what was prescribed for it; and everything they happened to touch was unclean. So the *bread of mourning*, then, was the bread set out as food for those mourning the corpse; even to taste it seemed fearsome for people anxious to avoid defilement from the corpse. Accordingly, he says, the *bread* itself was tainted and defiled for being offered as the first-fruits of the harvest, and those who *eat it will be defiled.* Instead, it will be useful *for their own selves*—that is, as their food—and *they will not enter the house of the Lord.* Now, we need to recognize that the Law also prescribed the offering of both sheaves and bread as the first-fruits of the harvest, whereas Israel transferred to graven images what was meant for the glory of God, despite God's clearly saying, "I shall not give my glory to another, nor my virtues to the graven images."[4]

It is therefore necessary to ask God for the necessities of life, and to express faith in him as giver and source of all our bodily and spiritual fertility. There is in fact no one other than he who sends the rain, as Scripture says; it is by his will that we are filled with the seasonal produce of the fields and blessings from on high, are nourished with the spiritual bread, and enjoy wine from heaven, "which gladdens the human heart." If we choose to have this attitude, we shall *inhabit the* holy *land;* we shall be with God, and we shall not *eat unclean food in Assyria.* It is in fact "the cosmic powers of this age, the spiritual forces of evil in the heavenly places,"[5] who pasture their adherents in unclean places. (185)

What will you do on the day of a festival, and on the days of the Lord's feast? (v.5) Since you have descended to such depths of folly and impiety, he says, and have become so loathsome and odious, what form of assistance will be left for you? Or what will you do or devise to avoid such a harsh and severe disaster when my *festival* is celebrated and the war consumes the offenders? God therefore mentions his own *feast,* that is, the occasion when Israel would be called to account for their sins against him. We must therefore not simply follow our inclinations heedlessly and

---

4. Dt 26.2; Lv 23.10; Is 42.8.
5. Jer 14.22; Ps 104.15; Eph 6.12.

take satisfaction in the present, influenced by our desires to the extent of offending God. Instead, we should consider the future as well, and strive to escape the effects of divine wrath; we shall thus be wise and appreciative of what is for our good.

For this reason, lo, they will proceed from the hardship of Egypt, Memphis will receive them, and Michmash will bury them. Ruin will succeed even to their money, thorns in their tents (v.6). When the Babylonians plundered Samaria, those able to escape scarcely took refuge in Egypt; and when they took Jerusalem itself in the time of Jeremiah's prophecy, an insignificant number was left from the tribes of Judah and Benjamin. They went to Egypt despite God's recommendation in the words of Jeremiah and his clear statement that they should not leave their native land (186) for Egypt, and his threat that, if they did so against his will, they would fall foul of equal or still worse troubles. The text goes as follows: "Thus says the Lord, If you turn your face towards Egypt and enter there to make your home, the sword that you fear will find you there."[6] In fact, when they trusted in the help of the Egyptians to resist the Babylonians, the Babylonians were consequently upset, and after the capture of Jerusalem and Samaria they turned against Egypt and easily vanquished them, the survivors from Judah perishing along with the Egyptians. Others, by contrast, succeeded in escaping the hardship in Egypt, and just made their escape by entering the country of Arcades, and dwelt in the heavily fortified cities of Memphis and Michmash, the latter city being quite close and more celebrated than the others; they died there, obviously after spending a long period, and being unable to return to Judea.

The prophet Jeremiah said again in similar terms, "Therefore thus says the Lord: Lo, I am determined to destroy all the survivors in Egypt; they will fall by the sword and by famine; from the least to the greatest they will waste away, and will become an object of opprobrium, ruin, and cursing. I shall also punish those in the land of Egypt as I punished Jerusalem by sword, famine, and death. None of the remnants of Judah dwelling in Egypt will survive to return to the land of Judah, where they hope to return

---

6. Jer 42.15–16.

safe and sound; they will not return."⁷ Do you hear that (187) they died in Egypt, with the divine wrath inflicted on them there? So when they avert hardship in Egypt, as they reach the famous city of Memphis, it *will receive them*, but they will die in Michmash, the text saying, *Michmash will bury them.*⁸ When God is in pursuit, therefore, no one will save the person at risk; wherever they go, they will fall foul of his anger.

While this is what he says will happen to them in Egypt, then, the text says also to those offending him with their own riches, "With their silver and their gold they made idols for themselves,"⁹ and consequently it was right that *ruin will succeed* to it, that is, it will be an inheritance for the destroyer. By *ruin*, in fact, he refers to the Assyrian for his savage and cruel fighting and taking captives. As well, he says, there will be a growth of *thorns in their tents:* the cities were reduced to such devastation as to be full of thorns, a sign of trackless and desolate country.

Accordingly, when you fail to use properly for his glory the good things given you by God, bodily or spiritual, and instead you shamefully commit what would offend him, and you are found provoking him, you will go off to *ruin* and will be allotted to Satan the plunderer as a nest of *thorns*, that is, fierce and culpable desires, producing no gentle fruits in your mind. This would be the experience of heretics in the first place, who impiously distort the benefit of the word to the undoing of the brethren, and "wound their conscience when it is weak,"¹⁰ despite Christ's suffering for us.

The days of punishment have come, the days of your retribution (188) *have come, and Israel will be distressed, like the demented prophet, someone spirit-filled* (v.7). It was normal for the people of Israel to reject the words of the holy prophets and place no importance on what came from God, despite the fact that they often suffered the calamities he had foretold. The God of all, for instance, pre-

---

7. Jer 44.11–14.
8. It is only the LXX text that contains a reference to Michmash; and while Cyril may be at a loss as to why this mention should occur of a city in northern Judea, he might have noted the appropriateness of reference to Memphis, the Egyptian city of cemeteries and pyramids.
9. 8.4.
10. 1 Cor 8.12.

dicted somewhere in the prophet Ezekiel, "Son of man, lo, the house of Israel is provoking me by saying, The vision that he sees is for many days ahead; he is prophesying for the future. Therefore, say to them, Thus says Lord Adonai: None of the words I shall speak will be delayed any longer; the word I speak I shall also fulfill, says Lord Adonai."[11] He says something like this here as well: *The days of punishment have come,* as if to say, Justice is close by, and its agent already at the very doors, disaster is at hand and war in sight. *The day of your retribution* is at hand. When you are *distressed,* O Israel, he is saying, there will be complete harm and punishment in equal measure for every false prophet along with you, *someone demented,* that is, inspired and deranged, who has lost his mind but who you think is *spirit-filled.* Together with the others, in fact, there have perished the priests of the high places as well as the worshipers of the idols and all who were soothsayers and false seers in Israel. You see, since those uttering oracles pretended to be demented and made a show of communicating messages, consequently he refers to such a one as someone *demented.* (189)

From the magnitude of your iniquities your frenzy has been magnified (v.7). By *magnitude of iniquities* he means Israel's manifold and multi-faceted worship. In a word, all of them were deceived and practiced idolatry, but they were divided into different forms of deceit, different ones performing different rituals and practicing false prophecy for their adherents. Some worshiped the heifers; others, Chemosh the idol of Moab; still others, Astarte; and there were others for Baal and the host of heaven. Consequently, God accused them in the statement of Jeremiah, "You have as many gods as towns, O Judah"; in other words, each town professes to have its own god. This same offense he rightly refers to as *magnitude of iniquities;* it is truly a crime and offense against God to forsake him and be devoted to sticks and stones and "the works of their hands," as Scripture says.[12]

By *frenzy* he refers to false prophecy. He is saying that, since *magnitude of iniquities* is found in your midst, consequently there is among you a magnitude also of *frenzy*—that is, false prophe-

11. Ezek 12.27–28.
12. Jer 2.28; 1.16.

cy—each one having his own form of false prophecy by which he prophesied. So it was surely wrong, unlawful, and truly profane, and not beyond the possibility of giving terrible offense and provocation to the God of all, to be in the habit of uttering false prophecy that was, as Scripture says, "from their hearts and not from the Lord's mouth."[13] Christians ought therefore to be on their guard against this fault; addiction to such practices would befit only the worshipers of demons. (190)

Ephraim is a lookout, a prophet with God, a tangled snare on all his ways (v.8). It is the custom of the divine Scripture to refer by *lookout* to the leaders and administrators of the peoples, raised to a position of respect; someone would supervise them if he was willing to live an upright and unassailable life. Somewhere, for instance, God said to the blessed prophet Ezekiel, "Son of man, I have appointed you lookout for the house of Israel; you will hear a word from my mouth and give them a warning from me."[14] Such lookouts, you see, normally not only proposed a life that was for those under guidance an example of virtue or of a manner of living as lawful as their own, but also introduced useful values and properly explained God's will. While some people who were subject to good *lookouts* and walked the straight and narrow were saved, however, others entrusted the line of their thinking to evil and depraved men, who kept "deceiving and being deceived,"[15] and had an attitude that was divorced from any beneficence or true knowledge.

He now charges those from the tribe of Ephraim, or Israel, with being in this condition, for it had as *a lookout a prophet with God*, as if you were to say that each false god had its own false prophet. As I said before, remember, they were divided into a range of multiple deceits, some serving Baal, some Chemosh, or Baal of Peor, and in each shrine cast statues were made, or handmade figures or images, and each one had a false prophet attending to it. The form of prophecy among them also differed; they gave vent as they pleased to their devotees as though it were useful and (191) vital. Since, then, there was *a lookout* for the

---

13. Jer 23.16.
14. Ezek 3.17.
15. 2 Tm 3.13.

people of Ephraim and its own *prophet* with each of the false gods, consequently they then turned without restraint to every shameful practice. This proved to be for it also *a tangled snare:* caught up in such awful polytheism, each *god* having its own *prophet,* they were unable to be controlled or make suitable progress. Furthermore, they set up a *lookout,* who withdrew them from reverence to God and hurtled them to the depths of ruin.

It is necessary, therefore, for those who want to live a lawful life to give heed not simply to teachers or those speaking from their own heart, but to those whose sincerity of love for God is confirmed by divine grace from on high. Accordingly, Christ also said, "Beware of false prophets, who come to you in sheep's clothing, but inwardly are ravenous wolves." We are in fact truthful in claiming that there is little difference from wild animals in those who devise and propose unholy heresies, "devouring Israel with open mouth";[16] they consume, as it were, simple souls by crushing them with the teeth of deceit. Let it be said, then, also of us, "God will break their teeth in their mouths, the Lord will tear out the fangs of the lions. They will disappear like water that runs away, he will draw his bow till they grow weak. They will be dissolved like melting wax."[17]

They planted madness in the house of the Lord. They corrupted themselves on the days of the hill. He will remember his iniquity, he will avenge his sins (v.9). By *madness* here he refers as usual to false prophecy, and by (192) *house of the Lord* to Israel. It was said somewhere in a statement of Jeremiah in the person of God to the assembly of the Jews, for instance, "Did you not call me house, father, and leader of your maidenhood?"[18] So he is astonished at the magnitude of the frenzy and the extraordinary degree of the lawless deeds; they had now sunk to such a degree of sacrilege, he says, as to *plant madness in the house of the Lord*—that is, false prophecy—and commit acts forbidden by the divine laws. *Plant* was well put: far from the crime coming to an end, the practice of impiety was now, as it were, planted and sunk deep; Israel did not put a stop to false seers and false prophets. When they committed

16. Jer 23.16; Mt 7.15; Is 9.12.
17. Ps 58.6–8; the final clause does not appear in the PG edition.
18. Jer 3.4.

such crimes, they were rightly called to account for their actions: *they corrupted themselves on the days of the hill,* for *he will remember their iniquity, he will avenge* all their *sins.*

The meaning of this phrase, *They corrupted themselves on the days of the hill,* come now, let us briefly explain. Such a phrase occurs in the book of Judges; as far as possible I shall give a brief explanation of it all, and abbreviate its length. "In those days there was no king in Israel; a man did what was right in his own eyes. There was a young man of Bethlehem in Judah who was a Levite, and he lived there. The man left Bethlehem, the city of Judah, to dwell in whatever place he could find, and came to the hill country of Ephraim as far as the house of Micah to make his way. Micah asked him, From where do you come? He replied to him, I am a Levite from Bethlehem of Judah, and I am on my way to dwell in whatever place I find. Micah said to him, Stay with me, and be to me a father and a priest, and I shall give you ten silver pieces per day, a set of clothes, and your living. (193) The Levite went and began to stay with the man, and the young man was like one of his sons to him. Micah paid the Levite, and he became his priest, and was in the house of Micah."[19] While Micah was an idolater, then, he hired the man from the line of Levi, he made him an attendant on the statue and assigned him to the needs of the idol.

What happened after this? The sacred text goes on as follows: "In those days the tribe of Dan was looking for a territory for itself, because to that point no territory had been allotted it amidst the tribes of Israel." Then they chose five men, and persuaded them to go ahead of them and spy out the land with a view to the possibility of taking it and making it their own territory. They reached, the text says, "the hill country of Ephraim to the house of Micah, and stayed there";[20] they were in the house of Micah, and recognized the Levite as a fellow tribesman from the language he used to them, since he spoke as a Hebrew to Hebrews. When they asked why, and learned that he was from the tribe of Levi but had been hired by Micah, who appointed him priest of his own idol, they should have commiserated with him as a cap-

19. Jgs 17.6–12.
20. Jgs 18.2.

tive who was deceived and on the run. But they immediately involved him in the wiles of their deceit, asking him to inquire of the idol and tell them if the project would turn out as planned—namely, getting control of the region which they had come to explore. He told them what they wanted as though it came from God. Those who had been sent and had spied out the land reported to those who had sent them that it was good and rich and would be taken without effort. When the men from the tribe of Dan heard a report to this effect, (194) six hundred of them went up bearing arms, and arrived at the house of Micah. "The five men who had gone to spy out the land of Laish reported to their fellows, Do you know that in this house there is an ephod, teraphim, and an idol of cast metal? Now decide what you will do."[21] ("Ephod" means "redemption," and "teraphim" means "relief," or "healing them"; an idol had the false reputation of being able to heal some people, since pagans sometimes invest their artifacts with such a reputation.) On learning this, the men from Dan lay hold of the statue, and persuaded the man from the bloodline of Levi to follow them and leave Micah. They went on the attack, were victorious, subjugated the land, and built a city they called Dan, giving it the name of their ancestor, being from the tribe and bloodline of Dan, as I said. In it they also set up the idol, offered sacrifices to it, and acquired a god along with the land, such being the extent of the stupidity to which they descended.

Consequently, God was now angry, and rightly so, at being insulted. Next, although all the people of Israel should have considered those from Dan implacable enemies and requited their impiety towards God, they even sided with them and judged their behavior commendable as though they had done no wrong. What the upshot of this indifference was, come now, let us proceed to say. When Israel was still without a king, a certain Levite dwelling on the hillside of Ephraim took a partner from Bethlehem. When the woman left for her father's place, the Levite followed (195) and again persuaded her to return and live with him. When this happened, in mid-journey he turned aside with

21. Jgs 18.14.

the woman to Gibeah, which means *hill*.²² Now, people of the tribe of Benjamin occupied Gibeah, or *hill*. While they were staying with a certain elder, however, in the middle of the night lawless men of the tribe of Benjamin arrived, as Scripture recounts, intending to force the Levite into incontinent behavior, both himself and others. Unashamed of their outrageous request, they seized the Levite's concubine and killed her after violating the woman all night long. He divided the body into parts and distributed them to the people of the tribe of Israel to bring to their notice the sin of the members the tribe of Benjamin towards strangers, their unbridled incontinence, and the fact that it resembled the sins of the Sodomites. Under pressure from this, all Israel rose up and attacked the tribe of Benjamin at Gibeah, that is, the *hill*. They destroyed them, numerous though they were, to such an extent that very few survived, and these scarcely managed to take refuge in the wilderness. An innumerable band of warriors from the whole of Israel also perished.²³

God would not allow the people of Israel to mingle with each other lest some from the tribe of Dan should venerate the statue from the house of Micah, and some from the other tribes should defy reason and make peace. Such an event occurred to God's displeasure also with the golden heifers: the two tribes of Judah and the ten tribes of Ephraim mingled, and, as *on the days of the hill*, a vast number fell and the vanquished perished along with the victors, a requirement of divine wrath. These things happened when Amaziah was king of Judah and Jehoash king of Israel; the latter took Jerusalem (196) in such a way as also to destroy a section of the wall four hundred cubits long.²⁴

---

22. Jgs 19. Cyril is showing the effects of Jerome's knowledge of Hebrew in offering etymologies above, and here perhaps observing that in the Heb. Gibeah the LXX had seen an identical form for "hill." As he is only relying on someone else, however, he fails to recognize the same solecism by the LXX at 10.9 and at Mi 7.4.

23. Jgs 20.1–35. The pathos of the incident of the abuse of the Levite's concubine and its aftermath—a celebrated "text of terror" in modern feminist commentators' view—attracts little sympathy from Cyril. Like the biblical author, he has another agenda in mind.

24. 2 Chr 25.21–23; 2 Kgs 13.12. Has this extraordinarily lengthy digression involving paraphrase of narratives from Judges 18–20 been prompted simply by the need to see Gibeah in the LXX "hill"?

Like a bunch of grapes in the desert I found Israel, and like an early fruit on the fig tree I saw their ancestors. But they went into Baal-peor, and practiced idolatry in shame, and loved ones became objects of loathing (v.10). He now tries to bring out the fact that it was not by accident but justly that destruction befell them. He says, note, I chose them as though *finding a bunch of grapes in the desert,* and picking a ripe *fruit from the fig tree.* In other words, I led them out of the country of the Egyptians, which was completely idolatrous and suffused with error, suffering utter deprivation of every good. So why was it the chosen who were snatched from my hand? They deviated to Baal of Peor, and left a relationship with me for *shame,* the sense of *practicing idolatry in shame,* by *shame* referring to Baal of Peor, which had the ugliest appearance of all, disedifying to see.[25]

If we love to be with God, then, and honor the one who called and chose us and plucked us from this worldly condition as if from a thorny *desert like a bunch of grapes and an early fig* that is attractive, we shall preserve unbroken our union with him, which is clearly of a spiritual kind. If, on the other hand, there is some inclination to what is ugly and what offends him, we shall be no different from the nations; we shall be *loved ones who became objects of loathing,* and duly hated. Scripture says, remember, "The righteousness of the righteous will not save them on the day they sin"; and very wisely the blessed Paul writes, "And so let the one who thinks he stands take heed lest he fall."[26] (197)

Ephraim flew away like a bird (v.11). All birds that are not tame and domesticated are kept in a cage and give pleasure to their owners; but if the opportunity arises for them to get out, they quickly take their leave, and fly with rapid flight to their normal environment. In some fashion, then, Israel like a *bird* was trapped by Moses and brought to God, enjoying untroubled satisfaction, guided by the Law and benefiting from care and mercy from on high. But it *flew away* again to what was in the beginning, as if escaping the hand of the catcher.

---

25. Nm 25.1–5. Like Theodore before him, and Theodoret in commentary on Ps 81, Cyril is taking *allotriôsis,* estrangement, in the sense of polytheism, idolatry.

26. Ezek 33.12; 1 Cor 10.12.

There is also another way to understand the verse. Many birds do not tolerate wintry climates, and transfer to other places, instinctively knowing what is for their good, as their maker intended. In a similar fashion Ephraim was afraid of the misfortunes of war, and *flew away* to Egypt.

Their glory is in births, pregnancies, and conceptions. Hence, even if they suckle their children, they will be deprived of offspring by men; hence woe is their lot (vv.11–12). Israel left its native land and went off to Egypt, and begged the ruler of the country to assist them. Surely it was not a case of God being impotent and unable to save them? Not at all: the divinity is omnipotent and more than capable of winning a war waged by the Assyrians. Now, it happened that the people of Ephraim, or Israel, suffered this fate because they abandoned the God who saved them, ridiculed as obsolete the idea of glorying in him alone, and believed (198) that they would be fearsome and invulnerable to their foes as a result of a growth in numbers and having large families beyond counting. The women in their midst, in fact, gave birth in accord with the promise and by way of blessing, since Moses had foretold, "There will be no one barren or infertile among the children of Israel." To scorn help from God on the basis of numerical growth, however, was very inane; rather, they should have had good sense and considered that it was with him and through him that "one man would pursue thousands, and two would rout tens of thousands."[27] Instead of boasting in God, therefore, he says, *their glory was in births, pregnancies, and conceptions* of the women in their midst. Let them realize, then, that even if they give birth to sons, even if they grow tired *suckling children*, they will repent of laboring in vain; they will lament complete and utter childlessness. The sword of the Babylonians would easily suffice to consume their whole race; *hence woe is their lot.* It is as if he were to say, "When God hurls woes upon you, who will bring satisfaction?" Scripture says, "If he closes the door on a person, who will open?"[28]

"It is therefore a fearsome thing to fall into the hands of the living God." We must therefore appease with our good behavior

27. Ex 23.26; Dt 32.30.
28. Jb 12.14.

the one offended, and seek salvation from him, trusting in no one else, and instead crying aloud, "I shall boast in God my Savior; the Lord God is my strength."[29]

My flesh from them (v.12). When God was threatening and saying of Ephraim, or all Israel, that it would perish, roots and all, lament its childlessness, and labor pointlessly in rearing its children, the prophet extracts himself (199) from vengeance, and prays to be delivered from wrath by saying, *My flesh from them,* the phrase *from them* to be taken to mean, "far from them." He means, in fact, I personally and all my race would be removed and at a distance from them, *flesh* sometimes meaning "race." We also take in this way, remember, the correct statement in Paul, who writes, "Now, I am speaking to you gentiles. Inasmuch, then, as I am an apostle to the gentiles, I glorify my ministry in order to make my own flesh jealous and save some of them."[30] It is customary with the holy prophets, when they frequently see awful and intolerable crimes of some people, to distance their own situation from these people's abominable behavior. The prophet Jeremiah, for instance, on seeing the Jews becoming guilty of countless crimes and offending God, said, "Lord almighty, I did not sit in the company of merrymakers; instead, I showed reverence for your hand, and sat alone, because I was filled with bitterness." There is need, then, to admire the blessed Paul when he writes to us in these terms: "Keep yourself pure, and do not participate in the sins of others."[31] Any pious person at all would therefore be right to say in reference to those offending God and not yet punished, *My flesh from them.*

Ephraim, as I saw him, presented his children as prey, and Ephraim led his children out for torture (v.13). The prophet now bewails Ephraim, or Israel, saying that it is responsible for its own childlessness and unbearable misfortune. As I see it, (200) both from your words, O Lord, he is saying, and from the facts themselves, Ephraim personally *presented his children as prey* and *for torture.* He

---

29. Heb 10.31; Hab 3.18–19. The final paragraph does not occur in the PG edition.

30. Rom 11.13–14. Antiochene and Alexandrian commentators struggle with this phrase in Hos 9.12, a verse that is corrupt in the Heb.

31. Jer 15.17; 1 Tm 5.22. The PG edition reads the next sentence to begin, "Any impious person . . ."

would not now blame others or rail against divine wrath if his thinking were correct; rather, he would blame his own folly and apostasy. You see, since he seriously offended the God who assisted and saved him, he willingly with his own hand, as it were, surrendered his very offspring to the cruelty of the nations, and presented them as booty and for captivity (the sense of *as prey* and *for torture,* or slaughter); of the men of Israel, the Babylonians did away with some; others they deported to their own country.

When we sin, therefore, we shall rather blame ourselves, not divine wrath, if we are thinking correctly; we scorned our duty, and proved indifferent in pleasing God. There is need to punish the insolent and inflexible person, who, as it were, says to the Lord of all, "Depart from me, I do not want to know your ways."[32]

Give to them, Lord: what will you give to them? Give them a childless womb and dry breasts (v.14). If the people of Israel were not going to acknowledge God, but rather to indulge a pointless and foolish hope in the belief that they would prevail over the enemy through a vast number of children, and that warlike classes would abound in their ranks, for this reason assistance from your hand would not have been needed nor the bearing of children by their women (the sense of *a childless womb*). Even should they give birth, (201) they should not rear the children, that is, they should be taken before maturity, and the race should decline before coming of age. In other words, once the arrogance inherent in them was deflated in this way, and the hope in a vast number of warriors then removed, they would have recourse to your mercy, and choose you as Savior and Redeemer. Such are the effects of love of God even now, the prophet is saying. In the same way he seeks both the glory of his Lord and the conversion of the bloodline of Israel under pressure of necessity if they do not have the fruit of a good intention.

Now, *a childless womb and dry breasts* in a spiritual sense would be fitting for evildoers and everyone who deceives and misleads those who usually keep to the straight and narrow (by faith, I

---

32. Jb 21.14.

mean) and "go straight on their way."³³ Their mind, you see, gives birth to nothing but false speech, illegitimate speculation, nor would they nourish their own children on deceit (by teaching, I mean). The churches of the evildoers will have *dry breasts* and be unable to be mothers to the deceived.

All their wickedness began in Gilgal, because it was there that I hated them for their evil pursuits. I shall drive them out of my house, I shall not continue to love them (v.15). Once again the God of all begins to list their crimes, recalling Gilgal, the city where in particular they venerated in a terribly wrong fashion handmade objects. It is the same thing over again, he is saying; the people of Israel have been guilty of profane worship in many ways. (202) By considering Gilgal you could see the extent of their inherent depravity: there I have witnessed all their wickedness; *there I hated them*, not on account of the place itself—a foolish idea—but rather in abhorrence of what was done in it. Accordingly, he says, I shall expel them, eject them from my court, and *drive them out* of relationship with me. I was right to *hate them*, and shall now threaten them, and would not in the future change to an attitude of love for them, guilty as they are of such crimes.

I expect, however, someone will ask, How then did he bring them back to Judea from Assyria, or how did he release them from captivity?³⁴ Surely he did not fail to have a change of heart and accord them clemency, mercy, and love? Yes, this would seem to be the case; admittedly, out of clemency he had mercy on them. The ones referred to, however, went into captivity and died from their punishment after the lapse of a long time. Just as he promised through Moses in Egypt to the people of Israel to bring everyone into the land which he swore to their ancestors, yet some were disobedient and did not enter it, "their bodies falling in the wilderness,"³⁵ and the land going rather as an inheritance to their offspring, so this is the interpretation to take in this case, too. Whereas the people referred to in the text died,

---

33. Prv 9.15.
34. We have noted that Cyril is not precise in referring to the respective enemies and fates of northern and southern kingdoms. At least, however, he is identifying some historical referent in the verse before giving it a christological dimension.
35. Heb 3.17.

you see, their successors in due course returned to Judea when Cyrus finally allowed it at the completion of their seventy years' residence in a foreign country.

They will be driven out of the house of God, or rather were driven out—that is, those who committed awful crimes against Christ, offended him indescribably, and used against him harsh and disparaging language; they will suffer his ineluctable wrath. It is, you see, not one of the prophets whom they have been guilty of provoking, but the very (203) Lord of the prophets. While all the other crimes they committed against themselves are glossed over, therefore, you could see *all their wickedness* and the enormity of their depravity in what was done against Christ alone, as it were.

All their leaders are disobedient. Ephraim suffered hardship, its roots were dried up, it will no longer bear fruit. Hence, even if they give birth, I shall kill what they longed for from the womb. God will reject them because they did not hearken to him, and they will be vagrants among the nations (vv.16–17). He says that no one among them was found upright, no one obedient, no one docile, whether lowly or important or in government or subject to authority. Consequently, he clearly declares that all alike have to perish, as though uprooted, resembling dried up and severed limbs of trees that are good only for cutting down, obviously shown to be fruitless. Now, the fact that fruitless trees deserve to be cut down the Savior himself teaches in giving orders for the fig tree that had no fruit, a figure of the Jewish synagogue, to be cut down: "Why does it waste the soil?"[36] Israel, then, was found to be fruitless, and would rightly be cut down, *no longer bearing fruit.* Even if it did, he says, I shall destroy what comes from it, namely, *what they longed for from the womb.*

Now, in my view there is need to give further consideration to the verse. What is the meaning of the statement, *All their leaders are disobedient?* Why was there need of submission by *the leaders?* (204) The verse therefore contains a reference to past facts; I shall proceed to explain it. In the absence of Moses Israel made a calf in the wilderness; he had gone up Mount Sinai to receive

---

36. Lk 13.7.

the Law. Then, when he came down, he was very upset at the transgression, smashed the calf, and in a way importuned the angry God by his characteristic sincerity and virtue; he fell down and besought him, "If you forgive them their sin, forgive; but if not, strike me also out of this book of yours that you have written." To the prophet God conceded mildness towards all, and went on to say, "I forgive them as you ask."[37] Do you see the great benefit that Israel derived from its leader's love of God, and how one person was sufficient to win God over by his submission and obedience on behalf of all? So he rightly charges[38] Israel for completely losing its way. Then, because they did not have any leader among them to chastise those who fell, recall them from error, or succeed by his own uprightness in life and virtue in diverting wrath when God was appealed to, as happened in the time of Moses, accordingly they will also be driven out, he says, and *will be vagrants among the nations*. This was their experience, at one time in being deported to Assyria, and now no less in their abhorrent frenzy against Christ; the people of Israel are everywhere exiles and refugees, living in the world with no city of their own; "I shall scatter them to every quarter," God said through the holy prophets.[39]

Accordingly, if our concern and attention is directed at having a relationship with God, let us submit our necks to him, and make our approach in loving obedience to Christ, who says, "Come to me, (205) all you who labor and are heavily burdened, and I shall give you rest. Take my yoke upon you."[40] This in fact is the way we shall be fruitful and resistant to assault, with our roots not dried up, our fruit not falling into decay, not wandering and removed from God, but close to him and with him, with a city on high in heaven, the mother of the firstborn, the nourishment of the saints, the pure residence of the spirits above.

---

37. Ex 32.32; Nm 14.20.
38. That is, in the Hosea passage under consideration here.
39. Ezek 5.10. Cyril has made an effort to see further levels of meaning in phrases from the verse, showing some relish in finding a reference to the plight of Jews of his day.
40. Mt 11.28–29.

COMMENTARY ON HOSEA,
CHAPTER TEN

Israel is a luxuriant vine, his crop abundant. He multiplied the altars in keeping with the great size of the crops, and erected pillars in keeping with the good things of his land. They divided their hearts, now they will be done away with. He will overturn their altars, their pillars will wear out (vv. 1–2).

FTER SAYING that Ephraim suffered in its roots and would be fruitless in the manner of those who have no children, since the savagery of the Assyrians consumed their offspring, he necessarily shows also that in the past they proved fruitful when they wisely lived a life in keeping with the Law. To its neighboring nations, in fact, it appeared like a lovely and *luxuriant vine* and was rightly admired. In regard to it, the blessed David also says somewhere in the book of Psalms to God the Savior of all, "You transferred a vine out of Egypt, you drove out the nations and planted it, you went as guide before it. It extended its branches to the sea, and its shoots to the river"; in fact, it was planted "in a horn and in a rich place," as the prophet says.[1] (206)

Instead of producing grapes, however, it bore thorns; in other words, in response to the vast number of good things given to it, it showed itself to be hand-in-glove, as it were, with iniquity; clearly it was hostile to God. In fact, it *multiplied altars* and *erected pillars:* the more it was enriched with good things from on high, the greater zeal it displayed for profane worship by bowing down to demons, erecting altars, and *dividing its heart* with the error of polytheism. But this, he says, would not last. How so? *He will overturn their altars,* and *their pillars will wear out,* obviously by being smashed and overthrown. Now, in *he* you would be correct in seeing a reference to the omnipotent God of all, or the person

---

1. Ps 80.8–9, 11; Is 5.1 LXX.

of the Babylonian, as demonstrated often before. It transpired, in fact, that in the cities of Samaria the very temples were burnt down and the statues seized.

It behoves us, therefore, to offer thanks joyfully for what we have from God, and not get caught up in the extent of our enjoyment and be misled into displeasing him. Instead, we should seek and exert ourselves to achieve with all enthusiasm the fruits of virtue, not divided by worldly passions or submitting our necks to Satan. It is in fact true, as Christ says, "No one can serve two masters: you will either hate the one and love the other, or be devoted to the one and despise the other." If we are *divided*, and "are jackals' portions," in the words of the psalmist,[2] we shall suffer complete deprivation of the one who is able to bring us enjoyment. (207)

Hence now they will say, We have no king, because we did not fear the Lord. But what will a king do for us? Uttering words, false pretexts, he will make a covenant (vv.3–4). He not only said that their altars will be shaken and pillars wear out, but added that they will also show repentance and mourning for their own stupidity. Thwarted in their hopes and deceived by the false statements of those in charge, they will finally and at a late stage understand; those among them who occupied the throne of the kingdom claimed that the golden heifers and security from the other idols would suffice for assistance, even if they did not have the divine Law, even if they chose not to observe the requirements imposed through Moses. Experience, however, showed them to be false. They saw those who had made this arrangement for them in the past and who had spoken in ill-advised fashion falling under the domination of the foe. Consequently, he says, *We have no king, because we did not fear the Lord;* lo, they said, lo, there is no one to give aid or resist the incursions of the Babylonians; instead, everyone has lost heart, the leaders are disbanded and have fallen. The cause of their weakness and ours is that *we did not fear the Lord.* What kind of benefit, he asks, comes from those in power? There was nothing from them except *false* words and futile *covenants* or promises (the divine Scripture normally referring to guarantees as *covenants*).

---

2. Mt 6.24; Ps 63.10. The PG edition abbreviates the final two sentences.

It is therefore wise and utterly commendable to trust rather in God, and not be influenced by the words of the deceivers to offend God. Instead, we should (208) rather avoid the effects of wrath before actually experiencing them, and not eventually lament the experience by being wise after the event.

Judgment will spring up like weeds in a barren field for the calf of the house of Ôn (vv.4–5). Weeds grow particularly in fields that are barren and not ploughed, and can get quite a grip on land lying alongside; they spread everywhere, and are not easily resisted by those wanting to check their propagation. Accordingly, he says that *judgment*—obviously by God—*like weeds in a barren field, springs up for the calf of the house of Ôn.* It is as if he were to say, From me will come a sentence of ruin and a decision for punishment, and *like weeds* will grip *the calf,* or idols of the temple in Bethel, which is indicated by *house of Ôn* (the other translators rendering it "the calf of the house of Bethel," whereas the Seventy put *house of Ôn* for "house of Bethel" for reasons already explained above, which we shall not weary you by repeating).[3] The Egyptian storytellers, in fact, claimed that Apis was child of the moon and nephew of the sun, *Ôn* meaning "sun" according to them, and that the heifer that Jeroboam made was a type of the Egyptians' Apis. So, he says, spreading *like a weed,* and overcoming everything (209) in its path, so will my *judgment* be *for the calf of the house of Ôn,* or Bethel; the divinity is omnipotent, after all, and nothing will resist his will. As Scripture says, "Who will turn away his uplifted hand?"[4]

The inhabitants of Samaria will dwell beside it, because its people grieved for it, and as they provoked it, they will rejoice in its glory. See, he makes clear the judgment befalling the calf, which spreads naturally like *weeds* in opposition to God's will. He also refers at this point to the historical situation, which must be mentioned;[5] we

---

3. Cyril makes a rod for his own back by including in this verse "for the house of Ôn" from the next verse. Though preferring not to rehearse what he said on the mention of Aven/Ôn in 5.8, he in fact repeats it, introducing also Apis and the sense of "sun" that he gives to Ôn in a phrase thought rather to mean "house of trouble" and to represent a case of "a sarcastic metonymy" for Beth-El, "house of God." See n. 13 on Hosea 5, above.

4. Is 14.17.

5. There is no bypassing the historical situation *(historia)* referred to in the verse—a principle Cyril religiously observes.

will take the oracle in the following way, and no other. It was the custom with all the idols' devotees at a time of distress and enemy onslaught to lay hold of the actual offerings in the shrines if there was a shortage of money. Accordingly, the books of Kings record that, when the king of Syria was besieging the cities of Samaria, Menahem the king of Israel at the time did not have resources sufficient to resist him, and sent ambassadors to Pul king of Assyria to persuade him with gifts to come to his aid and repel the Syrian. This is what actually happened: he took Damascus by force, and put to death Ader himself. The story goes, then, that when a vast weight of gold was required, Menahem then had no alternative but to steal one golden heifer and send it with the ambassadors.[6] Israel was distraught to see the dispatch of what they thought was a god. Consoling themselves with futile thoughts, they believed that it would be given an important place, (210) and that the Babylonian would set it up in a more splendid temple; they further thought it would be adored even by a greater number of nations, since the nations of the Persians and Medes were innumerable. So while Menahem dispatched the heifer made of pure gold, on receipt of it Pul smashed it, as they had a different idol, and had no interest in a calf. The story goes that it was found to be not golden, but a mixture of bronze and gold. This was the reason, the text says, that the Assyrian mocked Ephraim, that is, its king Menahem of the tribe of Ephraim, and in addition showed scorn for Israel's stupidity.

Having outlined the historical background, or at least the account of Hebrew tradition, come now, we need to return to our text; the sense of the verse is not clear or easily accessible. It says, then, *The inhabitants of Samaria will dwell beside it,* that is, those now in Samaria will *dwell beside it* in the sense of "dwell elsewhere," or "be deported elsewhere"—a reference to the calves, or heifers, which were dispatched to Babylon, as I said. *Its people grieved for them:* whose? Ôn's, in fact—that is, Apis's? But as they were seen to be *provoking* and dishonoring it by sending it to oth-

---

6. This is not quite the account of Menahem's buying off Tiglath-pileser III in 2 Kgs 15.19–20, where funds are collected rather from wealthy citizens; Cyril proceeds to admit that the story comes from "Hebrew tradition." The Antiochenes speak of gold from the heifers going rather to Egypt as insurance against the Assyrians.

ers, he says, likewise they will be perceived *in its glory,* for they thought it would be far more famous by being worshiped by a greater number of nations. Their hopes were dashed, however: it was broken up and became the occasion of mockery by the Babylonians. So "their pillar wore out,"[7] in the words of the prophet himself. Now, they *provoked* the calf,[8] not that (211) they really provoked it: how could senseless matter have that experience? Rather, the effect of the goings-on would have irritated it if it had really been a god and capable of experiencing the events.

Because it was carried away from it, and they bound it to Assyrians and took off gifts to King Jarib. Ephraim will receive it as a gift, and Israel will be shamed by his counsel (v.6). The prophetic verse explains itself to us: what it had said obscurely it tries to clarify. It was the calf, in fact, that *was carried away from* Israel, and *they bound it* (the text pokes fun). They took *gifts to King Jarib,* that is, the avenger:[9] he was called on to give assistance and, as it were, to avenge Samaria, which was being destroyed by the Syrians. But Pul *will receive* the heifer *as a gift* from *Ephraim,* by "Ephraim" meaning "the king of Israel." The text says, however, *Israel will be shamed by his counsel;* because he forsook the all-powerful God, as I said, and chose rather to adore heifers, he was an object of ridicule, and was found guilty of folly and vain and mindless stupidity. The prophet, therefore, or rather God, is right to say in the words of the saints in reference to those worshiping the works of their hands, "See, their heart is ashes, and they are deceived."[10]

Now, the verse would apply also to those undermining the true doctrines of the church: just as the smashing of the heifer convicted the people of Israel of stupidity, so, too, the smashing of those people's doctrine by inquiry, and the demolition of it by the force of truth, will prove to be the shame and reproach (212) of those who devise and sacrilegiously invent them, and accept such folly into their mind and heart.

Samaria cast off its king like a stick on the surface of the water. Altars

---

7. 10.2.

8. Cyril is unaware that the LXX has seen "provoked" in a similar Heb. form for "priests (will mourn)."

9. Unlike the Antiochenes, and with Jerome's help, Cyril sees in the proper name rather an unusual Heb. term for "the great (king)."

10. Wis 15.10.

of Ôn will be carried off, sins of Israel; thorns and thistles will grow up on their altars (vv.7–8). This verse in turn would also highlight the dissolute and disedifying behavior of Israel, or Samaria, even in regard to what they thought to be gods. That is not surprising. After all, how could people be genuine in regard to a great number of falsely-named gods made of sticks and stones when they sacrilegiously insulted him who by nature is the one true God by their infidelities and their recourse to any base thing at all? So he says the calf was *cast off* by those *in Samaria*, though believed by them to be god and king, and was cast off like a stick falling on the eddies of water and then carried at the whim of what moved it. Of the fact that the shrines will disappear along with the idols, that the altars will be destroyed and will become the place of *thorns* when their whole country is ravaged, there is no doubt. The altars he refers to as *sins of Israel*, and rightly so, raised as they were sacrilegiously as a reminder of their impiety towards God. He likewise gave the name Ôn, or Apis, to the heifers in both Bethel and Dan, to whose glory stood the altars. What God did not erect, therefore, will be utterly and completely destroyed. Something like this I take to be the meaning of the clear statement of another prophet, "They will build and I shall overthrow."[11] (213)

They will say to the mountains, Cover us, and to the hills, Fall on us (v.8). It is not that only in the two cities, namely, Dan and Bethel, were statues worshiped, though this case entails the golden heifers; on *the hills and the mountains* there were the idols of the neighboring nations, Baal, Baal of Peor, Astarte, and Chemosh. In this verse, therefore, he suggests that not only would the altars of Ôn be brought down—that is, of Apis, or the heifers—but all shrines everywhere on mountains and hills would fall. In fact, things will reach such a state of misery and terror that they will choose rather to be under *mountains and hills* than live to see the things they were forced unwillingly to endure. It must be realized that, in announcing to Jews the disasters that would befall them on account of their crimes against him, Christ used identical words: "Then you will say to the mountains, Cover us, and to

---

11. Mal 1.4.

the hills, Fall on us."[12] Excess of troubles, you see, and the enormity of disasters sometimes present death, harsh though it be, as very desirable to the general run of people. To the very *mountains and hills*, therefore, on which false worship and crimes of impiety towards God were committed, they will, as it were, say, *Fall on us* and anticipate the ferocity of the Babylonian sword and the inglorious and intolerable misery of life in captivity. (214)

From the time of the hills Israel sinned, there they stayed. War will not grip them on the hill, it came to the children of iniquity to instruct them. Peoples will be assembled against them when they are chastised for their double iniquity (vv.9–10). He says the apostasy that happened on both mountains and hills is older than the deceit in the case of the heifers. For instance, when the ten tribes took possession of Samaria, and shook off the yoke of the reign of Rehoboam, Jeroboam then introduced the heifers. But while in Jerusalem they practiced the deceit on both mountains and hills, since Solomon was making concessions and giving way to his foreign wives, and at that time erecting altars and shrines to their idols.[13] *From the time*, then, that the hills and diversions and false worship on them were considered, from that time Israel began offending. Now, clear proof of divine clemency would be the fact that for a long time he could not bring himself to punish the offenders; instead, he yielded and waited for the repentance of the deceived. They were very obdurate, however, and proved to be suffering a worse condition, proceeding from *the hills* to the novelty of the heifers.[14] By sacrificing to the demons on both mountains and hills, and seeming to be devoted to futile things, perhaps they thought—or, rather, they were firmly convinced—that they would *stay* firmly fixed in prosperity, and would prevail over weaker peoples and be invincible to foes—a usual ailment of those who are deceived.

When they went down to Egypt, therefore, with the capture (215) of Jerusalem by the Babylonian, the prophet Jeremiah advised them to avoid sacrificing to idols so that they might enjoy

---

12. Lk 23.30.   13. 1 Kgs 11.4–5.
14. This time Cyril does not note the LXX's reading "hill" in the identical form for Gibeah as he had (with Jerome's prompting) at 9.9.

mercy from the God who is able to save. But some people claimed that for this reason they would encounter trouble for reversing their decision to perform what was required and being guilty of decreasing honor for futile things. The text reads as follows: "A reply was made to Jeremiah by all the men who were aware that their wives were making offerings to other gods, and by all the women, a large assembly, and all the people resident in Pathros in the land of Egypt, saying: We shall not heed the word you have spoken to us in the name of the Lord. We shall continue to do everything that will come from our mouth, sacrificing to the queen of heaven, pouring libations to her as we have done along with our ancestors, our kings, and our rulers in the cities of Judah and outside Jerusalem. We were filled with bread, became prosperous, and experienced no troubles. When we stopped sacrificing to the queen of heaven, all our fortunes plummeted, and we perished by sword and famine."[15]

Accordingly, he accuses the people of Israel of the same idle tales and false hopes, and says about the *hills* that *there they stayed,* that is, that as they themselves admitted, or personally believed, it was *there* that they worshiped the statues, felt secure in their prosperity, and were fixed in irreversible good things. And as they were also convinced, absolutely no likelihood of distress will grip them on the hill if they decide to perform the prescribed rituals to the statues. They were deceived, however, he says, and their hopes dashed: *war* had come upon them as *children of iniquity,* and they would be *instructed* by experience itself that obduracy is harsh. Who would they be (216) who would bring them instruction? A mighty band of enemies, the meaning of the statement that *peoples will be assembled against them,* and the baleful effects of war will befall them *when they are chastised for their double iniquity.* What this is he made clearer to us in the statement of Jeremiah, "Heaven is appalled at this, and is utterly shocked, says the Lord, because my people have committed two evils: they have forsaken me, the fountain of living water, and dug for themselves broken cisterns which will not succeed in holding water."[16]

15. Jer 44.15–18.
16. Jer 2.12–13.

Ephraim was a heifer trained to be fond of victory, but I shall come upon the beauty of her neck. I shall mount Ephraim, but shall pass over Judah in silence (v.11). He compares Ephraim to a calf that is intractable, very proud, unaccustomed to keeping in check its drive to do whatever it wants, reluctant to be tamed, and endeavoring rather to gain the upper hand always and follow its impulses unswervingly as it pleases. Even if this is so, he says, it will yield, even if against its will; it will be tamed by the onset of disasters when God makes it submit as if personally achieving this feat and impairing *the beauty of its neck*, that is, by removing Israel's special feature. This was the monarchy in its midst, which incited its subject peoples to apostasy. So it will be brought to its knees under the weight of God (the sense I think of *I shall mount Ephraim*).

On the other hand, in the course of the divine plan, he says, *I shall pass over Judah in silence*, that is, I shall set Judah aside for a while, not subjecting her to punishment, not inflicting on her for the time being the effects of my wrath, (217) but putting up with her instead, and being lenient. For what reason? While Ephraim—that is, the ten tribes, as I have already said—deviated completely into performing the works of error, the two tribes in Jerusalem—namely, Judah and Benjamin—were often governed by upright and pious kings who dismissed the diversions of idolatry and persuaded the people to live a good and lawful life. Amaziah son of Joash was like this, a pious and righteous man; likewise Hezekiah, who was admired as much as the aforementioned, a devoted and godly man. Consequently, when the ten tribes were the first to experience captivity, and the Babylonian attacked Jerusalem, he caused no harm, instead retreating to his own country as a timid fugitive when in one night one hundred and eighty-five thousand Assyrians in a single night were felled by an angel.[17]

God therefore shows longsuffering and bears our weaknesses lest we grow indifferent and be found remiss in performing what is in accord with his will and pleasure.

Jacob will gain strength for him (v.11). I said that the Assyrian deployed his numerous forces, overcame the whole of Samaria, set

17. 2 Kgs 19.35–36. Sennacherib can be classed as Babylonian or Assyrian in the one breath by Cyril.

fire to the actual cities and the temples, and after that besieged Jerusalem but failed to take it since God protected it; a hundred and eighty-five thousand men were destroyed in a single night by an angel. (218) This it is, in my view, that he now foretells by saying, *Jacob will gain strength for him.* Who is the *him*—the Rabshakeh who was on the point of conducting the siege? On the other hand, he gave the name *Jacob* to the descendants of Jacob—I mean, Judah and Benjamin. Perhaps the text could be taken to refer to all Israel.

The sense of the prophecy is probably a reminder to us of a former event, as though God were fulfilling the promise made to the divinely inspired Jacob. After a human being, as it were, wrestled with him at night across the river Jabbok, at dawn, as day broke, God wanted to leave, saying, "Release me, dawn has broken." When he said he would not release him unless he blessed him, he then heard, "You gained strength with God, and prevailed with men."[18] Perhaps this is what the verse of the prophecy suggests to us in the present case, clarifying the words *Jacob will gain strength for him.* Consider the precision of the prophecy: not that Jacob will prevail over the Assyrians, but he *will gain strength*, it says; he gained strength from God, not by himself. (219)

Sow for yourselves righteousness, and reap the fruit of life. Enlighten yourselves with the light of knowledge, seek the Lord until the fruits of righteousness come to you (v.12). The style of exhortation is generally twofold: either by explaining to those opting for indolence the impending retribution we usually prompt them to change and with determination to choose an edifying life, or by proclaiming the honors accorded the upright we make those under instruction more zealous in taking a turn for the better and living in accord with law. This is what the God of all now does as well: the people being deceived he threatened with wars, calamities, deportation to foreign parts, incineration of cities, cruelty of fighters. Far from bringing a halt to the process of exhortation at this point, however, note once again a further method of benefiting

---

18. Gn 32.22–28. Theodore had also seen a reference to this Genesis incident, in which Jacob is given the name Israel, which may account for mention of both northern and southern names in the verse (Cyril also suggesting). The fifth tome closes at this point.

them: he bids them abandon the useless source of all their hardship and in its place adopt what is particularly likely to be of benefit, as in the case of farmers, *sowing righteousness, and reaping the fruit of life.* As blessed Paul in fact writes, "You will reap what you sow," and "Whoever sows bad things will reap evil," as (220) Scripture says, whereas the agent of righteousness will be filled with salvation and life, conspicuous and worthy of imitation, and will harvest the wine "that gladdens a person's heart."[19]

In addition there is need, however, for those wanting a good reputation to admit into their mind and heart the light of true knowledge, something that those who adore "creation instead of the Creator" do not have.[20] Now, how it would be possible to sow righteousness *and indeed* reap the fruit of life *and admit the bright light of knowledge* he himself suggested by adding, *Seek the Lord until the fruits of righteousness come to you.* Now, God would be sought by us, not in the sense of place—a fatuous notion, since the divinity is not localized—but in our state of soul, as it were, when our mind enthusiastically adopts everything pleasing to him and has regard for an upright and clear conscience that is not liable to correction from any quarter. When we find him in this way, you see, we shall be enriched by the acquisition of the other goods. Is Christ not right when he says, "Apart from me you can do nothing"?[21] This is quite beyond question, in my view, for people in the habit of thinking properly; possession of every good comes to us with God, through God, and from God.

It is, on the other hand, not only to the devotees of the idols to whom you would say, *Sow for yourselves righteousness,* and so on, but also to those who forsake the true faith, and instead devote themselves to "deceitful spirits through hypocrisy of demons, whose consciences are seared," as for instance Paul in his wisdom writes. These people *sow* through laborious dedication to knowledge and study—not, however, to works of *righteousness,* but to iniquity and impiety, "deceiving and deceived," and "wounding the weakened (221) conscience of the brethren for whom Christ died."[22] So they do not *reap the fruit of life,* but of

---

19. Gal 6.7; Prv 22.8; Ps 104.15.   20. Rom 1.25.
21. Jn 15.5.
22. 1 Tm 4.1–2; 2 Tm 3.13; 1 Cor 8.12.

punishment and judgment. Christ said, for example, "If any should scandalize one of the least of those who believe in me, it would be better for them if a millstone were hung around their neck and they were drowned in the depths of the sea."[23] Let them love the truth, therefore, this being the *light of knowledge;* this is the way God is sought, and from this *fruits of righteousness* will spring up for them *for life;* there will be a harvest of wine, not of the material kind but spiritual and through the Spirit, who gladdens the heart and mind.

Why did you pass over impiety in silence, and harvest its fruit and eat fruit that deceives? Because you hoped in your chariots, in the greatness of your power. Ruin will rise up among your people, and all your fortifications will be destroyed (vv.13–14). Once again he blames them for choosing on the basis of depraved pleasure to be inactive about things that did not deserve it, and being silent about foolish actions which were likely to give considerable offense to God. They should in fact, he says, have resisted with all their strength impiety towards me and corrected those recommending vile actions, thus gaining credit for doing so; but they kept silence and welcomed the forms of deceit. There was no one among them to resist those introducing novelties, to bring to bear the requirements of the Law and remind them of what was found in the inspired Scriptures; it is written, in fact, "You shall not have other gods than me," and again, "You shall not make yourself an idol."[24] But they gave altogether little importance to this, (222) keeping silence out of respect for impiety, that is, apostasy. They have therefore *harvested the fruit* of iniquity and *eaten fruit that deceives;* that is, they have had weak and blind hope. You see, whereas real fruit, which is capable of saving and bringing benefit, is love for God and the ornaments of righteousness, *fruit that deceives* would properly be understood as the fruit of impiety, eventually turning into something abominable.

What the *fruit that deceives* is like, therefore, which results from their impiety, he immediately demonstrates, going on to say, *Because you hoped in your chariots, in the greatness of your power. Ruin will rise up among your people, and all your fortifications will be de-*

23. Mt 18.6.
24. Ex 20.3–4.

stroyed. In other words, you have gravely offended by worshiping sticks and stones and dishonoring the one true God, who is God by nature. Then, when war was declared, and was at the very gates, far from seeking help from me, you placed your trust in your own *power* and the vast number of *chariots*, and expected to prevail over the might of the enemy, as though the favor and assistance of the false gods sufficed for you. This will prove to be *fruit that deceives* for you: destruction will befall the peoples, and the splendidly fortified city will be entirely brought down; after all, what God does not support collapses without any doubt.

Let this be said also by us, or rather by God, to those who are bent on paying heed to the sacrilegious heretics and who pretend to learn what is relevant to life and understanding. They *pass over impiety in silence,* being willing to listen to malcontents, despite their serious obligation to condemn them. They will therefore share in their folly, and *harvest the fruit* of iniquity; *they eat* (223) what deceives by accepting counterfeit and abhorrent knowledge, being drilled in twisted teachings and everything that runs contrary to the beauty of truth. There could be no doubting that all their greatness *will be destroyed* as God overturns it, and they will meet with destruction and ruin.

As prince Shalman[25] [*was destroyed in*] *the house of Jerubbaal, in the days of battle they dashed to the ground a mother with her children. So shall I do to you, house of Israel, in view of your wickedness* (vv.14–15). It is written in the book of Judges that at one time Israel made the mistake of following the Baals. Consequently, they offended God and were surrendered into the hands of Midian for seven years. They suffered the harsh oppression of their overlords to such an extent as even to live in caves, and survived only by hiding in them and by making a fortification of their difficult location, since they completely despaired of fighting.[26] It therefore happened that at times they were killed when they fell among the Midianites, the result being that women and children perished together, no quarter being given. Now, their rulers were Oreb and Zeeb, and Zebah and Zalumna.[27]

---

25. Greek: *Salmana;* see n. 27 below.
26. Jgs 6.1–2.
27. Jgs 7.25; 8.5. Cyril has seen the Midianite Zalumna in the Shalman of

The state of their misfortune reached a point where God had pity on Israel's hardship and raised up Gideon, who was also known as Jerubbaal by his father and countrymen for the following reason. At God's bidding through the voice of an angel, he destroyed the pillar of Baal and chopped down its grove, avoiding detection at night. When the inhabitants of the town at dawn arrived at the shrine in their zeal to perform the usual ritual, (224) they saw the Baal dislodged and the wood there cut down; they guessed it was due to Gideon's devotion, and attributed responsibility for the affair to him. They then went to his father and said, Give us your son so that we may kill him "because he destroyed the Baal." He replied, "Surely you are not avenging the Baal? If he is a god, let him take vengeance on the one who destroyed him"—hence Gideon's being given a different name from then on, Jerubbaal, which means, "Let Baal take vengeance."[28]

Just as *Shalman,* the leader of the Midianite horde, *dashed to the ground a mother with her children* from the *house* of Gideon, or Jerubbaal, then, he is saying, in the same way the cruel and inhuman general of the Assyrians will wage war on you without any compassion, and will *dash to the ground a mother with her children.* This will happen on account of your evil actions: the God of all, being a just judge, does not punish without reason. But if the sins of those offending him were taken to a surpassing degree, then he would inflict the effects of his wrath commensurately. If we are to avert his anger, we must avoid offending him or provoking to displeasure, as it were, God's mild nature, which is unwilling to be forced to act by the enormity of the failings.

Now, it should be realized that some previous exegetes claimed that it was not the Midianite ruler *Shalman* who *dashed to the ground a mother with her children* from the *house of Jerubbaal,* or Israel (the whole nation being understood by reference to the leaders); rather, it was Gideon who *dashed to the ground a mother with her children* in the *house* of Shalman. My view, however, is that

---

the Hosea text, as will Theodoret after him (who also makes a telling reference to Ps 83.11 citing the four Midianites), and finds a reference to the events in Judges.

28. Jgs 7.27–32.

it is not the latter view that is more convincing, but the former; just as at that time when Israel was attracted to the Baals, (225) the children along with their mothers were dashed to the ground by the hand of foreigners, so, too, at this later stage, when Ephraim was involved in idolatry, they were again dashed to the ground by the hand of savages, namely, the Assyrians, together with the women who bore their offspring. My view, therefore, is that the verse will be more persuasive and retain the resemblance between the ancient figure and more recent events if the force of the text is taken this way.

At dawn they were cast out, the king of Israel was cast out. Once again the other translators and indeed the Hebrew text are clear in saying, "They were cast out like dawn," as if to say, In a very short time, or quickly and without delay, Israel forfeited its relationship with God. The moment of dawn is very brief: once the light of the breaking day begins, it brings the dawn; the sun rises and releases its first beam, the dawn is dissolved and gone.[29] *Like dawn,* therefore—that is, in a brief moment that is soon over—they were cast out along with their leaders. This, in fact, is the way we shall interpret it; or we shall take it in a different sense: when God had not yet imposed penalties on human failings, or was displaying his longsuffering at greater length, it was not surprising that it compared him to people asleep at night. The blessed prophets, for instance, cry aloud to us in many ways to the same effect; Jeremiah in his wisdom said, "Surely you are not like someone asleep, or like a man unable to save?" The divinely inspired psalmist said at one time, "Wake up! Why are you sleeping, Lord? Arise! Do not (226) cast us off forever"; at another he looks to him to be awake and provide help for some people: "The Lord awoke as from sleep."[30]

He normally refers to *dawn,* therefore, as the time for awakening for them; at dawn we arise from sleep. When God exercises surveillance over them, then, and, as it were, gets up to inspect what they have done, they will be rejected and *cast out,* despite the extent of his longsuffering and his dozing over them, so to

---

29. Cyril may have noted that the Antioch text (in Theodore; Theodoret also reproduces it) typically offers both forms.

30. Jer 14.9; Pss 44.23; 78.65.

speak, in times past. *The king* also was *cast out* along with the mob, he says, as though the monarchy in Ephraim had not yet been removed. On return to Judea after the time of captivity, as I said, remember, they were all subject to one king, as of course in the beginning and before the time of captivity; members of the tribe of Judah reigned in Jerusalem, Israel being all one.[31]

31. We noted that, against the evidence of The Chronicler, Cyril believes the north joined fortunes with the south in the restoration (Pusey's text differing slightly from the PG edition at this point).

COMMENTARY ON HOSEA,
CHAPTER ELEVEN

Because Israel was an infant and I loved him, and I called his children to leave Egypt. Just as I called them, so they departed from my sight (vv. 1–2).

HE SENSE OF this probably gives rise to an objection on the part of some people. Take the case, for example, where someone thinks, or even openly says, If the people of the bloodline of Israel were due in time to be rejected, to leave God's presence, and to be loathsome and hated, why at all were they called in the first place? In response God very properly gives some kind of explanation by saying, *Israel was an infant and I loved him, and I called his children to leave Egypt*. (227) Jacob was a simple man, he is saying, who was given a different name: Israel; consequently, I loved him, saying even when they were in their mother's womb, "I loved Jacob, but hated Esau." Because *I loved him*, therefore, consequently I also rescued *his children* from the oppression of the Egyptians; "I shall show mercy to thousands who love me."[1] So what was the response of those who were honored and chosen on account of their fathers, who were honored by the grace of freedom, and liberated from slavery and hardship? Surely they honored me? Surely they were zealous to bring joy by their benevolence to the God who protected them? Not at all, he says: they abandoned the Lord, *departed* from the one who honored them, insulted the one who called them. *Departed:* in what way? Surely one by one and in small groups they defaulted on proper thinking and were inveigled into some people's deceits? By no means: they left in the way they were called, in vast

---

1. Mal 1.2–3; Ex 20.6. The opening verses of Hos 11 are noted both for the corrupt nature of the Heb. text and for moving sentiments on God's parental love that have been classed as one of the high points of the OT revelation of the divine nature. Cyril, on the other hand, turns them into a moral lesson, not mentioning the citation of them by Mt 2.15.

numbers, tribe by tribe, every family and household, in the way they left Egypt in the past.

We remember that Pharaoh had scarcely promised to release Israel when he wanted to know the numbers leaving, asking clearly, "Who are staying, and who are going?" Moses replied, "We shall go with our young people and our old people, with sons and daughters, our sheep and cattle."[2] So the call was for whole tribes and the whole population, families and households; and in the same way was the apostasy, which he suggests was extremely ugly by saying, *They departed from my sight.* In other words, those whom the Lord of all chose to hate he did not protect, in keeping with the verse sung in the Psalms, "Look upon me and have mercy on me." Scripture says, remember, "The eyes of the Lord are on the righteous," and he himself says somewhere, (228) "On whom shall my gaze fall if not on the lowly and peaceable, who trembles at my words?"[3]

They sacrificed to the Baals and offered incense to the carved images. I bound Ephraim together, I took him up in my arms. They did not know that I heal them in their human corruption, I drew them with bonds of my love (vv.2–4). He brings out the immeasurable clemency inherent in God, which befits him. I mean, it would be reasonable and fitting, and not improbable, that he would accord good things to those with faith in him already, who have acknowledged him and chosen to adore him alone; after all, anyone choosing to act properly honors his friend and supporter. But to do so, even to those who are profane and lack knowledge of him as the source of every good, reveals an immensity of lovingkindness and admiration and a proof of clemency truly befitting God. Accordingly, the Savior himself also said, when showing compassion for our situation and as God according mercy that is not at all due to people addicted to sin, on one occasion, "It is not the healthy who need a physician but those who are ill," and likewise at another time, "I have come to call not the righteous but sinners to repentance." Paul in his wisdom is also amazed at the incomparable longsuffering of the God who controls all, and he

---

2. Ex 10.8–9.
3. Pss 86.16; 119.132; 34.15; Is 66.2.

says, "Christ came into the world to save sinners, of whom I am the foremost."[4]

Accordingly, *they*—that is, the people of Israel—were deceived in Egypt, he says, and no longer knew the true God—me, that is; rather, they scorned me by offering sacrifices to *the Baals,* (229) that is, the idols, *offering incense to the carved images,* or the local deities. Since I am good and kind, however, *I bound Ephraim together* despite its being so depraved (referring to Israel as a whole by mention in this case of one tribe). The meaning of this he personally clarified by saying, *I took him up in my arms.* The comparison comes from what is done in the case of children: people picking up small babies in their hands *bind them together,* as it were, by holding their feet together. As I see it, everyone sitting down has to close their thighs and knees, which is the meaning of *I bound together,* as is also recorded of Abraham, that he *bound together* his son Isaac when he was expecting to sacrifice him to God.[5] Now, you should know that the Hebrew and even the other translators do not have the word *bound together,* saying instead, "I was like a nurse to Ephraim."[6] While I was like that with them, therefore, *they did not know,* that is, did not understand, did not sense that by destroying others among their adversaries I was achieving their improvement—the sense of *I heal them in their human corruption.* The Egyptians, in fact, were the first to be destroyed by the ten plagues when Pharaoh did not grant a release; after the Egyptians' plagues Hittites, Hivites, Amorites, Canaanites, and Jebusites perished;[7] Israel vanquished them and took possession of the promised land as God smoothed out everything rough for them and ensured that they could get the better of the enemy. They therefore do not appreciate, he is saying, that by destroying people of a type similar to them I improved their situation and drew them—that is, clasped and held them close—*with bonds of love.* Had they been wise, however, (230) they would have pondered and considered within themselves why

---

4. Mt 9.12–13; 1 Tm 1.15.
5. Gn 22.9.
6. Cyril did better with his initial educated guess involving the binding of feet, the Heb. term in this verse (a *hapax legomenon*) having to do with guidance in the use of feet, Zorell suggests.
7. Jos 24.11.

these nations were destroyed by God, on the one hand, and we were given admission, on the other; had they so understood it, that I hated the sinner and set no store by the worshiper of the demons, they would perhaps have ceased choosing to commit similar crimes.

There is surely need, therefore, for those who wish to give gladness to God with their self-control and sound thinking, to turn the wrath befalling others into an occasion for caution. From this it is easy to see that the vice of ingratitude is most regrettable, and the one falling victim to it would rightly be punished as if convicted of every wrong. The ingrate, he says, in fact, is like the blasphemer.

I shall be to them like someone striking a person on the cheek; I shall glance at him and prevail over him (v.4). Since he had said he loved them and took them in his arms like babies, and bound them together, as it were, with bonds of love, despite Ephraim's being profane and sinful, consequently he also says he will bring the sinner to conversion. "One whom the Lord loves he corrects, and he chastises every child he accepts," remember.[8] Note how he promises not to divest of the clemency befitting God even the manner of chastisement; he says the response to them will be like a blow on the cheek with a human hand, which could be understood as the action of a parent, combining anger with compassion and love, and simply striking with the hand lest the offense go completely uncorrected.

Since he loves, however, he also promises to *glance at him;* he accords supervision to those he chooses to honor, and *prevails* (231) over us, subduing with the skill and might proper to God those who opt to be infected with rebelliousness. After all, if he does not succeed by persuasion, he is obliged to have recourse to a better line of action, and by tribulation he brings us to what is for our benefit and necessary for salvation. Let the God of all therefore hear from us, "Lord, your correction brought us slight tribulation"—a slap, in fact—and again, "Correct us, Lord, but with justice and not in anger, lest you render us few in number."[9]

---

8. Prv 3.12.
9. Is 26.16; Jer 10.24.

Being corrected, you see, is not harsh for those who think aright, whereas being punished angrily is terrible and hard to bear, or rather is something ruinous.

Ephraim dwelt in the land of Egypt, and Assur was its king, because they were not willing to return. His sword was weakened in his cities, and met its end in his hands. They will feed off their schemes (vv.5–6). It is a fact that being separated from God by deviating perversely into commission of crimes, and that insulting him in some way by disobedience, despite his invitation to salvation, completely reduces us to the depths of evil. This fact blessed Paul clarifies in the words, "Beware, brethren, of refusing his invitation";[10] and it is not less clear from our text. On leaving his homeland, the text says, in fact, Ephraim in his depravity made Egypt his own country, as it were, out of fear of the misfortunes of war. But he became subject to *Assur* himself, and bent his neck to foreign rule, being reduced to such a point of hardship. Were you to ask the reason, you would listen to the words of the one who knows everything: (232) *They were not willing to return.* Though God offered an amnesty, in fact, and, as it were, bade them reform and return to his will by abandoning depravity and rising up from the depths of idolatry, they culpably ignored him and *were not willing to return.*[11] Consequently, [Ephraim] was then taken captive and became subject to those who hated him; *his sword was weakened in his cities, and it met its end in his hands.* That is, in no city of Ephraim was an able-bodied man found fit for wielding a sword; the hands of those who normally wielded it were limp and, as it were, loose. And when they planned and performed evil of their own, they ate the fruit of their own folly.

Presuming to dishonor the Savior by disobedience, therefore, is surely harsh, and even if the possibility of fleeing sin is proposed to some by clemency from God, indifference does not go unpunished. We *shall dwell in Egypt,* in fact; that is, we shall doubtless be fugitives and exiles. It is not a material land that we abandon in transferring to another, but the inheritance of the saints. We shall also be subject to *Assur,* obviously the ruler of this age, and be subject to him as slaves and captives, and under the yoke

---

10. Heb 12.25.
11. This sentence is not found in the PG edition.

of his will on account of the *weakening* of the *sword* among us and its coming to an *end*. There is no possibility, you see, no possibility for those addicted to sin to choose "God's armor" and "the sword of the Spirit, which is the word of God."[12] Now, by *sword* you would understand, as it were, the movement both warlike and godly of our mind directed against the passions and opposing the diabolical exploits; thus we tread the pious, blameless path and attach to our heads the ornaments of the evangelical way of life. (233).

His people dependent on their dwelling. God will be angry at his privileges, and will not exalt him (v.7). The sense of the verse is very difficult to explain and the composition of the text uneven, so there is need of considerable clarification for those wanting to understand it. Its meaning in brief is this: Ephraim departed for Egypt, and became subject to a king, the Assyrian. Then, as though someone were asking the question, "Why and in what manner was it allowed to suffer, or how did Israel come to serve foreigners?" he proceeds to give an explanation. He says firstly, "He was not willing to return" (v.5), that is, despite the offer of clemency, he was indifferent and disobedient to this extent. Next, "The sword was weakened in his cities" (v.6), that is, there was no one proven in military leadership to resist the Assyrians, since God had undermined their fighting power and by fear perhaps undermined the able-bodied fighters.

There is also, however, a different reason for his becoming subject to the Assyrian. What is that? *The people* (namely, Ephraim), as it were, *depended on* him (the Assyrian), and he wanted to remove him *from his dwelling* to that of the Persians and Medes. We do not claim that Ephraim himself wanted to suffer this fate; as far as his sins were concerned, however, he, as it were, sought to suffer such disasters, especially as it was possible to escape the wrath by opting for better and more appropriate behavior. He, so to speak, *depended* on the Assyrian, left his homeland, that is, *his dwelling*, and foolishly was anxious to proceed to the Assyrian's, despite God's expressly threatening to inflict such a fate on him (234) unless he decided to repent. Since they were so committed

---

12. Eph 6.11, 17. Having found the literal sense of the text difficult enough to explicate, Cyril has embarked on a spiritual application.

to this resolve, *God will be angry at his privileges,* by *privileges* referring to the special advantages of the peoples—namely, kings and leaders, who were deported with the masses as pitiable slaves and captives, because they had deceived those in their charge and proved to be a snare to those who could have kept to the straight and narrow, if they wished to, since leaders always lead their subjects. They will therefore be humbled and cast out, despite enjoying the highest reputation, fame attaching to the royal throne. God *will not exalt them,* however, for the kingdom of Ephraim is at an end, as I have often said.

We who are in Christ, therefore, must especially be on the alert for this inclination to depravity, clinging fast to God. If we do not do so, we shall willingly impose the yoke of the devil on ourselves, as if *depending* on love for him, and moving with complete enthusiasm to being henceforth subject to him and doing his will. If this were to happen, however, we would provoke God, and thus henceforth be base, with mind trampled into the ground, since God would disable us, unwilling that we should reach the good with valiant efforts.

How am I to feel towards you, Ephraim? Shall I be your protector, Israel? How am I to feel about you? I shall make you like Admah and like Zeboim. I have had a change of heart in this; I am stirred to compassion. I shall not give vent to the wrath of my anger, I shall not abandon (235) *Ephraim to destruction, because I am God and not human, the Holy One in your midst* (vv.8–9). He applied blame, suggesting that without any doubt the severest wrath should befall them for their sacrilegious behavior and extremely impious actions against God that left no room for mercy towards them. Since he is kind, however, the fount and origin of clemency, he cuts short that impulse, not as though he were unreasonably punishing something that happened by chance on the basis of thoughts of something better (the divine and ineffable nature would not be mistaken at any time in thoughts or actions most appropriate to it), but as though keeping in check what befits it and suppressing out of clemency what is particularly suited to them—namely, their utter ruin, and the need for their complete uprooting, as it were. Consequently, he says, *How am I to feel towards you?* In what way am I to proceed in dealing with your situation? *Shall I be your pro-*

tector and ally as well, and make you invulnerable to those wanting to plot against you? Then how will it happen? For those committing dreadful crimes against God, in fact, it would be more fitting to be punished than to prosper. Giving just deserts, then, and determining punishment to fit their crimes, *I shall make you like Admah and like Zeboim,* Sodomite cities which fire from on high destroyed to their very depths.[13]

I shall not do this, however, he says, despite a just demand for it to happen. Instead, I shall postpone it; having second thoughts, I shall not give vent to unmitigated anger. I would not consign Ephraim to complete destruction, despite its evil record. For what reason? Did they not deserve to suffer this fate? Yes, he says, but *I am God and not human;* that is, I am kind, not permitting myself to be overcome by angry impulse, a human passion. Why, then, do you still punish, he asks, (236) if you are God, who is not overcome by wrath, and proceeding rather by inherent clemency? I punish, he says, because I am not only good, being God, but in addition to this I am *holy,* hating iniquity, abhorring the defiled, repelling the ungodly, converting the sinner, and purging what is loathsome so that it may be associated again with me.

The prophet renders us a service, therefore, by crying out in the words, "Seek the Lord, and when you find him, call on him. When he comes near you, let the sinner abandon his ways and the lawless man his plans; let him turn back to the Lord, and he will find mercy." It behoves us, in fact, if being with God means much to us, with all our strength to avoid sinning, and to remember his saying, "You will be holy, because I am holy."[14]

And I shall not enter the city, I shall follow behind the Lord (vv.9–10). Sometimes precise knowledge of the future enters the minds of the holy prophets when the Holy Spirit illuminates them. Accordingly, amidst their own words, or those from God on high, they sometimes foretold the statements of some people repenting or giving thanks or exulting at God's promise to gladden them. We shall now find the blessed Hosea also having this

---

13. Dt 29.23.
14. Is 55.6–7; Lv 20.26.

experience: the God of all promised clemency and said he would not destroy sinners completely, because he is *God and not human,* the good one who is over all creation, not being like us. Some people acknowledged their own sins, as it were, and were somewhat embarrassed at the abundance of unexpected grace; so they promised to put a stop to what they had devised, (237) which was a means of offending God. What it was God has confirmed for us again through the prophet himself, saying a little earlier in censuring Judah itself and Ephraim, "Israel forgot the one who made him; he built shrines, and Judah made fortified cities. I shall send fire on his cities, and it will consume their foundations."[15] On the one hand, Ephraim, or Israel, built altars and shrines in Samaria for the idols, were drawn into apostasy, forgot God, set no store by sincerity of love for him, and kept provoking him. Judah likewise, on the other hand, although trusting in God, having been saved in times past by him and through him, roused him to wrath in many and varied ways, especially this one: when God threatened to send against them the Assyrian to devastate the land, it fortified its cities in the belief that even if God was unwilling, it would be saved by the fortification of the cities and would escape the hand of the enemy.

When God promised the benefits of his clemency even to those gravely offending him, therefore, those who were then saved said they would desist from their unlawful exploits and their schemes as well. Let Judah cry out, *I shall not enter the city;* that is, I shall have God as my wall; I shall count on hope in him for security; I shall run for cover to the right hand of the Savior; he alone will suffice for my salvation; I shall confess the complete futility and uselessness of expecting that, when war takes over the land, I shall be saved by entering the city—hence *I shall not enter the city.*[16] Let Israel, or Ephraim, on the other hand, likewise cry out in the other remark, namely, *I shall follow behind the Lord;* I shall put a stop to the former crimes, he means, and then

---

15. Hos 8.14.
16. Unaware that the clause in the Heb. is obscure and can also be rendered "I shall not come in wrath," Cyril engages in some creative commentary. Likewise with the opening clause of the next verse, which modern commentators see introducing a change of thought.

I shall adopt (238) the divine laws; I shall make the God of all my leader. If, on the other hand, you went after God's will, you would know him alone, show reverence for him, and worship no one other than him.

He will belch like a lion and will roar, and children of waters will be terrified. They will fly away like a bird from Egypt and like a dove from Assyria, and I shall restore them to their houses, says the Lord (vv. 10–11). With the passage of time and the arrival of the moment when Israel was due to be released from captivity, Cyrus son of Cambyses came to power over the Persians and Medes; with an imposing army and mighty force he campaigned against the lands of Babylon and Assyria, God appointing him to do so. The prophet Jeremiah, for instance, forecast the capture of Babylon, saying of the Medes and the Persians, "They will invade you and capture you, Babylon, without your knowing; you were found and taken, because you resisted the Lord." And of Cyrus, "A lion has gone up from its lair; it went out to destroy nations, and left its place to reduce your land to desolation; your cities will be destroyed through not being inhabited." Now, the fact that it was the God of all who gave power to Cyrus, the prophet Isaiah confirms in these words: "Thus says the Lord to my anointed one, Cyrus, whose right hand I have grasped, to subdue nations before him. (239) I shall smash the power of kings, and open doors before him, and cities will not remain closed. I shall go before you and level mountains; I shall smash bronze doors, and shatter iron bars, and reveal to you darkened treasuries, I shall open to you those unseen."[17] After being victorious, therefore, and taking Babylon by force, Cyrus released Israel; on their return they occupied their own land.

Commenting on this story, the prophet Hosea says, *He will belch like a lion.* Who will *belch*? Cyrus, obviously. It is like saying, The war under Cyrus against the Babylonians will sound fearsome and depressing, and when he roars like some lion crying out against the adversaries, *children of waters will be terrified.* By *terrified* he means aghast, and by *children of waters* the Babylonians, who are no match for the *children of waters* in fear, that is, swim-

---

17. Jer 50.24; 4.7; Is 45.1–3.

ming creatures in the sea, or fish, because they are timid and fearful, and are thus easily taken by the very experience. Fish are naturally affected by fear, fleeing noise and avoiding even the shadow of the angler. When Cyrus *roars*, therefore, he is saying, and utters a frightening and fearsome battle cry against Babylon, *the children of the waters* would be terrified, that is, the Babylonians, who are no match for fish in fear. Then like a *bird* and a *dove they will fly away from Egypt*, after having formerly fled to it, and those caught in the snares of captivity will take leave of Chaldea. They will now return and occupy their own land.

Since it is possible for us to enjoy good things by submitting the neck of our mind to God and living in subjection to him alone, let us not willingly (240) proceed to offend him and bring upon ourselves a spontaneous response. It is possible, as I said, to be firmly rooted in prosperity, giving gladness to the Lord by our lawful manner of living and our sincerity towards him.

Ephraim surrounded me with falsehood, and the house of Israel and Judah with impiety (v.12). Being good and compassionate by nature, God is quite loath to punish people; on the other hand, he has no choice in being roused to corrective anger when in some cases their crimes are excessive and innumerable. He teaches us this once more in the present verse, saying, as it were, As the eye of the divinity moved hither and thither and, so to speak, in circles, it was possible to see at every point the *falsehood* and *impiety* of both *Ephraim* and *Judah*. By *falsehood* he refers to the diversions of idolatry and the worship of futile objects, and perhaps by *impiety* insolence against God. After all, how could it fail to be dire and unlawful impiety to forsake the one who is God by nature and in truth, and stupidly to devote oneself to sticks and stones, or to adore creation instead of the Creator, and to endeavor to crown what was brought into being by him with tributes proper to the Lord?

Now God knows them, and a holy people will be called God's (v.12). Whereas it *surrounded me with falsehood and impiety*, he says—the house (241) of Ephraim and Judah, that is—nevertheless I shall even be kind in making a measured response to them, knowing them as I do, that they would not otherwise succeed in changing for the better than by suffering for the sins that give offense and that require a recognition of their sins. *God knows them*, therefore; that is, he is not ignorant of the way of conversion required of them. That event will not be without value for them: the result of it will be their being ranked among *God's holy peoples*. Once their inherent depravity is expunged with hardship and tribulation, they will be cleansed and sanctified, and will learn by experience that sincerity in love for God will be productive of complete enjoyment and prosperity for them, as of course the crimes of apostasy cast them into the depths of servitude and distress.

COMMENTARY ON HOSEA,
CHAPTER TWELVE

Ephraim, wicked spirit, pursued the heat. All day long he multiplied vain and futile things, made a treaty with Assyrians, and went to Egypt to trade with oil (v.1).

HE VERSE once again moves from the vulgar masses to those from the tribe of Ephraim who were ruling over Israel in Samaria, and whom he calls *wicked spirit* on account of their difficulty in adjusting their way of thinking and their extremely rebellious tendency to reject God. In fact, he says it *pursued the heat,* that is to say, although it was possible for it to be under my shade, it, as it were, independently made for the *heat.* Now, by *heat* he refers to burning by tribulation and the searing misfortune. The wise author of Proverbs, for instance, refers obscurely to hardship that way: "A sensible child is saved from the heat, but a lawless child becomes windswept (242) in the harvest." Ephraim, then, being a *wicked spirit, pursued the heat,* that is, sought out and willingly went after the *heat,* whereas sensible people at any rate say of God, "I longed to be in his shade, and took my seat there," by "shade" referring to the shelter of assistance that comes from God on high.[1]

That, however, was not what Ephraim did; it sought out the heat. How, and in what way? *All day long he multiplied vain and futile things,* that is, at every moment he performed and plotted frivolous and useless things. What were they? *He made a treaty with Assyrians.* He had already said on many occasions that some of the kings in Samaria and in Jerusalem endeavored at one time to buy from the Assyrians peace and thereby security, and at another time they called on Egypt for assistance, *going to trade* for the promise of support from them, and at the same time they

---

1. Prv 10.5 LXX; Song 2.3.

sent produce of their own country—to others, clearly. Now, Samaria was rich in oil, and the oil was precious in Egypt, since the land did not contain it.

Hope in human beings, therefore, is *vain and futile.* Let the one who trusts in God exult over the one who trusts in human beings, reciting the verse from the Psalms, "Behold a person who did not take God as his helper, hoping instead in the abundance of his wealth, and relying on his own futility. I, on the other hand, am like a fruitful olive in the house of God, I hoped in the mercy of God forever, and forever and ever."[2] It behoves sincere lovers and those who want to live securely to love as much as possible, to be under God's shade by not provoking him in any way, but rather avoiding offending him as if at the very gates of Hades.[3] (243)

The Lord has a judgment against Judah to avenge Jacob for his ways, and for his exploits he will repay him (v.2). Just as by mention of Ephraim he clearly suggested we should understand those who reigned from the tribe of Ephraim, so in this case [we should understand] those reigning at the time from the tribe of Judah by mention of the ruling tribe. After chiding Ephraim, then, or those from Ephraim who ruled in Israel, calling him a "wicked spirit," and saying "he multiplied vain and futile things" (v.1) by making a treaty with Assyrians and trading oil in Egypt, he now in turn blames those in Judah.[4] He says very properly that the God of all will enter into judgment *against* them as if *avenging Jacob*—I mean the patriarch—for being considerably wronged by his descendants' reluctance to think as he did or to adopt the ancestral attitude, and their refusal to imitate him as though it were a monumental error. He therefore promises to *avenge Jacob* for the wrong done to his reputation by his children's depravity, repaying the wrongdoers *for their ways, and for their exploits.*

---

2. Ps 52.7–8.

3. The final sentence is not found in the PG edition. Occasionally Cyril will insert a brief moral reflection, but his general approach to the text could not be called moralistic.

4. Though noting the inclusion of Judah in the satire, Cyril does not proceed (as do modern commentators) to question its appropriateness in the mission of this prophet to the north. Theodore had seen vengeance being taken on Jacob (the Jews generally, in his reading of it) rather than his being avenged.

In the womb he supplanted his brother, and in his struggles he strove against God. He strove against an angel, and got the better of him (vv.3–4). He helpfully lists the achievements of Jacob by way of refuting those who opt to think and do differently from them. His constant procedure, you see, is to rebut depravity by setting the good in opposition, and by contrasting it with what is commendable he is fond of criticising what is not. The fact that Jacob was gifted from infancy itself, (244) or rather even before birth, he tries to show by the clause, *In the womb he supplanted his brother.* You see, even if what happened was a working of divine power (we do not in fact claim that the infant as an embryo in the womb *supplanted* Esau by himself), nevertheless God was responsible for the child's achievement by foreknowledge of him as someone who would be good. Hence his saying, "I loved Jacob, but hated Esau."[5] Now, this happened by choice of grace, since God definitely chose the one who would be better, once again by foreknowledge, though in this case it was in the womb.

When he came to maturity, on the other hand—or, rather, was then counted as a man—*in his struggles he strove against God;* when in the course of the divine plan God exposed him to sweat and toil, he is saying, he did not show weakness. After all, was not sweat involved in leaving his ancestral home, going to Laban's, putting up with servitude, and performing the toil of a shepherd? Is there any question of this? So *in his* toil *he strove against God,* not that he fought God, but rather obeyed him, and, as it were, prevailed by carrying out what he was ordered. Though Jacob could have grown rich without sweat, and prospered by staying at home, God did not leave him untested; instead, using the occasion of his dread of Esau, he caused him to travel to a foreign country and city and submit to difficult toil so that he might preserve the sincerity of love for God, even amid tribulation itself, and duly be admired. So *in his* toil *he strove against God.* But he also says that *he strove against an angel, and got the better of him;* an angel, a form taken by God, wrestled with him; it was then that his hip was disabled. The divinely inspired Jacob, however, admits the great grace of the engagement, saying, "I have seen God face-to-face, and my life is preserved."[6] (245)

---

5. Mal 1.2–3.   6. Gn 32.30.

The mystery of Christ was prefigured in the bout with the angel; the descendants of Jacob were destined to oppose Christ, whom the verse from the prophets called "angel of great counsel."[7] And while some would be disabled by not adhering to the redemption won through him, others would confess that through him and in him they behold face-to-face the one who is by nature and in truth God. Emmanuel in fact gave us a glimpse of the Father in himself; as he said, "Whoever has seen me has seen the Father."[8] So the process of the contest prefigured the mystery; but God credited the achievement to Jacob.

They wept and implored me, in my house they found me, and there it was spoken to them. The Lord God Almighty will be his memorial (vv.4–5). He proceeds to cite other stories, at every point presenting Jacob to us as illustrious and well-proven. It is written in Genesis, for example, that Jacob's sons Levi and Simeon cruelly and inhumanely killed Shechemites when inflamed with rage about their sister Dinah, whom Hamor son of Shechem had raped.[9] Then the blessed Jacob was very apprehensive about this, and in the expectation that they would be destroyed along with their children and all their household, he immediately rebuked those who had done this: "You have caused me to be hated as someone evil by the inhabitants of the land, the Canaanites and Perizzites. I am few in number, and they will join together and attack me, and my house and I will be wiped out." While the young men in no way ceased their bravado, disputing with him in the words, "Are they to treat our sister as a whore?"[10] (246) the righteous man in his apprehension fell to imploring the saving God.

In his love for the righteous, God promised to rid him of his dread before long, saying, "Rise and go your way to the place [called] Bethel, and settle there; build an altar there to the God who appeared to you when you were on the run from your brother Esau." Then, when he was on the point of going up to Bethel and arriving at the divine house (the meaning of Bethel, "house of God"), the blessed Jacob proclaimed to all his household and everyone with him, "Remove the foreign gods from your midst,

---

7. Is 9.6 LXX. 8. Jn 14.9.
9. Gn 34.25–26. In fact, the guilty party was Shechem, son of Hamor.
10. Gn 34.30–31.

purify yourselves, change your clothes, and let us rise and go up to Bethel and make an altar there to God, who hearkened to me on the day of tribulation, who was with me and preserved me in the way I traveled. They gave Jacob the foreign gods that were in their possession and the rings in their ears; Jacob hid them under the terebinth in Shechem, and destroyed them to this day."[11] When this was done, the divinely inspired Jacob had high hopes; he was entirely rid of the Shechemites' hostility since God with his characteristic power had quelled those who were bent on fighting him. The sacred text says, in fact, "Fear of the Lord fell upon the cities round about them, and they did not pursue the children of Israel." When an altar was erected at Luz, that is, Bethel, "God appeared to Jacob, blessed him, and said, I am your God, increase and multiply; nations and companies of nations will spring from you, kings will emerge from your loins, and the land I gave to Abraham and Isaac I give to you, and to your offspring after you I shall give this land."[12] (247) The present prophetic oracle reminds us of these stories.

Whereas Jacob was a supplanter from the womb, therefore, you for your part are always supplanted instead of supplanting sin. Whereas he loved toil, and by his sweat he was proven to be sincere towards God, you revel in apostasy and are insolent, not according honor to the source of all your satisfaction. Your ancestors *wept and implored me,* he says;[13] if they suspected that they would suffer the effects of some peoples' plotting, they wept and implored me, expecting to be saved by me and only me; you, on the other hand, fortify cities, thinking that, should I be unwilling, you would survive and get the better of your adversaries. *In my house they found me,* for Jacob went up to Bethel, God appeared to him, and there the promise of blessing *was spoken to him,* as we recently explained; you in turn, on the other hand, do not seek

---

11. Gn 35.1–4. Cyril is acknowledging that "my house" in his text is a reference to Bethel. The Antioch biblical text speaks rather of "house of Ôn/Aven."

12. Gn 35.5–7, 9–12.

13. Theodoret will be at pains to point out that in the alternative versions (he is not able to trace their version to the Heb., which would have strengthened his case) these verbs are in the singular, Jacob being the subject. Cyril checks neither.

God in his house, but rather betake yourselves with great enthusiasm to the shrines of Baal. What you look for is not words from God but pronouncements from the demons. Whereas the divinely inspired Jacob went up to Bethel, God's house, and destroyed the idols, you, on the contrary, set up a statue as a god in opposition to God's house; they set up the golden heifer at Bethel, despite Bethel's meaning "God's house," as I said. Hence God says also in the statement of Jeremiah about the synagogue of the Jews, "Why has the beloved in my house made an abomination,"[14] that is, an idol? While the divinely inspired Jacob also ordered those going up to the house of God to purify themselves and change their very garments, (248) you are seen to be profane and unclean, and are not ashamed to enter the divine house with feet unwashed.

Now, since Jacob was like that, consequently *The Lord Almighty will be his memorial;* he is saved in memory of God, and enjoys unfading reputation, since God glorifies those who love him. Therefore—I repeat a matter that is vital for our benefit—our ancestors' glories will condemn us for failing to think like them and be adorned by similar habits and interests. We shall be condemned, not for wronging their souls alone, but, as it were, for undermining the ancestors' reputation and bringing shame on our forbears' nobility.[15]

You will turn back in your God. Observe mercy and justice, and stay close to your God forever (v.6). The promise of grace is combined with a threat, the verse coming from someone threatening rather than simply promising. The threat issues from love, however, the oracle coming from someone summoning to right thinking and to desire for comeliness. Although the divinely inspired Jacob was wise and faultless, he is saying, with godliness as the fruit of his own free will, you did not imitate your father. But you, too, *will turn back to your God;* that is, even if you are a spineless and arrogant apostate, you will nonetheless return, even if unwillingly, to live an upright life. You will return because you will have been chastened *in God,* that is, through God. Since sound rea-

---

14. Jer 11.15.
15. In the PG edition the verbs in the two closing sentences are in the second person.

soning did not persuade you to follow the straight and narrow (249) and be inclined to thinking as you ought, chastisement of every kind will be a decisive influence on you and firmly bring you to a beneficial frame of mind. This, as I see it, is the meaning we should take from the sentence, *You will turn back in your God*, which contains a threat, as I said, nicely combined with encouraging promises.

Then God goes on to announce to them, already chastised and submitted to punishment by him, *Observe mercy and justice, and stay close to your God forever.* In other words, just as if a master were to say with both compassion and irritation to a servant who had been corrected and submitted to chastisement by him, Be sensible and obedient, and don't scorn instructions from the master, in the same way, in my view, the God of all says to Ephraim, who has been struck in some fashion and corrected by the misfortunes of war, *Observe mercy and justice, and stay close to your God forever.* It would be like someone saying, Be aware that the reason why you were beaten is that you did not observe and respect what I love. By *mercy*, then, he means love ("love is the fulfillment of the Law, and does no wrong to the neighbor," in the statement of the blessed Paul),[16] by *justice* right behavior, or righteousness and observance of the divine will (the Law being referred to as *justice* in the divinely inspired Scripture), and *closeness to God forever* would highlight the mind's genuine desire and inclination for him, and not wanting to be attached to other things that are not gods, like creation, or sticks and stones. The person who is in the habit of excelling in good actions and preserving incorruptible faith within him will be close to God and near him in disposition; sin often intervenes and keeps God at a distance. (250) In the same way attachment to the views of unholy teachers of falsehood interferes with our relationship with him—of a spiritual kind, that is; accordingly, for those wanting to be near to God, whatever would keep them at a distance should be avoided.

Canaan, in his hand a balance of injustice, loved to oppress. Ephraim said, But I have grown rich, I have found respite for myself. None of his

---

16. Rom 13.10.

efforts will be found to benefit him because of the injustices he committed (vv.7–8). As far as pleasing God went, on the one hand, Ephraim *observed mercy and justice, and stayed close to him forever.* But when his sound thinking was lost and such precious and venerable values were set at naught, he became like the foreign Canaanites,[17] godless and impious, particularly given to habits of depravity, and unrestrainedly in thrall to the savage inclination to lust of foreigners. It was therefore necessary for Ephraim to be seen to imitate its forefather Jacob and choose to follow the path of his righteousness. Instead, it became *Canaanite: a balance of injustice* was found *in his hand,* that is, inequity and greed; he had given preference to accursed *oppression* like the nations that do not know God. The fact that he was wrong to do this he did not think worth considering; he took satisfaction only in growing rich and enjoying himself, as though God were not watching, no longer surveying people on earth, and not chastising rightly those who chose to do wrong.

Now, Ephraim's eagerness to grow rich by every means would be a clear proof of extreme folly, as would his setting at naught the crimes of robbery and violence, instead of then making a solemn pronouncement, as it were, (251) on the basis of extreme astonishment at what should have caused them shame instead. He said, in fact, *But I have grown rich, I have found respite for myself.* So what was God's response to this? *None of his efforts will be found to benefit him because of the injustices he committed;* it is true, in fact, that "wealth unjustly amassed will be vomited up," as Scripture says. To those bent on amassing it unjustly and growing rich from avarice, let the statement of the holy one be proclaimed: "It was better for you to execute justice and noble righteousness"; before the divine tribunal, in fact, "treasures are of no use to the lawless, whereas righteousness will rescue from death." The author of Proverbs says, "Better a small portion with fear of the Lord than vast treasures without fear"; and again the same author, "Better a slight yield with righteousness than a large income with injustice."[18] Sometimes, however, our behavior and

---

17. Cyril does not resonate with the sense of "merchant" in "Canaanite" as found in Ezek 17.4 and Zep 1.11, and used in mockery here.
18. Jb 20.15; 22.15; Prv 10.2; 15.16; 16.8.

the quality of our actions make us worthy of the nobility of holy parents, or, on the other hand, group us with sinful forbears; we would in fact in no way be different from those living in impiety if we were to imitate their doings. It was for this reason, we claim, that Ephraim was called *Canaan:* he had the outlook of foreigners. The Canaanites were foreigners, abominable for their godlessness. Accordingly, there are also some people who are reproached by fittingly being told in regard to their crimes, "Offspring of Canaan, not Judah."[19]

I, the Lord your God, who brought you up out of the land of Egypt, shall settle you again in tents as on a day of festival. I shall speak to the prophets, I multiplied visions and I took on a likeness at the hands of the prophets (vv.9–10). He called Ephraim *Canaan,* as I said, as a clear accusation of his having hated mercy and justice, and instead opting for (252) avarice, inequity, and every kind of injustice. Lo, once more he tries to bring out that he not only behaved this way to human beings, but in actual deeds declined closeness to God. So he accuses him of ignoring the Redeemer, of insulting with his foolish behavior the one who had brought him out of the house of slavery with signs and wonders, with great power and an uplifted arm. *I brought you up out of Egypt,* he says; by use of the term *brought out,* he reminds them of the things that were done for them up until their introduction into the land promised to the holy ancestors, which were countless and surpassed every marvel. The fact that it was inexcusable for them to forget them he emphasized by proceeding, *I shall settle you again in tents as on a day of festival.*

The nature of that occasion you will find out next. The Law given by Moses commanded that in the seventh month on the fifteenth day the feast of Tabernacles should be held. The occasion for it the lawgiver himself explains for us in reference to Tabernacles in Leviticus: "You shall celebrate it in the seventh month. You shall dwell in tents seven days. Every citizen in Israel will dwell in tents so that your generations may see that I made the children of Israel dwell in tents when I brought them out of the land of Egypt. I am the Lord your God."[20] The feast was

19. Susanna 56.
20. Lv 23.41–43.

celebrated, therefore, in memory of the exodus from Egypt. He then asks, How could you forget me, who brought you out of Egypt, when you are still living in tents, and in that fact you have an occasion for the feast? *I shall settle you again in tents as on a day of festival.* By *shall settle* he means, "am settling," or "making you settle" (253) in tents, on the days of the festival in those years. So the forgetfulness was inexcusable.

Perhaps, however, you were anxious to find out something of the future, and were curious about what concerns you. What need was there to make an approach to the false seers of Baal, or those of the false gods, and ask such questions of them, instead of wisely recalling that *I shall speak to the prophets, and I multiplied visions?* That is to say, every word of prophecy will come from me, or has already come, not from some other [source] of the false gods; knowledge of the future and remembrance of the past belong to me alone. The false seers and false prophets esteemed by you, he says, imitated me—the meaning of the clause, *I took on a likeness at the hands of the prophets.* You sought knowledge of the future from them. Then, feigning my words, and imitating the deeds of my prophets, they made utterances to you from their own hearts. Jeremiah the prophet, remember, put wooden stocks around his neck when God bade him do so; and in reference to his words the false prophet Hananiah took the stocks and smashed them, saying, "Thus says the Lord: Smash the yoke of the king of Babylon."[21] This, as I said, is the meaning of the clause, *I took on a likeness at the hands of the prophet.*

Ephraim's crime, then, was that, despite having a clear reminder of the feast of Tabernacles, in the course of the exodus from Egypt, it forgot God, and did not seek a response from him, though he was the one who *spoke to the prophets, and multiplied visions.* Instead, it was devoted to the deceits of the false prophets, who feigned God's [support] in word and deed. (254)

If it is not Gilead, surely there were false rulers sacrificing in Gilgal. Their altars like turtles in a dry field (v.11). In this he censures them for approaching false seers and false prophets, going up and sacrificing at Gilead and Gilgal. He takes as an example these two

---

21. Jer 27.2; 28.2.

cities in particular because in them the error was worse than in the others, and every form of piety towards God was rejected; everything was provocative in word and marked by extreme folly. For example, God said above in reference to Gilead, "There Gilead scorned me, a city producing futile things," that is, idols, there being makers of idols in it, and in reference to the other one, "All their wickedness began in Gilgal, because it was there that I hated them for their evil pursuits."[22]

There is need to make mention of something that happened in Gilead, for thus we shall understand the sense of the text. Pul king of the Assyrians, the first to attack Samaria, made the two tribes a kind of first-fruits across the Jordan, taking all of their cities, Gilead before the others. God mentions this, as if in passing, in saying, *If it is not Gilead:* if it is not, he means, Gilead will also now be saved;[23] and if it perishes, and it is not possible to convict Ephraim of intoxication because it is not seen now to be guilty, *surely there were false rulers sacrificing in Gilgal* and not true ones? Now, Gilgal is a city across the Jordan where assemblies of people, small and great, were particularly addicted to the defilements of idolatry. (255) So *if it is not Gilead,* is there anyone who dares to claim that *there were false rulers sacrificing in Gilgal* and not true ones? They were not shadows or dreams, however, and not some undistinguished people, but were prominent and important rulers and leaders,[24] erecting lofty and imposing altars for the statues, like *turtles* in *fields.* He calls them *turtles,* though not living beings—you should not think that—but piles of dirt which some people construct to conduct water to the hills. Thousands of such piles have been busily produced by farmers. By *rulers sacrificing* he means either generals and military leaders, or those of the bloodline of Levi, entrusted with leadership by the Law; they, too, were caught up with the others, and not a few worshiped the statues. It is written, for instance, in Ezekiel, "Hence the Lord God says this: No foreigner, uncircumcised in heart and uncir-

---

22. Hos 6.7–8; 9.15.
23. The PG text reads, "not be saved." The meaning of the verse is affected by the particle "surely," which can be accented as ἆρα or ἄρα; the Pusey edition shows Cyril reading the former (whether in the sense of "surely" or "surely not" is not clear), the Antioch text the latter.
24. The clause "They were not . . . leaders" is missing in the PG edition.

cumcised in the flesh, will enter my sanctuary, of all the foreigners in the midst of the house of Israel. The Levites, on the other hand, who went far from me when Israel went astray and were led astray from me in following their desires, will share their iniquity."[25]

Jacob went off to the country of Syria, Israel served for a wife, and for a wife he acted as sentry (v.12). The text returns to the question of the sincerity and simplicity of the ancestor, and to the knavery and impiety of his offspring. He admires, as it were, his endurance in small matters, then cites (256) the indifference of the ten tribes in important matters by way of accusation. After all, who could fail to admire Jacob for enduring such harsh and insupportable toil, and not declining to serve Laban for wives and marriages? Even if the ancestor's reward was insignificant, however—marriage was involved, I said—he still *acted as sentry* and kept faith with the one who promised marriage. Now, his labor was expended not for his own city or country or household; he was an exile living in a foreign land.

While Jacob was that kind of man, let us see also the crimes of the people of Israel. They were not sent to a foreign country; they were in the position of prisoners of war, in service to Egyptians, suffering hardship unrewarded, and were liberated by the power of God from the country of oppressors, and settled in a land promised to their ancestors. Now, the recompense proposed to them for observing the Law was not marriage; rather, it was an abundant source of every good, "a land flowing with milk and honey,"[26] the capacity to engage adversaries, glory and wealth as well as the pride that ensues from them, not to mention prosperity and enjoyment. They did not *act as sentry*, however; they transgressed, setting extremely little store by observance. It is therefore obvious that they abandoned their fathers' goodness to a great degree, and would not be sharers of the mercy accorded them. After all, the Judge is just.

By a prophet the Lord brought Israel up out of Egypt, and by a prophet he was guarded (v.13). In this he clarifies for us the reason for Is-

---

25. Ezek 44.9–10. Cyril might well raise the question of the meaning in the text of "rulers," the LXX seeing it in a similar Heb. form for "bulls."
26. Ex 3.8.

rael's not observing (257) the commandment imposed, for spurning God's words, "You shall have no other gods but me,"[27] and for refusing to emulate their fathers' goodness. He accuses the people of Israel, in fact, of being completely subject to human kingship, despite God's being their king through holy prophets and there being nothing lacking for them to be blessed. We remember, for instance, that while the blessed Samuel was still among them and acting as prophet, they wanted a king.[28] God was angered by this and gravely offended by the insult; but he designated Saul. So he makes the serious accusation that they became totally subject to human kingship, refusing to have God as king through a prophet; it was God, in fact, he says, who saved Israel, brought them out of the house of bondage through the mediation of Moses, who was both prophet and forerunner of prophets, and not only brought them out of *Egypt* but also preserved them, for they continued to worship the one who is God by nature and in truth. But when they became subject to a king, they lost their love for God; Solomon was the first to build altars and shrines to the Baals, then after him the accursed Jeroboam made golden heifers.[29]

Accordingly, he blames them for not observing the excellent divine plan [for them] to be ruled by God, I mean, through prophets, and preferring to fall under the hand of human beings, which proved to be the source of apostasy for them.

Ephraim enraged and provoked, and his blood will be poured out upon him, (258) *and the Lord will repay him for his reproach, according to the word of Ephraim* (v.14). In this he tries hard to show that choosing instead to be subject to the reign of human beings proved to be harsh, precarious, and productive of ruin for the people of Israel. Lo, he says, in fact, Ephraim—that is, Jeroboam of the tribe of Ephraim—*enraged and provoked* me, the Lord of all, and prompted every kind of provocation by introducing heifers and bestowing on them the glory belonging to me. Consequently, he proved responsible for his own ruin: *his blood will be poured out upon him.* Since, on setting up the heifers at Bethel

27. Ex 20.3.   28. 1 Sm 8.5.
29. 1 Kgs 11.5; 12.28.

and Dan, he announced to the people of Israel, "Enough of your going up to Jerusalem. Behold your gods, O Israel, who brought you out of the land of Egypt,"[30] consequently at that point, he says, very rightly he will repay to me, the Judge, the penalty for his *reproach*. Admittedly, in fact, it was a blatant insult and *reproach* to God, daring to ascribe to lifeless matter the marvelous and praiseworthy achievements worked by him. In keeping with Ephraim's *reproach*, therefore—that is, commensurately with his blasphemy and sacrilegious taunts—the effects of my wrath will come back upon him. In other words, just as God was deprived of the glory due to him and to him alone as far as deed and *word*[31] were concerned, so, too, they will be deprived of autonomy when the kingdom of Ephraim comes to an end in due course. As I previously mentioned, remember, after the return from Babylon no one from the ten tribes reigned any longer in Samaria; they were all in Jerusalem under one man, who at the time was from the tribe of Judah.

30. 1 Kgs 12.28.
31. This is perhaps an implied comment on the verse's final phrase, which Cyril finds in his text, but which in the Heb. and modern versions opens the next chapter.

COMMENTARY ON HOSEA,
CHAPTER THIRTEEN

He received ordinances in Israel, he assigned them to the Baal and died. He continued to sin, and they made for themselves an object molded from their silver in the form of idols, works made for them by craftsmen (vv.1–2).

N THIS IT is not the ten tribes individually that he blames, but Israel as a whole, saying that, though *ordinances* were given to them through Moses, through which they were instructed on how they should worship God and offer sacrifices in petition, they for their part dedicated them, as it were, to the Baal, or the idols (referring to the whole sometimes by mention of a part). In other words, they no longer sacrificed to God; instead, they celebrated festivals for the works of their own hands and offered them worship, first-fruits, adoration, gifts, thanksgiving offerings; they deprived God of his proper glory, and accorded it to the statues.

Having done this, however, Israel *died*, he says, and again *continued to sin*. It is like saying, He has been punished for doing this, he has perished for committing it, he knew the anger of the Lord, who inflicts on the deceived punishment unto death. Though he in no way put a stop to his own knavery, he would be apprehended for other crimes of equal gravity; we read in Numbers that the sons of Israel were unfaithful, inflamed with unlawful desires, and they had intercourse with Moabite women, and then paid the ultimate penalty for this. The text says, "Israel camped at Shittim. The people profaned themselves by committing fornication with the daughters of Moab, who invited them to the sacrifices of their idols; the people ate of their sacrifices and worshiped their idols, (260) and Israel was initiated in the rites of Baal of Peor. The Lord was very angry with Israel; the Lord said to Moses, Take all the rulers of the people and make an example of them for the Lord, exposing them to the sun, and the Lord's wrath will be averted from Israel. Moses said to the tribes of Israel, Each of you is to kill any of his family who has been initiated in the rites of Baal of Peor."¹ When this took effect, a vast number of the people of Israel lost their lives.

Consider, therefore, that by offering God's *ordinances* to idols at the time of Moses Israel died in misery; by being deceived it was slaughtered by its own swords, not by the hand of foreigners. Yet *it continued to sin: it made for itself an object molded from gold,*² and *works of a craftsman,* gods produced by the skill of artisans. Now, the verse, as it were, mocks their folly: they believed to be gods what they themselves had crafted. So let the psalmist cry aloud also to them, "Let all who make them be like them, and all who trust in them."³

They say, Sacrifice human beings: there are no more calves. For this reason they will be like a morning cloud and like dew at dawn that disappears, and like chaff that is blown off the threshing floor and like a haze from a chimney (vv.2–3). Once again he charges them not only with being guilty of impious behavior in molding into the form of idols the silver given by God, and in assigning the name of the divine glory to things made of wood and stone, (261) but also with being so caught up in such a degree of stupidity—or rather knavery and inhumanity and the ferocity proper to wild animals, or even worse than that—as not even to spare their own children, but even to sacrifice them to the demons. This was despite God's abominating the practice, and not allowing mention of it even to others, or even a report of it from anyone; the Lord has no love for blood, nor does he take satisfaction in the annihilation of people—far from it. Scripture says, remember, "He created all things for them to exist; the generative forces of the world maintain its welfare."⁴ Since the rebellious dragon, on the other hand, is the inventor and source of death, consequently he takes satisfaction in the slaughter of people. So the fact that the foolish statement on this is hated by God he clarifies by say-

---

1. Nm 25.1–5.
2. Is it from Theodore that Cyril, whose text speaks of silver idols, gets this mention of golden ones, appearing in the Antioch text?
3. Ps 115.8.
4. Wis 1.14.

ing, *They say, Sacrifice human beings: there are no more calves.* The saying is not mine, he means, nor would I ever make such a statement; it is they, the devil worshipers, who say there is need to *sacrifice human beings* to them.

He then mocks the idea and ridicules the practice, going on to say, They probably have no calves, and hence devote themselves to human sacrifice. So be it, he says, you are in error in devoting yourselves to statues and gods of molten metal. Why flood their altars with human blood? We read in the books of Kings that Jotham son of Ahaz, who reigned over Judah, "walked in the way of the kings of Israel, burning incense on the high places, even making his own son pass through the fire," and sacrificing to the demons the son born to him.[5] Since they committed such crimes, *they will be like a morning cloud and like dew, like chaff, and like a haze from a chimney,* (262) visible for a time but proceeding to ruination and ending in nothingness; morning cloud—mist, that is—dew, chaff, and haze from a chimney are evanescent, and soon disappear altogether, even in an hour. After all, what substance is composed of chaff or dew or haze from smoke?

I am the Lord your God, who establishes the heaven and creates the earth, and whose hands created all the host of heaven. I did not present them to you for you to follow after them (v.4). The ugliness of false belief is constantly under censure when true knowledge is brought to the fore, and, as it were, light shines as at night and in darkness, and the word acts as a guide to right thinking. The fact that the people of Israel were filled with every extreme folly, and went to an excess of miserable thinking in honoring molten figures and works of craftsmen and bypassing the one who is God in truth and by nature, he alleges by saying that he is the one who *establishes the heaven,* fixes *the earth* in place, and is maker of the stars. He reproaches them for passing by as hackneyed the possibility of learning the glory of the Creator from things that have been made, and making them the occasion of their own error. The reason they were made, however, was not that they might detract from divine glory when understood by people on earth

---

5. Cyril is going beyond the detail of 2 Kgs 16.3–4, which speaks rather of "Ahaz son of Jotham" and is not necessarily implying murder of a child. (Cyril's sixth tome concludes with comment on v.3.)

to support their assumption that gods exist, but that, as the sacred text says, "from the greatness and beauty of created things"[6] the mind of intelligent beings might by analogy arrive at an understanding (264) of the power and artistry of the maker. Accordingly, the Creator did not *present us* with creation so that it would be adored by us. He testified to this in advance through Moses, for instance, in saying, "On looking up to heaven and seeing the sun, moon, stars, and all the adornment of heaven, do not be misled into adoring them and worshiping them, when it was the Lord your God who allotted them to all the nations under heaven."[7] But the things that had been meant as a sign of seasons and given the role of lights they called gods and presumed to adore; and in their search for worse things than that the wretches honored metal and wooden objects as gods, adoring the products of coppersmiths and craftsmen.

I brought you up out of the land of Egypt; you are to know no God but me, and there is no one to save you except me; I fed you in the desert, in an uninhabited land, in their pastures (vv.5–6). In this there is a grave accusation of insensitivity, and forms of assistance are listed in a series, which highlight the magnitude of the ingratitude of the people of Israel. He accuses them, not as though they were unaware, in my view—how could they be?—but as though having consented to severe depravity and insensitive thinking, and, as it were, guilty of forgetting what they should have always remembered. In fact, while the accursed Jeroboam said, in setting up the heifers for them, "These are your gods, O Israel, who brought you out of the land of Egypt,"[8] they for their part, though aware that what was done for them was due to no one else than God, offered thanksgiving to handmade heifers, and convinced one another, goodness knows how, to attribute to them (265) the extraordinary degree of the divine achievements. As though they were intoxicated with the wine of Sodom, therefore, he pricks them, as it were, by saying that he was the one who brought them "out of the house of slavery," gave the order through Moses that "you shall have no other gods but me,"[9] and stated that it was he alone who would *save* them and effortlessly achieve whatever they

6. Wis 13.5.
7. Dt 4.19.
8. 1 Kgs 12.28.
9. Dt 32.32; Ex 20.2–3.

wanted, who would provide them with food in the wilderness, release springs of water in a land that was wild, inaccessible, and waterless, send down manna, bestow bread of angels from heaven, and, in the manner of a good shepherd, pasture them in prosperity *in their pastures* or journeys. The people of Israel, in fact, lacked no good in the wilderness, despite constantly moving from place to place, and camping in rough and infertile country.

There is need to be forever mindful, therefore, of what we have from God, and to keep far from our minds forgetfulness of it, productive as it is of ruin and provoking to anger the God who gives us complete prosperity. The ingrate, after all, is like a blasphemer, as was wisely remarked.[10]

They were filled to satiety, and their hearts were lifted up; hence they forgot me (v.6). Just as the most skillful physicians carefully consider the causes of disease, and thus strive to arrest it with the help of their expertise, in the same way, in my view, the God of all looks within our mind and heart and investigates the causes of the passions within us, and thus (266) checks the diseased mind with appropriate remedies. He charges the people of Israel, therefore, on the basis of prosperity, with falling victim to forgetting the one who provided them with everything necessary for life and all that was likely to shed the light of knowledge. This was despite the clear admonition in the Law, "Take care that you do not forget the Lord your God by failing to keep his commandments, judgments, and ordinances, which I am commending to you today. When you have eaten your fill, have built fine houses and dwell in them, and your sheep and your cattle have multiplied, your silver and gold are multiplied, and all your possessions multiplied, do not let your heart grow conceited, or forget the Lord your God, who brought you out of the land of Egypt, out of the house of bondage, who led you through that vast and terrifying wilderness, where there were venomous serpents and scorpions, and thirst because there was no water."[11] There was always, in fact, such sufficient enjoyment and conceitedness through unexpected honors as to cause you to forget God and enable the human mind to descend to every possible irregularity.

10. In comment on 11.4.
11. Dt 8.11–15.

In my view, Israel would have become sufficiently liable to accusation for kicking over the traces and finding in the extent of its prosperity an occasion for such a dire ailment; and when they overcame nations, with the help of the God who is all-powerful, they contracted arrogance, attributing somehow to themselves, and not to the God who protected them, the splendor of their achievements.

Luxurious living is therefore risky and difficult to manage, and is, as it were, a slippery path to apostasy from God; far better is moderate tribulation. The holy authors' statements confirm this for us; one said, "Lord, in tribulation I remembered you; by slight tribulation (267) your correction came to us"; and Paul in his wisdom cites tribulation as a kind of root and origin of every good for us: "Tribulation produces endurance; endurance, character; character, hope; and hope does not disappoint." The divinely inspired David also sings somewhere, "It was good for me that you humbled me so that I might learn your ordinances."[12]

I shall be to them like a panther and a leopard; in the path of the Assyrians I shall encounter them like a bear that is at a loss, and shall tear open the covering of their heart. Whelps of the forest will devour them there, and wild beasts of the countryside will dismember them (vv.7–8). Since in fact the extent of their prosperity proved to be productive of ruin for them and an occasion of apostasy, consequently tribulation will now be applied as in the case of sick people; the severe ailments and infections of the body would in no way yield to mild medicines, requiring instead knife and fire. Accordingly, since the magnitude of the divine clemency was of little benefit (not to say none at all) to the people of Israel, severity proper to wild animals is applied to them. Now, he compares himself to the most savage and ferocious wild animals with a particular name for cruelty—not that the divine and ineffable nature could ever act with such rage. It is rather a further lesson that, while the Assyrians will be found to be guilty of such unmitigated rage in their inhumanity and ferocity, not to mention other such things, it would seem that what happened was due to God since it was he who allowed it to happen, releasing on such grave sinners the wrath proper to the Assyrians.

12. Is 26.16; Rom 5.3–5; Ps 119.71.

In finding them, therefore, I will be *like a panther* (268) *and a leopard;* they will be deported to *the Assyrians; I shall encounter them like a bear that is at a loss,* perhaps meaning "starving," or "greatly distressed" in its search for its cubs (they say it is then that a wild beast reaches the height of natural frenzy);[13] *I shall tear open the covering of their heart,* by *covering* here meaning "security," since security of heart is the audacity that someone might have against foes, and, when it is torn open, feelings of fear enter in, with the result that the victory is given to the enemy even without a fight. So it is like saying, I shall reduce them to extreme fear, despite their being compared by contrast to a starving beast bereft of its young, namely, a *bear.* Now, the fact that, in being held by the bonds of captivity and carried off to the land of the Assyrians, they would make no withdrawal from evil, but instead vice would, as it were, follow them even there, he brought out by saying, *Whelps of the forest will devour them there, and wild beasts of the countryside will dismember them;* the Assyrian race is wild, and he compares it to *whelps of the forest* and *wild beasts,* which are much given to ferocity.

Who will help you in your dispersal, Israel? Where is this king of yours? Let him save you in all your cities and judge you, of whom you said, Give me a king and ruler. In my wrath I gave him to you, but in my anger I held back a core of iniquity (vv.9–11). I said a little above that God charges the people of Israel with opting, goodness knows how, to submit by preference to human yokes and to decline (269) the kingship of God himself, despite his reigning over the ancients through holy prophets. He said, remember, "By a prophet the Lord brought Israel up out of Egypt, and by a prophet he was guarded."[14] You, on the contrary, refused to serve under God, and shouted out to the blessed prophet Samuel, "See, you are old, and your sons do not walk in your way. Install a king now over us to judge us, like the other nations."[15] Since you seem really to have made your mind up, then, in setting up a king over

---

13. The interpretation that Cyril hazards he seems to derive from Theodore, who, however, is not as persistent as his successor in unpacking implicit or explicit figures of the author.
14. Hos 12.13.
15. 1 Sm 8.5.

yourself like the other nations, and you expected to be saved by him, *where is* he now? Lo, it is time for proof; let him wage war for you, let him arm himself splendidly, let him save the cities, let him protect those under his control, let him scatter the adversaries, let him vigorously repel those bent on wantonly devastating houses and cities.

Perhaps, however, you will reply, While it is clear that I did the asking, you did the granting, anointing Saul initially. True, he says, but it was *in my wrath I gave* you the leader, and *in my anger I held back a core of iniquity*,[16] wronged as I was by you. It is as if I was expelled from the royal chambers, and was very angry as far as your decision was concerned. Still, I appointed him, despite knowing it was not conducive to your good, my intention being that the experience of the events would clearly teach you that it was foolish and unhelpful, even if you opted for it. *Where is* he now? What good would he be for those involved in war? If, on the other hand, you were still subject to my compassion and authority, you would be seen to prevail completely over the foe. "Vain is human help," therefore, as Scripture says, and "unreliable a horse for salvation,"[17] in which rulers (270) hope, whereas God rescues without any difficulty whomever he chooses, and whomever he sees having regard for hope in him.

Ephraim, his sin is hidden; there will come for him pangs like those of a woman in labor. This son of yours has sense, because he will not cope with the destruction of his children (vv.12–13). This, in my view, is what is meant by the verse, "He conceived hardship and gave birth to iniquity."[18] In the beginning, remember, to avoid losing his throne when Israel kept performing sacrifices prescribed by Law by going up to Jerusalem for that purpose, Jeroboam devised the golden heifers. And, just as it admitted into its thinking some sowing of a wicked seed under the surface, like a *hidden sin*, nevertheless *there will come* the moment for birth *pangs*. It

---

16. The final (obscure) phrase in Cyril's biblical text is found at the beginning of the next verse in our Heb. and in the Antioch text. Other obscure phrases in the lemma Cyril wisely chooses to leave without comment, though he has made his usual creative attempt to wrest sense from it.

17. Pss 60.11; 33.17. This final sentence of Cyril's comment does not appear in the PG edition.

18. Ps 7.14.

could likewise be understood as the time of war and captivity: even if this did not happen to Ephraim itself, it would befall its offspring, or the successors to the throne in due course, because they proved to be imitators of his impiety.

So he is speaking, as it were, to the community[19] in Samaria, and saying, Who will save you? Surely *this son of yours has* no *sense?*[20] By *this* he either means the one reigning at the time, who had the reputation of being intelligent (something always befitting those in power), or suggests something else appropriate to the time when the prophetic word was given. Reigning over Judah in Jerusalem, in fact, was Ahaz, and in his "eleventh year Hoshea son of Elah became king over Israel in Samaria, and he did what was evil in the sight of the Lord." At that time, however, Shalmaneser king of Assyria waged a military campaign in Samaria, and "Hoshea became his vassal." But the Assyrian was very angry with him for the following reason: while he sent messengers to him demanding the customary tribute, he could not bring himself to do as directed by him, and sent a delegation to So king of Egypt asking for help from him. Offended by this, Shalmaneser besieged Samaria for three years, then apprehended Hoshea, threw him in chains, enrolled him among his servants, and deported Israel to the territory of Persians and Medes.[21]

The prophetic text, therefore, probably intends in these words to present Hoshea son of Elah, to whom he refers as *having sense,* as not really being intelligent, speaking ironically, as it were; to Israel someone seemed intelligent and capable of wise planning in choosing to call for help for themselves from Egypt, whereas executing such a plan was foolish and mindless. Who then, he asks, will rescue you from experiencing the unbearable calamities? *This son of yours has sense, because he will not cope with the destruction of his children;* he means that not even he *will cope with the destruction of his children,* since he will be taken captive and enslaved along with the others. He will go to the Assyrians. There is

---

19. Greek: *synagōgēn.*
20. The negative occurs, in fact (though this depends on Cyril's usage with ἆρα), in the Antioch text, as Cyril may have noted in Theodore, and he typically discusses possible interpretations.
21. 2 Kgs 17.1–6.

wisdom, therefore, in the psalmist's verse, "My strength and my praise is the Lord"; for with him are complete power and complete salvation, and there is no one beyond him who can save.[22]

I shall rescue them from the hand of Hades, and ransom them from death. Death, where is your vengeance?[23] *Hades, where is your goad?* (v.14) After mentioning the effects of his anger on sinners, and foretelling the future results of his being offended, (272) he returns to the clemency proper to God. The fact that, far from his being at odds with the whole race on earth and banishing them to unbridled and never-ending destruction, there will be some compassion and a summons to return in due time to the original condition through Christ, he mentions, adding that he will *rescue them from the hand of Hades, and ransom them from death,* obviously meaning those subject to him on account of the sin against the Creator and the original transgression of Adam.[24] Such a promise had in fact been made, not to Ephraim alone, or those of the bloodline of Israel, but to everyone on earth; the divinely inspired Paul writes, remember, "He is the God not only of Jews but also of gentiles, for he has justified the circumcised on the grounds of faith, and the uncircumcised through faith."[25]

In other words, he has ransomed us *from the hand of Hades,* that is, from the tyranny of death, and the form that that redemption takes is to be seen as the death of Christ. He willingly underwent execution on the cross for us, in fact, and disarmed principalities and powers by nailing to it the record that stood against us; then it was that "all iniquity stopped its mouth," and the power of death was undone with the removal of sin, this being the *victory of death and the goad of Hades.* Paul in his wisdom interpreted it this way for us, saying, "The goad of death is sin, and the power of sin is the Law." With the removal of the sin of all through Christ, therefore, we, too, would rightly say, *Death,*

---

22. Ps 118.14; Is 43.11.
23. Greek: *dikê;* the critical apparatus in the Pusey edition acknowledges the variant reading *nikê* (victory).
24. The phrasing strikes us as similar to "original sin"; certainly Cyril (like his Antiochene peers) is in no doubt of the Fall.
25. Rom 3.29–30. It is the rich Pauline development of this verse that encourages Cyril this time to move quickly from the promise of Israel's recovery to a christological dimension.

where is your victory? Hades, where is your goad? "If it is God who justified, who is there to condemn? It is Christ Jesus who died" for us, or rather, who "gave himself as a ransom for all," one person who is more worthy than all, through whom and in whom we have been enriched so as to return to incorruption.[26] (273)

Is consolation hidden from my eyes? Hence he will differentiate between brothers (vv.14–15). We shall read out the first clause of the verse as a question and as an aside, as would be suggested to us if we were to take it correctly. Human nature, he is saying, was affected by the diversity of sin, and took a decisive turn to transgression; consequently, it was rightly condemned to death. What the form of assistance will be for those so affected, or how the event will be averted, I shall next consider for myself, or rather, I have already determined. Surely there is no one among you who is so much a victim of derangement as to think and even claim that *consolation* is a form of encouragement that the divine and uncontaminated mind has not seen? After all, I am a craftsman, not completely unskilled, yet I have a good grasp of everything, and without delay I put my wishes into effect.

Admittedly, he says, *he will differentiate between brothers.* In this he announces to us in advance our Lord Jesus the Christ; he it is who is the *consolation* of all, the form that healing takes. The Father predestined him from eternity as Savior and Redeemer of those under death's control. He said that he would *differentiate between brothers.* What that means we heard Christ the Savior of us all saying, "Do not think that I have come to bring peace on earth; what I have come to bring is not peace but a sword. I have come to set a man against his father, a daughter against her mother, a daughter-in-law against her mother-in-law, and one's foes will be members of one's own household." And again in foretelling the future to the holy disciples, he says, "Brother will betray (274) brother to death," and a father will rise up against his sons.[27] You see, since he destroyed the tyranny of the devil, and rescued the deceived from the toils of idolatry, he so bound

---

26. Col 2.14–15; Ps 107.42; 1 Cor 15.56 (Cyril does not highlight Paul's citation of the Hosea text in a form where *nikê*, victory, replaces *dikê*, vengeance); Rom 8.33–34; 1 Tm 2.6.
27. Mt 10.34–36, 21.

them in love for himself that the believers even discounted physical affection, ignored brethren, fathers, houses, and family, and judged attachment to Christ sufficient for complete satisfaction. The blessed David, for instance, sings somewhere on the part of those who achieved that, "My father and my mother abandoned me, but the Lord adopted me."[28]

The Lord will inflict a burning wind from the desert upon him, and will dry up his veins and leave his springs exhausted; it will devastate his land, and all his desirable possessions (v.15). On the one hand, he transfers his attention to the personification of death, and on the other he likens Christ to the southerly *burning wind*, which he says will be introduced *from the desert* in due course. Now, there is need to realize, even before other matters, that the country of the Jews contains a wide and extensive desert located far to the south; if the wind were ever to blow strongly from that direction, they would be very apprehensive, since the country would dry out. Some people think that the actual underground *veins* of water are made more sluggish and are interrupted by the onset of the violent and fiery wind; so he delivers his words on the basis of what they know and have experienced. (275)

The prophetic verse told us, then, that Christ like a *burning wind* would beset death, and would *dry up* all *his veins and springs*. It very properly persists with the metaphor, therefore, and on the basis of what usually happens it gives a clarification of the mystery. We interpret *veins and springs* of death to mean the forms of destruction, or the evil powers in opposition; it is through them, as it were, that it supplies the vast number of those who are constantly perishing. This is also the way to understand *his desirable possessions;* you would rightly take the *possessions* that are perishing and precious to death to be the people on earth, or the evil powers in opposition, or some ungodly people on earth who minister to his perversity and destroy others in addition to themselves.[29] When the *burning wind* blows, therefore,

---

28. Ps 27.10.
29. If Cyril seems to be coming up with a series of arbitrary interpretations after concluding that the verse is metaphorical, it is equally arbitrary for the Antiochenes to presume we can find here an historical reference to Cyrus's conquest of Babylon.

he says, all the *land* of death will be *dried up*. The verse is presented still further in a metaphorical sense: it is as if you were perhaps to say, Death fed on people on earth like some pasture, but it will be dry, and death will find no feed. With Christ supplying life to all and allowing incorruption to be recalled, you see, corruption has been abolished.

Samaria will be wiped out because it rebelled against its God; they will fall by the sword, their babes will be dashed to the ground, and those with children in the womb will be torn open (v.16). After completing an excellent application of the text to Christ and foretelling the mystery of universal redemption, the blessed prophet once again laments the misfortunes of the offenders, as if he were also mourning those in (276) Samaria. Although they were in fact in a position to enjoy very lavishly the good things stemming from his clemency, they perversely brought down upon themselves the effects of his wrath by choosing to oppose God and set their own will against the Lord's commands as if to give the impression of going into battle against him or of being numbered among his true adversaries. Accordingly, having forfeited all mercy, they will fall to the sword, and novel forms of inhumanity will be devised against women and children; those not yet called into existence and life will endure untimely death along with newborn infants, and the enemies' sword will anticipate birth. Opposition to God is therefore a harsh thing, and is seen in truth and actual experience to be productive of ruin.

COMMENTARY ON HOSEA,
CHAPTER FOURTEEN

Return, O Israel, to the Lord your God, because you have grown weak through your iniquities. Take words with you, and return to the Lord your God. Speak to him, so that instead of receiving iniquities, you may receive good things, and we shall repay with the fruit of our lips. Assyria will not save us, we shall not ride on horses; let us no longer say "Our gods" to the works of our hands (vv. 1–3).

YOU COULD once again have considerable admiration here for the prophet's artistry and the economy of the expression; it is accomplished with appropriate respect, and is full of guidance from on high. He foretells, in fact, the redemption coming through Christ, and the fact that death will in due course give way, and the goad of Hades will be no more. Further, (277) no form of comfort and consolation at all could be imagined of which God is unaware. What more? There was need to advise on what to think and do in reference to their salvation, and, as it were, take pains to bring to sobriety those who were inebriated, not from wine but from worldly pleasure and a willingness to adopt the deceits of the demons.

Lest they succumb to indifference toward the promises of kindness and goodness, therefore, and set no store by the one in the habit of showing moderation, he consequently once more gives them a useful reminder of the calamities, saying that Samaria will be done away with because it resisted its God. He then proceeded to add to that what was sufficient to terrify and sadden the listeners: infants would be dashed to the ground, he says, and unborn children and their mothers destroyed before the womb discharged its longed-for burden into the light.[1] Having stunned them in advance with these terrors, therefore, he

---

1. Cyril paraphrases 13.16 (which in Heb. and LXX stands as 14.1, as also in the PG edition).

then chooses the moment to impart to the hearts of those being counseled an instruction summoning them to repentance, announcing clearly the need to change course and return to God. By saying *because you have grown weak through your iniquities,* he gives them to understand that their weakness will cease altogether along with their *iniquities;* and if the forms of apostasy are removed, the calamities will also disappear.

Now, he smooths out the manner of the *return* to God, properly saying that sinners will win benevolence and mercy from God, not by the proceeds of their wealth, not by offering gold, not by choosing to honor him with silver vessels, not with offerings of cattle, not by gladdening him with slaughter of sheep, but on condition that they make a gift of words, and choose to appease (278) the Lord of all and praise him; *Take words with you* he is saying, *speak to God, so that instead of receiving iniquity, you receive good things.*[2] In other words, lest you be punished in equal measure with your iniquities instead of abounding in the supply of good things, promise to offer to him what comes from your *lips,* thanksgiving hymns and confession, such things being the *fruits* of your tongue. But shout it out, he says, and make a firm promise that *Assyria will not save us, we shall not ride on horses;* nor shall we say *"Our gods" to the works of our hands,* which is a form of apostasy. It was on account of this that they offended, because they served the idols, and, while dishonoring the God who had always saved them, they placed their hope in human assistance. While they called on Assyria when under attack from Egypt, by contrast when Assyria in turn took up arms against Samaria, they bribed the mounted archers from Egypt, or those skilled in mounted attack. Consequently, they heard God's clear statement, "Woe to those who go down to Egypt for help, trusting in horses and chariots"; they were mocked, and rightly so, for eagerly taking as their protector "an Egyptian, a human being and not God, mere horseflesh," as Scripture says. So they promise to cease worshiping idols and continuing to put their hope in human beings. This reform of the guilty is an appeal for clemency

---

2. This difficult sentence Theodoret chooses to avoid citing textually. Cyril typically wrestles with it.

to the Lord of all, who says through the voice of the prophet, "Make a decisive turn from your crimes, house of Israel, and you will not be subject to punishment of iniquity."[3] (279)

In you he will have pity on an orphan. This statement comes from the prophet in his exhortation to repentance, his highlighting the Lord's mildness and calling into question the delay of the person intending to repent. Be in no doubt, O Israel, he is saying, that your prayers will be answered if you apply repentance; the God *in you* is in the habit of *having pity* and compassion *on orphans*. The divinely inspired David also says somewhere, "He upholds the orphan and widow,"[4] intending to highlight the lovingkindness of the divine and ineffable nature on the basis of one case or in the person of those who are particular objects of mercy. If, on the other hand, you wanted to apply to Israel itself the mention of *orphan*, since, as it were, it lost God its Father, despite his saying clearly, "My firstborn son Israel,"[5] I would say that this, too, is a correct interpretation.

There is therefore need for those who are really confident that the Lord of all is good and disposed to lovingkindness to be prompt to repent, and, by actions taken for the better, to remove the causes of previous falls.

I shall heal their dwellings, I shall love them openly, because my wrath has turned from them (v.4). The word from God is introduced as closely related, almost next door, as it were, with the promise to *heal* the weak and *love them openly,* that is, give a clearly stated demonstration of putting mercy and love into effect, as well as an increase in every good.[6] He indicates (280) in addition that he also put an end to his wrath against them, and would not desist from showing lovingkindness. Now, in this the verse probably not only reminds us of the conversion of those of the bloodline of Israel, but also combines it with the calling of the nations, because "not all Israelites belong to Israel." Instead, "those who follow the example of the faith that our ancestor Abraham had

---

3. Is 33.1, 3; Ezek 33.11; 18.30.   4. Ps 146.9.
5. Ex 4.22.
6. Cyril does not harp on "dwellings," which the LXX sees in a similar Heb. form for "apostasy." He prefers to give the obscure verse a spiritual interpretation.

before he was circumcised" are listed as children.[7] There is therefore a combined reference to the calling of the nations and their relationship to God in Christ through faith and holiness. In addition to this there is a suggestion also of the source of spiritual goods and the abundance of grace, namely, in Christ.

I shall be like dew to Israel (v.5), completely enriching and bedewing the mind of those called to repentance by consolation from on high, namely, through the Spirit, since dew comes from above.

He shall flower like a lily (v.5): he shall emit a sweet odor in Christ and the fragrance of a holy lifestyle, and will then be a choice bloom.

He will strike his root like a frankincense-tree;[8] *his branches will develop* (v.5). In this he indicates that the mind of believers is not easily shaken or readily overcome by evil spirits. It will in fact be as secure and firm as the growth of *the frankincense-tree,*[9] which sends its *root* to great depth. With its *branches* further up it spreads widely; as the root goes in all directions, the multiplication of saplings is very extensive.

He will be like a fruitful olive tree (v.6), that is, flourishing and fruitful, since it is that kind of plant.

And his fragrance like incense[10] (v.6). Incense is very fragrant. Consequently, the Law of Moses decreed that it should be sacred to God; it frequently required that flour offered for sacrifice had to be sprinkled with incense.[11] So the fruit of those called will be fragrant, he says, and very acceptable as a sacrifice to God, who loves virtue.

They will return and will sit in its shade (v.7). They will desist from their former crimes, he says, and will return in vigor to worship of "God living and true,"[12] and will be subject solely to him, looking to be saved from their enemies by no one else but him. The church from the nations fulfills this perfectly, and says of

---

7. Rom 9.6; 4.12.
8. "Frankincense-tree": Greek is *libanos*, which may also be translated as "Lebanon," as in v.7 below ("wine of Lebanon").
9. Greek: *to tou libanou phuton*, which may also be translated as "the plant of Lebanon."
10. Greek: *libanou.*   11. Lv 2.1; 15.16; 6.15.
12. 1 Thes 1.9.

the Savior of all in the Song of Songs, "I longed to be in his shade, and took my seat there." Let it be to those in the habit of doing so that the divinely inspired David also exclaims in the words, "By day the sun will not burn you, nor the moon by night." This was put into effect by God for the people of old when a cloud overshadowed them in the wilderness, nicely suggesting the tabernacle on high from God.[13] He properly speaks of their *sitting* there (282) so that the understanding should thus be gained of the stable and secure foundation of the attitude of the *returned.*

They will live and be intoxicated with grain (v.7). These gifts of return and stability are worthy of acceptance; they will be sharers in eternal life, he says, and abound in power, that is, spiritual power. This in fact is, in my view, the sense of the clause, *They will be strengthened by grain;* Scripture says, "Bread strengthens the human heart";[14] while bodies enjoy suitable foods, the divine word from on high invigorates the human soul. There is no doubt, in fact, that the person returning from error to knowledge of God would move from weakness to strength and rebound vigorously from the depths of depravity to a longing for virtue. Especially since it is really a fault of weakness, to lapse into indifference and worldly pleasures and to become addicted to worship of the idols, whereas it is a conspicuous achievement of spiritual strength to opt ardently for good works, and, in addition to this, to consider nothing better than love for God, and to follow unfailingly the path to this goal with fierce determination.

Like a vine its memory will blossom, like wine of Lebanon for Ephraim (v.7). God said somewhere to the mother of the Jews, that is, the synagogue, "I planted you as a fruitful vine completely genuine." The divine David sings to us about it somewhere, "You moved a vine out of Egypt, you drove out (283) nations, and planted it. You went as a guide before it. It extended its branches to the sea, and its offshoots as far as the river." Israel was therefore a vine

---

13. Song 2.3; Ps 121.6; Ex 13.21–22.
14. Ps 104.15. Is it the verb "strengthen" in this citation that has led Cyril to cite it in the lemma instead of the verb "intoxicate," or is it the fact that the Antioch text also reads "strengthen"? The PG edition "corrects" the "slip." Or are Pusey and PG misreading the lemma?

with many branches; but when it offended in many ways, "The Lord broke down its wall, all who pass that way pluck its grapes. A forest boar ravaged it, and a wild ass fed off it."[15] In other words, it was subjected to trampling by those bent on harming it, food for swine and asses—that is, pleasures and irrational follies—and was consequently polluted. But its *memory* (Israel's, that is) blossomed again in Christ. Now, by *memory* he means that not all have faith, but that the remnant is preserved as a reminder, as it were. To *Ephraim*,[16] or Israel, came grace from God *like wine of Lebanon*, that is, sweet-smelling and only slightly less fragrant than incense. Of such a nature is the word from Christ, the blessed David saying of it, "Wine gladdens the human heart"; to it the sacred word urges us to have enthusiastic recourse, saying, "Eat, drink, and become intoxicated, my friends."[17] What comes to the saints through Christ, you see, never reaches satiety, and is very useful in promoting inebriation.

What does it still have in common with idols? (v.8) If it enjoyed an abundant share of such venerable goods from on high, it would completely abandon the wish to be deceived and be devoted to the works of its own hands. In fact, what need would it still have of good things to go looking for them from another? Is not the search for such things by the deceived completely foolish? (284) What does lifeless matter provide to people? It was rightly said to them by God, "Do good, do harm, and we shall know that you are gods."[18] Such artifacts would never even do harm to people. How is this so? They would never do anything good or beneficial to them, either. Let them rightly give heed to this, then: "Let gods who did not make heaven or earth perish from the earth and from under this heaven."[19] He therefore suggests stability and resoluteness in love for God when he says, *What does it still have in common with idols?*

I humbled him, and I shall empower him (v.8). I am able to bring harm, he says, on those whom I see despising the ways of sincer-

---

15. Jer 2.21; Ps 80.8–13.
16. This final phrase of the lemma is placed at the beginning of the next verse in the Heb. and the Antioch text.
17. Ps 104.15; Song 5.1.   18. Is 41.23.
19. Jer 10.11.

ity towards me, and in turn I give strength to those who opt for virtuous behavior and for knowledge of the one who by nature and in truth is God. It was not from them, therefore, that harm came—that is, Israel's being weak—nor was the change to strength to be taken as a gift of the demons; instead, it is a God-given benefit, just as, of course, weakness was an effect of the movements of wrath. It is therefore with wisdom and godliness that the mighty David sings to us, "The Lord is my strength and my praise."[20]

I am like an evergreen cypress; your fruit is found to come from me (v.8). The cypress is a tree with such dense and abundant foliage that it gives the impression of a handmade canopy (285) not allowing passage of the sun's rays or showers of rain, even if they ever fall heavily on the ground. So the fact that those subject to God enjoy impenetrable protection or assistance he highlights by saying, *I am like an evergreen cypress.* Now, the fact that complete fruitfulness of those subject to God would come in no other way than in Christ and through Christ he personally confirms by saying in Gospel pronouncements, "Apart from me you can do nothing."[21] So let it rightly be said to each of the believers, if anyone should be conspicuous and praiseworthy and adorned with virtue, *Your fruit is found to come from me.*

Who is wise and will understand this? Or clever and will know it? Because the ways of the Lord are straight, and righteous people travel by them, whereas the impious will fail in them (v.9). He is definitely right to claim that the one who understands this is both wise and very intelligent; a grasp of the divine words is not readily available to those wanting to acquire it. Instead, you would not even be able to understand "a proverb and obscure saying, the words of the wise and their riddles," as Scripture says,[22] except through illumination from above, when Christ imparts to the mind and heart a kind of bright ray, namely, grace from him. Now, it teaches that, while the ability to travel the straight and narrow that is pleasing to God involves very little labor for those who love good order, it

---

20. Ps 118.14.
21. Jn 15.5.
22. Prv 1.6. Cyril would not agree with those modern commentators who see this final verse as a scribal addition.

is a difficult process for those of a different disposition. You see, whereas longing and enthusiasm for every kind of good thing invigorates the former, and encourages them to proceed at a rapid pace towards gaining a good reputation, (286) the tendency and inclination to depravity and sin would render the latter fearful and timid, lacking the ability from God to practice virtue because from the outset they had no regard for it and their purpose was not directed to it. If we are wise and prudent, therefore, we shall ask God for the ability to do what we ought, and in his lovingkindness he will doubtless grant it, and will fill us with spiritual strength through Christ, through whom and with whom be the glory to the God and Father together with the Holy Spirit, unto ages of ages. Amen.[23] (287)

23. The doxology closes what would have to be classed as a lengthy commentary on the first of the Twelve Prophets.

COMMENTARY ON THE PROPHET JOEL

PREFACE

HE DIVINELY inspired Joel probably prophesied at the time when those placed before him—namely, Hosea and Amos—would also be thought to have done so. The Hebrews, in fact, decided that he should be ranked with them and not after Micah.[1] His denunciation, at least in my opinion, is of the people of Israel, and he raises an extremely loud outcry against them for then reaching such a degree of insolence, stupidity, and insensitivity as not to be diverted from evil by anyone at all, and to succumb to calamities of such frequency, not to say successive occurrence, despite no interval occurring when some respite from trouble might be given, brief though it be. We shall find the blessed prophet Isaiah also speaking in similar terms; he said, remember, "The anger of the Lord of hosts was enkindled against his people, and he stretched out his hand against them and struck them. The mountains quaked, and their corpses were like dung in the open street. For all this, his anger was not turned away; (288) instead, his hand was still uplifted."[2]

You will understand how it was that they suffered one calamity after another, and how the hand of the striker remained uplifted as if still to inflict further blows on them. In other words, just as the worst illnesses sometimes require not a single incision but even more, so, too, the human mind, when it is a willing victim of insensitivity, requires very frequent striking if it is finally to re-

---

1. Cyril, typically and admirably tentative, debates points which occupy modern commentators also. Unlike the LXX (which arranges the first six books in order of length), the Heb. places them in supposed chronological order (as does the Antioch text, predictably, and as Jerome notes at this point—evidently decisive for Cyril). Beginning with this fact, Cyril makes a judgment on the moot point of the time of Joel's ministry as contemporaneous with that of Hosea and Amos in the eighth century. He is thus not swayed by the prophet's omission of mention of Israel and Samaria, a fact that influences most modern commentators to date the ministry after the exile.

2. Is 5.25.

cover the ability to learn how to operate to its advantage. The blessed prophet Joel therefore seems to have wisely applied chastisement to Israel as though it remained unmoved by the great number of previous punishments, and advised it at the same time to change from its involvement in turpitude to a choice for what pleased God. He added a promise of what was dearest to them if they decided to repent, and gave them confidence that they would find the Lord kind and mild.

While such is the thrust of his prophecy as a whole, we shall pursue the meanings of the text, and comment on each detail in succession.[3]

3. Having determined the narrative setting (*hypothesis;* see n. 3 on Joel 1, below) of the work, and identified the prophet's purpose (*skopos,* translated here as "thrust"), Cyril promises to work systematically through the text (as he had done with Hosea) to find the meanings, *theôriai*—a deliberately chosen plural.

COMMENTARY ON JOEL,
CHAPTER ONE

The word of the Lord that came to Joel son of Bethuel (v.1).

HE PROPHET says the *word of the Lord came to* him, his purpose being that we should accord faith to the prophecy in the firm and confident belief that what was foretold would definitely come to pass. The Savior himself also confirms us in this belief by saying, "Heaven and earth will pass away, but my words will not pass away." (289) Truth is in fact not falsehood, and whatever God says will be utterly reliable, since he is the one "who confirms the word of his servant, and verifies the counsel of his angels."[1] Artfully and wisely, therefore, he requires of the listeners the belief that, unlike some people, he is not telling lies or offering the wishes of his own heart; instead, by speaking in spirit from the mouth of the Lord he is making very clear pronouncements.

There was need for *son of Bethuel* to be added in case some other person than Joel himself be understood; the fact that many people bore such a name was a possibility, or rather even beyond dispute, but not all were sons of Bethuel. So, in my view, it was for the sake of certainty that *son of Bethuel* was also mentioned.[2]

Hear this, you elders, and give ear, all you inhabitants of the earth: have such things happened in your days, or in the days of your fathers? Tell your children about them, your children to their children, and their children to the next generation (vv.2–3). He refers the seniors to former times and memories, and bids them consider when or in what circumstances they actually saw calamities similar to those

---

1. Mt 24.35 (the PG edition including only the second clause); Is 44.26.
2. The "clarification" says something of Cyril's style of commentary: while he does not let the precision pass by, he does not bother himself about the identity of this Bethuel—a name known in the Bible from Rebekah's father in Gn 22.3, as also in Jos 19.4 and 1 Chr 4.30.

inflicted by divine wrath on their *fathers* or those after them. He goes on to say that there is need to ponder whether the accounts were novel and unfamiliar, and perhaps not known to anyone in the past. Other people also ought properly to realize whether *such things happened* to them, and the fact that they would be the basis[3] of unending recital not for one generation or even two or three, (290) but rather would extend much further. In other words, just as we claim that the highlights of the stories are worthy of hearing by the general run of people, and should give satisfaction to those interested, so the details of calamity and suffering seem likewise to deserve remembering. Such events, in fact, make an impression on the memory, as it were, and by delivering a more forceful impact from their extreme insolence they deserve to be remembered, being contrasted to the glories of pleasant events. While happy events leave memories that are not without benefit, so, too, in my view do unhappy and bitter ones; the former stir the listeners to a longing for virtue, whereas the latter instruct them to avoid the experience of evil before its onset. What brought other people punishment is the means of preventing our desire to be involved in similar pursuits.

What was left by the cutting locust the locust consumed, and what was left by the locust the young locust consumed, and what was left by the young locust the blight consumed (v.4). The statement of the holy prophets is generally obscure; they are loath to report the extremely unpleasant details of stories, and by introducing obscurity they allay the emotional response of the listeners, and by fabricating riddles and proverbs they bring considerable benefit. Sometimes the word comes to them in helpful metaphors, like the one occurring in the wise Ezekiel: "The eagle is a large bird with large wings, with a wide wingspan and generous talons. It set its sights on entering Lebanon, (291) took the top of the cedar, snapped off its tender summit, and bore it off to the land of Canaan."[4] He was in fact referring to the ruler of the land of the Babylonians, who cut off the chosen parts of Israel and took his booty home. The sacred text meant that there resulted lack of

---

3. Greek: *hypothesis*. See n. 3 on the Preface to the commentary on Joel, above.

4. Ezek 17.3–4.

produce from the fields, shortage of crops, and frequently extreme and lengthy famine throughout the land of the Jews; in the grip of hunger some people reached such a state of indigence as to pay fifty shekels for an ass's head. Women's fighting over their children demonstrated at times the severity of the shortages; when two women consumed one child, they sought judgment from the rulers on the one that was alive.[5]

If, therefore, the prophetic verse were suggesting to us in this the barren fields and destruction of crops, the fact would even be taken as intolerable; after all, how could the occurrence of sudden, numerous, and harsh plagues fail to be absolutely unbearable and fit to be mentioned? If, on the other hand, the interpretation brings us to other levels of understanding that are oblique and at some remove from the surface reference, the prophet by mention of *cutting locust, locust, young locust, blight,* and the ensuing dire and intolerable damage is probably suggesting the devastation at each particular period, and hinting at the conditions during the captivities.[6] Under them they expired and perished as though those responsible for the attacks consumed and destroyed them like crops in the field.

There were many individual attacks, therefore, (292) on the country of the Jews, and sometimes the neighboring nations and the kings of Egypt waged military campaigns. When Rehoboam was conducting the royal office in Jerusalem, in fact, Shishak king of Egypt came up, captured the palaces, emptied all the treasuries in them, took the golden spears and shields that Solomon had made, and returned home flushed with victory. Hazael the Syrian also inflicted severe blows on them. Pul king of Babylon captured the tribes across the Jordan; and in addition to him Pharaoh Neco king of Egypt campaigned against Samaria when

---

5. 2 Kgs 6.25, 27–29. Again Cyril does not risk underplaying his point of the masking of gruesome details by at least "prophetic" (in the sense of inspired) authors, mere historiographers not generally conceded to be *prophētai.*

6. While implicitly Cyril allows for the possibility of description by Joel of a factual locust plague—a possibility Theodoret along with some modern commentators favors—he prefers Theodore's option for oblique reference to foreign invaders. In fact, Cyril would suggest that we should always expect inspired authors (*prophētai*) to avoid factual description of distasteful realities, a position which goes against his position on the marriage of Hosea.

Josiah was in charge, and subjected the land to tribute, demanding a hundred gold talents.[7] So there were a great number of events at various times; but four sackings proved dire and worthy of mention. That is to say, when Hoshea son of Elah was reigning in Samaria, Shalmaneser the Assyrian conducted an expedition, and deported Israel to the territory of the Persians and Medes. Then, a short time later, when Jeremiah was prophesying, Nebuchadnezzar came with force against Jerusalem; eventually Israel was released by Cyrus son of Cambyses after the passage of seventy years. Then at another time came Antiochus, called Epiphanes; he reached Judea, burned the divine Temple, took the vessels in it, and forced the people throughout all Judea to relax the ancestral practices; it was then that the exploits of the Maccabees proved (293) really remarkable.[8] The fourth war of the Romans beset the people of Israel, and it was then that they were scattered to every wind.

The prophet, therefore, seems to want to bring his own message to us through such accounts indirectly and vaguely and in figurative form, suggesting obliquely by *cutting locust, locust, young locust,* and also *blight* the wars that broke out one by one, or the generals in charge, whom we have just mentioned.

If, on the other hand, you wanted to find a more moral content registered in these accounts, you would not be wide of the mark.[9] That is to say, if a soul were seen as being subject to frequent and successive attacks of passion, and, as it were, within a hair's breadth of losing virtue after virtue, the victim of one attack after another as a result of indifference, how would it not be true to say of it, *What was left by the cutting locust the locust consumed, and what was left by the locust the young locust consumed, and what was left by the young locust the blight consumed?* The wicked and unclean powers besetting our mind, you see, and in the habit of consuming it with insatiable teeth, do harm to the good in us like blight and the other scourges. Security, therefore, is good; the author of

---

7. 1 Kgs 14.25–27; 2 Kgs 13.3; 15.19; 23.33 (not quite the tribute Cyril nominates).

8. 2 Kgs 17.6; 25.8; 1 Mac 1.

9. Cyril had spoken before of "other levels of understanding" than the factual in this verse; and, after seeing an historical reference, he now turns to a spiritual one.

Proverbs brings us no little benefit by saying, "If the ruler's spirit rises against you, do not leave your post, because healing will put an end to grave sins."[10] In other words, passions that are chastised initially are curbed and halted; but if they follow a way to worse things that is wide and unchecked, they get a total grip on the soul, and cannot tolerate a thought that rebukes them. (294)

Wake up, you who are drunk on their wine, and weep; lament, all you who drink wine to excess, because gladness and joy have gone from your mouth (v.5). Once again you could easily gain from this, in my view, a clear understanding of how wise the divinely inspired Paul was in addressing those won over to salvation through faith in Christ. He said, on one occasion, "Sleeper, awake, rise from the dead, and Christ will shine on you," and likewise on another, to convince people to have a love for patience in hardship, he consequently said, "Endure discipline, since God is treating you as his children. After all, what child is there whom a parent does not discipline?"[11] Although he is loving, God punishes sinners, not willingly but in doing what is necessary to convert them, doing so to them by way of assistance. It is like a skillful physician applying extremely severe medication to the ill, turning the necessary pain into a remedy for their complaint.

Note, in fact, how he gave a glimpse in advance and a forewarning of the effects of wrath, as it were, "curbing their jaws with bridle and bit,"[12] as Scripture says, and in human terms he bids them proceed to transforming their mind by choosing to do what is better and more becoming: *Wake up, you who are drunk on their wine.* Do you hear how he now chastises them as stupefied and already intoxicated children, since, if they had been sober from the outset, the effects of the locust alone would have been a sufficient penalty for them? (295) Since they remained infirm, however, despite the initial imposition of wrath on them, a second follows, and after that a third, and so on to a fourth. But if they arise and become sober, and dispel from their minds the inebriation, as it were, of pleasure and a mistaken decision to sin, he then bids them proceed to a sense of what had befallen them, weeping and wailing over their own sins.

10. Eccl 10.4.
11. Eph 5.14; Heb 12.7.
12. Ps 32.9.

Now, it should be realized that for each of us there is a particular kind of *wine*, as it were, which inebriates the heart.[13] We have our own share of passions, so to speak: one person is drawn unrestrainedly to avarice, not to mention other vices, and another person likewise adopts a worldly mentality, weakened by fleshly delights, completely addicted to luxury and love of pleasure, and given to sin of any other kind. Now, we surrender ourselves to such abominable and ungodly passions, some of us with little enthusiasm, others in full flight, and keep unchecked the tendencies of our mind. Consequently, the prophet says, *Wake up, you who are drunk on their wine,* and he advises those who *drink wine to excess* that they need to lament; as I said just now, some pleasure-lovers do not exercise self-control when they have had enough, drinking instead *to excess* and going beyond every limit. Of these, he says, *gladness and joy have* disappeared from their *mouth;* Christ was right in saying that without any doubt "those who mourn now will be comforted."[14] It follows that those given to luxurious living will weep, because the outcome of insolence will be mourning (296) and lamenting, and those who embrace it are forced to become denizens of Hades. David also is right in saying to God, "There is no one to remember you in death; who will confess you in Hades?" and again, "The dead will not praise you, Lord, nor all who descend into Hades, whereas we the living will bless you, Lord."[15] If, on the other hand, the drift of the text is to be taken in an even more material sense, the *gladness and joy* of the victims will be completely abolished along with fruitfulness if the basis of the gladness is consumed by the locust and the other creatures. After all, there is no escaping the depression of calamitous events that generally give rise to grief and are quite capable, I say, of breaking the heart with harsh and intolerable sadness.

A nation will come up against my land, strong and beyond counting, its teeth a lion's teeth, and its fangs like its cub. It has reduced my vine to

---

13. Again, seeing little mileage in developing a factual or historical sense of the lemma, Cyril moves to a spiritual/moral level, and will later offer a further such sense.
14. Mt 5.4.
15. Pss 6.5; 115.17–18.

ruin, and my figs to smithereens. It stripped it bare and cast it aside; it left its branches white (vv.6–7). In his wish in some way to match the events, or what was expected to ensue from the events, and to prompt weeping in the process of repentance, he subtly outlines the future. By displaying the onset of horrors, as it were, he proposes to those suffering the blows something lamentable and mournful. To those bidden to grieve he teaches a song, (297) and urges them to recite it at that time, *A nation will come up against my land, strong and beyond counting,* which is hardly inferior to *lions and cubs* as far as the sharpness of the *fangs* is concerned. On the one hand, the event is real if applied to the cutting locust,[16] young locust, and locust; the event is ineluctable, and the advance of such creatures is quite irresistible, sufficient to cause complete destruction in the fields—of fruit and crops, I mean—and the ruin of *figs* and *vines*, causing the pasture to present an ugly and unpleasing appearance.

On the other hand, if the verse is applied in turn to the inhumanity of the raiders and the complete devastation of the country, it would suggest nothing other than the fact that while the whole country was ruined at their hands, the leaders were eliminated by them, though outstripping the measure of the common herd in importance and wealth—hence their being listed as *fig and vine*—before suffering decay. This is also what happens, of course, in the case of the material vines if the *teeth* of the locusts happen to lay hold of them: they suck out the sap of the plants, remove from them all the life-giving force, and before long dry them out and consequently cause them to be white in appearance. The *teeth* of the consuming foe totally consumed and reduced to an utterly useless state those who acted as *vines* or were in the role of *figs* by striking them with their swords or subjecting them to the yoke of slavery.

If, on the other hand, you wanted to take them spiritually as well, you could in turn apply such things to sinful people. Into their mind and heart, in the manner of a locust and young lo-

---

16. A patristic commentator looks for the reality (*alêtheia*) in the text, whether at the factual/historical level or at one or more other levels. So Cyril begins with the factual.

cust as well as the cutting locust, evil demons are constantly entering along with (298) passions of many kinds and forms, rendering [those people] useless and ugly in appearance after rejecting the bloom of piety and having no shoot of righteousness in them. I would claim, on the contrary, that it would befit them to weep incessantly and express their grief to God, to strive to attain forgiveness and assistance through constant prayer so that they might, even at a late stage, be wise and strong, and capable of escaping what has befallen them. Those people in particular would be in this condition whose mind was uncritically inclined to pay heed to people given to holding heterodox views and undermining the correct teachings of the church; of them you would rightly say, their *teeth a lion's teeth, and their fangs like its cub*. The *nation*, in fact, is ungodly, fraudulent, and destructive, devouring and consuming the mind of simple people with clever words so as to leave in them not a morsel of uprightness. They blight the Lord's vineyard, desiccating the garden, rendering it devoid of *figs*, and proving it to be wild and uncultivated; "their condemnation has not been idle" but "well deserved" in time.[17]

Those addicted to folly, therefore, will become the food of locust, young locust, and cutting locust, will remain bereft of anything to recommend them, and will have nothing at all blossoming in them. The wise and godly soul, on the other hand, richly adorned with the teachings of the truth, and with a heart fully in bloom and abounding, as it were, in the fruits of righteousness, will speak with complete forthrightness as the bride in the Song of Songs is understood to do: "Let my nephew come down to his garden, and eat the fruit of his trees."[18] (299) Sweet, in fact, sweet are the fruits of piety, and the trees of a true love of learning that belong to Christ the Savior of all, who is also our nephew, being born of our sister, as it were, the holy virgin.

Address to me lamentations for a bride clad in sackcloth lamenting

---

17. 2 Pt 2.3; Rom 3.8.
18. Song 5.1. The LXX renders as "nephew" a Heb. form that may mean "uncle" as well as "beloved." Cyril sees logic in the usage on the basis of Jesus' birth from Mary, whereas Theodoret in his commentary on the Song will see the church of the Jews (as distinct from the church from the nations) in that position.

her first husband (v.8). The repentance he requires of them is not idle, or passing, or indifferent, or what is taken to represent grief; instead, they are to take pains to match and zealously rival what is more distressing than other forms so that the hardship may be commensurate with the sins. A recently married maiden normally shows extreme grief for her deceased bridegroom, and normally feels such severe pangs in this case that her mind takes no account of advice, and no behavior seems to do justice to her grief. While women admittedly have a fondness for weeping and wailing, worst of all is that of the one who has the piteous sight of the bridegroom of her maidenhood and youth lying lifeless in death on the bridal couch. To her must be compared the mass of the Jewish people, he does well to say, who were confident of dispelling the divine wrath with their *lamentations* and averting the divine reaction directed ineluctably, as it were, against them, on the grounds that the Lord of all is "loving and kindly," and, in his love for humankind, "both rich in mercy and ready to relent from imposing troubles," as Scripture says.[19]

The synagogue of the Jews, however, has not *lamented* the (300) bridegroom from heaven, that is, Christ; in her frenzy she killed him. Consequently, she has been expelled from the divine bridal chambers and from the sacred nuptials, has completely forfeited her place in the feast and her inheritance, and has been cast out as far as possible from the hope of the saints. In her place has been invited the young and fresh bride from Lebanon, all-holy and wise, the beautiful dove[20]—namely, the church from the nations—who confesses the actual passion of the Lord, and, as it were, weeps in suffering with him, grieving, carrying his cross, and following him,[21] and thus longing to enter on account of love for him.

Now, Emmanuel could be understood as her *first* bridegroom, because, despite her infidelity and apparent adultery with Satan in the form of becoming deceived, she received the rebirth from on high with which we were enriched through the Spirit, denying the fleshly birth. It is written, in fact, of Christ, "He came to

---

19. Ps 86.5; Jon 4.2. 20. Song 2.14; 4.8.
21. Mt 16.24.

his own, and his own did not receive him. But to all who received him, who believed in his name, he gave power to become children of God, who were born, not of blood, or of the will of the flesh, or of the will of man, but of God."[22] Setting aside the fleshly birth, therefore, we make our own the spiritual birth, by which the church of the nations could be considered the pure and all-holy virgin, that is, those who have come to faith in Christ, to whom the divinely inspired Paul also writes wisely, "I promised you in marriage to one husband, to present you as a chaste virgin to Christ."[23]

Sacrifice and libation are abolished from the house of the Lord. Mourn, you priests (301) ministering at the altar, because the countryside languishes. Let the land mourn because grain crops languish, wine has dried up, oil has diminished, they have dried up (vv.9–10). It is as if one were to say clearly, Thanksgiving offerings have ceased; there is absolutely no one to offer sacrifice, to bring offerings and first-fruits of crops, the sacred sheaf offered to God as first-fruits of the wheat harvest, as prescribed by the law of Moses.[24] There is no one to put the seasonal first-fruits in a basket and go into the house of the Lord and devote the thanksgiving songs to God which were customarily uttered. Consequently, he bids the chosen people *mourn*—I mean the priests—bereaved not on account of the income they earned, but grieving exceedingly for the people in their care and being assigned to the sacred and commendable liturgy, the purpose being that they would give their attention to the God of all before everything else and imitate Moses the revealer himself, leader of Israel, who says to God, "I ask you, Lord, this people has committed a grave sin; if you forgive them the sin, forgive it, but if not, blot me also out of this book you have written."[25] The office of priesthood acts as mediator between God and the people, and to those assigned to such august worship would very properly belong, in my view, the right to offer prayers;[26] it is as if they devote their own life to God on

---

22. Jn 1.11–13. The PG edition abbreviates this citation, closing comment on the verse at that point.
23. 2 Cor 11.2.   24. Dt 26.2.
25. Ex 32.31–32.
26. As this question of priestly rights and responsibilities has been argued

behalf of everyone, and consume the sin offerings. This is also what the God of all says in the statement of Hosea, "They will eat the sins of my people, and in their iniquities they will take their lives";[27] that is, when the people commit iniquity by sinning against the Law, (302) it is then, he says, it is then that the priests of the divine altars will take to God their own lives on their behalf (by "will take" meaning "will offer" or "will consecrate"), since what is offered to God is taken.

Now, what was the occasion of this *mourning* for them? *The countryside languishes,* he says, as also *grain crops,* chewed up by the locusts' teeth and scorched by blight like fire; it burns, as it were, and dries out what is in the fields. The land itself, he says, must also lament, since its crops are destroyed: *grain crops languish, wine has dried up, oil has diminished, they have dried up,* that is, everything growing from it, and the things for which it was right to admire it as the mother and nourisher of good crops.

While this may suffice for us in reference to material things, every priest who is reputable will lament those who through considerable derangement do not achieve purification through faith and are not attracted to sanctification by Christ. In fact, they remain completely and utterly devoid of spiritual fruitfulness, and will experience extreme need of the way to nourishment and of transport to spiritual valor, lacking *grain* and *wine* and bereft of *oil.* The thinking is spiritual: to those, on the one hand, who achieve faith Christ offers himself as bread of life, having said, "I am the bread of life," and as the wine that gladdens the human heart.[28] Understand what I say: he anoints with *oil,* obviously the spiritual and sanctifying kind, (303) and as though with a spiritual participation in the Holy Spirit. Those, on the other hand, with an obdurate attitude, harsh and ungodly, and with an unbelieving and intractable mind, he renders

---

before, it may be possible that Cyril is exploring it again from his own situation rather than perhaps raising an issue of interest to modern commentators, namely, whether Joel himself was a prophet within the cult.

27. Hos 4.8, where Cyril wrestled with the term at length.
28. Jn 6.48; Ps 104.15. After a lengthy excursus on the reason why priests get particular mention, Cyril returns to Joel's picture of agricultural desolation. He first presents it "materially," then moves to a spiritual level that becomes even *mystikos.*

completely indigent, with no share at all in the good things just mentioned by us.

Now, it should be realized that Paul in his wisdom, when offering the Gospel of Christ to the nations, lamented, as it were, the unbelievers of Israel: "I have great sorrow and unceasing anguish in my heart for my brethren, my kindred according to the flesh, who are Israelites."[29] In this, as I remarked, the thinking is spiritual and obscure.

You farmers, lament your crops of wheat and barley, because the harvest has disappeared from the field. The vine has dried up and the figs are in short supply; mulberry, palm, apple, and all the trees of the field are dried up, because people stifled joy (vv.11–12). Devastation in the fields and the complete inability to harvest anything from them, sometimes despite long and hard work, indeed bring grief, sorrow, and lament to those who till the soil. The sight is now of choice trees in the orchard dry and dead, the vines spoilt like the crops, and the native forest itself ruined along with the orchard. *All the trees of the field are dried up,* he says, in fact, *because people stifled joy,* by *stifled joy* meaning that the occupants of the land made it a time of shame, reproach, and censure leading to penalties and retribution (304) when it was the appropriate time for them to harvest crops from the field, broaden their prosperity, fill the storehouses with grain, and for the harvesters to sing the vintage songs and take pleasure in the flocks of sheep, with abundant and lush fodder provided for them.[30]

Now, it would seem that the word *farmers* in this verse as well makes oblique reference to those of the Jewish ranks in authority at the time; they should have *lamented* the progress towards absolute ruin of everyone, so to speak, in the country or occupying the land, who could be understood to take the role of *wheat, barley,* and attractive *trees.* We might very appropriately apply the force of the ideas to the scribes and Pharisees in some way; though exercising the role of farm laborers, they vented their frenzy on Christ, killed the heir so as to get the orchard in their

---

29. Rom 9.2–4. Again Cyril insists that the treatment—his and Paul's—is *mystikos.* It is certainly at some distance from Joel's text.

30. Cyril is not to know that the LXX has produced an enigmatic phrase, "people stifled joy," by reading a form similar to the Heb. "wilt."

own hands and then become masters of the vineyard,[31] as if exulting over the numerous mass of their subjects like crops, and in the habit of plucking the finest ones among them, like a *mulberry* and *apple*. But the Roman war did away with them, consumed great and small, famous and notable, who, as I just said, are to be taken as *figs, vine, palm, apple,* and *trees,* as also in barley and wheat. They took different forms, in fact, there being no one standard of living in them all; since he once compared the land of the Jews to a *field,* and referred to the leaders as farm laborers, the thought continued the metaphor throughout, likening those subject to them in different fashions to *crops* and *trees.* (305)

If, on the other hand, you thought it appropriate to give the passage a moral dimension, your thinking would be correct; *vine, fig,* and the other *trees,* which normally mature into attractive fruit, should be compared with virtues and the good motions of the mind. If you were wise and prudent, attentive to the ornaments of virtue, you would produce an orchard of luxuriant growth in mind and heart, nourishing in yourself manifold virtues and every form of goodness. If, on the other hand, you were indolent and pleasure-loving, and quite inclined to dishonorable pursuits, you would doubtless *lament,* with your goodness withered, and your mind experiencing extreme fruitlessness. Prudent people should therefore be attentive to good things of the heart, which will doubtless accrue if they choose to gladden God, the giver of heavenly gifts, with their own goodness.[32]

Gird yourselves and beat your breasts, O priests, lament, you ministers at the altar, go in, pass the night in sackcloth as you serve God, because sacrifice and libation have departed from the house of our God (v.13). In this he elevates and, as it were, highlights what has happened and invests it with unbearable terrors by showing the extreme need of prayer through the requirement of mourning by the priests themselves. There is also an element of ingenuity in the thinking; be-

---

31. Mt 21.38–39.
32. After briefly commenting on the devastation of the countryside at a factual level (whatever its historical setting), Cyril relishes a christological application and then a moral one (without encouragement from Joel). This repeated progression from one level of meaning to another is not found in the Antiochenes, Theodore especially preferring to stay at the factual and if possible historical level.

cause they had unwisely attended to the shrines of the idols, and, despite God's punishing them with the effects of his wrath, they sought help from that quarter, the God of all helpfully allots (306) to his own ministers the conduct of prayer and the patient leadership in exercises of repentance in order that the sinners may realize that, unless they choose to seek what pleases God, and unless they offer prayers to him, they will not avert his wrath. The priestly class ought therefore, he says, to make available to the others, as it were, the effort involved in praying—*beating their breasts, lamenting,* wearing *sackcloth,* by which is meant rejection of luxurious living and inactivity, painful effort, and the pursuit of a saintly way of life that is upright and blameless.

He then clarifies the reason for the effort: *because sacrifice and libation have departed from the house of God.* A biting criticism; he is not saying that *sacrifice and libation* have been reduced or become less frequent, but *have departed,* which is suggestive of complete failure. It is truly a dire and grave charge against the leaders of the people if God is in no way worshiped by his subjects.

Sanctify a fast, proclaim worship, assemble the elders, all the dwellers of the land in the house of our God. Cry aloud to the Lord at length, Alas, alas, for the day! (vv.14–15) Once again he indicates the way in which they should manifest grief, presents himself to them as a wise commentator on the way of repentance, and clearly demonstrates what it is that makes the God of all gentle and benevolent. This way was, (307) in my view, the willingness to quell [divine] wrath, remove the offense, suppress the harm, restore to them a blissful way of life, and have good things bestowed on them. Hence his saying, *Sanctify a fast,* that is, perform a truly holy and blameless fast like an offering and in the manner of a sacrifice; what is required is not wasting the flesh with abstinence from food, but for them to fast from doing what would likely offend God. After all, if in the time of fasting we were not intending to abstain from our impulses, but to sting our inferiors "into quarrels and fighting, and strike the lowly with our fists," as Scripture says, we have not yet fasted in a holy and pure manner; our effort has gone for nothing, as God cries aloud, "I did not choose this fasting, says the Lord."[33]

33. Is 58.4–5.

COMMENTARY ON JOEL 1

It is therefore necessary to abstain from depravity and follow rigorously the teachings of the lawgiver, directing our heart towards whatever pleases him, submitting the neck of our mind, singing and saying, "See my lowliness and my trouble, and forgive all my sins," and in addition that prophetic statement, "Lo, here we come to you, for you are the Lord our God." This in fact is a spiritual offering and a sacrifice pure and pleasing to God "more than a young calf," more than a lamb of the flock, more than a kid from the goats, more than fine flour and incense, since "God is pleased with sacrifices" of a spiritual kind.[34] By *sanctifying a fast, let us proclaim worship*, that is, performance of the divine will, with which (308) is duly associated uprightness, docility in behavior, readiness for everything affecting piety.[35] Now, we shall perform the forms of *worship* when the elders are assembled in churches, *all the dwellers of the land* have congregated, constantly interceding all *day*, and firmly convinced that God will definitely have mercy. After all, he is "slow to anger, rich in mercy, and faithful," "pardoning iniquities, passing over transgressions, and not retaining his anger in witness, because he delights in mercy," as Scripture says.[36]

Because the day of the Lord is nigh, and it will come like hardship upon hardship. Food was destroyed before your eyes, and happiness and joy were dried up from the house of our God (vv.15–16). He says *the day of the Lord* is when the effects of his wrath were discharged, or the locust was dispatched on them and consumed what was in the fields, releasing the horrors of famine and need, and imparting the actual terror of death. Or it was the time when the Babylonians destroyed everything and fell upon cities and towns, causing trouble of one kind or another, and inflicted on the inhabitants of the land *hardship upon hardship*. The result was that they were allowed not even the briefest of respites, nor did any

---

34. Ps 25.18; Jer 3.22; Ps 69.31; Heb 13.16.
35. The LXX is reading "worship" in a form occurring in our Heb. as "assembly." A more serious failure of recognition by Cyril than this is his not detecting the apocalyptic motif "Day of the Lord" in this verse, the first of many occasions where keynotes of this genre go unregistered by him (as with his peers in Alexandria and Antioch), with obvious effect on his interpretation of The Twelve.
36. Ex 34.6; Mi 7.18.

useful interval occur when (309) those invested with the sequence of troubles could readily have derived in part at least some moderate comfort. Since it was when the fruit was ripe, when the crops were, as it were, summoning to them the reaper, and it was when the grapes were in need of packing and crushing that the onset of the locusts occurred, *food was destroyed before their eyes*, he said, as though snatched from sight after being set before them, as it were, and ready for enjoyment. He likewise confirms that *happiness and joy* were removed *from the house* of the Lord; they used to make sacrifices when exulting in the fruitfulness of the fields, and manifested forms of *happiness* by making thanksgiving offerings as a result of being abundantly surrounded by the good things of the land.

We shall find those who vented their frenzy on Christ also having this kind of experience; in their sight was the bread of life "who came down from heaven and gave life to the world," "the grain of wheat which fell into the ground" and produced a multiple yield, the spiritual wine which has the capacity to gladden the human heart.[37] But because they did not fail to be insolent in their unbelief, the spiritual *food* left their sight and, as it were, their midst; a share in every good deserted them, and *happiness and joy* were removed *from* their *house*. They have in fact been given over to desolation, and the wretches spend their days "without any king, any leader, (310) any sacrifices, any altar, any priesthood, any signs."[38]

Now, in another sense we claim the *food* and the *happiness and joy* have been removed from *their eyes*. Our Lord Jesus Christ said, remember, "not by bread alone will one live, but by every word that comes from the mouth of God."[39] No one would doubt that a word is the food of the mind. It was removed from the mass of the Jews, and they were in need of spiritual nourishment. They did not understand Moses; the divinely inspired Paul writes, "To this day, when they read the Old Testament, a veil lies over their heart."[40] They hated the oracles coming through Christ; hence all their spiritual food was destroyed—not that it suffered de-

---

37. Jn 6.33; 12.24; Ps 104.15.
38. Hos 3.4.
39. Mt 4.4.
40. 2 Cor 3.14–15.

struction in itself, but it was no longer available to those who suffered it, and there was absolutely none left as far as they were concerned. Our Lord Jesus Christ, by contrast, distributes it to those believing in him to enjoy and to revel in the good things from on high; it is written, "The Lord will not let the righteous person die of hunger, but he will overturn the life of the impious."[41]

Heifers leapt in their stalls, storehouses were destroyed, wine vats were overthrown because the grain dried up. What shall we put in them? Herds of oxen bellowed because there was no fodder for them, and the flocks of sheep disappeared (vv.17–18). Even to irrational beasts (3 11) the divinely inspired Scripture sometimes attributes reason, artfully investing the natures of things with different aspects of a joyful and elegant appearance, and, as it were, in moral terms describing the appropriate way to understand them. It is rather extraordinary for one to say that *heifers leapt* and *herds of oxen bellowed,* that is to say, they were subjected to unbearable pressure of hunger, and perhaps would have leapt up and died if they had a sense of what was happening. He says that *storehouses were destroyed* and *wine vats were overthrown,* perhaps because they were shown no attention on account of nothing being collected from the fields; instead, the sickle was unused on vine and grapes, and the sheaves were lying dry and unripe in the fields. He consequently asks, *What shall we put in them?* Now, the fact that the very pastures of the wilderness were destroyed along with the cultivated crops he makes clear by saying, *The flocks of sheep disappeared,* completely wiped out by starvation and deprived of their usual welcome fodder.

Now, he skillfully applies this to the Jews' misfortunes, since as I said they vented their frenzy against Christ the Savior of all.[42]

I shall cry aloud to you, Lord, because fire consumed the beauties of the wilderness, and flames burnt all the trees of the field. All the cattle of the countryside looked to you, because outlets of water were dried up, and fire consumed the beauties of the wilderness (vv.19–20). By *the beauties*

---

41. Prv 10.3.
42. Developing a convincing demonstration of the way in which this apocalyptic scenario is applicable to Jewish misfortunes might take even Cyril more than a simple assertion. He implies that it is axiomatic.

of the wilderness he perhaps refers to what (312) grew up of itself in the unploughed fields, and by *the trees of the field* he means the pedigree plants in orchards and gardens, implying that locust and blight devastated them in the manner of fire, as it were. He helpfully directs a well-developed prayer to God to persuade them to look to no one else for removal of the calamity by prayer, and instead to offer supplication to the only one who is capable of saving them and who also inflicts the distressing effects of his wrath. After all, it should not be thought, he well says, that such troubles occur independently, and are not imposed on them by divine initiative. The God of all personally says as much to us in the statement of another prophet, "Is there any trouble in the city which the Lord did not cause?"[43] In other words, there is nothing that normally causes harm to cities or towns which was not done with God's permission; he saves and frees from trouble those he chooses. He therefore urges them to seek relief from their distress from God, and cast away as far as possible the thought that it should be sought from the hand of the false gods and assistance asked from them. *Outlets of water were dried up*, he says; that is to say, with rain not bedewing the earth, and blight developing in addition, the locust armed, the young locust leaping, and the cutting locust crawling, there was no doubt that their necessities of life had been completely reduced to nothing at all. Fodder was also destroyed, and so it was utterly inevitable that cattle would also be lost.

Now, I would claim that it would behoove Jews at the end of the ages in turning back to God to cite such statements when suffering and lamenting the shortage of good things. (313) The good things of the mind have in fact been consumed as if by fire, in their case; the spiritual locust has destroyed them, and *outlets of water are dried up*. "He commanded the clouds not to send rain on them," Scripture says, and the land remained inaccessible and waterless, and will not be occupied.[44] In reference to us, on the other hand, who are justified by faith, God announces beforehand, and implied that there would be a most abundant sup-

---

43. Am 3.6. For Cyril's citation of this problematic text in comment on Hos 8.4, see note there, as well as for Chrysostom's efforts to prevent the abuse of it.
44. Is 5.6; Jer 50.43.

ply of gifts through Christ when he says, "On that day the mountains will drip sweet wine, the hills will flow with milk, all the outlets of Judah will flow with water, and a stream will emerge from the house of the Lord and water the torrent of rushes," and in another place, "I am the Lord God, I the God of Israel shall heed them and shall not forsake them; instead, I shall open rivers on the mountains and marshes in the midst of plains, I shall make the parched land into aqueducts."[45] We enjoy these benefits, then; and if they were to make progress to repentance, set their eyes on God, and in their own case say, *I shall cry to you, Lord,* they will be given *outlets of water,* and with us receive the spiritual water "from the fountains of salvation," drink from "the brook of enjoyment" from the God and Father, and have in their hearts the fountain of life.[46] It will be available to them for enjoyment and *the beauties of the wilderness,* that is, fine and abundant pasture, bringing them to the divine and evangelical knowledge, which is understood in Christ.

45. Jl 3.18; Is 41.17–18.
46. Is 12.3; Ps 36.8–9.

COMMENTARY ON JOEL, CHAPTER TWO

Sound a trumpet in Zion, proclaim in my holy mountain, and all the inhabitants of the earth will assemble, for a day of the Lord has come, because a day of darkness and gloom is nigh, a day of cloud and mist (vv.1–2).

ONCE AGAIN there is a nice description of war for us, and it would be factual in either case, whether taken as referring to a locust and young locust, or to the Babylonians if you prefer.[1] The war, in fact, had already come to the very doors, and was, as it were, bruited abroad throughout all the land of Zion, or in the whole of Judea, and so everything was filled with panic and alarm. *A day of the Lord has come*, note—that is, it was no longer merely a warning: the sufferings were before their eyes, and they were actually experiencing what had long been foretold,[2] that it would have been better for them to take a turn for the better, and avert the experience of the troubles before their onset and arrival. Far from allowing them to shrink from repentance, therefore, he bids them dismiss lassitude and indolence of mind, embrace activity with alacrity, and have the will to lend assistance to themselves in a noble spirit, obviously by appealing to God and annulling the faults of their former crimes by a turn for the better. Consequently, he says that *the day of the Lord is nigh*, when they will be, as it were, in *darkness and gloom*, afraid of hunger due to the locust, or of misery and destruction threatening them from the Assyrians.

A people numerous and strong will spread over the mountains like

---

1. Cyril is still ready to allow either interpretation of the plague in the previous chapter, whether from locusts or from Babylonians/Assyrians (he cites both here).
2. The apocalyptic motif means to Cyril only a divine warning of disaster that is factual/historical, "a nice description of war." Introduction of a different perspective by the author does not cross his mind; the troubles are at the door, and will just as soon be over.

dawn; its like has not occurred from the beginning, and will not occur again after it for generations of generations. Fire devouring what is in front of them, (315) and flame igniting what is behind them. As a garden of delight the land before it, and behind it a countryside of destruction. None of them will be saved* (vv.2–3). By *dawn* he is probably referring to the dew at dawn, which, when it completely covers *the mountains,* leaves nothing on them unmoistened. Or the first rays of the sun, and the initial glimmerings of the light of day, which reaches the tops of the mountains even before anything else, as it were, and lends a pink tinge to the hills. This is the way, he says, the *people numerous and strong will be over the mountains:* perhaps as locusts or, by comparison with them, the Assyrian is understood on the basis of incomparable numbers, since he says *its like has not occurred from the beginning,* nor will it ever be. Because whatever creeps in is immediately consumed by the onset of the locusts, anything that chances to survive is left to those that follow the first ones; he says, *Fire devouring what is in front of them, and flame igniting what is behind them* and following them. In my view, this is what a column of enemy would do: coming closely in the rear, they will without exception follow the insolence and cruelty of those preceding them. They will make the land like *a garden of delight,* utterly ravaging it and reveling in what is found there. The verse has a factual application, even if applied to the locust itself.[3]

Their appearance is like the appearance of horses, and they will charge just as cavalry do. (316) *They will leap forward like the sound of chariots on the crests of the mountains, and like the sound of flaming fire consuming straw, and like a people numerous and strong, arrayed for war* (vv.4–5). If the locust and the young locust advance on towns and cities, he says, they are not less fearsome than a warlike horse, stamping on the ground in such a way as to resemble the sound of *chariots.* In fact, they leap on all *the crests of the mountains,* charge down from every hill, and emit the sound of *fire* burning *straw.* It is said, you see, that the consumption of the contents of the fields is not done by them without noise, and

---

3. Committed to finding the *alētheia* of the text in fact or history, and yet clearly uneasy with the exotic description, Cyril advises the reader to look no further.

that they make a depressing and unpleasant clatter with their teeth as the fallen crops are demolished by them, like a wind fanning flames. It is not unlikely that he is comparing it to a mob of enemies; it moves in great numbers, and is hardly inferior to warriors in battle, being insatiable and almost invulnerable for its huge numbers—invincible, rather. The text itself seems to refer to the Assyrians. If, on the other hand, you wanted to see a reference also to the Roman army, which like locusts devastated Israel for its ungodly crimes against our Lord Jesus Christ, this would not be wrong, either.[4] (317)

In face of it peoples will be crushed (v.6). The onslaught of young locust and locust, as I said, is completely invincible and resistant to human beings.

Every countenance like the scorching of a pot (v.6). It is an actual fact that sometimes even the bloom of *countenances* withers and somehow turns black in an ugly fashion, changing color, as it were, with the mental anguish as a result of intolerable terrors and distress.[5]

They will run like soldiers, and like fighting men they will mount the walls (v.7). Their downward course resembles that of warriors, proof against both lethargy and terror; they will mount the very *walls*, with a kind of bold attack in mind.

They will each keep to their own course, and will not swerve from their own path, nor will each desert his brother (v.8). Though having no king, the locust advances in order from a single command. They say they move in groups, fly in ranks, are rarely scattered, and follow one another in the manner of brethren, with nature endowing them with mutual affection. (318)

They will advance laden with their armor (v.8). By *armor* I think he refers to their teeth, with which they fight and perform their actions as though in warfare—the consumption of fodder, felling of crops, parching of plants.

They will fall under their arrows and will not be brought to an end (v.8). Locusts do not strike the enemy with arrow points, nor is a

---

4. Cyril shrewdly notes elements of Joel's exact description of a locust plague, and finally essays a rather desperate christological reference.

5. It is good to be brief even when trying to do justice to an image that the LXX has created as a result of mistaking similar Hebrew forms.

bow drawn by them. How do they operate? They smite them, as it were, with the destruction of necessities and with the terrors of starvation and need. Now, the fact that the loss of the crops in the fields would not be the end of it for those suffering this disaster, and that instead they invaded their homes and cities and crowded in frighteningly when they were under attack from the locusts, or even the Assyrian himself, he brought out by saying, *they will not be brought to an end.* It is as if you were to say, "Even this will not be the last of the wrath: it will continue and surpass it." In fact, he says,

They will attack the city, charge onto its walls, climb up on its houses, and enter through the windows like thieves. In face of them the earth will be obliterated and heaven shaken; the sun and moon will be darkened, and the stars will not give their light (vv.9–10). You have heard[6] that they will fly down even on the very *walls,* (319) devastate the pasture in the manner, as it were, of people who steal others' clothes, enter *through the windows,* bring panic to the populace, and cause total confusion, so to speak, with the result that *heaven, sun,* and *moon* seem to shake, and even *stars* lose their light, so to speak. Now, in this the message once again comes to us in hyperbolic fashion,[7] presenting the calamity for the inhabitants of the land as intolerable and distressing. Yet the statement is reliable, even if again it is understood in reference to an army of men invading towns or a *city.* Like locusts, you see, they spread over everything, damaging the fields, harming the cities, mounting the walls, invading the very homes, and rivaling the terrors of an earthquake for ferocity.

The Lord will utter his voice in advance of his power, because vast is his army, because mighty are the effects of his words. Hence great is the day of the Lord, great and extremely spectacular: who will cope with it? (v.11) I previously took occasion to remark that the prophet's purpose is to present the calamity as dire and intolerable so that those who offended the lawgiver by deviating into depravity may begin

---

6. Though this is a written commentary, Cyril thinks of the acquaintance of most people with the Word as being aural.

7. Still trying to present the description as basically factual, Cyril has to admit that there is a cosmic dimension to the scenario that suggests a different perspective, which like his Antiochene peers he will call hyperbole, but which we recognize as apocalyptic.

to make a change for the better and be advised to come to their senses. The extraordinary degree of their sorrows, in fact, had the capacity of easily bringing people to the point of choosing under necessity to do what was pleasing to the one who was able to save and liberate them. He therefore says, *The Lord will utter his voice* (320) *in advance of his power,* presenting him as general and leader against the foe. Stirring on the troops and leading one's own *army* would in fact apply to no one better than to champions and leaders of others. Now, in this he highlights that fact that it was not independently that troubles made their assault, or simply out of chance, but rather that they were inflicted by God, obviously when he was offended and imposing holy retribution.

He alarms them by saying that there is a mighty *army,* and *mighty are the effects of his words.* It is absolutely impossible that whatever God orders to take place would not come into effect. He said to one of the holy prophets—Jeremiah it was—"Are not my words like flaming fire, says the Lord, and like a hammer that smashes rock?"[8] The word of God, in fact, penetrates everything, as it were, and nothing resists what he has said; rather, obdurate and inflexible things give way, being easily shattered and yielding even involuntarily to the Lord's wishes. *Great and extremely spectacular is the day,* he says, therefore, as a result of the news of the impending troubles coursing towards all people. *Who will cope with it?* In other words, no one on earth would be so stubborn and strong as to be able to resist the divine wrath. The divinely inspired David was very wise to cry aloud to God, "You are fearsome, and who will oppose you in your wrath?"[9]

The Lord our God now says, Turn back to me with all your heart, with fasting, with weeping, and with lamenting; (321) *rend your hearts and not your garments. Turn back to the Lord your God, because he is merciful and compassionate, longsuffering and rich in mercy, and repenting of the troubles. Who knows if he will turn and repent, and leave behind him a blessing, a sacrifice, and a drink offering to the Lord our God?* (v.14) From this you would learn very clearly that, on the one hand, he delivered the narratives for their own sake, and, on the other, he forecast the calamity that was harsh and ex-

8. Jer 23.29.
9. Ps 76.7.

tremely intolerable for them, with the sole purpose of persuading them to move to repentance. He does not allow them to despair, in fact; instead, he gives very clear confirmation that, if they chose a better frame of mind and brought their own ways into conformity with God's pleasure even if at a later stage, the effects of his wrath would completely cease, and their affairs would be transformed into widespread orderliness. He makes clear what this return would mean for them and what would be the form of prayer when he says, *The Lord our God now says, Turn back to me with all your heart.* Let the past be jettisoned, he says, and let what preceded be consigned to oblivion; present a better picture of yourselves in what follows, propitiate God with *fasting* and discipline, *weeping* and wailing. The enjoyment of satisfaction and delight will definitely follow those now opting to do this, in fact; just as indolence and immersion in pleasure finally result in complete upheaval into grief and punishment, so the outcome of simplicity and the discipline involved in repentance is widespread satisfaction. (322) It is therefore surely of benefit to weep for our sins and express a godly grief; as the blessed Paul writes, "Godly grief produces a repentance that leads to salvation and brings no regret." Christ himself also declares blessed those who "mourn now, for they will be comforted"; and the wise Solomon in a proverb tells us something similar: "Better to go into a house of grief than to go into a house of festivity."[10]

There is need to consider the full force of *fasting.* It appeases the Lord, quells wrath, averts punishment; by being hard on ourselves we very effectively allay the divine anger that is exercised and active against us, as it were, and we easily restrain the hand of the striker. In fact, if it is true that even by simply confessing our sins we are justified through God's compassion, how could you doubt that by wasting ourselves in the toils of self-denial and, as it were, paying the penalty we shall gain from God the forgiveness of our sins? He therefore bids us lament and *rend* ourselves, not so much our clothes as in a spiritual sense striking our *heart,* which is obdurate and resistant to the entry of fear of God. Paul writes to the Corinthians, for instance, "There is no restriction in

---

10. 2 Cor 7.10; Mt 5.4; Eccl 7.4.

our affections, but only in yours. In return—I speak to you as children—open wide your hearts also."[11] There is surely need, therefore, to expand our *heart* for God, as it were, and, so to speak, rend our mind to admit what is his; feigning grief by idly and to no purpose rending our clothes would not benefit (323) those choosing to do so. By contrast, it would bring no little benefit to open our heart and deposit what God wants, this being conducive to salvation.

Now, the fact that those who offer prayers will achieve their goal he confirms by saying that the Lord of all is kind, *rich in mercy, compassionate,* loving, *and repenting of the troubles.* In fact, even if he chooses to bring trouble on sinners, he is still gentle, and it will not be for long; he easily moves to provide for what is beneficial—the meaning, in my view, of *repenting of the troubles.* To offset the folly of those despairing of salvation, the prophet helpfully says, *Who knows if he will repent, and leave behind him a blessing?* In other words, he will give those who turn back a share in *blessing* so that they may offer *a drink offering and sacrifice* again to him, pleased and happy to offer thanksgiving.

Sound a trumpet in Zion, sanctify a fast, announce worship, gather the people, sanctify the assembly, select elders, gather together infants at the breast. Let the bridegroom leave his alcove, and the bride her chamber. Between the step and the altar the priests serving the Lord will weep, and they will say, Spare your people, O Lord, and do not make your inheritance a reproach for the nations to dominate them, lest they say among the nations, Where is their God? (vv.15–17). In this as well he firmly urges them to repentance, and instructs them helpfully to leave no form of zeal for this untried. (324) He says, in fact, that they should use a bold and piercing proclamation: *sanctify a fast, announce worship,* and gather in *assembly* those obliged to worship the God of all, who had been clearly offended. They would include "young men and maidens, old and young,"[12] and in addition to them newborn and suckling *infants,* even *bridegrooms* and newly married maidens issuing forth from *chambers* still garlanded, declining marital bliss, forsaking good fare and drink, and adopting instead an austere way of life; applause is suppressed,

---

11. 2 Cor 6.12–13.   12. Ps 148.12.

songs and blessings silenced that people sometimes offer customarily to the newlyweds, since they are grieving along with the grooms. There is in fact truth in what one of the sages tells us: "Like music in a time of mourning is ill-timed conversation."[13]

With the onset of divine wrath, therefore, it is necessary to mourn, not to be carried away with fine food and drink; the fact that untimely indulgence would not escape censure and retribution is clearly stated by one of the holy prophets in reference to the people of Israel: "On that day the Lord of hosts called to weeping and mourning, to shaven heads and the wearing of sackcloth, whereas they indulged in mirth, slaughtering calves, sacrificing sheep, and saying, Let us eat and drink, for tomorrow we die."[14] There was need, therefore, with the onset of wrath, to fall to weeping and wailing, and abandon drinking. The prophet actually says that the priestly and chosen class itself should also be involved with the mourners, and *between the steps* of the Temple *and the altar* (325) lament at length by crying out in these words, *Spare your people, O Lord, and do not make your inheritance a reproach for the nations to dominate them, lest they say among the nations, Where is their God?*

If there is reference only to the locusts, however, how is it they do not ask rather for relief from hunger and need? Instead, they are afraid of falling into the hands of the foe, and deplore ridicule and *reproach*. In all likelihood, therefore—in reality, I would even say—in the imagery of the locust the attack of the Assyrians is obliquely described.[15] If, however, you wanted to understand such events in reference to the locust itself, you would rightly marvel at the divine plan in the prophetic oracles; the very form of the punishment, as it were, bruited abroad the folly of Israel as well as the weakness inherent in them. They changed their God for "gods that are not gods,"[16] and dismissed the Lord of all

---

13. Sir 22.6.   14. Is 22.12–13.
15. Cyril has to this point typically allowed either interpretation of the description of the locust plague, whether factual or as an image of foreign invasion. Influenced by the cosmic scenario of the apocalyptic passage in this chapter, he is more inclined to disallow the former interpretation (still without identifying the different genre).
16. Jer 2.11: Cyril's first tome on Joel concludes with comment on this verse.

to worship the Baal. But, lo, they brought on the intolerable army of the locust; the young locust was armed, and they fell, and they got no assistance from the false gods. Instead, when vanquished by locust and young locust, what healing would they bring them as they worshiped them in the fight against the foe, under siege from the columns of the enemy? (326)

The Lord became jealous for his land, and spared his people. The Lord said in reply to his people, Lo, I am sending you grain, wine, and oil, and you will be satisfied with them. I shall no longer make you a reproach among the nations, and shall chase away from you the [enemy] from the north (vv.18–20). Consider the speedy course of mercy: serenity outstrips grief, in my view; and the grace of the compassionate one, the tears of repentance. In other words, he not only has mercy on those faring miserably, but also is jealous and vents his wrath on the offenders, who were responsible for the misery being inflicted on them. The God of all rebukes the Babylonians for being more cruel to the objects of divine wrath than was necessary, saying, "I gave them into your hand, but you showed them no mercy"; and also to the blessed prophet Zechariah, "The Lord says this: I am extremely jealous for Jerusalem and Zion. I am extremely wrathful towards the (327) nations who have conspired, the reason being that, while I was slightly wrathful, they conspired with evil intent."[17] Being *jealous for his people*, therefore, he promises to supply them abundantly with the necessities of life, satisfaction equivalent to the previous calamity, and a sufficiency of comestibles; in addition to this, protection against falling into the hands of the foe by becoming victims of slavery under them or living a pitiable life in misery. He promises further to wipe out *the [enemy] from the north*, that is, the Assyrians, their land lying to the north and somewhat to the east. If, on the other hand, you believed that an invasion of the locust was coming from the parts to the north of Judea, there is nothing to deny the accuracy of this interpretation.

---

17. Is 47.6; Zec 1.14–15. Typically, Cyril does not reconcile the different parties and periods concerned in the three prophetic passages; he finds it easier just to presume for the moment that all bear on the situation that Joel is addressing (whatever that is). His modern counterpart Stuart, we should also note, remarks that "nothing in the pericope gives the slightest hint as to date."

If, by contrast, the good things of the heart and the wealth of spiritual fruitfulness are ruined for some people with the onset of the herd of demons upon them like locusts, and principalities, powers, and authorities befalling them (of an evil kind, clearly),[18] let wailing commence, repentance be undertaken, tears be shed to God. Immediately, in fact, he will be heard saying in his lovingkindness, *Lo, I am giving you grain, wine, and oil,* presenting one's heart as productive soil, as a garden luxuriant with healthy crops, as a laden vineyard, and he lavishes oil on it, according to the psalmist, "You anoint my head with oil."[19] He will drive out from it *the [enemy] from the north,* that is, Satan, who freezes those in his power and does not allow them to simmer with the Spirit; (328) Paul also said that "the love of many will grow cold on account of the increase in lawlessness."[20] The intimates of Christ, on the other hand, will simmer with the Spirit, not yielding themselves to being frozen in wrongful pleasures; Scripture says, "They have crucified their own flesh with its passions and desires."[21]

And I shall drive him out to arid land; I shall disperse his advance column to the first sea and his rearguard to the last sea. Its stench will rise up and its smell will rise up, because he magnified his works. He develops the metaphor as he did in the beginning by citing locust and young locust, saying that what had been imposed on them by the will of God would be scattered to the very extremities of the land of the Jews, and would result in such an awful stench as to prove an intolerable plague upon people throughout the country. This verse in no way alters the need to interpret such things as applicable to the Babylonians once again; to the south of Jerusalem extends uninterrupted desert that borders upon the Indian ocean to the east and south, and to the west and north upon the neighboring sea of Palestine, which also borders upon Egypt. There the young locust and locust perish, he says, and its *smell* will be unpleasant—the locust's, as I just said. From

18. Eph 6.12. No one could complain that Cyril does not offer the reader a range of levels of meaning in a text.
19. Ps 23.5.
20. A dominical saying, in fact, recorded in Mt 24.12; even Homer nods. Instead of "simmer" (*zein*) above, the PG text has "live" (*zên*).
21. Cf. Gal 5.24.

the other point of view as well, the Babylonians, who inhabit a country further north and to the east, were done away with. We have often remarked that they were done away with at the time (329) of the reign of Hezekiah, and the *smell* of the fallen was so foul as to require almost seven months for the land to be cleansed and to be rid of the *stench* of the fallen; the prophet Ezekiel says as much somewhere, in fact.[22] Now, it would be clear that the land of the Babylonians is situated more to the north; God says in the words of the holy ones to those of the bloodline of Israel taken off into captivity, "O, O, flee from the north, says the Lord; escape to Zion, you inhabitants of daughter Babylon."[23]

Now, having driven out from us as well the locust—of the spiritual kind, I mean, that is, the depraved columns of the demons—Christ demolished them, dispatching them, as it were, into the depths of the *sea*,[24] he shut them up in Hades and in the innermost recesses of the deep. Yet their *stench* and *smell* rose up, proving to be foul and unpleasant for us, despite formerly not seeming to be so; we now finally know Satan for what he is, evil-smelling, whereas in our misery we thought him sweet-smelling and attractive when we were ensnared in the bonds of depravity and fell under his control. When Emmanuel was made manifest to us, however, crying aloud in these words, "I am a flower of the meadow, a lily of the valleys,"[25] then it was that we were finally invited to sample the sweet odor belonging to him, and abhorred the other's evil smell.

Have confidence, earth; rejoice and be glad, because the Lord has increased your productivity. Have confidence, cattle of the countryside, because (330) the countryside in the wilderness has blossomed, because a tree bore its fruit, and vine and fig tree showed their vigor. Children of Zion, be glad and rejoice in the Lord your God, because he has given you food for righteousness, and he will send you early and late rain as before; the threshing floors will be filled with grain, and the vats of wine and oil will be overflowing (vv.21–24). It is customary with the holy prophetic authors to give the text an overall and general meaning on the basis of details and particulars. This happens in what

---

22. Ezek 39.12.
24. See Mk 5.1–13.

23. Zec 2.6–7.
25. Song 2.1.

comes through Christ.²⁶ So once again the sense emerges for us in this way: when is the *earth to have confidence,* and when likewise *has the Lord increased productivity* in our case, if not when the Word, who is God, became man so as to shower the earth under heaven with good things from on high and prove to be for those who believe in him "like a river of peace, like a torrent" of enjoyment,²⁷ like *early and late rain,* and a giver of complete spiritual fruitfulness? Then it was, in fact, then it was that even for the most uncomprehending, who are called *cattle of the countryside,* a kind of spiritual fodder grew up, instruction by teachers; then it was that *the countryside in the wilderness blossomed.* By *wilderness* he refers to the church according to the saying in the prophets about it: "Rejoice, thirsty wilderness, let the wilderness exult and blossom like a lily."²⁸ *Countryside,* on the other hand, would be the leaders of peoples, skilled in guiding them, whose minds are, as it were, teeming and beautifully blooming with divine charisms from heaven, producing sweet odors from the flowers of teaching, and, as it were, growing fresh fodder. (331) They nourish the minds of those who have become like cattle so that they may even advance to the mentality proper to human beings.

He said also that *a tree bore its fruit, and vine and fig tree showed their vigor,* the solid message of the teachers, in my view, in which there is sweetness and in addition the means of gladdening, in a comparison to the fruit of *fig* and *vine.* Now, it would be very fitting to offer to people of a more materialistic attitude and the sloth typical of cattle an instruction that is more earthy, in form and content a natural fodder for those who teach the elements, and for the mature an understanding already received from on high, and, as it were, fruit springing from lovely *trees*—namely, the doctrine of the holy and consubstantial Trinity,²⁹ or moral teaching of an elevated level. The former he refers to as *cattle,* but to the more mature as *children of Zion,* whom he bids exult in *the Lord their God.* Our total satisfaction is Christ, in fact, and from

---

26. The factual and historical reference being vague, Cyril takes the opportunity to give the verses a spiritual and specifically christological interpretation, and then sacramental as well.
27. Is 66.12.
28. Is 35.1.
29. Cyril's expression is *homoousios Trias.*

him and through him comes complete fullness of good things and an abundant supply of heavenly graces to those who love him, understood as *early and late* fruit and as *grain filling the threshing floors, vats of wine* brimming over, and *oil* overflowing.

Now, it should be understood that the reality of the promise comes also in the form of sacramental fulfillment; the living water of holy baptism is given to us as *rain*, the bread of life as *grain*, and the blood as *wine*. Use of *oil* is also applied (332) in bringing those justified in Christ to maturity through holy Baptism.[30]

I shall repay you for the years when the locust consumed you, the young locust, the blight, the cutting locust, my great power, which I sent against you. You will eat aplenty and be filled, and you will praise the name of the Lord your God, who dealt wondrously with you (vv.25–26). As far as the factual sense of the text is concerned, he promises utter generosity equal in measure and effect to the locust's preceding invasion, and says that the provision of comestibles will be more extensive than the affliction befalling them at that time.

If, on the other hand, the verse of the prophecy were to be understood spiritually, our claim would be that Satan ravaged us, as it were, and in the manner of the *cutting locust, locust,* and even *blight* the unbearably destructive currents of various passions corrupted us. So we remained dry and fruitless, bare and bereft of any good, our mind set on no virtuous practice, undistinguished for doctrinal discernment, wasted, as it were, by spiritual malnutrition, and, in a word, deprived of all fruitfulness. But when we were enriched by Christ with confidence, having with him overcome the world and having been given authority "to walk on snakes and scorpions,"[31] then it was that we even enjoyed (333) *early and late* spiritual *rain*—that is, instruction in the law and encouragement from the Gospel; then it was that we sprouted up again and bore fruit; then it was that we *ate and were filled.* We confess Christ the Savior of all as Lord, proclaiming him as

---

30. The Fathers look for the reality, *alêtheia*, of a text. After finding it first in Christ's coming, Cyril then sees it at a sacramental *(mystikos)* level in the sacraments of initiation, Baptism and Eucharist, and it seems also in the anointing of Confirmation that completes baptism. Strangely, Theodoret does not follow this lead, though generally open to sacramental interpretations.

31. Jn 16.33; Lk 10.19.

wonder-worker, who gives to those who love him what surpasses description and expectation. We know no one else at all in addition to him; we have been taught to say in all earnestness, "Lord, beyond you we know no one; it is your name we call on."[32]

Now, note how the God of all, as it were, mocks and ridicules human things, referring to the *cutting locust* as his own *great power*, which he says was *sent against* them. We are not actually claiming that the cutting locust was really God's power, and great at that; rather, he is saying to those unable to bear the punishment involved in it, O you stubborn and arrogant people, who think nothing of offending me, I was not found dispatching fire from heaven upon you, I did not release thunder and hail, or anything else taken from on high; I only imposed what particularly befitted the glory of God. A miserable horde of lowly insects infested the country, you took fright at it, bewailed it, and perished. Perhaps the *cutting locust* is in some way very *great*, yet I consider it also *my great power*. The verse is therefore intended morally, and, so to speak, as a satire in which God, as it were, mocks those in the habit of showing scorn, the result being that if he wanted to punish them, the cutting locust would suffice at that time in place of great and invincible strength. (334)

Let heretics not engage in ribald mockery, or hold up to ridicule the glory of the Only-begotten, referred to as the *great power* of the cutting locust, even though the power of God himself may be described as an insect. In fact, the wretches risk going to the extreme of such abject ideas.

Let my people never be ashamed. You will know that I am in the midst of Israel, I am the Lord your God, and there is none besides me. My people in the future will never be ashamed (v.27). He makes a clear promise of the manner of the Incarnation, and the fact that he will live with those on earth by submitting himself to emptying and becoming like us, that is, a human being. Then it was, in fact, that he was *in the midst of Israel*, and we escaped ignominy and were rid of *shame*, as death was overcome, sin removed, true knowledge introduced; we no longer adore "the creation instead of the Creator,"[33] and accept no one else as God but him. Ac-

32. Is 26.13.
33. Rom 1.25.

cordingly, we are also enriched, hoping firmly in life, glory, and the living of a blessed life in sanctification and holiness.

After this I shall pour out some of my Spirit on all flesh, and your sons and your daughters will prophesy, and your elders will dream dreams (335) *and your young people will see visions. On my men slaves and my women slaves in those days I shall pour out some of my Spirit* (vv.28–29). Lo, he clearly promises the gift of the outpouring—that is, abundant provision—of the Holy Spirit, not selectively to a single prophet or two, but without distinction to all those worthy to receive it, something we say was achieved by the resurrection of Christ and his overcoming the power of death. In fact, he imparts it like first-fruits of such a venerable and praiseworthy grace to the holy disciples, breathing on them and saying, "Receive the Holy Spirit."[34] It was necessary, you see, it was necessary for the church's spiritual guides and future teachers of the world under the sun to be adorned before all with the gift of the Holy Spirit, and, as the ones called as first-fruits through faith to holiness, to be ornamented by divine grace from heaven. On the days of Pentecost, when the disciples were assembled in one house, offering the customary prayers to God, "There came a sound from heaven like the rush of a violent wind. Lo, divided tongues as of fire appeared among them and rested on each one of them, and they began to speak in other languages as the Spirit gave them utterance."[35] They gave utterance to prophecy, understanding and repeating (336) testimonies regarding Christ from the holy prophets, which were probably calculated to bring the listeners to obedience and the clear belief that the acceptable time had arrived, and the former prophecies through Law and Prophets regarding Christ had now come to fulfillment.

They therefore prophesied, speaking in every tongue, something also foretold by God through the holy ones; Scripture says, remember, "By people of strange tongues and by the lips of foreigners I shall speak to this people, yet even then they will not believe." The divinely inspired Paul also understood this, saying that the gift of tongues was provided as a sign to the Jews. Now,

---

34. Jn 20.22. The lemma begins chapter 3 in the Heb. text.
35. Acts 2.2–4. This would seem the place for Cyril to mention Peter's lengthy citation of the Joel passage, but he bypasses it; his focus is rather different.

the fact that with the descent of the Holy Spirit from heaven a great number were filled with the spirit of prophecy Paul clarifies in writing: "Let two or three prophets speak, and let the others practice discernment. If a revelation is made to someone sitting nearby, let the first person be silent, for you can all prophesy one by one."[36] In former times, remember, when Israel was offending through deep perversity, God said, "Lo, I am sending a famine upon the earth, not a famine of bread or a thirst for water, but a famine of hearing the word of the Lord. They will wander from east to west in search of the word of the Lord, and will not find it." And to the blessed Ezekiel, "I shall bind up your tongue and you will be speechless, and to them you will not appear as a man (337) reproving them, because they are a rebellious house." Now, as in the words of the psalmist, "The Lord is God, and he has appeared to us,"[37] our Lord Jesus Christ has shone upon us, forgiving our crimes, ridding us of blame, and shutting the mouth of sin; the outpouring of the Holy Spirit is now given to us; and God gladdens human nature, crowning it from above with the original glory, and lovingly returning it to the condition it originally enjoyed when sin had not yet deprived us of it.

We shall not, in fact, find Adam bereft of a prophetic spirit when he had not yet transgressed the divine commandment; instead, he was still firm and stable, and endowed with natural goods. When God formed the woman, for instance, and brought her to him, despite being told by no one who she was, where she came from, or how she had come into being, he announced at once, "This is now bone of my bones, and flesh of my flesh; she will be called my wife," or, according to the Hebrew, "wo-man," "because she was taken from her man."[38] The grace given to a human being proved fruitless, however, but was renewed in

36. Is 28.11; 1 Cor 14.21, 29–31.
37. Am 8.11–12; Ezek 3.26; Ps 118.27.
38. Gn 2.23, where Cyril sees Adam's observation as an index of a prophetic gift. On his further remark on the Hebrew text, Speiser's comment is apposite: "The assonance of Heb. 'is and 'issa has no etymological basis. It is another instance of symbolic play on words, except that the phonetic similarity this time is closer than usual. By an interesting coincidence, Eng. 'woman' (derived from 'wife of man') would offer a better linguistic foil than the Heb. noun."

Christ, the second Adam. Now, in what way was it renewed? As God, in fact, the Son is by nature also from God, truly born of the God and Father; the Spirit is proper to him, in him, and from him, (338) according to which, of course, by "him" is understood the God and Father. In so far as he became man, on the other hand, and is like us, he is said to have the Spirit imparted to him; it came down upon him, for instance, in the form of a dove when he became like us, as I said, and in the divine plan he was baptized like one of us.[39] Then it was that the Spirit proper to him is said to be given to him from on high on account of his humanity, and this is what the emptying means. Let this be the meaning, and no other, of the verse, "Though he was rich, he became poor for our sakes, so that by his poverty we might become rich."[40] The Spirit was in fact given to Adam in the beginning, as I said, but did not remain with human nature, which went in the direction of sin, took the path to transgression, and fell into every form of impurity.

Since, however, the Only-begotten, as I said, though rich became poor, and with us as man received the Spirit that was proper to him as though imparted, "it remained on him," as blessed John the evangelist said,[41] so that it might now also dwell in us, as already remaining in the second first-fruits of our race,[42] that is, Christ. This in fact is the reason why he is also called the second Adam;[43] it was through him that we were given an incomparably better reshaping and enjoy the great gain of rebirth in the Spirit, no longer having the first, by which I mean the birth according to the flesh, which leads to corruption and sin; as Scripture says, "The mindset of the flesh is death." Instead, it is the second

39. Mt 3.16. Cyril undertakes a precise exposition of christological or trinitarian doctrine only when the readers may otherwise gain a false understanding of a text.
40. Phil 2.7; 2 Cor 8.9.
41. Jn 1.32.
42. The "second first-fruits" is happier in Greek, *aparchê deutera*.
43. Cf. 1 Cor 15.45, 47, which speaks of Christ as "last Adam" and "second man." Kelly remarks of Cyril's fondness for this image: "The conception of Christ as the second Adam inaugurating a new, regenerated race of mankind demanded, he thought, a much more intimate union of the Word with the flesh than Nestorius postulated" (*Early Christian Doctrines*, 318.). It occurs to neither of the Antiochene commentators on this lemma to refer to Adam, first or second.

birth, from on high, which is of God through the Spirit, especially if it is true that "we are born not of blood, nor of the will (339) of man, but of God."[44] It is necessary, therefore, it is necessary that those numbered among God's children be enriched with the grace of the Holy Spirit. Christ brought this also into effect in us, as the divinely inspired Peter confirms in the words, "Being exalted at the right hand of God, and having received from the Father the promise of the Holy Spirit, he has poured out this that you see and hear." In fact, while as man he receives from the Father what is in him by nature, "he pours it out richly on us,"[45] because he is by nature God, even if he became flesh. *He pours it on all flesh.* This suggests not only those from the circumcision, but all those without distinction who are called through faith, be they from pagans in their error, be they small or great, slave or free, barbarians or Scythians; the grace of salvation in Christ is available to people throughout the world under heaven, because he is the "expectation of nations."[46]

If, on the other hand, some brazen people in their nonsense were to claim that *flesh* also means "cattle," let them be told that the sole thrust of prophecy is directed at the human race, and that "God is not concerned with oxen," as Paul says in his wisdom.[47] He says, *sons and daughters will prophesy,* implying in this the liberality of the grace and its equal application to all; the female sex would not be rejected by God if they performed with zeal what pleases him and opted for that attitude, nor would they be without a share in recompense and sanctification if they proved commendable in faith and (340) in the goodness of their actions. How so? They are deemed worthy of both grace and compassion, receive from God "the Spirit as a first installment,"[48] and are reckoned among the children. While he says, *elders will dream dreams,* then, *young people will see visions,* in my view meaning by advanced age pre-eminence and priority coming from quality of virtue, mature, as it were, with splendid achievements,

---

44. Rom 8.6; Jn 1.13.   45. Acts 2.33; Ti 3.6.
46. Col 3.11; Gn 49.10.   47. 1 Cor 9.9.
48. 2 Cor 1.22. Cyril seems unconscious of the backhanded compliment he is paying women by the rather patronizing expression of need to justify their receipt of the Spirit (just after disqualifying the cattle).

and distinguished and admirable for mature thinking. The divinely inspired Paul was like that; he saw in a *dream* a man from the people of Macedonia pleading in the words, "Cross over to Macedonia and help us," the text being found in these terms in the Acts of the wise apostles. Ananias, one of those approved by faith, had a *vision* of blessed Paul in person; when he went to Damascus, and Christ appeared to him on the way, he lost his sight by a lightning strike, and was cured by Christ. The text records it this way: "Now, there was a disciple in Damascus by the name of Ananias. The Lord said to him in a vision, Ananias, and he answered, Here I am. The Lord said to him, Get up and go to the street called 'straight,' and at the house of Judas look for a man of Tarsus named Saul."[49]

Do you hear how he spoke to Ananias in a vision? He was strong in faith, you see, youthful in outlook, his mind bent on goodness, unflinching in valor, (341) obviously of a spiritual kind. It seemed to be in a dream that the Macedonian made his plea to Paul; he was elderly in attitude, mature in mind, and filled with wisdom from on high. The wise John announces to those sanctified in Christ through faith, "I am writing to you, fathers, because you know him who is from the beginning. I am writing to you, young people, because you are strong and have conquered the evil one."[50] So he promises the outpouring of the Holy Spirit to those who serve him. Who, once again, would such people be? Would they without doubt be those who submit the neck of their mind to the Gospel oracles, abandoning the worship in type and putting an end to the deceits of paganism, as the phrase has it?

I shall give portents in heaven above and signs on earth below—blood, fire, and clouds of smoke. The sun will be turned into darkness

---

49. Acts 16.9; 9.4–11.
50. 1 Jn 2.14. It has been an extremely lengthy commentary on a passage which looms large in the NT in Peter's citation of vv.28–31 at Acts 2.17–21 on Pentecost. It is a citation that even Theodore could not ignore, though he did begin by launching into a tirade against those who thought that Old Testament people were familiar with the notion of the Holy Spirit. Cyril's focus differs: he wants to establish that the charism of prophecy as a gift of the Spirit can be documented (as promised by the Joel lemma) from Adam to Ananias and beyond. In the course of this development the Pentecost citation is ignored. Theodoret will take this lead without suppressing Peter's citation.

and the moon into blood before there comes the day of the Lord, great and spectacular (vv.30–31). In response to the impious behavior of the Jews—I mean that committed against Christ—even the very nature of the elements was upset, and creation, as it were, grieved to see its Lord insulted. The divine Temple was, so to speak, distressed equally with the mourners and suffered rupture; Scripture says, "The veil of the Temple was torn from top to bottom." *The sun* reduced its brightness and suppressed its rays, and did not deign to shine any longer on the inhabitants of the earth. This resulted, in fact, in darkness from the sixth hour to the ninth hour; the rocks were split; perhaps something unusual also happened to the orb of *the moon*, causing it to appear to be changed *into blood*.[51] While there was silence on the part of the holy evangelists about such an event, worthy of belief because it was on the basis of the prophecy, the fact that it was by the will of the Creator that not only did the signs happen in the sun, but, as it were, the whole of creation took on an ugly appearance unusual for it, would be clear from God's statement in Isaiah, "I shall clothe heaven with darkness, and make sackcloth its covering."[52] Now, when he says "heaven," he means that absolutely everything in heaven was enveloped in darkness like sackcloth in its mourning and grief, and, as it were, in appearing to be crying aloud.

While I would say that these were the *signs in heaven*, on earth the *blood, fire, and clouds of smoke* would suggest, in my view, the misfortunes of the Jews, which the harshest of wars heaped upon them at the hands of the Romans, their whole land flowing with blood. The celebrated Temple itself was destined to be set on fire along with the cities, and houses to be left in smoking ruins. Now, the fact that even before *the day, great and spectacular*, when the divine tribunal is set before everyone and Christ renders to everyone according to their deeds things such as those that will befall the Jews, he made mention of by saying, *before there comes the day of the Lord, great and spectacular*. Furthermore, it should be noted that even our Lord himself, when asked by the wise apostles about the end of the age and the circumstances of

---

51. Mt 27.51, 45.
52. Is 50.3.

the fall of Jerusalem, gave mixed signals, perhaps to leave them in ignorance of what would happen at the time.[53]

It will happen that everyone who calls on the name of the Lord will be saved, because on Mount Zion and in Jerusalem they will be saved, as the Lord said; good news will come to those whom the Lord has called (v.32). There will therefore be without any doubt, he is saying, signs and portents in heaven and on earth regarding the Jews' unholy actions. In this way there will be made available to them at least the effects of God's clemency—namely, salvation through faith, justification in Christ, the pledge of the Spirit, sanctification, the hope of the kingdom of heaven, God's ungrudging forgiveness of them even for the crimes against Christ. The divinely inspired Peter, for instance, severely censured the Jewish masses, crying out boldly that they killed the Savior and Redeemer of all by hanging him on a cross, that they "rejected the holy and righteous one, and asked to have a murderer given" them. He went on, "I know now, brethren, that you acted in ignorance, as did also your rulers. Repent, therefore, and be baptized, every one of you, in the name of the Lord Jesus, and you will receive the gift of the Holy Spirit; for the promise is for you and your (344) children."[54] Even if there be signs and portents, therefore, he is saying, *everyone will be saved who* adopts as his master the Lord of heaven and earth.

Now, the fact that the message of salvation was uttered first in Jerusalem itself, which murdered the Lord, and thus to be spread as well to all the nations through the holy apostles, would be clear from the prophet's words, *on Mount Zion and in Jerusalem they will be saved and given good news, those whom the Lord has called.* The divinely inspired Paul in fact writes, "One does not take this honor for oneself except when called by God";[55] so the blessed

---

53. Mt 16.27; 24.6. Even a reluctant Theodore had conceded that the events in Jerusalem at the time of the crucifixion represented the reality foretold "by metaphor or hyperbole" in the Joel lemma; Cyril is more definite and more specific about such realization of the prophecy. In this case significantly, however, he is prepared to adopt a longer perspective and allow for eventual fulfillment only at an eschaton when the human race is judged. The exception to his generally foreshortened perspective is a rare one, as his commentary on Zechariah will show.

54. Acts 5.30; 3.14, 17, 38–39.

55. Heb 5.4.

disciples were called selectively from the whole body, not moving to apostleship of their own volition, like that foolish Pharisee, or lawyer, who admitted himself to the rank of discipleship, going on to say, "Sir, I shall follow you wherever you go." Consequently, the Savior for his part rebuffed him when he caused unnecessary trouble and was, so to speak, nowhere near the Gospel requirements, saying, "Foxes have holes, and birds of heaven nests, whereas the Son of man has nowhere to lay his head," whereas to those suited to apostleship he announced, "Come, follow me, and I shall make you fish for people." Matthew, at any rate, he drew from the greediness of the tax office itself, and bade follow him;[56] he *was called* at will, especially since it was likely that they would be very capable of carrying out his decisions in a youthful fashion, even if the inventor and father of iniquity took possession of the traitor. (345)

56. Mt 8.19–20; 4.19; 9.9.

COMMENTARY ON JOEL, CHAPTER THREE

Because, lo, in those days and at that time, when I shall cancel the captivity of Judah and Jerusalem, I shall gather all the nations and bring them down to the valley of Jehoshaphat, and enter into judgment with them there on behalf of my people and my inheritance, Israel, who were scattered among the nations. They divided my land, cast lots for my people, gave the boys to prostitutes, sold the girls for wine, and drank it (vv.1–3).

HEN THE TEN tribes were plucked from the kingdom of Rehoboam and they were separated from Israel as a whole, the blessed prophets were sent to Ephraim and Judah. They spoke of the fate of both, since their kingship as a whole extended to the time of the captivity.[1] After the return from there to Jerusalem, however, and the eventual restoration, Haggai, Zechariah, and also Malachi prophesied to Israel; and it emerges that Ezra also foretold some few things happening at that time and in his own time. The text at hand, therefore, mentions events happening not at the time of the earlier prophets, but when the Lord finally allowed the people to return to Judea. The memorable character of what actually happened we shall describe as far as we can, drawing on the historical account given by Ezra for support.[2]

When the people of Israel had just returned to Judea, therefore, and recovered from paying tribute and the hardships of

---

1. The lemma begins chapter 4 in the Heb. text. There are different readings and punctuation in the Pusey and PG texts of the first two sentences of the commentary, affecting the meaning.
2. Again the apocalyptic nature of the material in this chapter is a challenge to the commentators. While Theodore typically wants to find a reference to history, and turns to the (equally apocalyptic) figure of Gog in Ezek 38–39, and Theodoret follows him, Cyril turns to canonical and apocryphal works attributed to Ezra, nuancing his original view that Joel's ministry was contemporary with that of Hosea and Amos.

slavery, they fell into indifference, and were not careful (346) to pursue and observe the oracles given through Moses. The Law in fact forbade sharing a bed with the daughters of foreigners; but they cared little for the decrees sent them by God, and they had relations with foreign women. Extremely angry at this, Ezra tore his garments, mourned for the people of Israel, and urged them to be rid of foreign women. Some were persuaded to do so, perhaps afraid of the effects of wrath and the future consequences if they did not decide to respect the Law, and took experience of the past as their teacher.[3]

When the large number of foreign women were expelled and left Jerusalem, inevitably the neighboring nations were then moved to anger by the considerable insult involved, and in addition they gave thought to the effect of this on themselves. Since [the Jews] were fortifying Jerusalem, you see, and were enthusiastically engaged in rebuilding the divine Temple itself, their rage was inflamed with the shafts of envy, and they took steps to be obstructive, probably pondering the thought that, if once again Israel enjoyed its former prominence, and had cities that were fortified and the God of all to assist it by reason of his being worshiped in a temple in the old ways, it would once again dominate and be intolerable to people everywhere and impose taxes on some of its neighbors, and they all would be captured and their land devastated if some of them chose even at this late stage to cast a hostile glance. For this reason they caused some people to hinder the work on the Temple itself and on the walls. Because their efforts were fruitless, however, since God was guiding the progress of the enterprise for the people of Israel, they then took up arms and decided to attack; but they were beaten and killed, (347) thanks to God's assistance.

Now, there was an assembly of those gathered for this purpose in *the valley of Jehoshaphat,* a place not many miles from Jerusalem in an easterly direction; they say it is bare and suited to cavalry. The fact that some very influential people were ill-disposed to those Israelites building the divine Temple, but had no effect, the blessed Ezra conveys: "In the time of Artaxerxes

---

3. Ex 34.16; 1 Esdras 8–9; cf. Neh 13.23–27.

king of the Persians a letter was written against the inhabitants of Judea and Jerusalem by Bishlam, Mithridates, Tabeel, Rehum, Beltethmus, the scribe Shimshai and the rest of their associates, residents of Samaria and other places."[4] The gist of the letter was as follows: the city of Jerusalem would have invincible power, in no way yielding to the kings of other places; instead, if it returned to its former position and rebelled very vigorously, it would be a cause of concern even to the rulers of Babylon in due course. The writers of this letter, however, as I said, achieved absolutely nothing.

Now, some people in Samaria urged those who had returned from Babylon to work with them and reside with them. They were unwilling, however, resisting those people's schemes, and for this reason they were greatly wearied. This is the text of the book of Ezra: "Those who were causing distress to Judah and Benjamin heard that the returned exiles were building a house to the Lord God of Israel; they approached Zerubbabel and the heads of the families, saying, Let us build with you, because we seek your God as you do, and we have been sacrificing to him since the (348) days of Esarhaddon king of Assyria, who brought us here. Zerubbabel, Joshua, and the rest of the heads of the families of Israel replied, You will have no part with us in building a house to our God, because we ourselves shall build this very house to the Lord our God, as Cyrus king of the Persians instructed us. The people of the land obstructed the work of the people of Judah and impeded their building, bribing them with the intention of frustrating their plan."[5] While they continued to scheme, however, their efforts were in vain. The fact that a secret plot was hatched and all the neighboring nations embarked on a military campaign, and were beaten and killed, you could learn from this same source. This is the text of the second book: "It happened that Sanballat and Tobiah, the Arabs and the Ammonites heard that the walls of Jerusalem were rising and the gaps were beginning to be closed. It seemed very evil to them, and all plotted to join forces and attack Jerusalem. We prayed to the

---

4. 1 Esdras 2.16.
5. Ezr 4.1–5.

Lord our God, and set a guard as a protection against them day and night. Judah said, The strength of the foe has been crushed, and a great crowd."[6]

While in these narratives there is no mention of *the valley*, the account in tradition conveys it to us as well. The prophecy is worthy of belief, giving us the name of the place of the battle. We claim it refers to this story in saying, to *gather all the nations to the valley of Jehoshaphat*. It is clear that, far from his bringing them against their will, they want to come and he will not hinder them. He will *enter into judgment with them* over Israel (349) and *his inheritance*, which they *divided* perhaps by snatching the remnants of the Babylonians, attacking at a time of distress, making a present of *the boys to prostitutes*, exposing the girls to vicious ways unfamiliar to them, and, as it were, trading them to other people's lascivious desires so as to make money thereby for feasting and drunkenness.

Now, when we ponder the redemption coming through Christ, we claim that something similar happened also in our time. He rescued us, remember, when we were captives and serving a cruel tyrant—I mean Satan—and restored us to the holy way of life of the Gospels, to habits that are easily learned, to the fortified city of the spiritual Jerusalem, "which is the church of the living God," in which he caused us to be built as precious stones "into a holy temple, a dwelling place for God in the Spirit."[7] The unholy mass of the demons was ignited by the pangs of envy, however, and they attacked the doctrines of truth; also they made frequent onslaughts against the saints, but without causing them any harm, for God was their protector and Christ encouraged them in the words, "You have tribulation in the world, but be confident: I have overcome the world."[8]

There is a silly old wives' tale current among the Jews, then, that in due course there will be judgment of all by God in *the valley of Jehoshaphat* after the dead have come to life. They believe that everyone throughout the world will be called to account for

---

6. Neh 4.7-10 (Nehemiah the "second book of Esdras" after Ezra).
7. 1 Tm 3.15; Eph 2.21-22.
8. Jn 16.33.

what has been done to them. It would not be inappropriate to ridicule their idea, since the divinely inspired Scripture states that the contents of prophecy have been fulfilled, and that the neighboring nations will be called to account by God after the war in *the valley of Jehoshaphat.* (350) They attacked the remnants of Israel, in fact, as I said, despite its suffering extreme distress, having been given over to the Babylonians.[9]

What are you to me, Tyre and Sidon, and the whole of Galilee of foreigners? Surely you are not visiting retribution on me, or nourishing a grievance against me? Swiftly and promptly I shall return your retribution upon your heads for your taking my silver and my gold, for introducing my choice things of beauty into your temples, for selling the children of Judah and the children of Israel to the children of the Greeks so as to remove them from their borders (vv.4–6). While every nation was ranged against Israel, therefore—Moabites, Idumeans, Jebusites, Ammonites, and the rest—I believe the people of Damascus initiated the plot and the project, along with Tyre and those called Philistines as far as Gath, a term also meaning *foreigners.*[10] Accordingly, it is also to them that the God of all says, *What are you to me, Tyre and Sidon, and the whole of Galilee of foreigners?* What grounds do you have for your ferocity, he asks, bringing distress on Israel, belaboring it in unholy fashion when it is severely subject to misfortunes at the hands of the Babylonians, cruelly invading and, as it were, mocking me its Savior, and resisting me, and daring to say hostile things to me—or, rather, actually do them?

Shortly, therefore, you will receive your *retribution.* It will come to you *upon your head;* you will pay me the penalty when I judge against you in *the valley of Jehoshaphat.* He accuses them of pilfering (351) the *choice things* of the Temple, stripping it of the gold-

---

9. Unable to respond to the wordplay involved in Jehoshaphat as "valley of judgment" or "Yahweh has judged," and seeing no reference to an eschatological judgment of the nations, Cyril is content to see an historical reference to the Babylonian captivity and a spiritual dimension in victory over the demons.

10. Cyril is right in noting the use of the name in two senses, and in implicitly rejecting Galilee (which the LXX has misread in "coastal cities")— and this without help from Jerome. He also seems to imply that a copyist may have written Galilee for Gath, which at least is in Philistia—an educated guess, if erroneous.

en vessels and devoting them to the worship of their own gods—an intolerable and insulting action, quite capable of offending God; he said, in fact, "I shall not surrender my glory to another, or my praise to statues."[11] After all, what does decoration of the temples of the idols with offerings to the divinities mean, other than to shout aloud the claim that the God of all comes second whereas they are pre-eminent in reason and know how to save their own worshipers? Far from stopping at the impiety of stripping my Temple of divine offerings, he says, *you sold the children of Judah and the children of Israel to the children of the Greeks*. Now, this probably happened when some of the people of Israel were deported to the lands of the nations, and perhaps the Tyrians or others who were merchants and involved in commerce bought them.[12]

On the other hand, the text would apply, it seems to me at any rate, also to the leaders of the unholy heresies, who, as it were, seize the *children* of the church and sell them to the sophistry of *the Greeks* so that, when filled with complicated ideas, they may prove to be malignant seekers—or, rather, disobedient and destructive—who undermine what is right, despite being obliged to live a simple life and meditate on the message of truth that is not to be sold.[13] [The effect of their efforts, therefore, is that] those who are deceived cross their own *borders*, the *borders* and country of the church's children, as it were, being the knowledge of the truth and the inclination to uprightness by those carefully examining any slightest detail. The *gold* and *silver* vessels and *choice things* of God could rightly refer in truth to people adorned with faith, (352) gilded with the ornaments of good deeds, and gleaming with the beauty of piety. If it happened, however, that one of such conspicuous people were caught in the toils of deceit, the victims of deceit would surely hear the statement, *You took my silver and my gold, and introduced my choice things into your temples*. It is a dire and ineluctable reproof: "When

---

11. Is 42.8.
12. Again the need to come up with some historical basis, even if fictional.
13. As an historical basis to a text can easily be surmised or even concocted, so with equal arbitrariness can a spiritual application be arrived at. Didymus would concur.

they sin against members of your own family, for whom Christ died,"[14] they offend Christ himself, by whom they will without any doubt be called to account for their sins against him.

Lo, I am stirring them up from the place where you sold them; I shall return your retribution upon your heads; I shall sell your sons and your daughters into the hands of the children of Judah; and they will sell them into captivity to a far distant nation, because the Lord has spoken (vv.7–8). He clearly states that the Tyrians' wiles and malignant enterprises against Israel would be ineffectual, and would have the opposite effect of bringing disaster on the wrongdoers; they would be caught up in troubles of equal magnitude when commensurate punishment fell on the *head,* as it were, of those guilty of unholy crimes. In other words, just as in their case they captured the nation from Judah and then gave them into slavery to be transported *to a far distant nation,* so their children would be sold by the hands of the Jews, and *the Lord has spoken,* confirming that such things would definitely happen. Now, nothing said by God is without fulfillment; (353) Christ, for instance, said, "Heaven and earth will pass away, but my words will not pass away."[15]

While this happened in actual fact, you would, if you chose to consider the spiritual dimension and be filled with hidden meanings, likewise ponder the fact that children of the Greeks who are carried away with sophistries, as well as heretics who in their convoluted and deceitful reasoning attribute their standing to themselves, entice some simpler people away from upright and blameless faith, which they would have from God; ensnaring them, as it were, in the toils of deceit and reducing them to the role of slaves, they transport them far from the *borders* of truth. The God of all, however, renders their malice ineffectual and forgives the deceived, but delivers to the people of *Judah* those who are *sons* of the deceivers in regard to instruction. The divinely inspired disciples could further be taken as the latter, as also everyone who announces the mystery of Christ; they bring freedom from the deceit of those people, convey them to a fine

---

14. 1 Cor 8.11–12.
15. Mt 24.35.

and desirable slavery—namely, under Christ—and, as it were, snatch them as captives and transfer them to their own attitude and mindset, which is far from those others'. There is visibly a great distance, in fact, between the mindset of the saints and that of such people. Christ also is said to take as *captives* those brought from the pagan deceit to the acknowledgment of the one who is God by nature; the blessed David said, "Ascending on high, you took captivity captive, and received gifts among human beings."[16]

Proclaim this among the nations: Sanctify a war, rouse up the fighters, draw near and ascend, all you men (354) *of war, hammer your ploughs into swords and your pruning hooks into spears. Let the weakling say, I am capable. Assemble and advance, all you nations round about, and gather there. Let the gentle person become a fighter. Arise and ascend, all you nations, to the valley of Jehoshaphat, because it is there I shall sit in judgment on all the nations round about* (vv.9–12). After threatening the nations with misfortunes of their own by contrast and with retribution commensurate with their unholy deeds, he shifts his focus to his own worshipers, bidding them not to be fearful and timid but vigorous, employing, as it were, a piercing *proclamation* for *the nations* to be assembled for battle and inflamed with zeal for the challenge, even if preferring an untroubled life opposed to war. This was part of his rendering them audacious, and persuading them that their confidence in him would mean their prevailing over the foe, under his protection. He therefore says, *Proclaim this among the nations: Sanctify a war.* What again is the meaning of *sanctify?* It is a way of saying this: Consecrate it to me, for I shall be the champion, and what is achieved will be to my glory; those who accord my glory to sticks and stones will die. Everything that is said to be *sanctified* is always offered to the glory of God. Hence his saying, *Sanctify a war, rouse up the fighters,* give voice, he says, *draw near, all you men of war.* The farmer is to abandon his dearest concerns and occupations, instead fashioning *a plough into a sword and a pruning hook into spears,* this being the time not for farming but for settling accounts for God, who has been dishonored. (355) If someone is a

---

16. Ps 68.18.

weakling, he says, let him take no account of his frailty, but even tell a lie in his own case, if he wishes, and say that he is up to it. Let no one absent himself from fighting, in fact.

All those *round about* Judea, therefore, he says, gather together, and *let the gentle person become a fighter;* that is, let him also be a fighter even if he is not inclined to anger. It is as if he were saying, let no one at all be left out, be he farmer, be he fearful or timid (the sense of *weakling*), be he *gentle* or pacifist, let him rouse himself for battle. I shall make no exceptions, in fact; *I shall sit in judgment* on everyone *in the valley of Jehoshaphat.* The meaning of *I shall sit in judgment* is "I shall be a competent judge," subjecting to retribution and punishment those who robbed my land, divided Israel by lot, surrendered the boys to prostitutes, traded the girls and drank them like wine.

Our Lord Jesus Christ would in turn make such a proclamation to the foes of the church; even if they were very numerous and employed every force in attacking the saints, they would collapse completely under him as protector. He would overthrow them and reinforce his own worshipers with faith, hope, love, and the gifts of his clemency.

Apply pruning hooks, because it is time for harvest; go in, tread it down, because the wine vat is full; the vessel overflows, because their wicked deeds are multiplied. Sounds rang out in the valley of judgment, because the day of the Lord is nigh in the valley of judgment. The sun and the moon will be darkened, and the stars will lose (356) *their brightness. The Lord will exclaim from Zion, and from Jerusalem will issue his voice; heaven and earth will be shaken* (vv.13–16). He had given orders for an assembly in the valley of Jehoshaphat of all the neighboring nations of the land of Judea as if at the sound of a trumpet—Arabians, Tyrians, Gathites, Philistines, Moabites, Idumeans, Ammonites, and Girgashites—the purpose being for them to die forthwith and be subjected to the Judge's imposition of harsh penalties. He now rouses the people of Israel to indomitable enthusiasm and invincible vigor, and to attack those assembled as ordered, saying they must be audacious, bold, and strong, not deterred by the fear of war, and not simply going there to fight, but considering it enjoyment and rating it as satisfying and pleasant in the manner of people harvesting the fruit of the vine. Consequently he says, *Apply pruning hooks, because it is time for harvest,* using *apply* to mean "wield" or "brandish" in the way people normally gather crops; in other words, they will be ready for destruction, disposed to cutting down. Let the enemy be plucked, he is saying, like grapes from the vine; let them be trampled down as though in wine vats, lying in heaps underfoot. *Go in, tread it down, because the wine vat is full;* that is, the vast number of the nations is brought together for destruction, and there is nothing to prevent their being under your feet. *The vessel overflows,* meaning by this the great quantity of those brought together for trampling; often the wine overflows the actual vats from the abundance of the grapes. (357) So by saying, *The vessel overflows,* he refers to the vast number of those lying underfoot.

Sounds rang out in the valley of judgment. What does this actually mean? It is customary with the holy prophets to foretell the future, and sometimes to use the very images of the events so as to give the impression of seeing what had already happened and hearing the sounds. The divinely inspired prophet Jeremiah, for instance, in foretelling what would happen to the Jews and the fact that Nebuchadnezzar in waging war would utterly perish, was caught up in a realistic, depressing vision of the war as if he were viewing even an immeasurable pile of corpses, and cried out, "Woe is me, my soul faints at the sight of the slaughtered!"[17] Such was the experience of the blessed Joel, in my view, perhaps getting a sensation of the din of warfare, and consequently saying, *Sounds rang out in the valley of judgment.* By *valley of judgment* he refers to the place of the battle, suggesting that the nations were assembled in it for no other purpose than to pay a severe penalty; and by *sounds rang out* he means either the wailing of the fallen in that place or the shouts of the victors; in battle the fallen normally lament and the victors rejoice over the fallen, uttering loud boasts. He says, *sun and moon will be darkened,* and the very *stars* will be without light. It is not that the elements will be affected this way at the time, but that the battle will bring darkness and, as it were, impart gloom to the sight of the vanquished; fear of death always brings darkness, and the magnitude of un-

---

17. Jer 4.31.

expected disaster dulls the mind and darkens the heart with gloom, as it were, from the excessive (358) sufferings.

He says, *the Lord will exclaim,* as an ally and protector, and as a general spurring-on of the people of Israel against the adversaries. Now, it would be particularly appropriate to the moment of the resurrection to say, *The Lord will exclaim from Zion;* as the divinely inspired Paul says, "The Lord himself with a cry of command, with the archangel's call and the sound of God's trumpet, will come down from heaven, and the dead in Christ will rise incorrupt."[18] The Law of Moses also foreshadowed this, bidding the people of Israel to sound the trumpet at the new moon; the new moon would be taken as a clear type of the future age that will be new after the first age, while the trumpet would be a type of the piercing sound of the archangel's call, the trumpet from God, which raises everyone lying in the ground, giving a bold and loud sound.[19] Now, it should be realized that the Lord himself also, in working the miracle upon Lazarus, arrived at the tomb, as the evangelist says, and cried out in a loud voice, "Lazarus, come out." How is this to be taken when God says through the prophet, "He will not wrangle or cry aloud, nor will his voice be heard abroad"?[20] The Savior's using a loud cry to rouse Lazarus is therefore a sign of the piercing trumpet and the sound from it, that is, at the endtime and from heaven.

The Lord will spare his people, and the Lord will empower the children of Israel. You will know that I am the Lord your God, who dwells in Zion on my holy mountain. Jerusalem will be holy, and aliens will nevermore pass through it (vv.16–17). When the crimes (359) of apostasy were registered against the people of Israel because they adored golden heifers and said sacrilegiously, "These, Israel, are your gods who led you out of the land of Egypt,"[21] at that time they were weak and vulnerable, ready prey for the enemy, and

---

18. 1 Thes 4.16; 1 Cor 15.52.

19. Nm 10.10. It is rare for Cyril to do what Didymus was inclined to do, that is, to begin elaborating on scriptural texts cited to support the lemma, which then becomes the subtext. A reader might retort, "There are no trumpets or new moons in Joel."

20. Jn 11.43; Is 42.2; 12.19. Cyril is prepared to concede that Joel's perspective is simply eschatological, though he makes no explicit comment on "the day of the Lord."

21. Ex 32.8.

consequently were dispatched into captivity. When they were shown mercy, however, and dwelt in their own land, thanks to God's wrath abating, they then proved invincible and irresistible to the foe, and they easily prevailed, despite the assembly of all nations in battle. He therefore says that they *would know* at least from their dominance over their adversaries that he was with them and was then resting on *Zion* as his *holy* city. Consequently he says that he *will spare* his peoples and make them strong; they would learn that, as I said just now, he was with them. He says, *Jerusalem will be holy*, completely rid of the former ungodliness, not involved in forms of worship of the false gods, with no further respect paid to false prophecy and charlatanism; instead, a lawful way of life would be in force, and eager attention would be given by them to irreproachable pursuits. He says none of *the nations* would pass through it when it was in this condition and had chosen to live this way, being invulnerable to all and no longer a ready victim, as previously, to any passersby so inclined, because it was well fortified by strength and assistance from me.

The reality of the text could also be found by applying it to the church of Christ, which cares for its own adherents and makes them superior to the enemy, strong and vigorous, bursting with spiritual health, knowing and (360) believing that God is in them through the Spirit. He dwells in our hearts through faith, in fact, and, as the evangelist John says, "From this we know that he is in us, from the Spirit he has given to us." The spiritual *Jerusalem* is entirely *holy* in reality—I mean the church, where there are the ranks of the saints; no *aliens* pass that way; Scripture says, "Those who belong to Christ have crucified the flesh with its passions and desires." There comes to mind also the statement of one of the sages, "If the spirit of the ruler rises against you, do not leave your post, for healing will put an end to grave sins";[22] their heart is secure, not open and accessible to unclean spirits, not easily admitting the assaults of the passions, not defiled by the false opinions of heterodox teachers, not shaken by deceitful ideas, but firm and strongly fortified by the doctrines of truth.[23]

22. Eph 3.17; 1 Jn 3.24; Gal 5.24; Eccl 10.4.
23. The final sentence is abbreviated in the PG edition.

On that day the mountains will drip sweet wine; the hills will flow with milk; all the outlets of Judah will flow with water; a stream will emerge from the house of the Lord and water the torrent of rushes (v.18). With Jerusalem shown to be holy and no longer accessible to foreigners on account of the residence in it of the Lord of all, when he has spared his own people, strengthened them, and rendered them superior to their adversaries, then it is that *the mountains will drip sweet wine,* (361) he says, *the hills will flow with milk, and all the outlets of Judah* will release their characteristic streams. *Outlets* I think refers to the outflow of the springs, or by another interpretation they would refer to channels of water. *Mountains* could be taken as those who opt for the heights of virtue, who by the achievements of a virtuous life surpass the measure of other people, and who are illustrious and conspicuous, as were the disciples and, surpassing others, the Baptist, of whom the Savior says, "Among those born of women no one has arisen greater than John the Baptist." These great and celebrated people, therefore, *will drip sweet wine,* and, oozing honey, as it were, they will present the message about the Savior in such a way that everyone who tastes it will cry out with joy, "How sweet your sayings in my mouth, better than honey and a honeycomb in my mouth,"[24] since the message of the saints is always sweet to those who love to be pleasing to God.

While such people should be understood to be *mountains,* then, and rightly so, we claim that the *hills* are those who, though somewhat inferior to their eminence and failing to reach the measure of their way of life, rival them and far excel the others. To the souls of those who have recently come to faith these people pour out the rational and guileless milk, providing nourishment suited to infants; while mature people need solid food, milk is most appropriate for infants.[25] We do not claim that it is their ability to pour out only milk to infants that is the measure of their thinking; after all, they are well equipped, if they choose, to be able to distribute (362) more substantial nourishment to those of a more solid disposition, as the sacred writer says, "Know

---

24. Mt 11.11; Ps 119.103.
25. 1 Pt 2.2; Heb 5.12–14.

well the souls of your flock." The divinely inspired disciples, for instance, although Christ has given countless commandments to us who came to faith from the nations, write authoritatively of the need to beware "of fornication, of what is strangled, and of blood, for it has seemed good to the Holy Spirit and to us to impose on you no further burden."[26] Do you hear how the precept is suited to infants, and supplied to those of weaker disposition in a similar way to milk?

Now, the fact that the spiritual *water* will also be abundant "to those planted in the house of the Lord" so that "they may blossom in the halls of our God"[27] when watered with the divine streams, and enriched with sayings from heaven above, he highlights by saying that *all the outlets of Judah will flow with water*—in other words, the blessed disciples also admit to being consoled by God. The first *outlets* of the spiritual water, however, would definitely be those outlets which are given as sources of good things to the saints by God through the Spirit; and the second *outlets of water* are their words to us, filling us with spiritual graces. Now, what would be the *stream emerging from the house of the Lord*, if not Christ? The blessed psalmist, in fact, refers to him in these terms in saying to the God and Father in heaven, "How you multiplied your mercy, O God! The sons of men will hope in the shadow of your wings. They will be intoxicated with the richness of your house, and you will give them to drink of the torrent of your delight, because with you is the fountain of life."[28] So Christ is the *stream* and *torrent* of life.

Torrent of rushes. While the prophet mentions a certain *torrent* where many rushes grow, they claim it is the same one as the Kidron torrent where the evangelist says our Lord Jesus Christ was found when the traitorous disciple with the cohort were searching for him.[29] Now, there is nothing distasteful in our seeing a likeness between the *torrent of rushes* and the church, to

---

26. Prv 27.23; Acts 15.28–29.
27. Ps 92.13.
28. Ps 36.7–9.
29. Jn 18.1–3, referring to the brook Kedron/Kidron. The LXX has seen "torrent of rushes" where our Heb. has "torrent of thorns" (the NRSV rendering it Wadi Shittim, of indefinite location).

which our Lord Jesus Christ "turned like a river of peace,"[30] around which he constantly flows, so to speak, giving drink to the ever-luxuriant rushes, that is, the souls of the saints; rushes are always fond of water and always luxuriant. If, on the other hand, rushes are seen to be sharp-pointed, this, too, is quite applicable; the virtue of the saints is not blunt, for, though lovers of meekness, they are fighters as well.

Egypt will become a wasteland, and Idumea a desolate countryside for the wrongs done to the children of Judah, in return for the innocent blood they have poured out in their land. Judea will be inhabited forever, and Jerusalem for generations of generations. I shall require their blood, and not hold them innocent; the Lord will dwell in Zion (vv.19–21). As far as the historical reference is concerned, then, (364) *Egypt* paid the penalty, being deprived of kingship when Cambyses' son Cyrus overthrew it, and *Idumea* sustained devastation, as events also confirm.[31] In this case, however, the prophetic text probably indicates to us the hidden divine plan, which the Only-begotten fulfilled when he became man. The divine Scripture, remember, is almost always interested in comparing the herds of demons, and those constantly opposed to the saints, to the practitioners of idolatry and people inclined to it. So he says that every enemy will perish, likening them to Egyptians and Idumeans; it is an unfailing promise of Christ about the church that "the gates of hell will not prevail against it."[32] He makes clear that an account of sins committed against people would doubtless be required of the evil powers and everyone guilty of sins like theirs, either by drawing some people into pagan error or distracting their minds to unworthy thoughts through zeal in teaching corrupt ideas.

For this reason he says that those making war on Zion would

---

30. Is 66.12. There being no factual or historical reference in this verse, Cyril seeks spiritual meaning(s) in either word, "torrent" or "rushes" (even if the latter is an erroneous version). He creates a connection with the torrent/brook Kedron that figures in the Passion narrative, which leads to a spiritual meaning of a phrase in Isaiah; then he moves to the rushes, and focuses on their sharp leaves, also a source of spiritual meaning. He does not ask how this bears on Joel's overall meaning.

31. Theodoret will accept this token historical reference from Cyril, who sees it as quite subordinate to the text's eschatological meaning.

32. Mt 16.18.

be devastated *in return for the innocent blood they have poured out* and for insupportable wrongs done to the *children of Judah,* that is, the saints, who are children of confession (Judah meaning "confession").[33] The blessed David also said somewhere in reference to those sacrilegiously done away with, "Because he who avenges blood was mindful of them; he did not forget the cry of the needy." The accusation is made against Satan under the figure of the Assyrian: "As a garment mixed with blood will not be pure, (365), so you will not be pure, either, because you polluted my land and destroyed my people; you will not abide forever."[34] Therefore, he says, those who wage war on Zion will disappear in ruin. On the other hand, *Judea will be inhabited forever, and Jerusalem for generations of generations,* not sacked and burnt, since the Lord and God as truth itself is reliable. That is the spiritual, the heavenly Jerusalem, the godly Zion on high, the beautiful and celebrated city, "whose architect and builder and craftsman is God."[35] May it come to pass that we arrive there through Christ, through whom and with whom be glory to the Father, together with the Holy Spirit forever. Amen. (366)

33. The etymology is a favorite one with Didymus.
34. Ps 9.12; Is 14.19–20.
35. Heb 9.10. The doxology closes Cyril's third tome and the Joel commentary as a whole.

www.ingramcontent.com/pod-product-compliance
Lightning Source LLC
Chambersburg PA
CBHW032027290426
44110CB00012B/706